Communicating Christian Thoughts on Voiceless Tribal Women

Communicating Christian Thoughts on Voiceless Tribal Women

A Sociological Perspective

I Lanusenla Ao

Christian World Imprints

&

Gossner Theological College

First Published in 2019 by

Christian World Imprints
Christian Publishing & Books from India
C-3, Shop No. 14, Ground Floor
Wazirpur Industrial Area, **Delhi-110052**
cwidelhi2017@gmail.com
www.ChristianWorldImprints.com
Phone: +91 11 41526079

&

Gossner Theological College
Main Road, **Ranchi-834001**
gtcranchi@rediffmail.com
Phone: +91 651 2350005

ISBN: 978-93-5148-383-0 (HB)
ISBN: 978-93-5148-384-7 (PB)

Cover Art: Toshimeren

Printed in India.

Contents

The book in its original form is a thesis submitted to the Senate of Serampore College towards the DTh degree and is published with written permission. The candidate is responsible for the title, contents and opinions expressed in it.

Acknowledgments

I owe my gratitude to God Almighty for enabling me and all those who stood by me helping in various ways during my studies. It was only because of God's grace and guidance along with the support, prayers, guidance, and valuable advice received from all my acquaintances that I could come this far.

I give my heartfelt thanks to my guide Rev. Dr M. Peter Singh, who had been a great mentor for me and shaped my thoughts innovatively. It is because of his understanding and constant encouragement and guidance that I could complete my work successfully.

I am grateful to the members of the Board of Directors of Leonard Theological College who sponsored me and willingly sent me for further studies for which act of kindness I shall be ever grateful to them. I am grateful to my former Principal, Revd Richard A. E. Rodgers, my colleagues, staff and students of the Leonard family who stood by me and supported me wholeheartedly.

My gratitude goes to South Asian Theological Research Institute (SATHRI) for granting me the scholarship in due time. I am also thankful to the former Deans of Research/SATHRI, Rev. Dr. H. Vanlalauva and Rev. Dr. P. G George for the valuable help they have rendered to me all throughout my studies.

I would like to thank all the professors and staff of the Tamilnadu Theological Seminary (TTS), who lent a helping hand in times of need throughout my studies. My heartfelt thanks go also to Rev. William Allberry who proofread my entire thesis very meticulously.

My thanks go to our former Deans of Research at Tamilnadu Theological Seminary, Dr Solomon Victus, Rev. Dr. Alfred Stephen and Rev. Dr John Jayaharan. I was able to process all my work through their guidance and corresponding between SATHRI, the college and me without delay.

I am thankful to all my family: my beloved husband John Lalnuntluanga, our sons Rema and Imcha, cousin Akangchila, my parents-in-law and family members, my parents, and all my family members who have been a great source of inspiration and a strong pillar behind my success.

I am thankful to all the Ao Naga tribal churches and all the organisations, church leaders, pastors and lay people, who had willingly spent their valuable time with me and allowed me to share their rich experiences and ideas, providing me the scope to think and receive information through them which I could put them into writing. My heartfelt thanks go to all my dear friends from whom I have received innumerable support during my studies; their service was beyond measure. My thanks also go to my cousin Toshimeren for bringing out a magnificent and meaningful cover design.

Lastly, but not the least, I am grateful to Rev. Dr. C.S.A. Kerketta, Principal, Gossner Theological College, Ranchi, Jharkhand, India, Rt. Rev. Johan Dang Moderator and Board members of the Gossner Evangelical Lutheran Church Assam and Chotanagpur, and Mr. Sudhanshu Kanda from Christian World Imprints who had collaborated in publishing my work.

May God bless you all.

I Lanusenla Ao

Glossary

ABAM:	Ao Baptist Arogo Mungdang.
Almāna:	silence (Widow in Hebrew word is almānāh).
Ao Senden:	Ao council.
Ao:	one of the tribes in Nagaland.
Arichujangr/ Arichununger:	the inmates of the Ariju.
Ariju:	a place/centre of learning for boys (educational centre among the Ao tribe).
Arijumen/ Arijujanger:	the boy of the Ariju.
Arogo:	Church
Asangchi:	child born out of wedlock having no father to claim.
Bat kol:	daughter of a voice in (Hebrew).
Chēra:	without source (In Greek for widow).
Chuzen:	the senior-most group in Ariju.
Clan:	in the context of the Ao tribe of Nagaland, any of the smaller in-group classifications with which each person is identified.
Customary Law:	habits that grew into customs through imitation and acquiescence in the values they symbolise.
Dao:	long knife use by the Naga tribes which functions both as implement for work and an important tool for defence.
Ekklesia:	a community where all members as equal citizens and friends.
Elangtsur:	the womenfolk of the same clan.
Feast of Merit:	auspicious occasion wherein Mithun (semi-domesticated bovine) or Bull is sacrificed.
G.B.s:	Gaon Boras (village heads).

Headhunting: Ao Naga tribe earlier laid emphasis on being a skilful hunter killing and chopping human heads.

Ita-Anu: moon and sun.

Kita-chir: a child born out of wedlock.

Kyriarchy: the rule of emperor/master/lord/father/husband over his subordinates.

Lijaba: in Ao Naga tribal community was considered as the creator of the world, the God of the fields and vegetation.

Log drum: a war drum used as a warning against invasions and attacks.

Menden: seat/government.

Meyutsungba: the only judge in heaven.

Moatsü: one of the festivals of Ao tribe celebrated after seeds have been sown in the field.

Morung: boys' dormitory which serves an important role as a place of learning.

Mungdang: Organisation/Association

Ola: voice (jungli Ao Naga tribal language). Uttering or sound produced by mouth. The emotions, feelings, ideas, that which enables a person to involve and participate in life.

Patir (M)/Putir (C)): a priest.

Patriarchy: the rule of father.

Peya: fermented rice.

Putu: of a generation.

SAMA: the first room of the Ariju.

Samen Menchen (M): body that exercises legislative, executive and judicial powers in a village

Senso: citizen.

Sobaliba: the moral principle.

Soba-Tiyaba/ Tiyar: alternative name given to the most supreme deity, creator and destine.

Tatar Putu Menden (C): body that exercises legislative, executive and judicial powers in a village

Tatar: chosen leader/holder of shares meat.

Tenapang: means "blooming period" this age-group is relieved from the menial duties taken up by the junior (Tzuir).

Teroktsungba: the most supreme deity.

Teroktsungba: often named as Soba-Tiyaba, creator and destiner.

Tipuli:	lived between heaven and earth.
Tir:	considered as religious head of the Ariju.
Tonglu:	from another founder clan of the village who will assist the Ungr.
Tsüki:	the female learning institution looked after by a widow or an unmarried elder woman of the same clan.
Tsukibutsüla:	a matron in the girls' dormitory called Tsüki.
Tsükimak:	visitation of girls dormitory during the special occasion/ festivals by Arijumen/Arijujanger.
Tsukir:	the girl of the Tsuki.
Tsüngrem mong:	a festival of the Ao tribe honouring the supreme deity.
Tzuir /Sungpur:	the youngest age group; Water (Tzuir) and wood (Sungpur) carrier.
Ungr:	nominated from among his clan he is entitled to be a member of the Tatar.
Watsü Mungdang:	the apex body of the Ao women organisation.
Yim mungdang :	village public meeting.
Zünga/Yanga:	a group of people born within a given period of three years, inclusive of both female and male constitute significant age-based group.
Züngatsur:	a male friend/s called to his female age group (Zünga/ Yanga).

Introduction

1. Elaboration of the Problem

In the Ao Naga tribal[1] community the structure of polity for local self-government at the village level is democratic. The village being an independent democratic republic has its own governance systems and laws. A council of elders, called the *Putu Menden* or *Tatar Menden* oversees all matters of common interest, and nothing can be done without its approval or sanction. The *Putu Menden* – which roughly translates as 'seat/government' *(menden)* of a generation *(putu)* – is the federal assembly of elders representing different founding clans of the village. There are broadly five established *putus (generations)* amongst the Aos and each *putu* rules the village for 30 years in a cyclical pattern. Within each *putu* are seven to nine age/peer groups units called *Zünga*. Each *Zünga* consists of people born within a three-year period, and this forms the order of precedence within each *Putu*. The elders hold forth over their juniors and accordingly the work distribution and roles and, responsibilities in each *Putu* are established. Within the time frame of 30 years governance of a *Putu*, different *züngas* succeed one another as and when the time arises. At the end of the allocated 30 years, all councillors of that outgoing *Putu* vacate their position and a new *Putu Menden* takes over.[2] All the decisions made are supreme, and the matters discussed there are final. A similar arrangement can be noticed even in places such as Mokokchung Town, the urban centre of the Ao area which is also the seat of the *Ao Senden*. The *Senden* is the apex body of the Ao community. Though Mokokchung is declared

---

[1] The Ao Naga tribal community is one of the major tribes in the North-eastern state of Nagaland in India. Mokokchung town is the district headquarters for the Aos in Nagaland. The area consists of six mountain ranges: Tzurangkong, Japukong, Changkikong, Asetkong, Langpangkong, and Ongpangkong range. Each range consists of around eight to sixteen villages. The total villages are approximately around sixty in number. Many Aos are scattered and settled in various other parts of towns and cities too. Almost all are Christians.

[2] Amba Jamir, "Understanding Local Self Governance in Nagaland – An essence of the institutions and their activities" http://www.scribd.com/doc/51638389/Local-Self-Governance-in-Nagaland-India?olddoc accessed on (23.2.12).

a municipality, the *Senden* seems to have a place and role not dissimilar to that of the *Putu Menden* in the village(s).

It can be asserted that the widespread adoption of Christianity and Christian ideals as well as the pursuit of modern education significantly increased the status of women and their participation in various aspects of Ao Naga tribal community life. However, women do not have any role in the official functioning of traditional institutions; they are not given any chance to participate in decision-making bodies. Women are invisible when it comes to the decision-making process in the village council. Only male members decide and women are not allowed to participate in the decision-making; even to come and listen is prohibited and considered as taboo. The understanding is that "[i]t is a taboo for women to appear on a political platform or to participate in any village council or public meeting ... Women's role is simply to follow and cooperate with the men's decision without any complaint."[3] In Ao society, the silencing of women's voice happens along with other axes of oppression. Silencing consists of instinctively disregarding what a woman is saying, not listening, wanting to interrupt, ignoring their opinions, making mockery of what women say, and reducing women to sexual appearance. The mentality of silencing is an outcome of the age-old practice of patriarchy. This is very much visible in the the Ao Naga tribal community of Nagaland. The denial of rights in land holding systems, discrimination against women in decision-making bodies, exclusion of women as members in the village council, etc., are some examples. The Ao Naga tribal community which is supposedly run on democratic principles does not really show justice in practice. It is, therefore, not surprising to find that the Ao Naga tribal society considers women as "non-citizens." This is an outcome of the whole worldview being conditioned by the inherited customary[4] pattern of thought, and action. Women are denied full participation in the society. When probed on this particular aspect of social functioning, normally the response that comes from male respondents is: "Traditions and our customary practices do not permit

[3] N. Limatula Longkumer, "Christianity and Naga Women," in *Transforming Theology for Empowering Women: A Theological and Hermeneutical Reflection in the Context of North East India*, edited by R.L. Hnuni (Jorhat: Women's Studies, ETC,1999), 56.

[4] The customary law is considered as tpart and parcel of the people's culture and tradition, whose origin lies in habits that grew into customs. Adino Vitso, *Customary Law and Women. The Chakhesang Nagas* (New Delhi: Regency Publications, 2003), 2. When a whole community adopts a particular habit it becomes its custom. In traditional societies that did not have written laws, the customary law maintained social order, prescribed rules of conduct to individuals and regulated human behaviour. The tribe cherished its laws as intrinsic to its identity. The customary law thus provided some formal rules of behaviour, enforcement procedures and punishment for violation, thus turning it into a guardian of its values and norms. K. S. Singh, ed., *Tribal Ethnography, Customary Law and Change* (New Delhi: Concept Publishing Company, 1993), 17.

women to participate."[5] Monalisa Changkija indicates that: "Aos are still very much dictated and directed by customs and traditions that keep the personal, private, public and professional life well-oiled."[6]

1.1. Impact of Modernisation in Ao Naga Tribal Society

Even though the Ao Naga tribal community still functions through the traditional system of administration, other areas of development such as their lifestyles and living standards have changed tremendously. About 95% of the youngsters received at least primary education, and many highly qualified male and female members hold government administrative offices and other business positions in many places. New means of transport and communication facilities are easily available and allow one to move easily to even a remote corner within a few minutes. Modern means of advancement like electronic machines, vehicles, televisions, computers, internet, mobiles connectivity etc. are easily accessible and readily adopted by the people in the community.

It is noticed that most of the traditional socio-cultural practices and structures seem irrelevant in Ao Naga tribal community today. In many ways traditional practices which were once considered noble, admirable and appreciable seem to be gradually fading away. People are no longer static or inert in their thoughts and actions but dynamic and mobile as the time changes. For example, life at Morung[7] for men, tsuki[8] for women, head-hunting, etc., are not practised any more. So also the customary laws need to be re-examined. It is said: "One cannot conclude … that the customary laws should be accepted or rejected in their totality. One can only say that they should not remain intact because they are equitable but have elements of inequity that need to be changed."[9]

---

[5] L. Imsutoshi Jamir, "Morality of Inter-subjectivity: Toward Inclusive Tribal Community," *Journal of Tribal Studies*, XVI/1 (Jan-June, 2010): 16-31.

[6] Monalisa Changkija, "*Ariju:* The Traditional Seat of Learning in Ao Society," in *Glimpses from the North-East* (Shillong: National Knowledge Commission, 2009), 23.

[7] The Morung, (*Ariju* in Ao Naga) or the bachelor dormitory was an important educational institution for Ao Naga tribal society. Like many other Nagas, the Ao Naga culture, customs, and traditions, were conveyed through folk music and dance, folk tales by word of mouth from one generation to the other. Handy work such as wood carving etc. were learned in the Morung. Apart from other activities Announcements of meetings, the death of a villager, warnings of impending dangers, etc., were made from the Morung with the beating of log drum. http://en.wikipedia.org/wiki/Naga_people accessed on (23.7.12).

[8] *Tsuki* is a girls' dormitory. Like *Ariju* for boys, it is an educational institution for woman. In *Tsuki* girls learnt all theories and practices. Panger Imchen, *Ancient Ao Naga Religion and Culture* (New Delhi: Har Anand Publications, 1993), 101. It is mentioned that *Tsuki* and *Ariju* were two distinct social organization which existed and function well in correspondence with one another. Imnuksungla LKR, "Tradition of Tsuki (Girl's Dormitory) And Its Contribution to Ao Naga Women's Solidarity"(M.Th. dissertation, Tamilnadu Theological Seminary, 2007), 22.

[9] Walter Fernandes, Melville Pereira, Vizalenu Khatso, *Customary Laws in North East India : Impact On Women* (New Delhi: National Commission for Women, n.d), 4. http://ncw.nic.in/

However, some of the traditional practices that are kept alive today are such as village guard called *tsutemmonger*, whose duty is to guard the village throughout the day while everyone is busy at the paddy fields, to alert the villagers during emergencies such as fire, sickness, death, accident etc. They also deliver official letters and messages to other villages[10] and perform related social work called by the village council in times of need.[11]

2. Importance of the Problem

There is a perceivable lack of women's participation in decision-making bodies in the Ao Naga tribal community. This is representative of the low status of women in all walks of lives, and is symptomatic of a lack of communitarian ethos in the community. Hence, there is a need to strive for an egalitarian community geared towards engendering equal participation and mutual co-existence in decision-making bodies. It is proposed that "voice" is one of the important components in a feminist communication theory that attempts to overturn the gender injustice that deprives women of their fundamental human rights. And it is further proposed that "media" is an effective means of communication for such a social change here envisioned.

The study will contribute towards an attempt to:

- locate how traditional practices in decision-making bodies negate women's participation.
- examine how the age-old practices of the traditional Ao Naga tribal community consider women as inferior beings in decision-making bodies.
- determine how this flawed concept of human worth that has been imbibed in the Ao Naga tribal community could be corrected.
- find ways to bring all human beings together in all walks of life without any discrimination among the Ao Naga Traditional tribal community.
- unearth the Implications of Communication for the assertion of fundamental human rights in the Ao Naga tribal community.
- promote Voice as an important component in Communication Theory.
- advocate Media as an effective means for social change.

The researcher has studied and investigated the problem, posing certain questions. Questions such as, how far are the traditional practices such as

pdfreports/Customary%20Law.pdf accessed on (25-7-12).

[10] Monalisa Changkija, "*Ariju*: The Traditional Seat of Learning in Ao Society," 18.

[11] Social work called by village council (*Yimten* in Ao Naga) which is usually done by men (not for all men in the village but only those who practise *jhum* cultivation. Their main work is to clear and maintain footpaths used by the farmers between the cultivated areas (paddy fields) and the village.

composition and functioning of decision-making bodies relevant in the Ao Naga tribal community today? What are the reasons behind barring women from participation in decision-making bodies in the Ao Naga tribal community? Are people aware of the denial of rights to half of the population, i.e., women, in decision-making bodies in the community? How far are people willing to change the traditional nature of a so-called democratic system of self-governance that does not consider women's voice as voice? What is the response of the common people towards traditional methods of decision-making body today? What are the responses of women towards the traditional practices in decision-making-bodies? How do menfolk feel about women not being counted as partners in decision-making bodies? Do they have the awareness that it amounts to a negation of the basic principles of Christian communication, i.e., the right to participation and the right to information?

How do women cope with being rendered voiceless and left out completely from the decision-making process that decides what directions their community and by extension their families, take? Do they resist at all? Assuming that they do resist, what are the strategies adopted for resisting and/or coping with such an arrangement and practice? These are some of the questions the research addressed.

2.1. Women in Ao Naga Tribal Community

Women are denied the right to raise voice which is the utmost medium of communication and means of human interaction. Language that binds individuals together which enables us to be together in qualitatively different ways from animals which reveals the essence of the human being: to-be-with-other, and to-be-in-relationship. Sharing of views and listening to what is being discussed become an important means of communication in decision-making. Language which is the genuine model of all communications that enables us to become members of a shared culture[12] is denied by traditional socio-cultural structures to a large section of society, i.e., women, in the Ao Naga Tribal community.

Some of the blame for women being excluded from participation in the public domain can be directly attributed to the socio-cultural and traditional structures of the Ao Naga tribal community. It says:

> The political consequence of the Naga tradition and culture on the women is their almost total eclipse from the administrative and decision-making bodies and institutions, which continue till date.[13]

At one point of time, Ao women were discouraged by parents from attending school and receiving education. Their roles and responsibilities were to look after

---

[12] Michael Traber, "Why communication studies in theological education", in *Communication in Theological Education: New Directions*, edited by, Michael Traber (Delhi: ISPCK, 2005), 10-11.

[13] Toshimenla Jamir, "Gender Dimensions of Electoral Politics in Nagaland." https://indianfolklore.org/journals/index.php/Ish/article/viewFile/522/612 accessed on (20.7.12).

the siblings, to help parents at work and in the paddy fields, and to assist in the household chores. In short, the duty of a woman was to be confined at home, which undermined the potentialities of a woman. This relegation of women is conditioned by the patriarchal socio-cultural mind-set that considers women as inferior beings.

The socio-cultural tradition provides two perspectives in the Ao Naga tribal community in terms of the relationship between women and men. The role of women is associated with or in the private sphere and the role of the men is associated in the public sphere. The public sphere operates outside the family and has its social values, status and power. The private sphere is linked with reproductive labour, within the home, the work of maintaining body and soul together through cooking, cleaning, sewing, socializing and child rearing and educating children, keeping up the practices and rituals of the culture and the community. The concepts of the "ideal woman" have been based on her role in the private sphere. The image of the independent woman is not esteemed in the society.[14] This concept is still prevalent in the minds of the people in the Ao Naga tribal community today.

It is obvious that the division of labour allotted to males and females in Ao Naga Tribal society is quite distinct even now. The society gives due recognition to men's hard work and hold it in high esteem, whereas the hard work of women is counted as secondary. Womenfolk even today contribute the major work such as cutting trees, clearing weeds without differentiating from men in *jhum* cultivation in the village. An interview by Imnuksungla LKR confirmed that during the time of head-hunting women carried a major task. Along with domestic work they took up other responsibilities including *jhum* cultivation when men were away for hunting game.[15] The prejudices and biased nature of the patriarchal socio-cultural structures that undermine women's capabilities remains prominent in Ao Naga tribal community, as the statement quoted below attests:

> There were *Arijus* for girls too but because women have a secondary position in a basically patriarchal Naga society, *Arijus* for girls were never accorded the importance they should have been given … In the girls' *Ariju*, they were taught the traditional roles and responsibilities accorded to women in any patriarchal society. And the girls' *Ariju* functioned much like the boys' except for training in warfare and other activities that were held to be men's prerogative.[16]

---

[14] A. Asola Jamir, "The image of women in selected Naga folklore and its impact on Naga Women Today", in *Communication and Naga Culture*, edited by L. Imsutoshi Jamir, C. Alitemjen Longkumer (Dimapur: Tribal Development and Communication Centre, 2008), 91-92.

[15] Imnuksungla LKR, "Tradition of Tsuki (Girl's Dormitory) And Its Contribution to Ao Naga Women's Solidarity" (M.Th. dissertation, Tamilnadu Theological Seminary, 2007), 22.

[16] Monalisa Changkija, *"Ariju*: The Traditional Seat of Learning in Ao Society," 22. *Ariju* for girls and *tsuki* are used interchangeably in this paper.

It was during the time of head-hunting when the villagers waged wars against others that it became necessary for everyone both strong and weak to be with a larger group to assure safety and security. Imnuksungla LKR has rightly brought out that:

> Even though women have enjoyed protection and security, the dominating social structures had made them more dependent and subjugated. As it was done in the name of assuring total security, they become more and more voiceless, since they themselves internalised such patriarchal arrangements, they were not even fully conscious of being dominated and not having space. The uncertainty in life due to constant warfare and the productive process of child bearing, nurturing and up bringing brought women into a precarious situation ... Women who were slogging in the *jhum* and in the homes did not have much time and space to develop other skills. This kind of factor divides men from the women.[17]

In Ao Naga tribal society people still cherish and are associated with varieties of folklore[18] that are considered as rich cultural heritage for the common people. However, in most cases, these are folklores that manifest a multiplicity of women's images in which they are alternatively viewed as impure, destructive, opponents and witches. Most significantly these images leave a deep imprint upon women's self-perception that paralyses their potentialities.[19]

At the same time, the Ao Naga tribal community fails to recognise the success stories of Ao women who were once the forerunners in the whole of the Ao Naga community. For example, Ongangla the diviner, Akangla a great diplomat, and Yongyintemla a great musician were women whose wisdom and knowledge brought tremendous success to the whole of the Ao Naga tribal community.[20]

2.2. Voice: A New Paradigm of Womanist Communication Theology

It is true that silence can speak more than language in communication. However, voice here becomes more important because there is a necessity to raise voice

---

[17] Imnuksungla LKR, "Tradition of Tsuki (Girl's Dormitory) And Its Contribution to Ao Naga Women's Solidarity", 78.

[18] In Ao Naga tribal society folklore such as the story of "the wicked stepmother", "the story of Kongrola and her slaves", "the story of an unstable wife" etc. is commonly narrated among the people in the community. A. Asola Jamir, "The image of women in selected Naga folklore and its impact on Naga Women Today", in *Communication and Naga Culture,* edited by L. Imsutoshi Jamir, C. Alitemjen Longkumer (Dimapur: Tribal Development and Communication Centre, 2008), 80-85.

[19] Ibid., 97.

[20] N. Limatula Longkumer, "Rediscovering Women's Role and Status in Society," in *Transforming Theology for Empowering Women: A Theological and Hermeneutical Reflection in the Context of North East India,* edited by R.L. Hnuni (ETC, Jorhat: Women's Studies, 1999), 35ff.

and speak out the truth, to dismantle the distortive patriarchal structures of misrepresentation and misinterpretation of gender roles in society. And it is through voice that it is possible to reconstruct and restore the neglected beings. Therefore, a new paradigm of womanist communication theology ought to assert the centrality of voice in engendering women's power towards refashioning a new theology of the Reign of God.[21] This requires a critical deconstruction of texts and theologies, a reconstruction through re-reading and re-interpreting the text and appropriation of women's voices in society.

3. Definition of Terms

Voice is defined in the Oxford Advanced Learner's Dictionary as sound from mouth, the right to express your opinion and influence decisions, a particular attitude, opinion or feeling that is expressed, make your voice heard, with one voice, etc.[22]

Voice, generally is understood as the sound uttered by the mouth, especially that uttered by human beings in speech or song.[23] It is understood as an expression; a medium or agency of expression, the right or opportunity to express a choice or opinion. The Oxford Dictionary defines voice as the ability to speak and a particular opinion or attitude expressed: *a dissenting voice, a worried tone of voice.*[24] Voice establishes one's right to communicate, to resist, to support, to share, give opinion, to accommodate, and to suggest one's own experiences. Here, voice can mean all round development of oneself "when voiced" it will lead to free and fair well-being in one's own existence as "a complete human."

The Ao Naga tribal community belongs to one of the major tribes in the North-eastern state of Nagaland, India. Almost all the members have now Christians. It covers an area of 1,615 km and is bounded by Assam to its north, Wokha to its west, Tuensang to its east, and Zunheboto to its south. Three dialects are spoken by Aos: Chungli, Mongsen, and Changki. Chungli Ao and Mongsen Ao are spoken in the majority of the Ao villages.

4. Scope and Limitations of the Study

The study focuses on the issues and problems related to women's participation in decision-making bodies in the Ao Naga Tribal community. It concentrates on the village council and its decision-making bodies, especially the *Yimmungdang*

---

[21] Ivy, "Engendering Women Power Towards the Reign of God" Paper presented in Pre-Governing Council Seminar at Tamilnadu Theological Seminary, Madurai (7.8.12).

[22] "Voice," *Oxford Advanced Learner's Dictionary* (2010), CD-ROM, 8th Edition.

[23] Meaning of Voice. thefreedictionary.com/voice accessed on (3.9.12).

[24] "Voice" in http://oxforddictionaries.com/definition/english/voice?q=voice accessed on (3.9.12).

(general meeting).[25] The researcher conducted the field research in six ranges/areas selecting two villages from each range/area of Ao country including three urban areas and some cities.

5. Previous Research

Related research and studies connected to tribal women and culture in North East India are readily available. These are published accounts from religious studies as well as secular fields both by native researchers and others. Sociologists, historians, anthropologists, and proponents of gender studies have written about the tribal women and cultures of North East India. The last few decades have witnessed a number of articles, books, edited books, published and unpublished theses, journals, newspapers etc., written particularly on the tribal Naga women and culture related issues in North East India. Some of the contributors among many are Rita Manchanda,[26] Meneno Vamuzo,[27] M. Akang,[28] K. Meru,[29] and Limatula Longkumer.[30] Some of the Ao Naga scholars have incidentally touched on the subject but so far nobody has directly dealt with the Ao Naga tribal community and women on decision-making bodies.

Lanuyanger Ao's research, *Women's Relation To Property in Ao-Naga Customary Law of Inheritance*[31] described how the customary law of inheritance in Ao-Naga society denies equal rights to some people, particularly women who cannot inherit their father's property. The researcher analysed and studied the true nature of the problem involved and provides a new perspective to the struggles of women.

---

[25] On the day of the *Yimmungdang*, the whole village (community) is not allowed to go anywhere beyond the village limits, even to work in the fields. However, women are not allowed to participate in this decision-making process which supposedly involves everyone.

[26] Rita Manchanda, "Naga Women Making a Difference: Peace Building in Northeastern India," edited by Sanam Naraghi Anderlini, Women Waging Peace Policy Commission, January, 2005. http://www.inclusivesecurity.org/wpcontent/uploads/2012/08/13_naga_women_making_a_difference_peace_building_in_northeastern_india.pdf accessed on 15.1.13.

[27] Meneno Vamuzo, "Narratives of Peace: Naga Women in the Self Determination Struggle," http://www.yorku.ca/intent/issue6/articles/pdfs/menenovamuzoarticle.pdf accessed on 15.1.13.

[28] M. Akang, "Akidang Ao Yimli Nung Tetzurtem Jenjang Meyiba Reprangshiba (Looking back at the Status of women in old Ao society), in *Shisa Lemsa Kaket*, edited by Ruth and Chubala, (N.p.: n.p., 1989), 2.

[29] K. Meru, "The rule of women before and now", *Highlander*, 1978, 20.

[30] Limatula Longkumer, ed., *No More Sorrow in God's Garden of Justice: Tribal Women Doing Theology*, Women Studies Series 4 (Eastern Theological College, Jorhat: Women's Study centre, 2007).

[31] Lanuyanger Ao, "Women's Relation to Property in Ao-Naga Customary Law of Inheritance" (M.Th. dissertation, Tamilnadu Theological Seminary, 1995).

Narola Imchen, in *Women in Church and Society: The Story of Ao Naga Women*[32] deals with the condition of Ao Naga women in church and society. She brings out the traditional patriarchal nature and practices that are prevalent in Ao Naga society. The patriarchal mind-set which lingers in the minds of Ao Naga society, preventing women from developing and coming up to the forefront for equal participation with men. The researcher therefore at the end suggested being partners both in the church as well as in society.

Aphuno Chase Roy's *Women in Transition: Angami Naga Women From 1878 to the Present*[33] deals with the experiences and struggles of women from another Naga tribe, i.e. the Angami. However, it is of importance for the present research by providing parallels as well as counterpoints to the issue under consideration.

In *A Womanist Theological Critique on the Naga Traditional Worldview*[34] Lovely Awomi James critiqued the traditional worldview of the Nagas. It mentioned that the social context of the Nagas particularly men-women relationship needs serious reflection which requires to reconceptualise the idea of sexuality and gender. It refutes and challenges the romanticism of the Naga traditional culture and worldview that do not necessitate fullness of life. The researcher urges that it is a necessity to redefine "theology" and "worldview."

In addition to those mentioned above, the Tribal Study Centre at Eastern Theological College contributes a number of writings on women in north east India. But so far nobody has undertaken a detailed study on the subject of women in decision-making bodies in the Ao Naga tribal community. The researcher, therefore, focused and located the real life situation of present Ao Naga tribal women and re-examined it from the communication studies perspective. The socio-cultural tradition of Ao Naga tribal community denying women the right to information and communication in decision-making bodies was addressed.

Nonetheless, the intention of this research was not to reject the entire socio-cultural structure which has its own significance and import. The intent, rather, was to observe and critique the views and belief systems that had failed to recognise women's voice as voice in the Ao Naga tribal community.

6. Method of Research

The research employed library research and the empirical study method. In connection with this, both quantitative and qualitative research methods were employed. The qualitative research method included personal interviews and focus group discussion. Questionnaires were distributed in applying the

[32] Narola Imchen, *Women in Church and Society: The Story of Ao Naga Women* (Jorhat: Eastern Theological College, 2001).

[33] Aphuno Chase Roy, *Women in Transition: Angami Naga Women From 1878 to the Present* (Kohima: Published by the Author, 2004).

[34] Lovely Awomi James, "A Womanist Theological Critique on the Naga Traditional Worldview" (D.Th. dissertation, Federated Faculty for Research in Religion and Culture, 2010).

quantitative research method. The researcher then engaged in survey and observation of both rural and urban set ups in order to determine if there are distinct attitudes regarding the traditional practices in decision-making bodies. Specific attention was given to two villages from each range and three urban areas in Ao Naga tribal society. The researcher had used ethnography,[35] in order to know the attitudes of the people (that is their like and dislike) towards the functioning of traditional practices in decision-making bodies, employing interviews in the selected villages and towns. To get to know more of their insights the researcher interviewed both female members and male members. The participants were selected from a cross section of society such as educated people, lay people, church leaders, young group, and old age group. Three-hundred questionnaires were distributed to various sections of the Ao Naga Tribal community and fifty personal interviews were conducted. Through this study the researcher had been able to indicate the socio-cultural, political, economic and religious conditions of the present day Ao Naga tribal community.

6.1. Methodological Considerations

The exclusion of women in decision-making bodies in the Ao Naga tribal community is an important issue that needs to be brought into special consideration. Therefore, this study is to attempt and to explore the possibilities for accommodation in decision-making bodies and to strive for mutual co-existence in communicating with one another in the Ao Naga tribal community. There is a need for a holistic approach that would be applied to deal with the issue. The approach would incorporate raising awareness and conscientising people about the imbalance in social life and functioning.

The study employed some of the important theoretical works of the feminist communication scholars. Scholars such as Lana F. Rakow and Laura A. Wackwitz asserted "Voice" as one of the most important components in communication theory, especially feminist communication theory.[36] Julia

---

[35] Ethnography comes from anthropology, which includes an empirical and theoretical approach. It involves field work, detailed holistic description and analysis of cultures. According to Hammersley and Atkinson, the 'ethnographer participates in people's lives for an extended period of time, watching what happens, listening to what is said, asking questions.' M. Hammersley and Atkinson, P, *Ethnography: Principles and Practice* (London: Tavistock Books, 1983), 2.

Sometimes it is called 'thick descriptions' of 'the multiplicity of complex conceptual structures'. It includes verbal, non-verbal, "taken-for-granted assumptions that operate within cultural life". Chris Barker, *Cultural Studies: Theory and Practice* third edition, (Los Angeles, London, New Delhi, Singapore: Sage Publications, 2008), 32.

[36] Lana F. Rakow and Laura A. Wackwitz mentioned that the significant work by critical feminist scholars to "reclaim," "discover," and "give voice to" those who have not been heard in public discourse is an important phase of the work on voice. They observed and shared that this will lead to strengthen the theoretical and political pitfalls and therefore, need to address why

T. Wood asserts critical theories that are concerned with an aim to identify prevailing structures and practices that create or uphold disadvantage, inequity, or oppression and strive to point the way towards alternatives that promote more egalitarian possibilities for individuals, relationships, groups, and societies.[37]

Virginia Woolf wrote about the power structures of patriarchal system and introduced some of the critical strategies such as the concepts like "difference," "the other," "representation" and "signifying practices."[38]

Rakow and Wackwitz offer a critique of the widespread use of the term "voice" by feminist scholars and scholars of colour that "its significance can be taken for granted and its complexity overlooked."[39] They further opine that scholars often use it "uncritically, without precision, explanation, or definition."[40] Along with the work of these two scholars, our use of the term presupposes "a political means and ends in which what is said has an effect."[41] And the end goal "must be a reconstituted communal and political life in which all members of a

---

feminists should be concerned with voice. Their subjectivity cannot be taken for granted and their authenticity to speak as and for group identity can be challenged. Nana and Laura raised their voice to express their concerns on Why Voice? Lana F. Rakow, Laura A. Wackwitz "Voice in Feminist Communication Theory," in *Feminist Communication Theory,* edited by Lana F. Rakow and Laura A. Wackwitz (Thousand Oaks, London, New Delhi: SAGE Publications, 2004), 94.

[37] Critical theories investigate interactive influence between cultural practices and structures; and the political, material, social, personal, professional, and economic lives of members of a culture, especially those who do not occupy dominant status and the privileges it confers. In other words, critical theories ask how cultural structures and practices shape the lives of members of a cultural and, conversely, how members' lives and activities shape cultural structures and practices. Critical theorists are particularly interested in identifying how dominant groups manage to privilege their interests and perspectives and impose them on less-powerful groups. At the same time, critical theorists want to understand how oppressed groups become empowered and, in some cases, change dominant patterns and perhaps the ideologies that underlie them. Critical theorists allow critiquing not only official forms of power such as laws, but also "tiny, everyday" practices that reproduce and sustain particular ideologies and their attendant inequities. Julia T. Wood, "Critical Feminist Theories: A Provocative Perspectives on Families," in *Engaging Theories in Family Communication: Multiple Perspectives,* edited by Dawn O. Braithwaite, Leslie A. Baxter (Thousand Oaks, London, New Delhi: SAGE Publications, 2006), 201–202.

[38] Critical cultural studies provide a critique of patriarchal culture that probed the relations of power that helped to perpetuate the systematic subordination of women. Helping us to see (sexual) identity as a cultural construction and how representation functions with relation to repression. Showing how contexts of difference can challenge simple notions of identity and how culture can be seen as gendered. Making us aware of the role of what are now known as 'signifying practices'. Demonstrating the importance of historical contexts and concepts like gender, "difference" and "other." Providing an effective demonstration of a key area of resistance and struggle in contemporary culture. David Walton, *Introducing Cultural Studies: Learning Through Practice* (New Delhi: SAGE Publications, 2008), 256.

[39] Lana F. Rakow, Laura A. Wackwitz "Voice in Feminist Communication Theory," in *Feminist Communication Theory,* 95.

[40] Ibid.

[41] Ibid.

community and within a society have a voice that is heard, acknowledged, and taken into account in setting and adjusting the course of our local and collective lives."[42] Thus, it is necessary to establish, at the outset, the strictures for our usage of the term "voice" for the purpose of this research.

[42] Ibid.

Chapter 1

Epistemological Considerations of the term "Voice"

Introduction

Voice is that which can be heard by all, pronounced by all, which means that every individual has her/his own right to voice. This chapter presents the importance of Voice from various arenas dealing with three main segments in relation to voice. In the first section, a definition and detailed treatment of voice, *ola*[43] in the Ao language, would be brought in so as to recognise and establish the significance of voice in Ao Naga tribal society. It will be argued that voice is about the freedom and equality that one must possess.

Here we will seek to understand voice in relation to speech, language, reason, silence, dialogue, talk, etc. The second and third sections deal with the Christian biblical concept of voice. An attempt will be made to show voice as an important agency of all ages in communicating and building the interrelationship between God, Christ, nature and humankind.

1.1. Defining "Voice"

Voice is generally understood as sound produced by vertebrates by means of lungs, larynx, or syrinx; especially: sound so produced by human beings.[44] It is understood as an expression; a medium or agency of expression, the right or opportunity to express a choice or opinion. The Oxford Dictionary defines it as the ability to speak and a particular opinion or attitude expressed: *a dissenting*

---

[43] *Ola* is voice in *Chungli* dialect, the Ao Naga tribal language.

[44] "Voice" http://www.merriam-webster.com/dictionary/voice accessed on 3.9.12.

voice, a worried tone of voice.[45] Voice can also be spoken of as a window into the inner soul. One's innermost ideas, when voiced, reveal what goes on inside one's mind. Furthermore, it can lead to nurturing of oneself on the path to becoming a more complete being; it can help in the self-development of a free and fair well-being in one's own existence, in enabling one to become a complete human.

"Voice" implies a subject who speaks (or writes). Moreover, it is both a set of sonic, material, and literary practices shaped by culturally and historically specific moments and a category invoked in discourse about personal agency, communication and representation, and political power.[46]

In his treatise on politics entitled *Politics*, the Greek philosopher Aristotle distinguishes mere voice (*phóné*) from "speech" (*logos*). He sees the former as the capacity that humans share with most animals, the capacity of communicating basic sensations of pain and the like, while the latter is the medium of political deliberation and action.[47] Voice, used in the sense of Aristotle's "speech" (*logos*), establishes one's right to communicate, to resist, to support and to suggest one's own experiences. Here, voice can mean freedom of speech, the ability to talk and converse without any hindrance from one person to another.

In "Saved From Silence: Finding Women's Voice in Preaching", Mary Donovan Turner and Mary Lin Hudson described the importance of the use of "Voice" as metaphor in one of the sub-points, "Claiming the Importance of Voice". They asserted that voice arises from the recognition of the importance of individuality, self-expression, and truth through relationship. Here, voice becomes an important means to signal the growing cultural acknowledgement of the right to self-expression in today's dominant metaphor for power relations between persons and groups in the society.[48]

According to Britzman, "A commitment to voice attests to the right of speaking and being represented."[49] Christine Ashby further remarked that "voice is the right and the ability to make oneself heard and to have one's experiences and perspectives available to others; to participate in the construction of the self and to decide how to represent that self to others."[50]

---

[45] "Voice" http://oxforddictionaries.com/definition/english/voice?q=voice accessed on 3.9.12.

[46] Cf. Amanda Weidman, "Anthropology and the Voice", Anthropology News, 52:13. doi: 10.1111/j.1556-3502.2011.52113.x accessed on 15.2.15.

[47] Aristotle, *Politics* (Harmondsworth: Penguin, 1992), en.m.wikipedia.org/wiki/mo., accessed on 12.5.2012.

[48] Mary Donovan Turner, Mary Lin Hudson, *Saved from Silence: Finding Women's Voice in Preaching* (Danver: Mary Donovan Turner and Mary Lin Hudson, 1999), 16.

[49] Quoted in Christine Ashby, "Whose "Voice" is it anyway?: Giving voice and qualitative research involving individuals that type to communicate," *Disability Studies Quarterly* dsq-sds.org/article/view/1723/1771 (31Oct. 2012).

[50] Ibid.

Therefore, it should be asked why voice is important in communication. The term "Voice" in communication is not just an ordinary noise or sound that is produced or passed on to others by a person or thing. Rather, it is more of an emotional expression that denotes an individual who shares and exchanges her/his own views, ideas, feelings, emotions, knowledge, and wisdom to others and that can be heard by all.

It may be claimed that the written word or printed language/literature carries more weight than oral language in today's technological world. Walter Ong, who valued literature more than the oral/spoken word, said, "… I propose to skirt it, without losing sight of it, and to discuss the value of literary content against the background of the spoken word, in which literature has its pristine and its permanent roots."[51] Ong was right to a certain extent, as technological advancement has a firm grip on writing, and printing has become much easier ever since. Literature rather than human utterance certainly made it possible for word of mouth to be put down in writing or printing, due to which human histories can be preserved and made accessible for all.

The present study places emphasis on voice, that is, the human utterances in oral communication through which interpersonal communication takes place and face-to-face interaction is conceivable. The reason for choosing to place oral communication higher than written language is owing to the 'cultural context' of the Ao Naga tribal community, where oral communication is not only an indispensable part but the primary component in the functioning of the decision-making bodies. People come together, assemble at a given time, talk, raise their voices, share their concerns and make decisions instantly. In such a context, written literature does not relate or occupy any significant role at that moment but it is through 'human voice' that communication takes place and deliberations and decisions that affect the community occur.

Turner and Hudson, in *Voice as Distinctive Self,*[52] mentioned the qualities of distinctiveness and uniqueness to each voice symbolising a person's self. One such example is to be found in the story of Isaac in the Hebrew Scriptures. Isaac, in his old age, was blind and was lying in his bed when his son Jacob, claiming to be his firstborn son Esau, approached him expecting his blessings. When Isaac heard the voice, he could easily sense and differentiate that it was Jacob and not Esau.[53] Mary Donovan Turner, Mary Lin Hudson wrote that:

> Voice, then, not only symbolizes the self; it symbolizes a distinct, unique self. Although the voice can change its pitch, pace and inflection

[51] Walter J. Ong, "From Mimesis to Irony: The Distancing of Voice," *The Oral Aural* http://harlotofthearts.org/index.php/harlot/article/view/163 accessed on 15.1.15.

[52] Mary Donovan Turner, Mary Lin Hudson, *Saved from Silence: Finding Women's Voice in Preaching,* 9.

[53] Ibid.

reflecting a seemingly endless variety of emotions and feelings, there is a recognizable quality to it. The voice is wedded to each person in a way that is particular and undeniable.[54]

1.2. Voice in relation to Speech, Language, Reason and Talk

Speech, language, reason and talk are interlinked. These are all part of a voice. The speech we deliver, the language we speak, the way we reason, and the way we talk with one another is communication.

1.2.1. Speech-Language

Turner and Hudson defined the chronological function of the human body – how it is connected and works simultaneously with its body parts to become complete beings. It is said that in order for sound to be produced, that "spirit" must meet and move the body's vocal cords, the vacuum, and a vibrating pattern. These vibrations carry the energy of one's being into the universe through sound. Turner and Hudson describe the act of speaking as involving physical experience: "Sound emitted by the vocal cords is amplified when it passes through the rest of the body. The physical experience of speaking includes an awareness of sound resonating through various parts. Through the movement of lips, tongue, soft palate, and facial muscles this sound is transformed to speech."[55] Vincent Casaregola[56] also upholds that speech is vital in life. Casaregola maintains that: "Speech, as sound, is in many ways merely moving air, and yet like the air, despite seeming ephemeral, it is essential."[57]

On the other hand, without the function of the brain there won't be any possibility of human voice. Erling Berge has righty observed the coordination between human brain and other body organs: "The spoken language is not just words following each other like in a text. It is also intonation, rhythm and melody. These convey feelings and moods. They are interpreted by the right part of the brain constructs out of the supplied words."[58] It is from the cooperation of brain, breath, and body that voice results. Berge continues to say that it is not only the listener but the speaker herself/hiself have been touched: "Within every voice is the effort of a human being to express self. Voice signals the presence of the one

[54] Mary Donovan Turner, Mary Lin Hudson, *Saved from Silence: Finding Women's Voice in Preaching*, 9.

[55] Ibid., 8.

[56] Vincent Casaregola, "The 'Exact Location' of the Voice: Walter Ong and the 'Embodiment' of Discourse," http://www.media-ecology.org/publications/MEA_proceedings/v10/7_exact_location.pdf accessed on 15.1.15.

[57] Ibid., 68.

[58] Erling Berge, "Language and Culture: On the Possibility of an Emerging Cartoon-based language," in *Communication and Society: The Emerging Human Concerns*, edited by, Kamlesh Mahajan (New Delhi: Classical Publishing Company, 1990), 164.

who speaks. Not only does the sound of a voice affect the one who hears it; the speaker is affected also. As people vocalize their experiences, they learn about themselves, others, and the world."[59]

Voice is interlinked with speech[60] and language. Michael Traber in his writing also mentioned that, "humans, in distinction from plants and animals, are the living being capable of speech .... It means to say that only speech ables the human being to be the living being he or she is as human being."[61] Speech and language are inextricably linked; they are interconnected with one another. As it is said, "there is no language without speech, and no speech outside language."[62] One cannot separate these two from each other; they exist in relation with one another "in a relation of reciprocal comprehensiveness."[63] Roland Barthes sums it up when he said that "a language is at the same time the product and the instrument of speech: their relationship is therefore a genuinely dialectical one."[64] So also, when one speaks out, voice naturally flows to communicate, and speaking originally comes to us as breathing. Therefore, voice, speech, and language are integral to each other.

One very unique feature in human communication is language. Animals do communicate with their own tone of voice but they carry limited number of messages. Jean Aitchison in "Defining language" mentioned Hockett's eight features of the essential nature of language. These are: *use of vocal-auditory channel, arbitrariness, semanticity, cultural transmission, duality, displacement, structure-dependence and creativity*.[65] Hockett discussed all the design features of human language to identify and see whether it is present in animal communication. Finally, it is observed that, even though some animals possess some of the features, for instance bird song has duality, and bee dancing has a greater degree of displacement, but no animal system can be proved to have semanticity or to use structure-dependent operations.[66] According to Plato and Aristotle, human

---

[59] Erling Berge, "Language and Culture: On the Possibility of an Emerging Cartoon-based language," in *Communication and Society: The Emerging Human Concerns*, edited by, Kamlesh Mahajan (New Delhi: Classical Publishing Company, 1990), 164.

[60] "Speech is the ability to speak," in Oxford Advance Learner's Dictionary 9th edition, www.oxfordlearnersdicyionaries.com/definition/english/speech?q=speech, accessed on 16.3.15.

[61] Michael Traber, "Communication is Inscribed in Human Nature: A Philosophical Inquiry into the Right to Communicate," www.direitoacomunicacao.org.br/content.php?option=com..., accessed on 21.2.2014.

[62] Roland Barthes, "Language and Speech (langue and parole)," in *Communication Studies: An Introductory Reader*, edited by John Corner, Jeremy Hawthorn (London: Edward Arnold Pty Ltd, 1983), 78.

[63] Ibid.

[64] Ibid., 79.

[65] Jean Aitchison, "Defining language," in *Communication Studies: an Introductory Reader*, edited by John Corner, Jeremy Hawthorn (London: Edward Arnold Pty Ltd, 1983), 69.

[66] Ibid., 76

beings are termed as "the animal possessing speech," (*zoon logon echon*) and Aristotle further distinct and defined other creatures as *alogon*, meaning without speech (*logos*).[67] It is, therefore, concluded that there is no such animal that could creatively communicate or talk to another animal as human beings who talk and learn languages.

It is assumed that forms of symbolic interaction or communication through language emerged some 50,000 years ago. Language becomes an essential part or type of communication which we call "conversation."[68] Paul A. Soukup's essay, mentioned six communication images and the first image of communication is linguistic:

> Language, with its syntactic, semantic, and pragmatic characteristics, fundamentally defines communication for those who accept this image. As an analogue for communication, language highlights grammar, symbols, and linguistic acts. Thus, the perspective of those who choose this image tends to be somewhat structural and in search of interpretive tools. People with this view also ask about the relationship between language forms and language contents; thus, questions of narrative, anecdote, and story arise as do questions about the fundamental operation of language, particularly in affective expression through metaphor, symbol, or parable.[69]

Language is a tool for representing experience, and tools contribute to creative endeavours only when used.[70] Casaregola affirms the relation of human sound, speech, and language: "When we speak together we bathe in sound. This is not ephemeral. It is, quite literally, the embodiment of language."[71] In order to have mutual respect, sharing experiences and reflections within individuals among its social group and community, the oral and written forms of language must pass back and forth between persons who both speak and listen or read and write. Without them, individuals remain isolated from others; and without tools for representing their experiences, people also remain isolated from the

[67] Philip Lee, "Introduction," in *Many Voices, One Vision: Right to Communicate in Practice,* edited by Philip Lee (Penang: Southbound; London: WACC, 2004), 2.

[68] Cees J. Hamelink, "Grounding the human right to communicate," in *Many Voices, One Vision: Right to Communicate in Practice,* edited by, Philip Lee (Penang: Southbound, 2004), 24.

[69] Paul A. Soukup, *Communication and Theology: Introduction and Review of the Literature* (London: World Association for Christian Communication, 1983), 27.

[70] Mary Field Belenky, Blythe McVicker Clinchy, et.al., *Women's Ways of Knowing: The Development of Self, Voice, and Mind,* 10th ed. (New York: Basic Books, A Member of the Perseus Books Groups, 1997). 25.

[71] Vincent Casaregola, "The "Exact Location" of the Voice, op. cit., 68.

self.[72] S. Wesley Ariarajah also rightly states that: "Languages are innate to people's being; it is difficult to separate a people's language from their culture, history and emotions."[73] Michael Traber talks about the importance of language which is essential for every humanbeings. It is mentioned that:

> The essence of the human being as a social being is constituted and perfected by language. Being-together-in-the-world, or being intersubjective, is realised and actualised in the self-transcendence of communication. When we are deprived of this togetherness we cannot live lives worthy of human nature. Language is thus the symbolic human construct that allows the forging and maintenance of relationships.[74]

1.2.2. Reason - Language

St Thomas Aquinas (1223–74), the medieval theologian, translated the Greek *logos* into Latin as "reason." This means that the speech and reason, or rationality, became the keystone of philosophical thinkers.[75] Philip Lee also mentioned about the connection between reason and language it is visible through his writing which says:

> It is reason that enables human beings to justify their beliefs and actions; to make moral judgements (criticise); to choose; to contemplate past and future; and to imagine. Reason makes them aware of themselves (self-conscious), aware of their state of mind and of others from whom they knowingly distinguish themselves.
>
> To carry out these tasks, reason requires language. People's "passage from a natural to a cultural state – the single major act in [their] history – is at every point interwoven with their speech faculties ... Language is the ability to represent the world in signs, initially by speaking (using a recognised system of sounds), and later by writing (using a recognised system of symbols).[76]

Reason and language therefore, connects and support each other in one's life.

---

[72] Mary Field Belenky, Blythe McVicker Clinchy, et.al., *Women's Ways of Knowing: The Development of Self, Voice, and Mind*, 26.

[73] S. Wesley Ariarajah, "Creating a 'Culture of Dialogue' in a Multicultural and Pluralist Society," in *Communication Reconciliation: Challenges Facing the 21st Century*, edited by Philip Lee (Geneva: World Council of Churches, 2001), 3.

[74] Michael Traber, "Communication is Inscribed in Human Nature, op. cit.

[75] Philip Lee, "Introduction," in *Many Voices, One Vision,* op. cit., 2.

[76] Ibid.

1.2.3. Talking

Talking, or the spoken word, means that it is the voice that speaks out of the vocal cords through the mouth. Communication takes place more in talking than listening. It is said that "the key to success seems to be the ability to speak well."[77] When one speaks or talks, there is a chance of acquiring respect and admiration. On the other hand, talking gives one a chance to release energy, which means to release tensions as well. When one expresses her/his sad emotions verbally, it relieves her/his inner pain. Sharing your problem and speaking out with someone gives you immense joy. Adler and Rodman asserts: "It is also helpful to share your excitement with others by talking about it, for keeping it inside often leaves you feeling as if you might burst."[78] The importance of oral element can be seen in the media like television or film, and one cannot imagine the existence of radio without the voice as a medium. B.F. Jackson claims is true when he said: "From our first year to our last day, spoken communication is essential to life."[79]

1.3. Voice in Relation to Freedom and Equality.

1.3.1. Freedom

Michael Traber, in speaking of "Communication in Freedom, Equality and Solidarity,"[80] explains the interrelationship between language and freedom, equality and solidarity. He said that language and freedom are intertwined and freedom is an integral part of human nature which is a precondition of humans to be moral beings. Genuine freedom means to become more truly human and humane and that it can be experienced only through interaction with one human being to another. Traber goes on to say that: "Deprivation of freedom makes genuine communication impossible, and the first sign of repression in groups and societies is the curtailment of freedom of speech."[81] Traber continues to assert: "Freedom means being part of, and thus being able to participate in, life-in-common."[82] If an individual is deprived of her/his freedom that means genuine communication is impossible.[83] Michael Traber in his book mentioned the fabric of freedom which says:

> Freedom, it should be noted, is not primarily orientated towards objects but towards people. Only in the free encounter with others

---

[77] Ronald B. Adler, George Rodman, Understanding Human Communication, op. cit., 86.

[78] Ibid.

[79] B.F. Jackson, Jr., "Spoken Communication: A Medium," in *You And Communication In The Church: Skills And Techniques* by, B. F. Jackson, Jr., (Waco, Texas: Word Books, Publisher, 1974), 18.

[80] Michael Traber, "Communication is Inscribed in Human Nature, op. cit., 3.

[81] Ibid.

[82] Ibid., 4.

[83] Philip Lee, "Introduction," in *Many Voices, One Vision,* op. cit., 3.

> can genuine freedom be experienced. An intersubjective approach to the notion of freedom also establishes the rationale for the limitations of freedom, which are enshrined in the customary and codified laws of all societies.[84]

Being free to us does not mean total rejection or ignorance of the rights and responsibilities of given norms in a given community. It is not to overpower the rights of others but to exercise one's own rights and duty with utmost care and responsibility that is, the freedom of speech for all.

1.3.2. Equality

Freedom of speech is connected to equality. According to Traber, equality means when everyone in the community is considered as equal beings then only genuine freedom takes place. Genuine freedom will not be achieved if one considers others, as inferior being. For instance, if in the community men consider women as "inferior" human beings then that is not a true freedom. If one party discriminates against another race, ethnicity, religion, or sex and age, etc., then freedom and equality will disappear.[85]

The true sense of equality is unity in diversity. Knowing the difference, respecting and recognising the difference itself is equality which is unconditional. As it is said:

> Equality ... does not deny the reality of specific social identities, loyalties or preferential interests. Equality does not mean homogeneity or uniformity. Neither does it contradict the special roles and ranks which societies confer on individuals and groups of people.[86]

1.4. Voice as Non-Verbal Communication

In communication, another form of nonverbal communication is voice. Paralanguage is the term used by social scientists to describe nonverbal, vocal messages.[87] Even when the words are muffled, listeners may follow only the pitch, rate, volume, number and length of pauses and disfluencies (such as stammering, use of "uh," "um," "er," and so on)[88] but can still ascertain the speaker's emotions. The most important aspect of voice seems to be inflection variations in volume, rate and pitch that make you sound more expressive. It is explained that the impact of paralinguistic cues is strong because when vocal factors contradict a

---

[84] Michael Traber, "Communication is Inscribed in Human Nature, op. cit., 4.

[85] Ibid.

[86] Ibid.

[87] Ronald B. Adler, George Rodman, *Understanding Human Communication*, Third Edition (New York: Holt, Rinehart and Winston, INC., 1988), 116.

[88] Ibid.

verbal message, listeners judge the speaker's intention from the paralanguage and not from the words themselves.[89] Walter J. Ong in *Hermeneutic Forever: Voice, Text, Digitization, and the "I,"*[90] also explained that "any *use* of words, oral, textual, or digitized, is not just words but is also a speech *act*... entangled in all sorts of other nonverbal matters—these persons speaking and these listeners listening, the physical setting, the mood, ... and much else.[91] In the book, *The Dynamics of Human Communication,*[92] it was also stated that nonverbal communication is the main style of communicating feelings and emotions. Words normally carry *content information* whereas nonverbal communication expresses *affective information.* For example, from the way you look at someone you may communicate love, hate, dislike, interest, trust ... etc. which is a full range of human emotions which you do not always express verbally.[93]

1.5. Voice is Counter to the Culture of Silence

In most cases, voice cannot be controlled by any person for any reason. Voice is a gift from God, a gift of life for every living creature. Voice can be an utterance or an expression of joy or sadness, but voice is not silent, as the "discourse on voice assumes a fully conscious, fully speaking, 'unique, fixed and coherent self.'"[94]

In speaking for broadening the conceptualization of voice beyond verbal speech, Ashby argues that in some exceptional cases, silence does speak louder than the words of a language. Silence can be speech or, at least, a part of speech. There may be times when choosing not to speak is more resistance than oppression.[95] One such example will be found in an article by Evangeline Anderson-Rajkumar,[96]

---

[89] Ronald B. Adler, George Rodman, *Understanding Human Communication*, Third Edition (New York: Holt, Rinehart and Winston, INC., 1988), 116.

[90] Walter J. Ong, "Hermeneutic Forever. Voice, Text, Digitization, and the 'I'." http://journal.oraltradition.org/files/articles/10i/5_ong.pdf accessed on 15.1.15.

[91] Ibid.

[92] Gail E. Myers, Michele Tolela Myers, *The Dynamics of Human Communication: A Laboratory Approach 5th ed.* (New York: McGraw-Hill Book Company, 1988), 169-170.

[93] Ibid.

[94] Quoted in Christine Ashby, "Whose "Voice" is it anyway?: Giving voice and qualitative research involving individuals that type to communicate" in *Disability Studies Quarterly* dsq-sds.org/article/view/1723/1771, accessed on 31.10.2012.

[95] Ibid.

[96] Parattai Annan, an "original Dalit thinker and Dalit theologian" spelt out the importance of the agency of the option of Silence that a Dalit chose when she was the sole witness to the village headman raping and killing a woman in the forest. She felt silent for days and months together and refused to speak. The villagers interpreted this as being affected by the spirits in the forest. ... The silent dumb woman regains her "speech" ... She calls out to the Village headman by name and asks him to confess to the killing of the adivasi. See Evangeline Anderson-Rajkumar, "Decoding 'Silence-Voice-Speech' as an epistemological tool for a theology of engagement," in *God of Life, Lead us to Justice and peace: A Theological Reflection in the Context of India today* edited by H. Vanlalauva (Serampore: Department of Research/SATHRI, 2012), 80-81.

"Therefore, when the odds of patriarchy, class, caste are heavily loaded against a person, there may be a sudden decision to fall silent and this silence should not be measured in terms of lack of sound, voice, speech."[97]

Clyde H. Reid, in dealing with *The Role of Silence in Oral Communication,* wrote about silence in a small group verbal communication. It is affirmed that silence occurs in group interaction occasionally. Silence happens due to several reasons. It can be either a tense, awkward silence or a creative silence during which group members are reflecting, listening to the echoes of their minds, and waiting for fresh insight to emerge. In such a situation, in order to find out the reasons of their silence we can only tell by asking group members to express what they were feeling after the silence has been broken.[98]

Reid believed that language and silence have an integral relationship. He says that silence enriches oral communication: "Speaking needs silence for its own refreshment. Speaking flows out of the silence and is more likely to be heard and more likely to be relevant because of the silence."[99]

In other circumstances, we will need to consider the example from Christine Ashby who argued against voice as speech in the case of the disability. She added that if we continue to conceptualize voice as speech, certain persons with disabilities will be constructed as being without one. Therefore, one has to be rational as to how voice of disability can be heard and not only listen to a normative voice. For this, to think of voice more broadly as the ability to express oneself and be heard by others, that can encompass typed text, non-verbal communication, gestural communication or silence, which leaves the door open for a more expansive conceptualization of participation and engagement.[100] Our human physical body can also carry a lot of meanings and can communicate with the people much faster than the spoken voice. Leonie Kelleher states rightly that: "Before a person speaks, bodies elicit feelings of excitement and admiration, attraction and desire, envy and distaste."[101]

In speaking of those who are "Seen But Never Heard," Mary Field Belenky and others had explained some of the life stories of women who experienced their childhood lives in isolation, blanketed with silence, whose families were cut off

---

[97] Evangeline Anderson-Rajkumar, "Decoding 'Silence-Voice-Speech' as an epistemological tool for a theology of engagement," in *God of Life, Lead us to Justice and peace: A Theological Reflection in the Context of India Today* edited by H. Vanlalauva (Serampore: Department of Research/ SATHRI, 2012), 81.

[98] Clyde H. Reid, "Spoken Communication in Small Groups," in *You and Communication in the Church: Skills and Techniques* by B. F. Jackson, Jr., (Waco, Texas: Word Books, Publisher, 1974), 106-7.

[99] Ibid.

[100] Ibid.

[101] Leonie Kelleher, "Story Telling: Silence and Voice-Hope, Trust, Knowledge-Reflections on Aboriginal Heritage Legislation." http://www.tasa.org.au/uploads/2011/05/LeonieKelleherPaper.pdf accessed on 13.12.2013.

from the broader community, and communication such as discussion with family members and others too discouraged. This results in the denial of opportunities for play and dialogue, and hampers, the growth of a child. Belenky and others used an example of Lev Vygotsky and his colleagues who also suggested that exterior dialogues are a necessary precursor to inner speech and an awareness of one's own thought process, and argued that play itself is a precursor to symbolization and meaning-making.[102] It is said that:

> In the ordinary course of development, the use of play metaphors gives way to language – a consensually validated symbol system – allowing for more precise communication of meanings between persons. Outer speech becomes increasingly internalised as it is transformed into inner speech. Impulsive behaviour gives way to behaviour that is guided by the actor's own symbolic representations of hopes, plans, and meanings. Without playing, conversing, listening to others, and drawing out their own voice, people fail to develop a sense that they can talk and think things through.[103]

In some societies, cultural norms maintained the system of silence for certain sections of people, normally women and children. One's own voice is restricted by socio-cultural norms. Here in this case silencing refer not just to quieting, but also to censorship, suppression, marginalization, trivialization, exclusion, ghettoization, and other forms of discounting.[104]

As for Paulo Freire, the culture of silence means that, "the masses are 'mute,'... prohibited from creatively taking part in the transformations of their society and therefore prohibited from being ... They are nevertheless alienated from the power responsible for their silence."[105] The illiterate do not know that

---

[102] Mary Field Belenky, Blythe McVicker Clinchy, et.al, *Women's Ways of Knowing*, op.cit., 33.

[103] Ibid.

[104] Leonie Kelleher, "Story Telling: Silence and Voice-Hope, Trust, Knowledge-Reflections on Aboriginal Heritage Legislation." http://www.tasa.org.au/uploads/2011/05/LeonieKelleherPaper.pdf 13.12.13.

[105] Paulo Freire, *Cultural Action for Freedom*, (Cambridge, Massachussets: Penguin Books, 1972), 30. The context in which Paulo Freire developed his theory for the education of illiterates, especially adults, was based on his experience as well as the experiences faced by common people in Brazil. Freire "based on the conviction that a human being, no matter how "ignorant" or submerged in the "culture of silence," is capable of looking critically at his (sic) world in a dialogical encounters with others, and that provided with the proper tools for such an encounter he (sic) can gradually perceive his (sic) personal and social reality and deal critically with it." See Paulo Freire, *Pedagogy of the Oppressed*, (New York: The Continuum Publishing Corporation, 1982) back cover. The common people at that time, in all private and public life, were crushed by the external power and authority such as the power of the landlords, governors, captains, and viceroys. These aristocrats were controlling commerce and they were the ones who governed municipalities. The common people were excluded from the elective process, and forbidden to enter into their (the one who controls) communities. A democratic urban life was impossible in that condition because

they have the transforming power, and creative and re-creative ability, but they were blinded by the myth of their own culture, i.e. the "natural inferiority." They were "prevented from having a "structural perception" of the fact involving them, they do not know that they cannot "have a voice," that is, that they cannot exercise the right to participate consciously in the socio-historical transformation of their society, because their work does not belong to them."[106]

Freire says that since the common people or the dependent society are normally a silent society, their voice becomes inauthentic, their thinking and expression are those of the "culture of silence" and just a mere echo of the voice of the dominant or the metropolis. The dominant/metropolis speaks, and thus this culture "has a voice."[107]

The oppressed themselves develop self-deprecation which is derived from the internalization of the oppressors' opinions. The oppressor often made the oppressed believe that they are useless, know nothing, and are incapable of learning anything – that they are sick, lazy, and unproductive – so in the end they become convinced of their own unfitness.[108]

In response to the marginalisation of some sections of society, Freire therefore concluded in his *Banking Model of Education Versus Problem-Posing Education* that an "authentic education is not carried on by "A" *for* "B" or by "A" *about* "B," but rather by A" *with* "B," mediated by the world – a world which impresses and challenges both parties, giving rise to views or opinions about it."[109] The "Revolutionary leaders cannot think *about* the people, or *for* the people, but only *with* the people."[110] One's own voice is valid and nobody can represent

---

the common people were already impoverished, absorbed and suffocated by the economic power of the great estates. The common people were set aside without civic rights, any experience of self-government or dialogue. Freire had lived among such condition in Brazil. See Paulo Freire, *Education for Critical Consciousness* (London: Sheed and Ward, 1979), 26.

[106] Ibid.

[107] Paulo Freire expressed that the 'culture of silence' is not something created or transported or constructed or imposed on it by the Metropolis/dominator to the Third World/dominated but this culture is the result of the structural relations between the dominated and the dominators.

Why do we speak about culture? Freire said this because revolution is always cultural. Why we have been speaking about cultural action and cultural revolution? it is because cultural action for freedom has been carried out in opposition to the dominating power elite. Cultural revolution proposes freedom as its goal without being subordinated to the revolutionary regime. "Cultural action, on the contrary, if sponsored by the oppressive regime, can be a strategy for domination, in which case it can never become cultural revolution." See Paulo Freire, *Cultural Action for Freedom*, 57-82.

[108] Paulo Freire, *Pedagogy of the Oppressed,* (New York: The Continuum Publishing Corporation, 1982), 49.

[109] Paulo Freire, *Education for Critical Consciousness* (London: Sheed and Ward, 1979), 82.

[110] "Paulo Freire's *Pedogogy of the Oppressed,"* http://www.sonoma.edu/users/d/daniels/Freire_summary.html accessed on 11.9.13.

someone else except by her/his own self. For that it is not about, for, or by her/him but rather with her/him.[111]

Voice, speech, language, talk, silence, reason etc. that are discussed above communicate to us powerfully as tools for empowerment and kindling for transformation in the community where people who are subdued and ostracized in various ways. One does agree with Evangeline Anderson-Rajkumar who used the words "Silence-Voice-Speech" as one hyphenated triadic concept emphasising the enormous potential by using this triad as analytical tool to study the experience of power-powerlessness, patriarchy, violence, caste, class, race, etc. and other dominant ideologies and issues in society.[112] Evangeline Anderson-Rajkumar states that: "'Silence-Voice-Speech' as 'Voice of Dissent' is a necessary theological and ethical category to construct a theology of liberation as well as a Theology of Engagement."[113] Through voice, speech, language, talk, reason, silence etc. an individual being conveys powerful messages.

1.6. Voice as Dialogue

Why is voice important in dialogue? Can dialogue be possible in the absence of human voice? Yes, dialogue is possible when it is written in a book or conversations in a book. However, for example, a formal or informal discussion between two parties or countries normally bears more fruitful and instant results when one communicates face to face and makes voice to voice contact. Turner and Hudson mentioned Carol Gilligan and Jean Baker Miller who say that when the self is brought fully into relationship with others, it results in honest dialogue.[114] It writes that:

> As an important component of the self in dialogue, voice represents the valuing of emerging differences and the full participation of all persons in a conversation that leads to connection and understanding. It is essential to the development of authentic community. In the same way, voice presupposes a social world, the presence of others whom we address and who also respond to us. Voice is central to understanding the relationship of trust, belonging and intimacy between God and community.[115]

---

111 This idea has been borrowed from Paulo Freire, the Brazilian educationist.

112 Evangeline Anderson-Rajkumar, "Decoding 'Silence-Voice-Speech' as an epistemological tool for a theology of engagement," 76.

113 Ibid.,79.

114 Mary Donovan Turner, Mary Lin Hudson, *Saved from Silence: Finding Women's Voice in Preaching* (Denver: Mary Donovan Turner and Mary Lin Hudson, 1999), 16.

115 Ibid.

Cees J. Hamelink writes that, "... in communities people need to share language in conversation in order to understand each other. Mutual understanding is not possible without dialogue."[116]

As it is said, the essence of dialogue itself is the word. It is the word which is an important instrument that makes dialogue possible. Within the word, we find two dimensions that are reflection and action. These two cannot be separated because if one suffers the other one also gets affected. Action and reflection becomes praxis. If action and reflection fails to go along, then it negates the true praxis and makes dialogue impossible.[117] Therefore, Paulo Freire states that: "Thus, to speak a true word is to transform the world."[118]

Human existence cannot be silent, but made manifest in word, in work, in action-reflection. According to Freire: "... word is not the privilege of some few men [*sic*], but the right of every man [*sic*]. Consequently, no one can say a true word alone – nor can he say *for* another, in a perspective act which robs others of their words."[119] Therefore, dialogue cannot occur between those who deny others the right to speak their word and those whose right to speak has been denied them.[120]

One of the methods that Freire adopted on education is a dialogical process of communication. This method of education is not limited to literacy training alone but rather to conscientise people of their rights. Conscientisation means to have a critical awareness of reality and of the capacity to transform it through dialogue. In one's life, if one wants to achieve purpose and meaning, then one must seek insight through dialogue.

Freire illustrated that both teacher and pupils combine in a common purpose seeking truth about relevant problems, while respecting others' opinions.[121] Thus "through dialogue the teacher-of-the-students and the students-of-the-teacher cease to exist and a new term emerges teacher-student with student-teachers. The teacher is no longer merely the one-who-teaches but one who is himself taught in dialogue with the students who in their turn while being taught also teach."[122]

It is affirmed that true dialogue is about love, humility, hope and faith without which there will not be any meaningful dialogue. Grounded in love,

---

[116] Cees J. Hamelink, "Grounding the human right to communicate," in *Many Voices, One Vision: Right to Communicate in Practice*, 25.

[117] Paulo Freire, *Pedagogy of the Oppressed,* (New York: The Continuum Publishing Corporation, 1982), 75.

[118] Ibid.

[119] Ibid., 76.

[120] Ibid.

[121] Ninan Koshy, "Introduction to Paulo Freire," in *Education for Liberation: Addresses by Paulo Freire and Critical Reflections on Indian Education* (Whitefield, Bangalore: Ecumenical Christian Centre, 1983), 15.

[122] Ibid.

humility, faith and hope brings horizontal relationship in which mutual trust between the dialoguers emerge.[123] Freire calim is true when he says that: "Without dialogue there is no communication, and without communication there can be no true education."[124]

1.7. Storytelling is Voice

Storytelling is also considered as one of the important means of communication which is voice. Leonie Kelleher has rightly pointed out that: "Storytelling reverses silence. It both gives voice and is a type of voice. Storytelling, including giving voice to self, is core to formation of positive imagery and to creation."[125] This is illustrated by the experience of the Aboriginals, the indigenous people of Australia. The Indigenous people of Australia had their voice silenced, even their philosophical standpoint, language and knowledge systems. They were occupied and subjugated leading to depression, their relationships were severed and they missed opportunities for learning and achievement. As the *Bringing Them Home* report concluded, the only hope and solace for the Indigenous people was to continue to record the testimonies of the excluded. In such a condition, a little relief of pain or a small change may come about through sympathy, listening, ensuring individuals do not self-silence, which has profound positive effect. Kelleher also attested that: "Voice is a primary mechanism in the management of past trauma."[126]

1.8. Voice in the Old Testament

In the Old Testament, God revealed God-self to humankind through various forms. In all these, one of the most unique and ultimate sources of God's communication with humankind is through the divine spoken "Voice." The voice of God had been heard by different people, at different times, and on various occasions. It is received through messengers, angels, prophets/prophetesses, judges, and sometimes kings. They are the mediators between God and human beings; they are entrusted and commissioned by God. God's voice is heard in various forms through different ways. John H. Skilton writes that a person knows in the deepest recesses of her/his being that that voice is true. To deny that voice would be to cut herself/himself off from hope, light, reason, and reality; it would be to deny her/himself and to deny God.[127]

---

[123] Paulo Freire, *Pedagogy of the Oppressed,* (New York: The Continuum Publishing Corporation, 1982), 77-79.

[124] Ibid., 81.

[125] Leonie Kelleher, "Story Telling: Silence and Voice-Hope, op. cit., 6.

[126] Ibid.

[127] John H. Skilton, "The Voice of God's Word," *Westminster Theological Journal,* 60/2 (1 September, 1998): 189.

The voice of God comes to the people in various circumstances. It includes all concerning instructions, impending danger or catastrophes, punishment, prosperity, and good news. It is also received by individuals, judges, and the leaders. God spoke directly to the people, sometimes through signs and miracles, and through dreams and visions. God commands and directs as has witness in the Scriptures for example, in Psalms 147:15 that says; "He sends out his command to the earth; his word runs swiftly," in Isaiah 59:21 it says; "The Spirit of the Lord rests on Isaiah and fills his mouth with everlasting words, and in Ezekiel 37:1-10 we find the prophet Ezekiel who was commanded by the Spirit of the Lord to speak to the valley of dry bones and Ezekiel followed the instruction which had goes forth through his breath, voice, and lips, and the dry bones are brought to life.[128] In the life of Aaron he obeys and listens to God's instructions, "Go into the wilderness to meet Moses." Aaron spoke all the words that the LORD had spoken to Moses, and performed the signs in the sight of the people (Ex. 4: 27, 30).

God is also a listening God, who hears and listens to the voice of the people. In the Scripture we find in Genesis 4: 9 ff God who hears the cry of the slain Abel and holds his brother Cain accountable, in I Kings 21:17 ff God condemns Ahab and Jezebel for killing the poor man Naboth, and in Exoduc 3:7ff God also spoke to Moses because God hears the cry of the slaves in Egypt.[129] As it is said that "God's Spirit is often conceived as the divine voice that breathes through particular and diverse human voices, and makes God heard and known in the believing community."[130]

1.9. The Voice of God in the Creation Story

In the first chapter of Genesis, we find that everything God created on each of the six days of Creation Week was by His word. Genesis 1:2 clearly mentioned the presence of God's Spirit over the water, "... and the Spirit of God was hovering over the face of the waters." In the Scripture, the Spirit is often associated with voice. In the Hebrew Bible, *ruach* is a feminine noun that speaks of both divine and human breath.[131] *Ruach* can also mean "spirit," "wind," or "breath." The writer means to say that a wind was fanning the waters, or that the Spirit of God was participating in the creation event.[132] After this, God began to voice saying, "Let there be light," and there was light. With those first words the creation event begins to unfold as God speaks into being sky, earth, seas, plants, life, lights, living

[128] Andrea Hollingsworth, "Spirit and voice: toward a feminist Pentecostal pneumatology," *Pneuma*, 29/2 (2007): 205.

[129] *The Ecumenical Review*, 57/2, (April, 2005):197.

[130] Andrea Hollingsworth, "Spirit and voice: toward a feminist Pentecostal pneumatology," *Pneuma*, 29/2 (2007): 205.

[131] Ibid.

[132] "Who really is the God of Genesis? Genesis the word of God," http://creation.com/who-really-is-the-god-of-genesis accessed on 12.3.12.

creatures, and finally human beings. According to Turner and Hudson, "Speech demonstrates God's agency and authority in the world."[133]

The formula God used on each day was "And God said ...," and it was so. God's satisfaction was expressed through the uttered voice, as mentioned in the scripture, "God saw everything that he had made, and indeed, it was very good ..." (Gen.1:31).[134] Therefore, creation of the world itself is a manifestation of the character of God. God shaped it with an intimacy that expressed God's concern and pronounced it a worthy expression by calling it "very good."[135]

In these entire creation events, one very special item that God had created in God's image was humankind, both female and male. The voice of God had expressed something very special into the cosmos, that is, humankind. Then God said, "Let us make humankind in our image, according to our likeness ..." (Gen.1:26-7). Of all the wonders of creation God addresses only humans. God's gift to humankind is the ability to listen and to speak. God had given the authority not only to listen and to speak but also to take up the responsibility over the inhabited earth.

1.10. The Significance of God's Voice

The voice of God is revealed to humankind in very different and various ways as we can find in the Hebrew Scriptures as well as from the New Testament. The Hebrew term *bat kol* (Hebrew בת קול), literally means daughter of a voice, and concerns a "heavenly or divine voice which proclaims God's will or judgment." The characteristic attributes of the *bat kol* are the invisibility of the speaker and a certain remarkable quality in the sound, which is considered to be a heavenly voice.[136]

In Deuteronomy 4:12, we see that "... the Lord spoke to you out of the fire. You heard the sound of words but saw no form; there was only a voice". In this account, God reveals God-self to humans through the organs of hearing, not through those of sight. God's voice came to the prophet Ezekiel, who saw many visions and said, "... I heard the voice of someone speaking, (Ezek. 1:28c); similarly, Elijah recognized God by a "still, small voice," that addressed him (I Kings 19:12–13; compare Job 4:16); sometimes God's voice rang from the heights, from Jerusalem, from Zion (Ezek. 1:25; Jer. 25:30; Joel 4:16–17; Am. 1:2, etc.); and God's voice was heard in the thunder and in the roar of the sea.[137]

---

133 Mary Donovan Turner, Mary Lin Hudson, *Saved from Silence: Finding Women's Voice in Preaching,* (St Louis: Chalice Press, 1999), 20.

134 "Who really the God of Genesis?, op. cit.

135 William Dyrness, *Themes in Old Testament Theology* (UK: Paternoster Press, 1979), 26.

136 "*bat kol,*" http://www.jewishencyclopedia.com/articles/2651-bat-kol accessed on 12.3.12.

137 Ibid.

1.10.1. God's Word is Voice

Isaiah 9:7 tells us that 'The Lord sent a word.' The term "sent," which is borrowed from the commissioning of the prophet (Isa. 6:8; 61:1; Jer.1:7 et.al.) is transferred to the word: "It shall succeed in that for which I sent it" (cf. Ps. 107:20; 147:15, 18). Thereby something of the character of the prophet himself is transferred to the word.[138]

"For as the rain and the snow come down from heaven, and do not return there until they have watered the earth, making it bring forth and sprout, giving seed to the sower and bread to the eater, so shall my word be that goes out from my mouth; it shall not return to me empty, but it shall accomplish that which I purpose, and succeed in the thing for which I sent it." (Isa. 55:10f.) A voice says, "Cry out! And I said, "What shall I cry? All people are grass, their constancy is like the flower of the field .... The grass withers, the flower fades; but the word of our God will stand for ever." (Isa. 40:6-8).[139]

We wonder and imagine how powerful the presence of God's voice was among the people over the past years. The intimate voice of God was prevalent within humankind as we see in the creation account. 1 Kings 19:11-13 talks about the voice of God that was revealed to the prophet. When the prophet tried to search God, the prophet could not see the Lord in the wind nor in a powerful earthquake that shook the ground beneath his feet, nor could the prophet see the Lord in the fire that flashed in the wilderness. But finally, the prophet heard a different sound, the sound of a "still small voice." God was not in the earth, the wind, the fire; he was in that still, small voice.[140]

1.10.2. The Voice of God with Humankind

The mutual act and involvement of God in conversation with people and the promises made with humankind is obvious.[141] One of the examples in the Old Testament attests this, when David inquired of the Lord, "Shall I go and attack these Philistines? The LORD said to David, Go and attack the Philistines and save Keilah. But David's men said to him, Look, we are afraid here in Judah; how much more than if we go to Keilah against the armies of the Philistines? Then David inquired of the LORD again. The LORD answered him, Yes, go down to Keilah; for I will give the Philistines into your hand." (1 Sam. 23:2-4).

Another conversation will be seen between God and Elijah. "Then the word of the Lord came to him, saying, what are you doing here, Elijah? He answered,

---

[138] Ibid., 239.

[139] Ibid., 238.

[140] David Capes, "Where did the title 'The Voice' come from?" (7 December 2012), Personal letter to the author (15 December 2012).

[141] Paul S. Chung, "God's Mission as Word Event in an Age of World Christianity: An Asian Linguistic-Transcultural Model." *International Review of Mission*, 98/2 (November, 2009): 17- 328.

I have been very zealous for the Lord, the God of hosts; for the Israelites have forsaken your covenant, thrown down your altars, and killed your prophets with the sword. I alone am left, and they are seeking my life, to take it away." (1 Kings 19:8-10).

On many occasions, the voice of God had been received directly by an individual. As we know from the call of Samuel by God, God spoke to Samuel in a voice in the night. The LORD came ... calling as before, "Samuel! Samuel!" And Samuel said, "Speak, for your servant is listening" (1 Sam. 3:10). The essential nature and character of the word assert God's power and the effectiveness of the divine voice to humankind. Jeremiah 15:16 says, "Your words were found, and I ate them, and your words became to me a joy and the delight of my heart; for I am called by your name, O LORD, God of hosts."

1.10.3. The Voice of God in the Whirlwind and a Burning Bush

The voice of God is manifested in Job out of the whirlwind. "Who is this that darkens counsel by words without knowledge? Gird up your loins like a man, I will question you, and you shall declare to me." (Job 38:1–3). When the LORD saw that he had turned aside to see, God called to him out of the bush, Moses, Moses! And he said, here I am (Ex. 3:4).

1.10.4. The Voice of God in Dreams and in Visions

Dreams and visions are some of the channels through which God communicated to humankind in the past as we find in the scripture. "While the words were still in the king's mouth, a voice came from heaven: O King Nebuchadnezzar, to you it is declared: The kingdom has departed from you!" (Dan. 4:31). Dreams are spoken of as a passageway through which God can speak. Some of the examples are, in Genesis 31:11 God spoke to Jacob, "in a dream," to Abimelech in Genesis 20:3, "in a dream by night." In Genesis 37:6, "Joseph dreamed a dream" concerning what would happen in the future. In Genesis 40:8, a Butler and a Baker in prison with Joseph, both "dreamed dreams." In Genesis 41:1, Pharaoh dreamed and asked Joseph to interpret the dream for him; the meaning was that he saw, "Seven years of plenty and seven years of famine." As we read 1 Kings 3, it is in a dream that Solomon was given a choice of choosing anything he desired. He chose "wisdom to judge God's people" and, because he chose wisdom, God gave him wisdom and, in addition, God promised him riches and honour.[142]

1.10.5. The Voice of God through an Angel

God's voice comes through an angel as we see in the life of Elijah. While he was sleeping, an angel touched Elijah and said, "Get up and eat." He ate and drank, and lay down again. "The angel of the LORD came a second time, touched

---

[142] "Are dreams real?" http://www.angelfire.com/nt/theology/theology/02rev.html, accessed on 13.10.12.

him, and said, "Get up and eat, otherwise the journey will be too much for you" (1 Kings 19:5–7). To Moses God spoke through an angel. There the angel of the LORD appeared to him in a flame of fire out of a bush; he looked, and the bush was blazing, yet it was not consumed (Ex. 3:2).

1.10.6. The Voice of God through Prophetesses and Prophets

Prophets and prophetesses were the mediators or seers; they were the channels through whom God had communicated to the people in the past. The prophetesses/prophets occasionally speak directly of the process of reception and transmission of the word.[143] The Hebrew Scriptures indeed included women prophets sparingly, though they were prominent at that time. Prophetesses such as Deborah who was a Judge, a counsellor, and a warrior too (Judg. 4 and 5);[144] prophetess Miriam was a woman who the people led the people in a victory song after the crossing of the Red Sea (Ex. 15:20–21); Huldah the prophetess remained the single most powerful Deuteronomistic voice in Israel in the absence of Jeremiah (2 Kings 22; 2 Chro. 34); prophetess Noadiah was mentioned very little (Neh. 6:14); and the nameless woman prophet, the wife of the prophet Isaiah (Isa. 8:3): [145] these were the women whose voices were powerful and heard by the people in Israel.

As we have seen, the prophet Jeremiah says, "the Lord put out his hand and touched my mouth; and the LORD said to me, now I have put my words in your mouth. See, today I appoint you over nations and over kingdoms, to pluck up and to pull down, to destroy and to overthrow, to build and to plant (Jer. 1:9,11f.). Is not my word like fire, says Yahweh, and like a hammer which breaks the rock in pieces?" (Jer. 23:28f; cf. 23:18ff).[146]

God had chosen and commissioned special people as prophetesses/prophets. On several occasions, the voice of God passed through them to individuals as well as to the nation at large. It was a vocation for the prophetesses/prophets to carry out the task that had been assigned to them by God. In the book of Amos, it says, "… the lion has roared; who will not fear? The Lord GOD has spoken; who can but prophesy? (Am. 3:8). Jeremiah uttered to God, O LORD, you have enticed me, and I was enticed; you have overpowered me, and you have prevailed …" (Jer. 20:7ff).

We also see other prophets like Gad (2 Sam. 24:11; 1 Kings 12:22). When David rose in the morning, the word of the Lord came to the prophet Gad, David's seer, saying, "Go and say to David: Thus says the Lord … (2 Sam. 24:11-12). But,

---

[143] Werner H. Schmidt, *The Faith of the Old Testament*, translated by John Sturdy (Oxford: Basil Blackwell, 1986), 236.

[144] Gabriele Dietrich, *A New Thing On Earth: Hopes and Fears facing Feminist Theology*, (Delhi: ISPCK, 2004), 78-9.

[145] Tal Ilan, "Huldah, the Deuteronomic Prophetess of the Book of Kings," http://www.lectio.unibe.ch/10_1/ilan.html accessed on 19.2.13

[146] Ibid., 237.

that same night the word of the Lord came to Nathan, saying … (1 Chron.17:3). The word of God came to Shemaiah the man of God …" (1 Kings 12:22). All these examples bring to us that the voice of God was communicated to the people directly through prophetess/prophets.

1.10.7. The Voice of God in Judgement

The voice of God is not only to announce news to the people but also to bring in judgment. As we find in Daniel 4:31 While the words were still in the king's mouth, a voice came from heaven "O King Nebuchadnezzar, to you it is declared: The kingdom has departed from you!"

Jeremiah expressly attested that the word of God means the prophetic message that participates in God's power and that is not only to announce but also to bring in the judgment. The word "sent" by God is certainly that spoken by the prophetesses/prophets, which is regarded as the cause of the catastrophe. In Jeremiah 5:14 it says, "… therefore thus says the LORD, the God of hosts: Because they have spoken this word, I am now making my words in your mouth a fire, and this people wood, and the fire shall devour them."

Hosea 6:5 says, "Therefore I have hewn them by the prophets, I have killed them by the words of my mouth, and my judgment goes forth as the light (Hos. 6:5). As in Isaiah 9:8 it says, … the Lord sent a word against Jacob, and it fell on Israel ... Is not my word like fire, says Yahweh, and like a hammer which breaks the rock in pieces?"

1.10.8. The Voice of Abrasiveness and Insistence

Human beings do not only listen to God's voice in silence; rather they converse with God. The interaction between God and human beings is seen in many instances in the bible. One such example is the lament psalms in which, "… anything, everything is brought to speech as the psalmist names the reality of the world as he knows it and directs his misery, pain and betrayal to God."[147] The voice of the people is not always for the adoration and admonishment of God but sometimes in a provocative and requisite manner that asks God for their deliverance. The lament psalms are expressions of grief by the nation as well as individuals.

In Psalm 64:1 David expressed his deep emotion and raised his voice before God. "Hear my voice, O God, in my complaint; preserve my life from the dread enemy. And also in Psalm 141:1 I call upon you, O LORD; come quickly to me; give ear to my voice when I call to you."

In my distress, I called upon the Lord; to my God I cried for help. From his temple he heard my voice, and my cry to him reached his ears (Ps. 18: 6). Evening and morning and at noon I utter my complaint and moan, and he will hear my

---

147 Mary Donovan Turner, Mary Lin Hudson, *Saved from Silence: Finding Women's Voice in Preaching,* (St Louis: Chalice Press, 1999), 21.

voice (Ps. 55: 17). I had said in my alarm, "I am driven far from your sight." But, you heard my supplications when I cried out to you for help (Ps. 31: 22).

Walter Brueggemann in *Voice as Counter to Violence* speaks about the lament psalms, arguing that they are that which "insist upon Israel's finding voice, a voice that tends to be abrasive and insistent." Brueggemann mentioned that a lament psalm is a Jewish refusal of silence before God, which is not cultural, sociological, or psychological, but that which is theological. The Jewish belief is that either on earth or by heaven the adequate relationship with God permits and requires a human voice that will speak out against every wrong perpetrator.[148]

Some of Brueggemann's sharing and/or explanations about the lament psalms 39 are highlighted here. In verse 4, we will notice the speaker who with the change of tone expresses to God, "Lord, let me know my end, and what is the measure of my days; let me know how fleeting my life is?" Here it is said that, "the speaker names Yahweh for the first time." Immediately after the address, things begin to change as has mentioned: "The cause of trouble has now become an open question in the relationship."[149]

There are dissimilarities between verse 4 and verses 5–6. Verse 4 is about "serene, trustful petition." But verses 5–6 are about "accusation." Therefore, it is observed that they are the strange combination of "deference and accusation." The speaker is speaking to God saying, "You have reduced all human life and my human life to meaninglessness." Brueggemann go on to say that, "Israel speaks in this psalm on the conviction that to speak seriously about meaninglessness is to render meaning. Speech turns meaninglessness into meaningfulness!"[150]

Here the point is that the human voice becomes a powerful tool to seek God's providence, to address the problem, to question God, and to strengthen the relationship with God. Voice is the powerful agent that has been reciprocally communicated between God and human beings in the past and present, and it will continue till the end of time as it is the provision from God.

1.11. The Voice of God through Jesus Christ.

The manifestation of God is seen through Jesus Christ in the New Testament. The direct conversation and relationship between God and humankind has been replaced by the presence of Jesus Christ on earth. Peter T. O'Brien has rightly brought in that, "God's being is made manifest in Christ, so that to see him is to

---

[148] Walter Brueggemann, "Voice as Counter to Violence" in *Calvin Theological Journal* 36 (2001): 22-23.

[149] Ibid.

[150] Ibid.

see what God is like (Heb.1:3b)."[151] The word of God is alive and active.[152] And this is represented through the usage of the term "Logos" in John's gospel. The Greek term λόγος (Logos) represents not only single meaning but it carries a number of meanings. It can mean "word," "speech," "matter," "thing," "command," "message," "account," "reckoning," "settlement," "respect," "reason," and so on.[153] John the Baptist mentioned the word 'voice' in his testimony, confirming what we have asserted, "I am the voice of the one crying out in the wilderness, 'Make straight the way of the Lord,' " (Jn. 1:23).[154] For Paul Christ is the "image of God" (2 Cor. 4:4; Col. 1:15). It is greatly believe in Marianne Meye Thompson's writing that talks about: "Adoration, the recognition of the icon of God in the human face, both occur on the basis and in the light of the encounter with the word, that is to say, with the actual person of Jesus Christ."[155]

In the New Testament, mention of "a voice from heaven" occurs in the following passages: Mt 3:17; Mk 1:11; Lk 3:22 (at the baptism of Jesus); Mt 17:5; Mk 9:7; Lk 9:35 (at the transfiguration); Jn. 12:28 (shortly before the Passion); Acts 9:4; Acts 22:7; Acts 26:14 (conversion of Paul), and Acts 10:13, Acts 10:15 (instruction of Peter concerning the clean and unclean). Andrea Hollingsworth writes: "After the resurrection, God's Spirit falls in the form of tongues of fire in the upper room at Pentecost, filling the men and women present with power to voice loudly and clearly the good news of the risen Christ to all people (Acts 2:1-13)."[156]

Thompson highlighted the characterization of God in the Gospel of John (the Fourth Gospel). When dealing with *The Actions of God*, she mentioned the actions attributed to God in the Gospel. These are either implied or assumed, or understood indirectly through the actions of Jesus. Examples such as, "all things came into being through him, and without him not one thing came into being" (Jn.1:3) and "the Law indeed was given through Moses; grace and truth came through Jesus Christ" (Jn. 1:17) are statements by the narrator of the Gospel that imply God's actions.

---

[151] Peter T. O'Brien, "God as the Speaking God: "Theology" in the Letter to the Hebrews," in *Understanding the Times: New Testament Studies in the 21st Century*, edited by Andreas J. Kostenberger, Robert W. Yarbrough, (Nottingham: Crossway Books, a publishing ministry of Good News Publishers, 2011), 201.

[152] Ibid., 207.

[153] William F. Arndt and F. Wilbur Gingrich, *A Greek-English Lexicon of the New Testament and Other Early Christian Literature* (Chicago: The University of Chicago Press, 1957), 478-80.

[154] "New Revised Standard Version Catholic edition for India," (Bangalore: Thomas Nelson, 1993), 92.

[155] Marianne Meye Thompson, "God's Voice You Have Never Heard, God's Form You Have Never Seen: The Characterization Of God In The Gospel Of John," *Semeia*, no. 66 (January 1, 1993): 30.

[156] Andrea Hollingsworth, "Spirit and voice: toward a feminist Pentecostal pneumatology," *Pneuma*, 29/2 (2007): 205.

God is characterized as equal with everyone, "indiscriminately gracious, healing, life-giving, judging, liberating, illuminating, revealing."[157] All these show that God is actively participant with Jesus Christ in the making, involvement, and achieving, and is also the one who is active and present. In John 12:28, we see God's direct voice in response to Jesus' prayer "Father, glorify your name," then a voice came from heaven, saying, "I have glorified it, and I will glorify it again."[158]

The Gospel of Luke and Acts counted the human voice as very important in the divine realm through the story of Jesus and his followers' empowerment for proclamation. Peter T. O'Brien brought certain characteristics of God's word from the letter to the Hebrews. These are:

- God's word is *personal.* Here it says, God spoke directly and personally to his Son, to angels, and the first hearers, and now speaks to us (Heb.1:2).
- Divine word is *living.* It means that both women and men receive new life through God's announcement to them by his Son Jesus Christ.
- God's address to his people is a word that is *clear* and wholly *trustworthy.* God wants us to listen to his voice and understand to the word he said, by believing and acting upon it.
- God's voice from the scriptures was a *spoken* word to the congregation - it was oral.[159]

As Hebrew 4:12 says, "The word of God is living ..." This means that the scripture carries a vital message, a life-giving power. Elmer E. Flack mentions that, "God speaks the Word, and men [sic], receiving it, are born anew through faith. The presence of God will be felt in the Church, in, through, and under the Word."[160]

1.12. The Voice for Widows and Women

The word for "widow" in Hebrew is "*almānāh.*" This word denotes a negative connotation. Its root word is *"alem,"* which means "unable to speak." "Thus, the widow was "the silent one." Almānāh was used specially to designate the widow as helpless or exposed to oppression and harsh treatment. Therefore, "widowhood," "*almānah*" means "silence."[161] Similarly, in the Greek:

---

[157] Andrea Hollingsworth, "Spirit and voice: toward a feminist Pentecostal pneumatology," *Pneuma,* 29/2 (2007): 205.

[158] Ibid., 194-8.

[159] Peter T. O'Brien, "God as the Speaking God, op. cit., 215-6.

[160] Elmer E. Flack, "The Approach to the Word of God" in *Old Testament Commentary: A General Introduction to and A Commentary on The Books owf The Old Testament,* edited by Herbert C. Alleman, Elmer E. Flack (Pennsylvania: The Muhlenberg Press Philadelphia, 1949), 7.

[161] Prema Vakayil, *Women Shall Prophesy: Anna, The Prophetess (Lk 2:36-38): A Study in Luke's Feminine Perspective* (Bangalore: Asian Trading Corporation, 2007), 51-52.

> The Greek word for widow *chēra* means "without source (widowed)." *Chēra* is related to the preposition *chōris*, meaning 'without' or 'apart from', and is used adverbially to mean 'separately' or 'by itself'. It is also related to the noun *chōra* 'region or empty place'. The original meaning is 'a person without' or 'left without.' In the New Testament the term signifies a woman left without a husband. Hence some scholars are of the opinion that *chēra* can mean not only a widow in the modern sense of the word but also a woman living without a husband ... *chēra* simply denotes a celibate woman. 'Widow' frequently connoted not only marital but also economic status. A widow was often left without money or financial support as well, as a result of being left without a husband. The term *chēra* has strong social and financial overtones more appropriate to a widow than a widower. Thus a Greek woman who was left without a spouse was left a 'widow', a person without a source of support, silent and needy.[162]

The terming of the word "widow" itself shows us that she is regarded valueless, meaningless, hopeless and lifeless. She is left with no voice which means dead. Timothy C. Morgan says that in the whole of Scripture, the treatment of widows is a yardstick of community justice. It is very few times widows are seen as anything more than needy and defined by their loss.[163] A ray of hope appears in the midst of hopelessness when Jesus intervenes.

Mark 12:43–44 talks about Jesus's appreciation and acceptance of a poor widow who cast two copper coins into the temple treasury. Jesus said to his disciples, "Truly I tell you, this poor widow has put in more than all those who are contributing to the treasury. For all of them have contributed out of their abundance; but she out of her poverty has put in everything she had, all she had to live on." Luke 7 clearly brings to us that widows, slaves, and sinful women receive salvation through Jesus. In the writing of Patricia Datchuck Sánchez, "Jesus did not avoid those with whom others refused to associate; he purposely sought them out ... While others tried to silence and shun the needy, Jesus sought them, healed them and restored them to society."[164]

The constant use of the word 'woman' by Jesus is not a negative connotation but rather an expression of love and sympathy towards women. Jesus did recognise and called women as having "great faith" where in contrast, he often points out the "little faith" in his male disciples. Jesus addressed "woman" (*gynai*) in many

---

[162] Prema Vakayil, *Women Shall Prophesy: Anna, The Prophetess (Lk 2:36-38): A Study in Luke's Feminine Perspective* (Bangalore: Asian Trading Corporation, 2007), 54-55.

[163] Timothy C. Morgan, "Learning from Widows," *Christianity Today*, 53/5 (May, 2009): 7-7.

[164] Patricia Datchuck Sánchez, "The Word Scripted for Life" *National Catholic Reporter*, 50/1 (25th October, 2013): 27-27.

instances while he interacts with women. Thus he addressed his mother (at Cana, Jn. 2:4; and at the cross, (Jn. 19:26), Mary Magdalene (at the tomb after the resurrection, Jn. 20:13, 15), a crippled woman who was healed (Lk. 13:12), the Samaritan woman at the well (Jn. 4:21), and the adulteress saved from stoning (Jn. 8:10).[165]

It was the woman disciples who followed Jesus Christ till the end of his life. They were faithful followers of Christ who stood by him in his ministry, who assisted him, showed hospitality towards him and his disciples, followed him to the cross and his burial place, kept vigilance over his body, and who also witnessed his resurrection and ascension to heaven. Lydia Neufeld Harder has brought in her writing saying:

> All of the women thus knew that his ignominious death had been transformed into life, not only for Jesus but also for them. The resurrection signified the vindication of the suffering but also the vindication of the message of the reign of God which Jesus had proclaimed and lived. They had not followed him in vain. The power already exhibited in Jesus' life was stronger than the power of death.[166]

1.13. Communicating Without Barriers

The mission and ministry of Jesus began by bringing a voice to the voiceless in society. God's continuing communication to the world has been manifested through Jesus Christ. We see Jesus's response to the cries and yearnings of the excluded and the disempowered in many instances such as the bent-over woman, the man with a withered hand, the blind beggar, lepers, the Syrophoenician/ Canaanite woman, the Samaritan woman, the multitudes, etc. Jesus broke down the barriers between disabled people, and between socially, culturally and religiously ostracised citizens, and participated with them. Jesus had dialogue with them and allowed them to live meaningful lives by giving voice to the voiceless.

1.13.1. The Conversation between Jesus and the Syro-Phoenician Woman/Canaanite Woman

Matthew 15:21-28 brings out a remarkable story which was the turning point that shed light for women of all generations. This passage contains the story of Jesus and the nameless Canaanite woman, who is identified as the Syro-Phoenician woman in Mark's gospel. According to the biblical tradition the Gentiles or the

---

[165] Deb Beatty Mel, "Jesus and the Canaanite Woman: An Exception for Exceptional Faith," *Priscilla Papers,* 23/4 (Autumn, 2009): 8-12.

[166] Lydia Neufeld Harder, "The witness of women: dying to sin and rising to life" *Vision* (Spring, 2006): 19.

Canaanites are identified as enemies of Israel.[167] This passage talks about the longing for hope and assurance from Jesus, the relentless efforts that she had made by raising her voice despite being surrounded by many opposition. Her bold decision of seeking an approval of Jesus's healing power for her daughter's illness was an extraordinary step she had undertaken. It has been clearly stated in Gail R. O'Day's writing that: "The woman impinges on Jesus from all sides and does not hesitate to make her presence felt and demands known."[168]

O'Day points out that Mt. 15:21-28 is neither a miracle story nor a saying of Jesus but is counted as dialogue. It is all about the conversation between the Canaanite woman and Jesus. Mt. 15:21-28 is said to have a resemblance between the Canaanite woman's words of petition and the cries for salvation and deliverance in Israel's lament psalms. It is because most of the psalms are of laments which are either from an individual or of communal prayers. O'Day continued that: "The laments confront God with startling candor, placing full-bodied pleas and petition for help and deliverance boldly before God ... these human experiences had to be handed over to God in disciplined, liberated speech in order for transformation to become a reality."[169]

The response of Jesus towards the Canaanite woman shows that her petition did not go in vain, as we see in Mt. 15:28. O'Day writes: "In response to the woman's unrelenting insistence, Jesus says, 'O woman great is your faith! Be it done for you as you desire'. Jesus's words give voice to what the woman's words have already demonstrated: her faith."[170] Gail had concluded by saying that, "[I]n the voice of this marginal woman who would not be silenced even when no one seems to listen, we hear the resilience of faith. The Canaanite woman's faith insisted on the fulfilment of the gospel promise ... persistent, vigorous, and confident in God's faithfulness to God's promises."[171] A similar comment was made by Thomas E. Boomershine about the woman where he said that she had crossed the boundaries between enemies: "She had shown courage and a perseverant faith."[172]

1.13.2. The Conversation between Jesus and the Samaritan Woman

John 4:1–42 tells us of the conversation between Jesus and the Samaritan woman. This is another example which shows that both parties in a conversation, that is,

---

[167] Gail R. O'Day, "Surprised By Faith: Jesus And The Canaanite Women," in *A Feminist Companion To Mathew* edited by, Amy-Jill Levine, Marianne Blickenstaff, (Cleveland: The Pilgrim Press, 2001), 114-115.

[168] Ibid., 118-119.

[169] Ibid., 117.

[170] Ibid., 123.

[171] Ibid., 125.

[172] Thomas E. Boomershine, *Story Journey: An Invitation to the Gospel as Storytelling* (Nashville: Abingdon Press, 1988), 115.

Jesus and the Samaritan woman, played significant roles. Some of the major steps that were taken by Jesus and the Samaritan woman in this story are visible. Firstly, Jesus spoke with the "Samaritan" woman. In doing so, he broke the Jewish socio-cultural and religious laws. Secondly, Jesus spoke with a "woman," which means that Jesus had violated the Jewish law and reconstituted a new law. In that new law there is no social, cultural, and religious or gender discrimination. On the other hand, the Samaritan woman took bold steps to speak with the outsider. She was risking her life by going against her tradition since women at that time were not even allowed to speak in public. Teresa Okure in "Jesus and the Samaritan Woman (Jn. 4:1-42) in Africa" talks of this Samaritan woman as one who took up the responsibility by risking herself before the world.[173] Okure continue to say that: "In this Samaritan setting, the woman is the victim of racial, religious, and gender prejudice."[174]

The Samaritan Woman was very much aware of the strain relationship between her people and the Jews, and the problems that entails for a Jewish man who would speak with a Samaritan woman (both "you a Jew" and "me a Samaritan woman" in 4:9 are in emphatic positions). However, she firmly stood her ground, and she could reason and reach her own conclusions in her dialogue with Jesus. Contrary to critics who view her character as dependent on the men from her town to tell her that Jesus is the Messiah, she is not afraid to engage in conversation with a Jewish male. When convinced that Jesus is the Messiah, she runs to the town and persuades the people to come meet Jesus for themselves. The dialogue with the woman, steadily Jesus leads her to surpass the barriers of prejudice and the stigmas of racism and sexism, and to know and accept God's free gift in himself, who offers to all who believe in him salvation, "living water," and the Holy Spirit.[175]

Here, Jesus demonstrated with an action by maintaining no distinction between clean and unclean; Jesus ignores the Jewish warning about speaking to a woman because "Jews viewed Samaritans with distaste, and in fact the rabbis especially shunned Samaritan women, whom they viewed as perpetually unclean, menstruants from the cradle."[176] But, the fact is that it was the conversation with a woman at a Samaritan well that had prepared the way for the triumph of the Word of God at Samaria.[177]

---

[173] Teresa Okure, "Jesus and the Samaritan Woman (Jn 4:1-42) in Africa," *Theological Studies* 70/2 (2009): 108-9.

[174] J. Lyle Story, "The Discipleship of Women - From Jesus' Birth to the Empty Tomb," *Priscilla Papers*, 21/1 (winter, 2007): 14-20.

[175] Teresa Okure, "Jesus and the Samaritan Woman (Jn 4:1-42) in Africa," *Theological Studies* 70/2 (2009): 408-9.

[176] Quoted in J. Lyle Story, "The Discipleship of Women - From Jesus' Birth to the Empty Tomb," *Priscilla Papers*, 21/1 (winter, 2007): 14-20.

[177] Ibid.

Jean-Marc Chappuis, writing on "Jesus and the Samaritan Woman: The Variable Geometry of Communication," talks about one of Jesus' mission accomplishments and explains how Jesus establishes communication between people:

> Mission is the combat he is pursuing, of light against darkness, truth against error and falsehood, sincerity against hypocrisy. It consists in giving a voice to those who have no voice, in making clear what is confused, in promoting true human relationships, in denouncing idols and bringing to light God's icons in this world. He establishes communication between people as a new covenant, by promoting in them the new humanity, freed from the baleful power of separation and possessed by the beneficent power of reconciliation and peace.[178]

1.13.3. The Gospel of Mark and the Voice of Women

It is often asserted that "... discipleship in Mark is understood as a literal following of Jesus and of his example."[179] The Markan text shows female disciples as faithful followers of Jesus, great witnesses of the death, burial, and resurrection of Jesus. Female disciples were the ones who first proclaimed the good news of Jesus's resurrection to the male disciples. When we see the passion narrative, some of the male disciples betrayed and denied Jesus and they even abandoned Jesus and fled to a hiding place.[180]

It is a woman who recognizes Jesus' suffering Messiahship and, in a prophetic-sign action, anoints Jesus for his burial, while "some" of the disciples reprimand her. Further, it is a servant woman who challenges Peter to act on his promise not to betray Jesus. In doing so she unmasks and exposes him for what he is, a betrayer.[181]

David E. Malick also considers the encounter of a Syrophoenician/ Canaanite woman and Jesus in Mark 7:24–28 significant. A woman understood what Jesus had said in a parable, unlike the disciples who did not understand his sermon when he spoke in a parable (Mk. 7:14-18). She not only understands the metaphor Jesus spoke to her, but immediately adapts it to persuade him to provide her with the overflow of his blessings to Israel. When we see the following verse accordingly, Jesus tells the woman that her request has been granted. It is also a clear indication that this Gentile woman is unique in Mark's gospel because she understands Jesus's parables, engages with his words beyond the Twelve, and

---

[178] Jean-Marc Chappuis, "Jesus and the Samaritan Woman: The Variable Geometry of Communication," *Ecumenical Review*, (January 1, 1982): 15.

[179] Elisabeth Schüssler Fiorenza, *In Memory of Her: A Feminist Theological Reconstruction of Christian Origins* (New York: Crossroad, 1988), 316.

[180] Ibid., 319.

[181] Ibid., 321.

thereby sets forth the significant theology that Gentiles may share in the blessings to Israel.[182]

Thus, the gospel of Mark unveils women's extraordinary gifts of faithfulness that stood till the end in their struggle for salvation in Christ. It has been manifested that the not so important ones in the Isrealite tradition are being recognised: "Those who are the farthest from the center of religious and political power, the slaves, the children, the Gentiles, the women, become the paradigms of true discipleship."[183]

1.13.4. The Gospel of John and the Voice of Women

The Fourth gospel is considered one of the important milestones in the Bible because it has brought out how the discipleship and leadership of the community consists of both women and men. In this Gospel, the evangelist gives women a prominent place in the narrative. Here, in this narrative the beginning and ending are about Jesus's public ministry with stories about a woman. Indeed, it also often mentions the "Word" along with wine, water, bread, light, truth, way, vine and door, as the essential aspect of human life or for the fullness of life.

John highlighted women like Martha and Mary Magdalene whose voice turned the wheel of the new era of witness and proclamation and salvation to all humanity. Martha did not keep herself mute after receiving the revelation and expressing her faith in Jesus' word, but she raised her voice and called Mary (Jn. 11:28), just as Andrew and Philip called Peter and Nathanael. She became the spokeswoman for the messianic faith of the community as the "beloved disciples" of Christ. Her confession was not just in response to the miracle of Jesus but it was the response to Jesus's revelation and challenge.[184]

As found in John 20:11-18, Mary Magdalene became the first witness of the resurrection who went to the disciples and announced to them: "I have seen the Lord." The significant role played through Mary Magdalene in the resurrection time has been witnessed: "She communicated the message to them which he had given to her. Thus she is the primary apostolic witness to the resurrection."[185] Unlike Mark 16 that did not allow Mary Magdalene's voice to be heard in John 20 there is an exchange of roles, or the reversal of the (more or less contemporary) prohibition on women's speaking.[186] In Ingrid Maisch's writing it is aslo seen that, "Mary is *not* to be silent, but to *speak*; she is to *teach* her brothers by *speaking* of

---

[182] David E. Malick, "An Examination of Jesus's View of Women through Three Intercalations in the Gospel of Mark," *Priscilla Papers*, 27/3 (Summer 2013): 4-15.

[183] Elisabeth Schüssler Fiorenza, *In Memory of Her*, op. cit., 323.

[184] Ibid., 326-329.

[185] Ibid., 333.

[186] Ingrid Maisch, *Between Contempt and Veneration ... Mary Magdalene: Image of a Woman through the Centuries*, (Minnesota: The Liturgical Press Collegeville, 1998), 180.

what she has experienced."[187] Elisabeth Schussler Fiorenza, in her work *In Memory of Her: A Feminist Theological Reconstruction of Christian Origins*, concluded by saying that:

> The writers of Mark and John have made it impossible for the Christian church to forget the invitation of Jesus to follow him on the way to the cross. Therefore, wherever the gospel is preached and heard, promulgated and read, what the women have done is not totally forgotten because the Gospel story remembers that the discipleship and apostolic leadership of women are integral parts of Jesus' "alternative" praxis of *agape* and service.[188]

1.14. Mary Magdalene's Voice in the Nag Hammadi Library

The Nag Hammadi[189] library demonstrates Mary Magdalene's traditions very different from those of the Christian Testament. Jane Schaberg gave nine points which are shown in at least four texts:

> (1) Mary is prominent among the followers of Jesus; (2) she exists in a textual world of male-centred language and kyriarchal ideology; (3) she speaks boldly; (4) she is a visionary; (5) she is praised for her superior understanding; (6) she is identified as the intimate companion of Jesus; (7) she plays a leadership role in relationship to the male disciples; (8) she is opposed by or has an open conflict with one or more of the male disciples; (9) she is defended.[190]

Jane Schaberg and Melanie Johnson-Debaufre, brought out Mary Magdalene's less significance in the Christian Testament where she is considered as important but not prominent: "Like all the characters other than Jesus, she speaks very little; in her case, only among the figures to the empty tomb, to the risen Jesus, and then to the disciples about the resurrection, except in Mark where she is said to remain silent out of fear."[191] However, the Nag Hammadi

---

[187] Ingrid Maisch, *Between Contempt and Veneration ... Mary Magdalene: Image of a Woman through the Centuries*, (Minnesota: The Liturgical Press Collegeville, 1998), 180-181.

[188] Elisabeth Schüssler Fiorenza, *In Memory of Her*, op. cit., 334.

[189] The thirteen books found in Egypt in 1945 by a peasant named Muhammad Ali while he was digging for nitrates for fertilizer near the town of Nag Hammadi in Upper Egypt are now named after the town and called Nag Hammadi library. The Nag Hammadi library contains fifty-two religious texts-Christian, Jewish, and pagan. The books were hidden in a jar around 400 CE, possibly to preserve them from Roman Christian "heresy" hunters. Jane Schaberg, Melanie Johnson-Debaufre, *Mary Magdalene Understood*, (New York, London: The Continuum International Publishing Group Inc, 2006), 67-8.

[190] Ibid., 70-71.

[191] Ibid.

text gives us a ray of hope in hopelessness by bringing to us Mary Magdalene's voice into this male dominated society. Mary Magdalene interrupts the voices of the Christian Testament and the Church Fathers. As she speaks boldly from the outside, she can teach us to read the canonical texts in new ways.[192]

1.15. Paul's Voice in the Ministry

The immense contribution of Paul towards the foundation of the early Christian movement cannot be simply erased. Throughout his mission and ministry, Paul was able to communicate to a large audience by endorsing the inclusion of all people in the church, which in turn contributed to the movement's appeal and agility. Paul had a positive attitude towards women because when we examine carefully it was women who had contributed enormously to the making of mission and ministry during Paul's time. This is why it appears that Paul's theology allowed for significant gender inclusivity that was later lost.[193] Sarah Casey stated that inclusive attitude was not maintained in the later Christian churches, it is therefore this loss of inclusivity that has led people to read Paul incorrectly, through the lens of the Deutero-Pauline literature and the later church, rather than letting Paul's letters stand on their own.[194]

1.15.1. The Voice of Jesus to Paul

The call of the apostle Paul himself has been manifested through the "voice" from heaven. Voice plays a prominent role in the life of Paul which has brought a complete revolution in Christian history.

It is written that God showed the miracle to Saul of Tarsus, a Pharisee from Jerusalem and led him to conversion where he changed his name from Saul to Paul after he converted from Judaism to Christianity. Before God called Paul, the high priest had authorized him and commanded him to persecute and to arrest every follower of Jesus in the city of Damascus. When he and his companions were on the way to Damascus to arrest Jesus's followers, a bright light struck him down to the ground and he heard a voice saying to him, "Saul, Saul, why do you persecute me?" He asked, "Who are you, Lord?" The reply came, "I am

---

[192] The thirteen books found in Egypt in 1945 by a peasant named Muhammad Ali while he was digging for nitrates for fertilizer near the town of Nag Hammadi in Upper Egypt are now named after the town and called Nag Hammadi library. The Nag Hammadi library contains fifty-two religious texts-Christian, Jewish, and pagan. The books were hidden in a jar around 400 CE, possibly to preserve them from Roman Christian "heresy" hunters. Jane Schaberg, Melanie Johnson-Debaufre, *Mary Magdalene Understood*, (New York, London: The Continuum International Publishing Group Inc, 2006), 96.

[193] Sarah Casey, "For You Are All One in Christ (Gal 3:28): The Role of Women in the Pauline Churches" (2010). *Honors Projects.* http://digitalcommons.iwu.edu/religion_honproj/18, accessed on 10.9.2012.

[194] Ibid.

Jesus, whom you are persecuting" (Acts 9:1-19; retold in Acts 22:6-21 and Acts 26:12-18).[195]

1.15.2. Paul and Women

One of the most controversial and much debated passages among other letters concerning women in the church is the First Letter of Paul to the Corinthians 14:34-35 which says that, "women should be silent in the churches. For they are not permitted to speak, but should be subordinate, as the law also says. If there is anything they desire to know, let them ask their husbands at home. For it is shameful for a woman to speak in church." Some of the assumptions made by the scholars about these statements follow.

Some believe that the passage is culturally conditioned. Others hold that what Paul prohibits in 1 Corinthians 14:34-35 is some kind of disruptive speech. Some take the word "speaking" in these verses to indicate speaking in tongues. Others have suggested that the women were largely uneducated and were interrupting the proceedings with questions, which were better dealt with by their husbands in their homes. Another suggestion is that Paul is quoting an assertion made by some in Corinth who wanted to exclude women from speaking in church.[196]

Neil Elliott, in his book *Liberating Paul: The Justice of God and the Politics of Apostle*, brought out his evaluation of the ideas of scholars like Antoinette Clark Wire and Elisabeth Schüssler Fiorenza under the sub-heading "Paul and Women: The Curious Persistence of 1 Corinthians 14: 34-35." There, he showed how both the scholars recognised and agreed that the emancipatory aspects of Paul's letters were being compromised by the stubbornly patriarchal sliver in 1 Corinthians 14:34-35.[197] At the same time, a scholar like L. Ann Jervis observed that Paul wrote these words out of concern that some women's speech was detrimental to the Corinthian assembly's exercise of prophecy, not because it was spoken by women, but because it was self-focused rather than loving which did not belong in church. Therefore, it destroyed peace, order and loving which was the mark of Christian prophecy.[198] Gabriele Dietrich also holds the opinion that the letters of Paul, especially the pastoral letters, contributed much to obscure the feminist content of Jesus's personality, life and message by paving a way towards

---

[195] "The Conversion of Paul-Story Summary," Christianity.about.com/od/biblestorysumm, accessed on 16.3.2015.

[196] James Greenbury, "1 Corinthians 14:34-35: Evaluation Of Prophecy Revisited," *Journal of the Evangelical Theological Society*, 51/4 (December 2008): 721.

[197] Neil Elliott, *Liberating Paul: The Justice of God and the Politics of Apostle*, (Bangalore: Theological Publications In India, 2006), 53.

[198] L. Ann Jervis, "1 Corinthians 14:34-35 A Reconsideration of Paul's Limitation of The Free Speech of Some Corinthian Women," *in Journal for the Study of the New Testament* No. 58 (June 1995), 73.

the ferocious misogynism of the church Fathers. However, she added that Paul's confused texts about women have to be read in the light of his wider message.[199]

In whatever or whichever way we look at Paul towards women in the canonical biblical text today, we can still remember and witness the inclusivity in Paul towards women who had chosen to travel and live in communities where women were present and women were among the active contributors in the churches during his time. As we look at Paul's letters, "the women in the churches he addresses seem to be important members of those churches, and he speaks of them with respect and positive regard."[200] Some of the prominent women in the church who played a major role during Paul's time will be seen in his personal letters as we go through the lists of greetings. Norbert Baumert's writing asserts: "This testifies to an interior freedom in his relationships with women and his esteem for them…"[201] Now we shall look at some of the women whom Paul had mentioned in his writings.

1.15.3. The Women in Philippi: Lydia, Euodia, Syntyche.

When Paul visited Philippi for the first time there seems to have been no synagogue since it is mentioned that he normally looked out the worship place wherever he went. There in Philippi, Paul came across a group of Jewish women (presumably married to pagans), who met to pray on Saturdays down by the river. Paul had met along with them, a woman by the name Lydia of Thyatira, who is said to be a vigorous, independent woman running an important business. She was a convert and later she has been an asset for the mission and ministry of Christ.[202] She invited Paul and his companions, Timothy and Silas, to live in her house as the following passage confirms:

> On the sabbath day we went outside the gate by the river, where we supposed there was a place of prayer; and we sat down and spoke to the women who had gathered there. A certain woman named Lydia, a worshipper of God, was listening to us; she was from the city of Thyatira and a dealer in purple cloth. The Lord opened her heart to listen eagerly to what was said by Paul. When she and her household were baptized, she urged us, saying, "If you have judged me to be

---

[199] Gabriele Dietrich, *A New Thing On Earth: Hopes and Fears facing Feminist Theology*, 72.

[200] Sandra Hack Polaski, "Paul and Real Women," *Word & World*, 30/4 (Fall 2010): 392.

[201] Norbert Baumert, *Woman and Man in Paul: Overcoming a Misunderstanding,* (Minnesota: The Liturgical Press, 1996), 199.

[202] Jerome Murphy- O'Connor, Op, "Paul's first stop in Europe: Philippi", http://www.catholicbiblical.ca/scripture.blogs/pauls-first-stop-in-europe-philippi/ accessed on 15.1.13.

> faithful to the Lord, come and stay at my home." And she prevailed upon us (Acts 16:11-15).[203]

When Paul looked back on his days in Philippi what he remembered above all was "your partnership in the gospel from the first day [in Europe] until now" (Philippians 1:5).[204] We see in the letter that Paul underlines the prominence of women in the evangelisation of Philippi:

> I urge Euodia and I urge Syntyche to be of the same mind in the Lord. Yes, and I ask you also, my loyal companion, help these women, for they have struggled beside me in the work of the gospel, together with Clement and the rest of my co-workers, whose names are in the book of life" (Philippians 4:2–3).[205]

We can gather from the passage above that Lydia, a "woman," was the first convert mentioned in Acts in Macedonia after Paul had received the Macedonian call. She was an extraordinary woman who had shown her hospitality, her wealth and her determinant power for the establishment of her service and to hold on to the gospel of Christ (Acts 16:40). It is assumed that the church in Philippi grew and flourished because Paul wrote them a letter probably around AD 61 about ten years after he first met Lydia.[206] This is testified through the greetings of Paul, which mentions that it was sent by "Paul and Timothy, servants of Christ Jesus, to all the saints in Christ Jesus who are in Philippi, with the bishops and deacons" (Phil. 1:1).

1.15.4. Priscilla and Aquila's Joint Efforts in the Service of God

Paul's constant appreciation of Priscilla and Aquila will be seen in the letters. The letter to the Corinthian church from Ephesus in his final greetings mentioned clearly about the hard work done by the couple for the service of the Lord. As in I Corinthians 16:19 it says that, "the churches of Asia send greetings. Aquila and Prisca, together with the church in their house, greet you warmly in the Lord." The letter of Paul to the Romans 16:3-5 says, "Greet Prisca and Aquila, who work with me in Christ Jesus, and who risked their necks for my life, to whom not only I give thanks, but also all the churches of the Gentiles. Greet also the church in their house."

---

[203] "What did Paul really think about women? A study of the apostle Paul and his interactions with women" http://www.christdeaf.org/bible/WhatDidPaulThinkOfWomen.pdf accessed on 15.1.13.

[204] Jerome Murphy- O'Cornor, Op, "Paul First Stop in Europe: Philippi", op. cit.

[205] Ibid.

[206] "What did Paul really think about women? op. cit.

i. *Phoebe*

We find Phoebe as an active and important woman in the service of God whom Paul referred to in the greetings section of his letter to the Romans. " I commend to you our sister Phoebe, a deacon of the church at Cenchreae, so that you may welcome her in the Lord as is fitting for the saints, and help her in whatever she may require from you, for she has been a benefactor of many and of myself as well" (Rom.16:1).

Gregory R. Perry mentioned that for Paul, deacons are exemplary men and women who exercise their varied gifts, carry out works of relief and restoration (1 Tim. 3:8-13; 5:9-10; cf. Acts 6:3; 9:36, 39), and execute commissioned tasks (Rom. 16:1-2) to display God's multifaceted wisdom through the church to those rulers and authorities whose lordship in this age is being nullified (1 Cor. 1:28; 2:6, 8; 15:24; Eph. 3:10).[207]

Gregory R. Perry writes, "Paul's emphatic description of Phoebe as "a patroness for many … stresses her role as an advocate or forerunner for Paul and others into the élite circles of Corinth and Cenchreae, Corinth's south-eastern port."[208] Though a Gentile woman, Phoebe had accepted and helped Paul, a Jewish man, who describes her not as "common" or "unclean" but as "our sister."[209]

Gregory had concluded in his writing that Paul's clear description of Phoebe as a "deacon of the church in Cenchreae" in Romans 16:1 dignifies it by commending Phoebe and by recognizing women among the candidates who were being evaluated for diaconal office at Ephesus.[210]

1.15.5. Other Women

The salutation of the letter to Philemon addresses three people: Philemon, Apphia, and Archippus, in that order, and the church in "your" house (Philem. 1-2). Apphia, the one female name, is identified simply as "the sister." She might have been a significant lady whom Paul had to mention in his letter specifically. It is possible that, she is an important enough leader in the church, which may meet in her house, so that she needs to be addressed along with the male leaders.[211]

We also find, in 1 Corinthians 1:11, a passing reference to "Chloe's people," who had brought a report to Paul. We do not clearly know about these people but they are under Chloe's patronage. Whoever they may be, they travel on behalf

---

[207] Gregory R. Perry, "Phoebe of Cenchreae and 'Women' of Ephesus: 'Deacons' the Earliest Churches," *Presbyterion*, 36/1 (Spring 2010), 12.

[208] Ibid., 17.

[209] Ibid., 17-18.

[210] Ibid., 33-4.

[211] Sandra Hack Polaski, "Paul and Real Women, op. cit" 392.

of the church or at least the faction of the church to which Chloe belongs to communicate with Paul.[212]

In Colossians 4:15, a woman named Nympha and the church in her house are also mentioned in Paul's final greetings and instruction, and he not only greets brothers but sisters in Laodicea are also acknowledged. Another good example of Paul giving room for women's voices can be gathered from his mention of Timothy's grandmother Lois and mother Eunice. These two women were excellent teachers, strong in faith and through whose constant teachings and instructions of faith Timothy was raised to become a faithful follower of Christ (II Tim.1:5). In Romans 16: 6, "Greet Mary, who has worked very hard among you." In v. 12, Tryphena and Tryphosa are described as "workers in the Lord" Persis is identified as having "worked hard in the Lord" Rufus's mother, in v. 13, is said by Paul to be "a mother to me also." Paul also includes in his greetings Julia and the sister of Nereus in v. 15.[213]

The writing of Paul in Galatians 3:28 clearly mention the 'oneness in Christ'. He says, "There is no longer Jew or Greek, there is no longer slave or free, there is no longer male and female; for all of you are one in Christ Jesus." (Gal 3:28). In the writng of Sandra Hack Polaski it is mentioned that: "This quotation is no throwaway; rather, it points toward the new reality that Paul perceives God to be about in this "new creation" .... It remains, for us as for Paul, a goal toward which to strive. That is, indeed, good news for women."[214] As Doug Heidebrecht also added this passage (Gal. 3:28) is so intricately woven into the fabric of Paul's epistles that its meaning and significance cannot be detached from the larger tapestry of the New Testament. When Gal. 3:28 is read against the backdrop of the New Testament, an integrated picture of the implications of the gospel becomes apparent.[215]

Through the reading of Paul's letters carefully, we can understand that Paul had included and respected women in the foundation of the churches during his time. Women were active participants involved in the ministry of the churches in the region during that time. Narola Imchen has mentioned in her writing that: "Often women of the house where the believers met acted as the leaders of such house churches. Therefore, though the designation as pastor was not given to them, yet the way they functioned was what the pastor would do in the later years."[216] Women were also the agents of change, faithful followers of Christ, active participants in the churches as pastors, and in society. Their voice was

---

212 Sandra Hack Polaski, "Paul and Real Women, op.cit" 393.

213 Ibid., 394.

214 Ibid., 398.

215 Doug Heidebrecht, "Distinction and Function in the Church: Reading Gal. 3:28 in Context," *Direction* 34/2 (Fall 2005), 190.

216 Narola Imchen, *Women in the History of Christianity* (N.p.: Tribal Development and Communication Centre, 2010), 40.

raised; they were accepted and recognised by the people and they also worked hard for the glory of God.

1.16. "Voice" in the Ao Naga Tribal Community

The word *Ola* is voice in *Chungli*, the prestige dialect of the Ao Nagas. *Ola* denotes both voice and sound. Human speech or utterance of word by mouth is called *ola*. The sound of a person or an animal can be both called as *ola*. The shouting or sounds produce in a group, or crowd are also called *ola*.

Apart from all those mentioned above, what we would like to bring in here is the human voice *ola*. We are speaking about *ola* that comes out from one's own mouth. It is not simply uttering or sound produced by mouth but with emotions, feelings, ideas, that which she/he is able to involve and participate in life with loved ones, friends, family members and in the larger group/community affairs. Voice that comes out from one's own word of mouth (orally expressed) as an expression of joy, solidarity, sympathy, sadness, reasoning, thoughts etc. to one another is *ola*.

With the manifold manifestations of voice having been outlined in this chapter, the next chapter will deal with various theoretical considerations that underpin our attempts at defining the meaning and role of voice in communication and outlining its place in society.

Chapter 2

Voice, Gender and Communication: Theorizing Cultural Studies

Introduction

Theory is an essential component in a research which presents a systematic way of understanding events, behaviours and/or situations.[217] Theory is a tool that enables us to identify a problem and to plan a means for altering the situation. Theory explains how some feature of human behaviour or performance is organised. The components of theory are concepts and principles and they serve two important functions. In these functions, they help us to understand or explain what we see and to figure out how to bring about change.[218] Therefore, theory becomes a necessity to help shape the area of research.

The approach taken in this study is not purely that of the communication perspective alone but it also holds an interdisciplinary approach. Along with communication studies, it embraces cultural studies, gender studies, social studies, and biblical studies as well. We find a unique co-relation within them in which each of these studies conveys its diverse meanings that help us to bring out the distinctive meaning of "voice."

In any area of research, there is a certain set of norms based on reason which help shape and validate the research stance. Here, the researcher seeks to highlight various definitions of perspectives on voice, and this will establish the theoretical and perspectival underpinnings of the study on the voice of women in decision-making particularly in the Ao Naga tribal community.

---

[217] "Social and behavioral theories", http://www.esourceresearch.org/Default.aspx?TabId=727, accessed on 3.4.15.

[218] "What is theory?", http://www.jou.ufl.edu/faculty/mleslie/spring96/theory.html, accessed on 13.4.15.

Before going into a detailed study on the interconnectedness of voice, Gender and communication, we will begin by raising the question why feminist communication theory is relevant in our society today. For this, one should have a proper idea of what feminism really is. While talking about feminism in communication, one must be clear that simply understanding feminism as hatred of men or dominion over others is illogical and irrational.[219]

2.1. Understanding of the Word Feminism

Feminism is to be understood in a broader sense. G. Sen and C. Crown write that when one talks about feminism, it does not end in captivating a distinct body but includes diverse forms:

> Feminism cannot be monolithic in its issues, goals and strategies, since it constitutes the political expression of the concerns of women from *different* regions, classes, nationalities, and ethnic backgrounds. There is and must be a diversity of feminism, responsive to the different needs and concerns of different women, and defined by them for themselves.[220]

Maria Mies writes: "Within a patriarchal system "equality" for women can only mean that women become like those patriarchal men."[221] As Mies says, in reality most women who call themselves feminists do not agree with such a prospect, and they too, have no such intention to gain hope from such a demand (equality) within such a system. Mies continues to say that: "It is,

---

[219] There are debates about searching for the uniformity and universality of feminism. What exactly is feminism all about, for whom, by whom, for what and why? This question was raised by scholars and thinkers all over the world. It is suggested that the women's struggle is not just a single entity but a multiple one. It differs from place to place, period to period, language to language, location to location, culture to culture etc. in differing ways. It is, therefore, the diversity of women's struggles around the world that constitutes a challenge to the claim that feminism is a western invention. The global women's conference exemplified this: "There has never been a shared theory of gender oppression or male dominance; a unified vision of justice and liberation; a common approach to the production of knowledge; agreed knowledge of the extent of women's differences; or a consensus on truths about gender." Since then, any definition of feminism can be contested. However, this western concept of feminism has been reviewed since the nineteenth century; women's movements from all over the world came together and took initiation they sought mutual consensus. "... Feminism addresses women across their social differences, on the grounds that common interests can be found wherever gender relations are unjust. If women really have nothing in common, and no gendered inequalities or injustices exist, the rationale of feminism disappears." Caroline Ramazanoglu, Janet Holland, *Feminist Methodology: Challenges and Choices* (New Delhi: SAGE Publications, 2002), 6-7.

[220] G. Sen and C. Crown, *Development Crises and Alternative Visions: Third World Women's Perspectives* (New York: Monthly Review Press, 1987), 1-19.

[221] Maria Mies, *Patriarchy and Accumulation on a World Scale: Women in the International Division of Labour* (London: Zed Books Ltd., 1986), 37.

therefore, wrong, as many men fear that the feminists only want to replace male dominance by female dominance, because that is what 'equality' means for most of them: equality of privileges."[222] The main intention of feminist movements is all about building up a non-hierarchic, non-centralized society where no elite lives on exploitation of and domination over others. This means that the feminist movement is basically an anarchist movement which seeks not to establish a new power equation by adding to one (male) power elite another (female) power elite.[223] Patrice M. Buzzanell asserts:

> The incorporation of masculinities is a logical outgrowth of a contemporary feminist agenda that prioritizes inclusion of difference in theorizing. Feminism is "not *just* about women, but about oppression, and ways to create life and work experiences that are honest, sensitive and open to all types of voices (*including* men's)."[224]

In line with the above statement, feminist communication also aims to identify, critique, and change inequities and discrimination, particularly those that are based on sex and gender.[225] Maria Mies has rightly pointed out how androcentric chauvinism had conceptualised in theories and methods in the disciplines, thereby making it necessary to contain in all the disciplines as mentioned below:

> Feminist research, in view of its roots in the Women's Liberation Movement, 'would have to cut across all the disciplines'... that Women's Studies could not just be added on to the existing disciplines as a new hyphen sociology, psychology, and so on. As feminist research, it was of necessity a *criticism of the prevailing paradigm of science* and social science, which had not only made women and their contribution *invisible,* but was most profoundly imbued with androcentric, that

---

[222] Maria Mies, *Patriarchy and Accumulation on a World Scale: Women in the International Division of Labour* (London: Zed Books Ltd., 1986), 37.

[223] Ibid.

[224] It is an attempt to generate further feminist organizational and managerial communication theory, research, and practice. This work leads to an inclusive, representative, and diverse. It is about presenting and publicizing the voices of those who are silenced, ignored, and misunderstood because of either taken-for-granted practices or deliberate attempts to quash resistance. The very theoretical elements and frameworks that we have here, are taken as the bases of discipline. See Patrice M. Buzzanell, *Rethinking Organizational and Managerial Communication from Feminist Perspectives* (New Delhi: Sage Publications, 200), 259.

[225] Julia T. Wood, "Critical Feminist Theories: A provocative perspective on families," in *Engaging Theories in Family Communication: Multiple Perspectives,* edited by Dawn O. Braithwaite, Leslie A. Baxter (Thousand Oaks, London, New Delhi: SAGE Publications, 2006), 200.

> is, male-centred prejudices, both in its general assumptions and conceptualizations and in its theories and methods.[226]

Chandrakala Padia in *Theorizing Feminism*[227] discusses the historical background on feminist theory developed in the West. In this, she talks about the concept history of feminism: Liberal Feminism,[228] Marxist/Socialist Feminism,[229] Radical Feminism[230] and Postmodern Feminism.[231] One cannot simply reject or ignore their concepts which in one way or the other occurred according to the needs in their given time, location and situation. For example, the concept of postmodern feminist thought seems relevant to our study:

> The postmodern feminists ... focused on local and specific facts and on historically accurate analysis, and with due regard to the varying spatio-temporal and cultural contexts of situations and happenings. In general, they called for the recognition and celebration of difference(s), and stressed the importance of renewed attention to dissident voices that have been silenced forcibly.[232]

2.1.1. Christian Feminist Thought

Elisabeth Schüssler Fiorenza observed that Christian feminists attempt to transform their religious "home bases" by introducing women into theological discourse as new thinking and speaking subjects. She further observed that such theologians are able to claim their own religious voice, heritage, and community

---

[226] Maria Mies, Vandana Shiva, *Ecofeminism* (Jaipur: Rawat Publications, 2010), 37.

[227] Chandrakala Padia, *Theorizing Feminism* (Jaipur: Rawat Publications, 2011), 12-19.

[228] Liberal feminism is an individualistic form of feminist theory, which focuses on women's ability to maintain their equality through their own actions and choices. Liberal feminism argues that society holds the false belief that women are, by nature, less intellectually and physically capable than men; ... Liberal feminism believes that "female subordination is rooted in a set of customary and legal constraints that blocks women's entrance to and success in the so-called public world". See, en.m.wikipedia.org/wiki/Liberal_feminism, accessed on 19.3.2015.

[229] Marxist Feminism is a branch of feminism focused on investigation and explaining the ways in which women are oppressed through systems of capitalism and private property. See, "Feminist Perspectives on Class and Work", Published 1st October, 2004, revised on 12th October, 2010, plato.stanford.edu/entries/feminism-class, accessed on 19.3.2015.

[230] 'Radical feminism is a philosophy emphasizing the patriarchal roots of inequality between men and women, or more specifically, social dominance of women by men', See, "What is Radical feminism?", womenhistory.about.com/od/feminism, accessed on 19.3.2015.

[231] 'Postmodern feminism viewed positively towards women and its historic value for shaping the structure of gender equality today'. See, Aaron Ashba, "Postmodern feminism", (24th January, 2008). feminism-gender.blogspot.com, accessed on 19.3.2015.

[232] Chandrakala Padia, *Theorizing Feminism*, 19.

in the struggle for liberation by critically reflecting on their own location within institutionalised biblical religions.[233]

The African-American suffragist Anna Julia Cooper's contribution to feminist biblical interpretation was described by Fiorenza in her writing. Cooper's contribution consists of an inclusive vision and a radical democratic interpretive framework. Cooper not only emphasises the right of wo/men to speak publicly but also stresses that the whole world needs to hear the voices of wo/men. Wo/men's struggles are linked with "every wrong that needs a voice."[234] Elisabeth Schüssler Fiorenza affirms that changes would take place from the church itself saying that:

> The bible does not serve only religious but also and especially political right-wing interests that deny democratic rights and human dignity to wo/men. If women want to change society and state, then they cannot stop before church doors. Bible, religion, and church are important institutions which must be changed.[235]

Feminist analyses agree that the Bible is written not only in androcentric or kyriocentric languages and symbols, but also is deeply entrenched in kyriarchal[236] cultures and societies.[237] For the African-American theorist Karen Baker Fletcher, as quoted by Fiorenza, equality and freedom were not simply physical states or states of mind but rather political-spiritual realities.[238] For Fiorenza, the feminist emancipatory tradition of religious agency, justice, and equality of wo/men claimed the authority and right of wo/men to interpret experience, tradition, and religion from their own interests and perspective. Fiorenza continues: "This tradition has insisted that equality, freedom, and democracy cannot be realised if wo/men's

---

[233] Elisabeth Schüssler Fiorenza, *Sharing Her Word: Feminist Biblical Interpretation in Context* (Edinburgh: T&T Clark, 1998), 26.

[234] Elisabeth Schüssler Fiorenza, *Sharing Her Word: Feminist Biblical Interpretation in Context* (Edinburgh: T&T Clark, 1998), 55.

[235] Ibid., 66.

[236] Kyriarchy is derived from the Greek words κύριος or *kyrios* (lord or master) and ἄρχω or *archō* (to lead, rule, govern). Kyriarchy means "rule by a lord," and αρχή/*arche* "authority, leadership," it is a social system or set of connecting social systems built around domination, oppression, and submission. "Kyriarchy encompasses sexism, racism, homophobia, economic injustice, and other forms of dominating hierarchies in which the subordination of one person or group to another is internalized and institutionalized." Elisabeth Schüssler Fiorenza coined the term "kyriarchy" in 1992 when she published her book, *But She Said: Feminist Practices of Biblical Interpretation*. See Sian Ferguson, "kyriarchy 101: We're Not Just Fighting the patriarchy Anymore" (23 April, 2014), everydayfeminism.com/2014/04/kyri...accessed on 6.2.15.

[237] Elisabeth Schüssler Fiorenza, *Sharing Her Word,* op. cit., 67.

[238] Ibid., 71.

voices are not raised or are not heard and heeded in the struggle for justice and liberation for everyone regardless of sex, class, nationality, or religion."[239]

Gayatri Chakravorty Spivak has said that reading and observation direct us to see "that a feminist historian of the subaltern must raise the question of woman as a structural rather than marginal issue in each of the many different types and culture."[240] Since the institution of communal power structures was based on kin and clan in the pre-capitalist societies, this was already encompassed and widely practised. It is there that the importance of sexual difference in the arrangement of such power is foreclosed so that sexuality is seen only as one element among the many that drive this "social organisation of production." Commonly, the visibility of women figure is not encouraged to perform in the public.[241]

Fiorenza stated that a critical feminist model of reading for liberation employs biblical interpretation not just as theological but also as a cultural-religious practice of resistance and change.[242] It is also suggested that not only does it use historical-and literary-critical, ideology-critical and theo-ethical evaluation methods which place emphasis on the rhetoric of the biblical text in its historical context.[243] Fiorenza continues to say that: "It also employs methods of storytelling, role play, biblio-drama, poetry, pictorial arts, dance, music, ritual for creating a "different" religious imagination."[244]

April D. DeConick stated that, as long as the Bible's deflation of the female body as part of the natural order of creation is viewed as sacred, as holy misogyny, no realistic argument can remove it. As long as the Bible's story of the suppression of woman is looked at as God's deserved decree laid upon all women for all time, there can be no liberation.[245]

2.1.2. Critical Feminist Theories in Communication

Critical feminist theories in communication identify, question, and seek to reform the patriarchal ideologies that give rise to oppression, as well as the asymmetrical rights, opportunities, roles, and so on. Julia T. Wood contends that the critique mounted by critical feminists' theories is not confined to matters of sex or gender inequality but is also aimed at efforts to devalue and oppress any groups that do not reflect the standpoint and interests of those who hold dominant positions

---

[239] Ibid., 87.

[240] Gayatri Chakravorty Spivak, "Subaltern Studies: Deconstructing Historiography" *in Subaltern Studies IV: Writings on South Asian History and Society*, edited by Ranajit Guha (Delhi: Oxford University Press, 1985-1994), 361.

[241] Ibid.

[242] Elisabeth Schüssler Fiorenza, *Sharing Her Word,* op. cit., 87.

[243] Ibid.

[244] Ibid.

[245] April D. DeConick, *Holy Misogyny: Why the Sex and Gender Conflicts in the Early Church Still Matter* (New York: The Continuum International Publishing Group, 2011), 153.

in cultural life. She says that very few take note of women's and children's perspectives on family life.[246] Ramona R. Rush too supports the above statements when she says: "Attending to these neglected facets of and perspectives on families is a priority for critical feminist theory and research."[247] According to Wood, such critical theories are concerned with and aim to identify prevailing structures and practices that create or uphold disadvantage, inequity, or oppression and to point the way towards alternatives that promote more egalitarian possibilities for individuals, relationships, groups, and societies. They are concerned with social change, to make a difference in how cultures operate and how those operations affect people in material and non-material ways.[248]

Critical theories investigate interactive influence between cultural practices and structures on the one hand and, on the other, the political, material, social, personal, professional, and economic lives of members of a culture, especially those who do not inhabit dominant status and the privileges such position offers. In other words, critical theories ask how cultural structures and practices shape the lives of members of a community and, conversely, how members' lives and activities shape cultural structures and practices. Critical theorists are particularly interested in identifying how dominant groups manage to privilege their welfares and perspectives and impose them on less-powerful groups. At the same time, critical theorists want to understand how oppressed groups become empowered and, in some cases, change dominant patterns and perhaps the ideologies that underlie them. Critical theorists allow the critiquing of not only official forms of power such as laws, but also "tiny, everyday" practices that reproduce and sustain particular ideologies and their attendant inequities.[249]

2.1.3. Voice in Feminist Communication Theory

Lana F. Rakow and Laura A. Wackwitz[250] talk about "voice" in feminist communication theory. "Voice" is considered as one of the important concepts in communication studies. In connection with voice, they have put forward language, talk, and stories that are interrelated and connect as a medium of power for feminist communication theory.

---

[246] Julia T. Wood, "Critical Feminist Theories: A provocative perspective on families," op. cit., 200.

[247] Ramona R. Rush, "Ten Tenets for Deeper Communications: Transforming Communications Theory and Research," in *Women Transforming Communications: Global Intersections,* edited by Donna Allen, Ramona R. Rush and Susan J. Kaufman (Thousand Oaks, London, New Delhi: SAGE Publications, 1996), 201-202.

[248] Ibid.

[249] Julia T. Wood, "Critical Feminist Theories: A provocative perspective on families," op. cit., 200.

[250] Lana F. Rakow, Laura A. Wackwitz "Voice in Feminist Communication Theory," in *Feminist Communication Theory,* edited by Lana F. Rakow and Laura A. Wackwitz (Thousand Oaks, London, New Delhi: SAGE Publications, 2004), 94.

The concept of voice as a methodology to recover women's experiences, meanings, and resistance to their subordinate positions becomes very important in the study. In expressing their views on voice, Rakow and Wackwitz assert that the most important breakthroughs by feminists in communication was in challenging what was considered truth in the field about language, interaction, and rhetoric. This challenged the assumptions about the neutrality of language, the functionalism of interaction, and the motivations behind western principles of persuasion, all of which they mentioned as having come under the scrutiny. These challenges include "feminist insights about the politics of meaning making and the structure and consequences of discourse within which women are spoken to or about or must stake their claims as persons who have a right to be heard."[251]

Rakow and Wackwitz asserted that the work of critical feminist scholars who have done significant work to "reclaim," "discover," and "give voice to" those who have not been heard in public discourse is an important phase of the work on voice. They observed and shared that this will lead to strengthening of the theoretical and political pitfalls; hence the need to address why feminists should be concerned with voice. Their subjectivity cannot be taken for granted, and their authenticity to speak as and for group identity can be challenged.[252]

Transnational feminism is another term used for feminist communication scholarship today. Among the pioneering scholars Gayatri Spivak, Chandra Mohanty, Jacqui Alexander, and Doreen Massey are behind this theory. The work of such scholars paved the way for interrogating gender in ways that emphasise the importance of recognizing how unequal global relations (of culture and economy) continually articulate the politics of gender in the local context, and how local relations are at work in larger global processes.[253] Raka Shome contends that transnational feminist perspective is not the same as, and must be distinguished from, multicultural feminism. This, she says, is because most of the critical racial/multicultural feminism has been performed by American academics and avoids global issues of power and struggle. Shome goes on to say: "Consequently, multicultural feminism has remained tied to the logic of the (U.S.) nation state and has often shored up the ideology of American exceptionalism at the same time that it has purported to expose the racialized and gendered violences of that ideology."[254]

Transnational feminist and communication studies therefore maintain and question the lack of attention to the cultural and economic inequities of

---

[251] Lana F. Rakow, Laura A. Wackwitz "Voice in Feminist Communication Theory," in *Feminist Communication Theory,* edited by Lana F. Rakow and Laura A. Wackwitz (Thousand Oaks, London, New Delhi: SAGE Publications, 2004), 94.

[252] Ibid., 95.

[253] Raka Shome, "Transnational Feminism and Communication Studies," in *the Communication Review 9* (Routledge: Taylor & Francis Group, 2006), 255-256.

[254] Ibid.

globalization in any interrogation of gender itself which is imbricated in, and reinforcing of, global inequalities. It is in such a force us to confront how histories, geographies, nations, cultures, and economies remain simultaneously *connected* and *disconnected* in complex and unpredictable ways in the continual making and unmaking of gender.[255]

A tremendous challenge was made by journalist Fran P. Hosken from 1975 onwards with the launch of Women's International Network (WIN) News.[256] Hosken claims: "It was to develop a global communication system by, for, and about women, to which women and women's organizations everywhere had ready access to speak for themselves; …to communicate about their own concerns and issues regarding political barriers and of manipulation by main stream media."[257] She toiled tirelessly for the success of this work, and through her relentless effort it was made possible and became a landmark for feminist communication scholars. Among the many issues raised therein through programming such as, "Reporting on Female Genital Mutilation," and "Exposing the Facts on Violence Against Women Worldwide," are some of the turning points that impacted and brought changes to the world at large.[258]

Luz Estella Porras and H. Leslie Steeves's work on "Feminism in a Post-Development Age" is pretty relevant to bring in because they highlight that post-development feminists examine the contradictions of integrating women into development. They bring out how post-development feminists argue that development is gendered, that women and men engage and experience the impacts of modernization and globalization in different ways, and that women in their local contexts and social groups deal in varied and multifaceted ways with poverty and gender inequality. For instance, when modernizing agencies or non-governmental groups put forward welfare projects, women's lives do not necessarily progress, and the culture of gender oppression remains unchallenged.[259]

The emergence of local level movements gains political supremacy, establishing collective identities that connect with places and actions thrilled with cultural meanings. It has been demonstrated in Latin America that new social movements have emerged, which are not only about economic issues but also about culture and identity dimensions of people's lives and have significant connection

---

[255] Raka Shome, "Transnational Feminism and Communication Studies," in *the Communication Review 9* (Routledge: Taylor & Francis Group, 2006), 255-256.

[256] Fran P. Hosken, "Women and International Communication," in *Women Transforming Communications: Global Intersections,* edited by Donna Allen, Ramona R. Rush and Susan J. Kaufman (Thousand Oaks, London, New Delhi: SAGE Publications, 1996), 211.

[257] Ibid.

[258] Ibid.

[259] Luz Estella Porras and H. Leslie Steeves, "Feminism in a Post-Development Age," in *Development Communication: Reframing the Role of the Media,* edited by Thomas L. Mcphail (Chichester, United Kingdom: Blackwell Publishing Ltd, 2009), 152.

to place and surroundings. Therefore, post-development feminists recognize that feminism is plural, and the many ways in which ethnicity, sexual orientation, class, race, political militancy, and more further define the mobilization of women and ground conceptions of social justice.[260]

Post-development feminism states that, communication is not only about mass media arrangements, social marketing or information campaigns, but about a wide range of communication opportunities in which the voices of women are expressed and the nuanced paradoxical, complex threads of life are shared.[261] Communication efforts may embrace exploration of the variety of *modes* local communities use to communicate within themselves and to make meanings of their experience, place, history, identities, resources, and engagements to the global world.[262]

2.2. Postcolonial Reading

It is also imperative to include the postcolonial reading on all the socio-cultural, political, and religious structures in a given community either in "evaluating, analysing, and re-interpreting the text within the given contexts."[263] One finds it difficult to give a clear cut definition of postcolonial reading strategy, whether it is a "method," of reading or a "criticism," or a "theory," or "mental attitude," with "a subversive stance towards the dominant knowledge."[264] C. I. David Joy suggested that, since postcolonial insight involves considerable deconstruction of the past, it could be termed as "a critical and reflective reading strategy based on particular ideological and theological positions."[265]

Postmodernity has added a powerful and significant terminology such as "the subaltern, the dominance of the striking narrative, the constitutive nature of discourse, the importance of language and representation, the formation of identity, the impossibility of distancing knowledge from subjectivity."[266] Methodologically, postmodernity has the quality of distracting single and linear

---

[260] Luz Estella Porras and H. Leslie Steeves, "Feminism in a Post-Development Age," in *Development Communication: Reframing the Role of the Media,* edited by Thomas L. Mcphail (Chichester, United Kingdom: Blackwell Publishing Ltd, 2009), 153.

[261] Ibid., 154.

[262] Ibid.

[263] C. I. David Joy, *Hermeneutics: Foundations and New Trends: A Postcolonial Reading of John 4* (Delhi: ISPCK, 2012), 40.

[264] Ibid.

[265] Ibid.

[266] Nelly P. Stromquist, "Voice, Harmony and Fugue in Global Feminism," in *A Feminist Critique of Education: 15 Years of Gender Education*, edited by Christine Skelton and Becky Francis (London/New York: Routledge, 2005), 127.

accounts, of deconstructing apparently innocuous texts, of presenting the voices of peoples formerly ignored.[267]

The old usage of the words like "commonwealth," "third world," "orientals," and others are being new edition with a common term "postcolonial."[268] One of the relevant definitions on postcolonialism in this study shows that:

> Postcolonial critique focuses on forces of oppression and coercive domination that operate in the contemporary world: the politics of anti-colonialism and neo-colonialism, race, gender, nationalism, class and ethnicities define its terrain. Interest in oppression of the past will always be guided by the relation of that history to the present. In that sense, postcolonial theory's intellectual commitment will always be to seek to develop new forms of engaged theoretical work that contributes to the creation of dynamic ideological and social transformation.[269]

To rationalise and write from the point of view of their own painful experiences and in their own context becomes necessary; so also many Indian scholars came up to challenge the unjust traditional structures imposed upon the common people such as women, Dalits, subalterns and the oppressed classes who are still living in deplorable conditions. Biblical scholars have suggested that a proper understanding of the context is essential in proposing a new paradigm for liberation. Since postcolonial theory has brought substantial challenges in the fields of literature, politics, history and sociology, biblical hermeneutics have found this theory an effective inter-disciplinary tool in re-mapping the new location of biblical interpretations.[270]

Along with this, it is also essential to evaluate and expose the unchallenged socio-cultural structures in a given society from the postcolonial perspective and theory. It is clear that postcolonial concerns and cultural issues go hand in hand where they share common concerns of conflict, confrontation and justice. Joy writes that: "It is significant as the notions of culture are transmitted through symbols of human life. Therefore, the signs and symbols in the texts need to be interpreted in the light of local cultures and religious values."[271] Trinh T. Minh-Ha in *Post-Colonial Studies Reader* has also shared the concerns that:

> The pitting of anti-racist and anti-sexist struggles against one another allows some vocal fighters to dismiss blatantly the existence of either

---

[267] Ibid.

[268] C. I. David Joy, *Hermeneutics: Foundations and New Trends: A Postcolonial Reading of John 4*, 43.

[269] Robert C. Young, *Postcolonialism* (London: Blackwell, 2001), 11.

[270] C. I. David Joy, *Hermeneutics: Foundations and New Trends: A Postcolonial Reading of John 4*, 45.

[271] Ibid., 56.

> racism or sexism within their lines of action, as if oppression only comes in separate, monolithic forms. Thus, to understand how pervasively dominance operates via the concept of hegemony or of absent totality in plurality is to understand that the work of decolonization will have to continue within the women's movement ...[272]

2.3. Cultural Studies and Communication

Cultural studies is said to have come up from an academic field grounded in critical theory and literary criticism. Its main concerns are the political nature of contemporary culture, as well as its historical foundations, conflicts, and defining traits. Here, we see how a particular medium or message relates to matters of ideology, social class, nationality, ethnicity, sexuality, and/or gender. Cultural studies cannot be counted as a separate entity; rather it incorporates multiple approaches such as feminist theory, critical theory, media theory, film/ video studies, communication studies, etc., which are to be studied from cultural phenomena in various societies.[273] One must examine as to how cultural studies can be achieved to maintain its stance on human ground for viable living: "Thus, cultural studies seek to understand the ways in which meaning is generated, disseminated, and produced through various practices, beliefs, institutions, and political, economic, or social structures within a given culture."[274]

2.3.1. Defining Cultural Studies

In attempting to define cultural studies, it should be noted that it is more than a common term. Pertti Alasuutari mentioned in his book *Researching Culture: Qualitative Method and Cultural Studies* that the studies or researcher who have been, or could be, argued to represent cultural studies share a kind of "centre position," a distancing from various forms of reductionism. Pertti Alasuutari states that: "'Culture' is taken seriously, it is granted some independence, but at the same time it is emphasized that the practices and symbolics of everyday life must not be treated in isolation from question of power and politics."[275] Cultural studies address the particular features and problems of present-day development in the contemporary society. Chris Barker also maintains that: "The forms of power that cultural studies explore are diverse and include gender, race, class, colonialism, etc. A cultural study seeks to explore the connections between these

---

[272] Trinh T. Minh-Ha, "Writing Postcoloniality and Feminism," in *Post-Colonial Studies Reader*, edited by Bill Ashcroft, Gareth Griffiths and Helen Tiffin (London: Routledge, 1995), 268.

[273] "Cultural Studies," http://www.huminities.uci.edu acessed on 28. 9. 2011.

[274] Ibid.

[275] Pertti Alasuutari, *Researching Culture: Qualitative Method and Cultural Studies* (New Delhi: SAGE Publications, 1995), 23ff.

forms of power and to develop ways of thinking about culture and power that can be utilized by agents in the pursuit of change."[276]

Cultural studies is considered as a new discipline similar to that of classical sociology. Several individuals like Vilfredo Pareto, Emile Durkheim and Max Weber, "[converge] upon a single theory" known as sociology. Now it could be argued that corners of sociology, anthropology and literary criticism have been cut off to form and give space to it.[277]

An attempt has been made to bring these together under one umbrella to universalize them into "sciences," but they often lose their grip on or blur the initial problem they were formed to deal with. For example, literary criticism: today cartoons, films, videos and television are far more important for common people than literature. So, also anthropology was born to study foreign cultures and less complex societies in remote places, but as time changes the meanings do not apply any more in the society. It has been new edition by the "western" artefacts, television programmes, and economic networks in and around the world. Finally, sociology was born to question how the modern industrial society should be understood, but many of these post-war, "post-industrial" developments in society have been evaded, which was the intention of established academic sociology. Therefore, cultural studies can now be seen as another generation of sociology which is the discipline to study the present social and cultural conditions, what is called "postmodern condition."[278]

David Walton says that cultural studies or culture are not "fixed categories." Hence there is no definite clear-cut definition. He used the examples of the character Gollum, from *The Lord of the Rings*. Gollum habitually stutters and adds the letter 's' to many words; therefore Walton said, "We can imagine the subtitle of this section being spat out of his mouth as 'identifying 'cultures' and 'cultural studies.'"[279] In cultural studies, the other aspects that tend to complicate

---

[276] Chris Barker, *Cultural Studies: Theory and Practice,* 3rd ed. (Los Angeles, London, Singapore, New Delhi: SAGE Publications Ltd, 2008), 6.

[277] Chris Barker, *Cultural Studies: Theory and Practice,* 3rd ed. (Los Angeles, London, Singapore, New Delhi: SAGE Publications Ltd, 2008), 6.

[278] Here, we have Chris Barker who brought the ideas of some of the postmodern writers like Lyotard, Rorty, and Foucault who say that "knowledge is not metaphysical, transcendental or universal but specific to particular times and spaces", which means that for postmodernism, knowledge is perspectival in character. It says that "there can be no one totalizing knowledge that is able to grasp the 'objective' character of the world. Rather, we have and require multiple viewpoints or truths by which to interpret a complex, heterogeneous human existence". Therefore, it is argued by postmodernism that knowledge is specific to language-games; local, plural and diverse. Chris Barker, *Cultural Studies: Theory and Practice,* 3rd edition. (New Delhi: SAGE Publications Ltd, 2008), 21.

[279] David Walton, *Introducing Cultural Studies: Learning through Practice* (New Delhi: SAGE Publications, 2008), 288.

fixing identity are concerned with synchronic and diachronic factors which can also be called synchronic versus diachronic approaches.[280]

2.3.2. Development of Cultural Studies

Cultural studies originated and were introduced in Britain in the late 1950s and were continued by the Centre for Contemporary Cultural Studies in Birmingham. Richard Hoggart coined the term cultural studies in 1964, followed by Stuart Hall, and later cultural studies have moved to the other continents as well.[281]

In order to understand the changing political circumstances of class, politics, and culture in the United Kingdom, scholars at the Centre for Contemporary Cultural Studies turned to the work of Antonio Gramsci, an Italian thinker of the 1920s and 30s. In Gramsci modified classical Marxism found culture to be a key instrument of political and social control.[282] Gramsci's ideology in cultural studies is also mentioned by the Indian communication scholars such as Krishna Menon[283] and M. Peter Singh had remarked on:

> Building on Gramsci's theory of hegemony and counter hegemony, cultural studies analysis cultural forms of domination and seek counter hegemonic forces of resistance and struggle. In order to do this, cultural studies need to develop critical tools to dismantle the harmful social practices, while simultaneously rethinking the project of human emancipation. Secondly, cultural studies must engage the intellectuals themselves to address their own critical role in the production and

---

[280] A synchronic analysis tends to ignore longer historical transformations in order to concentrate on a specific period of time. So, if it is possible to focus on particular stages of development, then it is possible that the identity of something will alter not only with relation to *how* we look but *when* we look. A diachronic approach has to take into account longer historical transformations which demands that the specific findings of a synchronic approach are appreciated with relation to a wider chronological view. One way of understanding the two mutual correcting strategies is to see one like a detailed close-up photograph, made possible by a power zoom, and the other like one taken with a wide-angle lens that takes in as much of the landscape as possible. Walton, David, *Introducing Cultural Studies: Learning through Practice* (New Delhi: SAGE Publications, 2008), 288.

[281] Pertti Alasuutari, *Researching Culture: Qualitative Method and Cultural Studies,* op. cit., 23.

[282] There was an uprising of an international intellectual movement from the 1970s onward in Great Britain. Pioneer scholars such as Stuart Hall, Paul Willis, Dick Hebdige, Tony Jefferson, Angela McRobbie and many other cultural studies scholars employed Marxist methods of analysis, exploring the relationships between cultural forms (the superstructure) and that of the political economy (the base). However, there was a tremendous shift in Britain where the politically formidable British working classes were in decline; this shift in loyalty from the Labour Party to the Conservative Party was antithetical to the interest of the working class. It was this that Hall and the other Marxist theorists had to explain in terms of cultural politics. "Cultural studies" http://en.wikipedia.org/wiki/Cultural_studies, accessed on 28-9-11.

[283] Krishna Menon, *Research Methods for Media and Cultural Studies* (Delhi: Manglam Publications, 2010), 51.

legitimation of social relations. This shows that cultural studies cannot be used as merely as an academic discipline in universities, rather it should become a collective endeavour of society.[284]

2.3.3. The Characteristic of Cultural Studies

Scholars in the United Kingdom and the United States developed somewhat different versions of cultural studies after the inception of the field in the late 1970s. The British version of cultural studies developed in the 1950s and 1960s, mainly under the influence of political, left-wing views, and criticisms of popular culture as "capitalist" mass culture; it absorbed some of the ideas of the Frankfurt School critique of the "culture industry" (i.e., mass culture). This emerges in the writings of early British cultural studies scholars like Raymond Williams, Stuart Hall and others.[285]

The Birmingham School, where the concept of "cultural studies" had originated, referred to culture as something like *collective subjectivity* which means a way of life or outlook adopted by a community or a social class. Here it opposes the formerly predominant *hierarchic* notion where culture referred to the best and most glorious achievements of a people or civilization. These approaches were imported by the Birmingham School from Marxist-inspired studies of working-class culture such as the research on the arts or literature.[286]

In the United States, "cultural studies were grounded in a pragmatic, liberal-pluralist tradition."[287] The American version of cultural studies initially concerned itself more with understanding the subjective and appropriative side of audience reactions to, and uses of, mass culture. However, these two distinctions between the American and British strands also are no longer relevant.

In the meantime, other approaches to cultural studies such as feminist cultural studies and later American developments of the field diverged from the Marxist view. They criticized the Marxist assumption of a single, dominant meaning, shared by all for any cultural product. Later on, other developing countries including those in Latin America developed their own theories depending on their own relevant situation and context.

The book *Doing Cultural Studies: The Case of the Sony Walkman* by Paul du Gay and others seeks to challenge the notion that those who produce commodities control the meanings that people attribute to them. Feminist cultural analyst, theorist and art historian Griselda Pollock contributed to cultural studies from viewpoints of art history and psychoanalysis.

---

[284] M. Peter Singh, *Cybertheology* (New Delhi: ISPCK, 2009), 99.

[285] Chris Barker, *Cultural Studies,* op. cit., 25.

[286] Ibid.

[287] Ibid.

Stuart Hall and John Fiske developed the act of consuming with cultural identity. They criticized the traditional view of assuming a passive consumer especially by underlining the different ways people read, receive, and interpret cultural texts. On this view, a consumer can appropriate, actively reject, or challenge the meaning of a product. These different approaches have shifted the focus away from the *production* of items.

In cultural studies *text* includes all the meaningful artefacts of culture such as written language, films, photographs, fashion, etc. So, also the discipline widens the concept of "culture." For the cultural studies researcher, it is not only limited to traditional high culture (the culture of the ruling social group) but also popular culture, everyday meanings and practices. Now the recent approach is comparative cultural studies, based on the discipline of comparative literature and cultural studies.

2.3.4. Cultural Studies and Communication

Cultural studies and communication are two separate fields that are interlinked in a number of ways. Cultural studies and communication support and complement each other and are inseparable. Cultural studies emerged from the mid-1950s onwards as a response to the rise of Nazism in Germany, Fascism in Italy, Spain and Portugal, and Stalinism in the Soviet Union. Different scholars reacted and worked in distinct historical conjunctures to particular political, social and economic conditions.[288] Douglas Kellner in his writing, "Communication vs. Cultural Studies: Overcoming the Divide,"[289] came up with comprehensive approach to study of media, culture, and communications by overcoming the limitations of dominant and alternative approaches. The history of bifurcation of the field (i.e., communication and cultural studies) is documented in the 1983 *Journal of Communications* issue entitled *Ferment in the Field.* The culturalist approach during that time was largely textual, centred on the analysis and criticism of text as cultural artefact, using methods primarily derived from the humanities, whereas the method of communication research employed more empirical approaches or methodologies, i.e. quantitative empirical studies of specific cases or domains, or broadly historical research. Some of the topics are analyses of the political economy of the media, audience reception and study of media effects, media history, and interaction of media institutions with other domains of society. Their conflicting approaches led to a bifurcation of the field of media communication into specialized sub-areas with competing models and methods.

Kellner argued that the "Frankfurt school overcame this bifurcation of the field by taking both culture and communications into their analytical focus and

[288] Krishna Menon, *Research Methods for Media and Cultural Studies,* op. cit., 49.

[289] Douglas Kellner, "Communication vs. Cultural Studies: Overcoming the Divide," http://www.uta.edu/huma/illuminations/kell4.htm, accessed on 19.10.2011.

by conceptualizing the nature and effects of both within the framework of critical social theory."[290] Therefore the Frankfurt school provides a model to overcome contemporary divisions in the study of media, culture, and communications and integrated within critical social theory which has become an important part of a theory of contemporary society, and playing more significant roles.

Kellner also mentioned that while the Frankfurt School was fully occupied with critical social theory and cultural criticism, cultural studies of the Birmingham school were blooming with postmodern theories. Thus, other attempts have appeared which overcome the bifurcation of the field of culture and communications. These theories, such as political economy, social theory, cultural analysis, philosophical speculation, and political critique, overcome the disciplinary crisis by employing specialization which bifurcates the field of study of the media, culture, and communications into separate and competing disciplines. These alternative approaches also destabilize the discipline and open up the study of culture and communications to the fields of history and society. They draw on a disparate range of disciplines to theorize the complexity and contradictions of the multiple effects of a vast range of forms of media/culture/communications in our lives and, to different extents, demonstrate how these forces serve as instruments of domination, but also offer resources for resistance and change.[291] Kellner at the end suggested a multiperspectival approach to communication and cultural studies, asserting that:

> What is important is the adoption of a multiperspectival approach that prevents excessively one-sided definitions of the field and arbitrary policing of methods, approaches, and perspectives ... That is, I am suggesting that if one views the very field of communications and culture as a continuum, one sees that it is arbitrary to cut up the field in a way to separate the two domains ... It seems obvious that the domain of media, culture, and communications is central to the economy, polity, social life, and other domains of contemporary experience, and that therefore the field of communications must be open to other academic fields and by definition be multidisciplinary. It would be useful for academic departments of communications, or cultural studies, to engage individuals trained in various disciplines to carry out studies of media, culture, communications, and society ... those who study media, culture, and communications as a vocation can utilize perspectives and positions developed in other disciplines to help study and understand their objects. In this way, it would be

---

290 Ibid.

291 Douglas Kellner, "Communication vs. Cultural Studies: Overcoming the Divide," http://www.uta.edu/huma/illuminations/kell4.htm, accessed on 19.10.2011.

possible to overcome the one-sidedness and limitations of any given academic discipline.[292]

Thus, Kellner's notion about multiperspectival and multidisciplinary approach to communication and cultural studies is relevant to relate in our study in this research as well. Along with Kellner, Noel Williams follows the same line on cultural studies and communication as multidisciplinary. Williams says, "I tend to see media studies and cultural studies as centrally concerned with human communication."[293]

The report of a policy workshop held at the Institute of Social Studies, The Hague, brought out the concern for the development of an alternative communication system in an alternative model of media research. This model talks about how to generate participation and to reinforce the cultural identity of all participating groups, countries or regions, which was most needed at the time when a dominant model of development of communication systems was characterised by global transnational control.[294]

The workshop which was held at The Hague seems to be still relevant in our society even today. One of the key concepts towards the promotion of the approaches to communications research on methodological and theoretical framework that they suggested was an alternative, participatory, horizontal, or marginal, all of which have something in common.

Certain points listed under the sub-heading "participatory research" may be considered worthy of a relook even today. It is said that when Cultural and communicative counteractions proceeds that can help the voiceless to be heard within a system which is characterised by verticality.[295] Following are some of the objectives suggested in the workshop under participatory research:

a. To articulate the logic and rationale that lies beneath these forms of 'liberating' communication.
b. To realize one's capabilities as a researcher and those of the social sector with which one works in order to observe social reality and thus to become an agent of social change.
c. To understand the forms and circumstances in which alternative communications emerge under oppressive situations; to understand the types of inter-relationships that sectors of society establish as they are affected by political or economic oppression; to understand the

---

[292] Ibid.

[293] Noel Williams, *How to Get a 2: 1 in Media, Communication and Cultural Studies* (London, Thousand Oaks, New Delhi: SAGE Publications, 2004), 3.

[294] *Major Areas of Concern: Problems and Developments in Communications Research in Third World Realities* (Hague: The Report of a Policy Workshop held at the Institute of Social Studies, 1980), 4-22.

[295] Ibid.

> richness of experience in such situations and to use them to promote the authentic democratization of communications systems at local, national and international levels.[296]

Sylvie I. Cohen, in "mobilizing communities for participation and empowerment" has brought about a "People-centred development approach." This approach stressed equal participation in all the decision-making and power and the importance of being active participants in all stages of planning, resource mobilization and allocation, acting and maintenance of the system without limiting on gender or weaker sections of society.[297]

Pramod K. Nayar expressed that "a Cultural Studies approach gives voice to the voiceless." Cultural studies aims at constructive dissent and debate and gives attention to the politics of cultural forms and narratives. It moves towards egalitarianism and shows constant vigilance to socio-political oppression and injustice, allowing a pedagogic practice that infuses literature and culture with democracy, justice and emancipation.[298]

2.3.5. James W. Carey's Cultural Approach to Communication

James W. Carey, a twentieth century American communications theorist pioneered two alternative conceptions of communication – a transmission view of communication and a ritual view of communication. He says that a transmission view of communication is the commonest in all culture – perhaps in all industrial cultures – and is defined through terms such as "imparting," "sending," "transmitting," or "giving information to others."[299] Carey says that in the nineteenth century it was formed from a metaphor of geography or transportation, but today the movements of goods, people and information are seen as essentially identical processes, and both were described by the common noun "communication." Thus, he states: "Our basic orientation to communication remains grounded, at the deepest roots of our thinking, in the idea of transmission: communication is a process whereby messages are transmitted and distributed in space for the control of distance and people."[300]

---

[296] Ibid., 21.

[297] Sylvie I. Cohen, "Mobilizing Communities for Participation and Empowerment," in *Communication and Human Values: Participatory Communication for Social Change,* edited by Jan Servaes, Thomas L Jacobson and Shirley A White (Thousand Oaks, London, New Delhi: SAGE Publications, 2002), 226.

[298] Pramod K. Nayar, *Reading Culture: Theory, Praxis, Politics* (New Delhi: SAGE Publications, 2006), 44.

[299] James W. Carey, "A Cultural Approach To Communication," in *Theorizing Communication: Readings Across Traditions,* edited by Robert T. Craig, Heidi L. Muller (Los Angeles, London, New Delhi, Singapore: SAGE Publications, 2007,) 38.

[300] Ibid.

In a ritual view, Carey explained that communication is linked to terms such as "sharing," "participation," "association," "fellowship," and "the possession of a common faith." This definition exploits the ancient identity and common roots of the terms "commonness," "communion," "community," and "communication." Carey continues: "A ritual view of communication is directed not toward the extension of messages in space but toward the maintenance of society in time; not the act of imparting information but the representation of shared beliefs."[301] Here we have understood that Carey's message through these models of communication is that the transmission view is the extension of messages across geography for the purpose of control, and that the ritual view is the sacred ceremony that draws persons together in fellowship and commonality.

Carey asserts that "... we are almost always coerced by our traditions into seeing it as a network of power, administration, decision, and control – as a political order. Alternatively, we have seen society essentially as relations of property, production, and trade – an economic order."[302] However for Carey society means more than what has been described. He follows along the same vein as Raymond Williams when talking about society which "includes the sharing of aesthetic experience, religious ideas, personal values and sentiments, and intellectual notions – a ritual order."[303] As Carey notices that we are blinded by the chaos of modern culture such as politics, trade, and therapy. We are paying the penalty for the long abuse of fundamental communicative processes such as the advance in communication technology, to matters of government and trade. Whereas we could rarely notice the opportunities to expand people's powers to learn and exchange ideas and experience. Therefore, Carey's ritual model is another tool "to give us a way in which to rebuild a model of and for communication of some restorative value in reshaping our common culture."[304]

Cultural studies have centred on three kinds of approach; "ethnography, which has often been linked with culturalist approaches and a stress on "lived experience"; a range of textual approaches, which have tended to draw from semiotics, post-structuralism and Derridean deconstruction; and a series of reception studies, which are eclectic in their theoretical roots."[305] In communication studies, the ethnography of communication is also known as the ethnography of speaking; it considers discourse as pivotal to the study of social life. The qualitative communication inquiry draws inspiration from anthropological

---

[301] Ibid., 40.

[302] James W. Carey, "A Cultural Approach To Communication," in *Theorizing Communication: Readings Across Traditions,* edited by Robert T. Craig, Heidi L. Muller (Los Angeles, London, New Delhi, Singapore: SAGE Publications, 2007,) 40.

[303] Ibid.

[304] Ibid., 48.

[305] M. Hammersley and Atkinson, P, *Ethnography: Principles and Practice* (London: Tavistock Books, 1983), 2.

and sociolinguistic approaches to language.[306] Human expression such as body language consists of kinesic (the study of human movement), proxemic (the study of social distance), postural, gestural, and paralinguistic are part of the methods of ethnography in addition to linguistic.

Sociolinguistics and *folklore* are the two streams of empirical study that came together to form the ethnography of the communication research programme. The concern of sociolinguistics is with the relationship between linguistic forms (especially grammatical rules and vocabularies) and their social uses and meanings. On the other hand, folklorists study oral and material cultures. Its study involves the collection of examples of *in situ* speech or musical performance in order to develop an understanding of their culture and historical origins and functions. Sociolinguistics stresses the social practice of language whereas folklore studies stress the artful performance of feeling and thought in regional, ethnic, or national cultures.[307]

2.3.6. British and American Cultural Studies

During the course of its development, cultural studies could be said to have developed along two main strands, namely, the British and American. The British version of cultural studies was developed in the 1950s and 1960s mainly under the influence of Richard Hoggart, Raymond Williams, Stuart Hall and others at the Centre for Contemporary Cultural Studies at the University of Birmingham. It started out as a socialist and working class-oriented project that assumed that the industrial working class was a force of progressive social change and that it could be mobilized and organized to struggle against the inequalities of the existing capitalist societies and for a more egalitarian socialist one. It went on to combine theoretical models and insights drawn from Marxism, post-structuralism, critical race theory and feminism with tools drawn from the disciplines of sociology, history, ethnography, and media studies. Hence, it included overtly political left-wing views and criticisms of popular culture as "capitalist" mass culture. It absorbed some of the ideas of the Frankfurt School critique of the "culture industry" (i.e., mass culture).

In contrast, 'American' cultural studies adopted a pragmatic approach grounded in a liberal-pluralist tradition. It initially laid emphasis on in-depth analysis of audience groups and understanding the subjective and appropriative dimension of their reactions to and uses of mass culture. For instance, proponents of American cultural studies would focus on the liberative aspects of fandom. However, the distinction between American and British strands has gradually faded.

---

[306] Thomas R. Lindlof, *Qualitative Communication Research Methods* (Thousand Oaks, London, New Delhi: Sage Publications, 1995), 46.

[307] Thomas R. Lindlof, *Qualitative Communication Research Methods* (Thousand Oaks, London, New Delhi: Sage Publications, 1995), 46-47.

2.4. Interconnection of Voice, Gender, and Communication

Julia T Wood, in *Gendered Lives* says that gender, culture, and communication are interlinked and are hitched to the whole universe. What gender means depends heavily on cultural values and practices; a culture's definitions of masculinity and femininity shape expectations about how individual women and men should communicate; and how individuals communicate establishes meanings of gender that, in turn, influence cultural views.[308]

In order to know in detail what gender, culture, and communication mean to us, we will explore how they are linked to each other. At the same time, we must remember that they do not exist on their own but rather co-relate with many other elements such as religion, history, politics, society, identity, patriarchy, etc., which are interwoven in this web.

2.4.1 Gender

Sex and gender have often been used interchangeably but they carry different meanings: "Sex is a designation based on biology, whereas gender is socially constructed and expressed."[309] Normally in most cases sex and gender go together, like women as feminine and men as masculine. But, this is not so in all cases, because just as some women possess masculine nature in their characters so also some men possess feminine nature in their characters. Wood states that: "Sex and gender are inconsistent for transgendered individuals, who have the physical characteristics of one sex but identify strongly as the other sex."[310] It is therefore observed that the influences of biological development do not completely

---

[308] Julia T Wood, *Gendered Lives: Communication, Gender, and Culture,* 8th edition (Boston: Wadsworth Cengage Learning, 2009), 20.

[309] Ibid.

[310] While we search for the meaning of gender the concept of Androgyny is important to note here. In the 1970s, researchers coined the word androgyny by combining the Greek words *aner* or *andros*, which means "man," and the Greek word *gyne*, which means "woman." Therefore, androgynous individuals embody qualities that are considered both feminine and masculine. Androgynous women and men are both nurturing and assertive, both strong and sensitive.

The anthropologist Margaret Mead (1935/1968) reported three distinct gender patterns in the New Guinea societies in her study. Among Arapesh people, both women and men conformed closely to what we consider feminine behaviour. Both were passive, peaceful, and deferential, and both nurtured others, especially young children. The Mundugumor tribe socialized both women and men to be aggressive, independent, and competitive. Mothers were not nurturant and spent very little time with new born babies, weaning them early instead. Within the Tchambuli society, women were domineering and sexually aggressive, whereas men were considered delicate and taught to wear decorative clothes and curl their hair so they would be attractive to women.

When it comes to transgendered and transsexed individuals, transgendered is the term for individuals who feel that their biologically assigned sex is inconsistent with their true sexual identity – that they are women, despite having male bodies, or men despite having women's bodies. These meanings are communicated through structures and practices that pervade our daily existence, creating the illusion that there are two and only two sexes, two and only two genders, and the gender

determine one's behaviour, personality, etc. Biology also does not stipulate the meaning that members of a culture assign to particular behaviours – which ones are valued, which ones devalued. It is all depends on how we perceive and treat differences and not by biological differences.

Wood added that gender is a classification that society makes based on genetic and biological factors which most endures throughout their lives. Gender is neither innate nor stable. It is a social, symbolic construct that varies across cultures, over time within a given culture, and over the course of individuals' life spans.

What gender means and how we express it depend on a society's values, beliefs, and preferred ways of organising collective life. It is a societal structure that is defined by individuals as they interact with others. One is born male or female (sex), but one learns to act in masculine and/or feminine ways (gender). For example, for men to be masculine is to be strong, ambitious, successful, rational, and emotionally controlled. These are regarded as "real men" who don't cry in public, and "real men" who are successful and powerful in their professional and public lives. In opposite to masculinity, femininity is termed as "physically attractive, deferential, emotionally expressive, nurturing, and concerned with people and relationships. Those who embody the cultural definition of femininity still don't allow themselves to outdo men ..."[311] Thus, gender distinction such as male and female as masculinity and femininity are not *natural* but *acquired*.[312] Society teaches us how to behave as female/male in a particular place and time. All the norms and values as (we consider normal) are constructed and shaped by society. Right from the beginning of infancy we are encouraged to learn how to embody the gender that society prescribes for us.[313] Shefali Moitra pointed out that: "... the attributes associate with male-gender roles have been valorized whereas the female-gender roles have been pejoratized. Therefore, gender does not simply symbolize difference, it also symbolizes discrimination."[314]

The eighteenth-century woman's claim for participation in intellectual life can be seen in the assertion by Londa Scheibinger that 'the mind has no sex'. This sentiment is also echoed by the character of Anne Elliot in Jane Austen's *Persuasion*, who argued against the biased and exclusive male-oriented modes of

---

prescriptions which society embraces are the natural, normal ways for women and men to be. Julia T Wood, *Gendered Lives: Communication, Gender, and Culture,* 8th edition, 21-30.

311 Ibid., 23-24.

312 Mary Evans, *Gender and Social Theory* (Berkshire: Open University Press, 2003, Indian Reprint, 2009), 17.

313 Julia T Wood, *Gendered Lives: Communication, Gender, and Culture,* 8th edition, op. cit., 23-24.

314 Shefali Moitra, *Feminist Thought: Androcentrism, Communication and Objectivity* (Kolkata: Munshiram Manoharlal Pubilshers Pvt, Ltd./Centre of Advanced Study in Philosophy Jadavpur University, 2002),78.

reproducing social knowledge and staked a claim for the recognition of women's intellectual and moral abilities.[315]

Between 1970 and 1975, scholars raised the issue of discrimination faced by women in industrial societies both by western capitalist and state socialist societies. Some of the prominent writings are Shulamith Firestone's *The Dialectic of Sex*,[316] Sheila Rowbotham's *Hidden from History*,[317] Kate Millett's *Sexual Politics*[318] *etc.* For them, the social world of the late twentieth century was depicted, in these writings, as a world which was misogynistic and exploitative of women. They attacked the literature and philosophy of the west whose history was written on the vested interest and supremacy of men, whereas a total lack of public voice for women either in political or in institutional life was deemed visible. These feminist authors had shown their anger and conviction, and they demanded to rethink and to restructure gender relations in the west as well as across the globe.[319] Virginia Wolf in *Women and Fiction* says: "In future, granted time, and books, and a little space in the house for herself, literature will become for women, as for men, an art to be studied. Women's gift will be trained and strengthened."[320]

Jürgen Habermas's earlier classic work on the origins of modernity that has traced the emergence of a distinctly "public" space where citizens could debate without prejudice, through open and rational interchange, a community of discourse with free and democratic social order seems irrelevant because in this public space (origins of modernity) reason reigned, but the argument based on religious insights was excluded. Therefore, Habermas suggested that something is "missing" in secular reasoning in the shape of transcendental and metaphysical values. In his recent work on "post-secular" he expressed and emphasised the role of religion in the public square that has taken a new turn in social theory and political philosophy. However, Elaine Graham asserts that religion is not the only factor that has "gone missing" in the post-secular reconfiguration of belief, civic identity and the body politic. Graham in her writing observed that there is a

---

[315] *Against this,* Hegel claimed in *The Philosophy of Right that* the mind (women) *did* have a sex. According to him, feminine qualities were intuition, affection, and subjectivity. For him these qualities are essential in the family and not in the public ethical life. Thus in the nineteenth century women was considered as inferior beings but men were viewed as creatures of objectivity and rationality. (The thesis proposed by Hegel was not, however, about the intellectual inferiority of women, but about the intellectual *inclination* of women). Mary Evans, *Gender and Social Theory*, op. cit., 18.

[316] Shulamith Firestone, *The Dialectic of Sex: The Case for Feminist Revolution*, (New York: William Morrow and Company, Inc., 1970).

[317] Sheila Rowbotham, *Hidden From History: 300 Years of Women's Oppression and the Fight Against It*, (London: Pluto Press, 1973).

[318] Kate Millett, *Sexual Politics*, (New York: Doubleday, 1970).

[319] Mary Evans, *Gender and Social Theory*, op. cit., 10.

[320] Virginia Wolf, "Women and Fiction," in *The Feminist Critique of Language: A reader*. edited by Deborah Cameron, 2nd edition (London/New York: Routledge 1998), 52.

danger of gender, particularly women, disappearing from this new post-secular chapter in the debate about religion, politics and identity.[321]

Similar to Graham's critical observation about gender disparity,[322] we also find a similar idea in Errol Miller's assertion about equality in the representation of women and men.[323] He said that we find equal representation only at the highest level of political in nation characterised by little or no diversity. For example, the voice of gender equality will be heard within a specific circle that shares and distributes equally the available material resources, because the filters of ethnicity/race, religion, region, class, etc., virtually would not exist and the generation filter sufficiently permeable to allow effective transmission.

In contrast, there are nations with diverse social composition such as a newly constructed common identity who among formerly disparate groups and limited material resources had found inequitable distribution in society. In such social groups voice of gender equity might be just a mere whisper, as the filters of ethnicity/race, religion, region, class, caste, etc., would block transmission in the face of inter-group conflicts. It is therefore, patriarchal patterns prevail at all levels of the political apparatus where group solidarity and loyalty stifle notions of gender equality.[324] Gender injustice such as sexual division of labour is also common in many places.

Ivy mentioned in her writing about the impact on women the division of labour among genders which says that:

> The gender division of labour impacts upon women's time, income, nutrition and health. It also impacts crucially on their access to, and control and management of natural resources, their perceived ability to take community level decisions, and the value society places on their contributions. The question of access and control over productive resources is linked to the issues of poverty, lack of skills and information, and lack of effective organizational forms for women to express their needs and concerns in the environment sectors.[325]

Muthuraj Swamy says that any approach to the sexual division of labour should look critically into the socio-cultural and historical factors which are connected to the various human social developments. It is said that the myths about women's work are associated with mind-sets where the inherited socio-

---

[321] Elaine Graham, "What's missing? Gender, reason and the post-secular," *Political Theology*, 13/2 (April, 2012), 235.

[322] Elaine Graham, "What's missing? Gender, reason and the post-secular," *Political Theology*, 13/2 (April, 2012), 235.

[323] Errol Miller, "Gender, Power and Politics: An Alternative Perspective," in *Gender, Peace and Conflict*, edited by Inger Skjelsbaek and Dan Smith (Delhi: SAGE Publications, 2001), 99.

[324] Ibid.

[325] Ivy, *Voices from Narmada: Doing Ecofeminist Theology* (Delhi: ISPCK, 2009), 117.

cultural stereotypes further help the patriarchal-capitalist structures. Therefore, a holistic approach of sexual division of labour is the need of the hour to challenge and eliminate the existing stereotypes and destructive forces of capitalism and development.[326]

Some of the approaches that failed to establish gender equity in society are like the neo-classical approach which establishes that the economic issues that decide the nature, the amount and the extent of women's work did not really touch the core of women's problems because the nature of socio-cultural and other factors that determine women's work is not put into account and therefore leads to the sexual division of labour. The Marxist approach often remains silent about the division between men workers and women workers even though the approach highlighted the struggles of the working community in the context of capitalistic domination where the activities of the labour force were controlled. So, also from the anthropological perspective the issue of women's work particularly in relation to patriarchy was discussed, but above all, how these perspectives can be extended to understand women's work in the unrecognised domestic sector was put into serious consideration.[327]

Just as Graham says that it has been her contention that the post-secular invites us to think about "what's missing" in secular reasoning, it is at the same time "also an opportunity to acknowledge and correct the gendered nature of our thinking about faith and reason, private and public, sacred and secular, tyranny and freedom." Graham has shown that just as feminist interventions into the discourse of the Western Enlightenment which was a part of critical debate about the nature and trajectory of modernity,[328] Clara Greed's writing has attested that, "now the opportunity has been brought to us by post-secularism to discuss and expose the dualism that halts women's lives from religious, sociological and spatial perspectives."[329]

2.4.2. Gender and Religion

From the religious point of view, everything seems absolute but the element that hinders the growth of human (mostly women) seems unchecked. As it is said, religions may be doctrinally pluralistic, but their practiced form is far from egalitarian. It can be as exploitative as anything else. It is obvious to see from some of the examples in India too how political and religious fundamentalists used

---

[326] Muthuraj Swamy, "Women's Work and Sexual Division of Labour: Critiques from Feminist Perspectives," in *Women's Issues and Reflections*, edited by, Christina Manohar (Delhi: ISPCK, 2012), 120-121.

[327] Ibid.,119.

[328] Elaine Graham, "What's Missing? op. cit., 244.

[329] Clara Greed, "A Feminist Critique of the Post-secular City: God and Gender," in *Post-Secular Cities: Space, Theory and Practice*, edited by, Justin Beaumont and Christopher R. Baker (London: Ashgate, 2011), 108.

women as tool for power and control mechanism. The injunctions on compulsory *purdah* for women by Islamic fundamentalists in Kashmir, the BJP-ABVP's objection to western clothes on Indian women are the signs of fundamentalists' need for control. For the interests of fundamentalists' purpose women's clothes, sexuality, behaviour, and rights are used.[330]

Even the biblical texts, which all Christians consider sacred, are not free from gender biases. Take, for example, the story of the fall in Genesis 3 itself depicts the fall into patriarchy which justifies women's subordination in a patriarchal society. The moral lesson has been taken out from this passage like a marriage drama between Mr. Adam and Mrs. Eve, in which the woman, beguiled by the snake, tempts her husband, who without being suspicious listens to her and falls into a mortal trap. However at the very outset, Mr. who was already well informed not to eat from the tree, while Mrs. was not yet in the picture. Here, the woman is depicted as the origin of sin, evil and death and not as givers of Life. Gabriele Dietrich expresses that, "this subordination of women is not inherent in God's good creation, nor is it envisaged in the new community, which Jesus was trying to create and which prefigures the new relationship in God's reign."[331] She says, "[d] ismantling the attachment to wealth and the attachment to power and hierarchy needs to go together with dismantling patriarchy," patriarchy itself is sin.[332]

Religion was neglected in a secularist agenda. Which means many of the contemporary feminists accepted the postmodernism that open up critical spaces for seeking and challenging the constitution of modernity along gendered lines. The androcentric concepts of subjectivity, reason and personhood were highlighted by the postmodern feminists. Post-Enlightment first-and second-wave feminism[333] also benefited from a modernist appeal to autonomy, freedom

---

[330] Pramod K. Nayar, *Reading Culture: Theory, praxis, Politics* (New Delhi: SAGE Publications, 2006), 38-41.

[331] To have a clearer understanding about division of gender in the biblical texts we bring an example, in Gen. 1:26-31, which mentioned "Adam" as a generic term, "human being," made from adamah, Mother Earth. So, the question of patriarchal subordination does not arise here. Both male and female are made in the image of God. Thus, Gen.1 is said that it belongs to the priestly source, compiled in the time of Babylonian Exile. And it is said that Gen. 2 and 3 belong to the Jahvist source which belongs to the 8th century when kingship and patriarchy were in full power. It is said that differentiation into male and female happens only from chapter 3:18 onwards, and in that, it talks about equality and companionship. Also who was first is not a question because Earth and all other creatures are the first that has created. Here, the term "Helper" that is used does not express subordination either. It can be used among equals. See, Dietrich, *Wise Like Snakes, Innocent Like Doves: Thirty Biblical Reflections in Feminist Perspective* (Delhi: ISPCK, 2011).

[332] Ibid., 85.

[333] The history of feminist movements up to the present day is often considered to consist of three "waves." The first wave refers to the movements of 19th and 20th centuries where women demanded right to vote, education, employment, and marriage laws and sought to highlight the plight of middle-class women. The second wave begins in 1960's-1980's which was referred to the campaign for legal and social equality for women on abortion, birth control, and overall reproductive

from external constraint and self-determination. However, it has been gradually realised and noticed that the Enlightenment feminism unconsciously acquired to a secularist agenda, but had neglected on the part of most of western feminist scholarship of religion and theology.[334]

Graham points out that the analysis of post-secular society is an imperative to "make space for theorising a meaningful way about the role of religion in women's lives, and the de-and recontextualizations of the relationship between religion, culture and gender." Therefore, through this related approach of "faith" and "reason" might inform discourses around the construction of gender identity, relations and representations.[335]

Examining patriarchy from another angle, we put forward the assertion from Errol Miller who says that, *Equality is a unified whole*. In his description about patriarchy, Miller says that the radical feminist scholars' definition of patriarchy is confined solely to gender[336] and Weber's definition[337] of patriarchy included only the elements of gender and generation and omitted the kinship relations that normally exist between the older and younger men and women who constitute the household. Thus, Miller says that "patriarchy needs to be defined because that system of reciprocal social obligations in which final authority rests with the older men of the kinship collective, who exercise that authority over its individual male and female members in the overall interest of the collectives."[338] Miller therefore in alignment with these two definitions of patriarchy gender and generation, added the element of genealogy in the definition. In his view, gender and generation elements relate mainly to the internal relation, of the collectives, whereas the genealogy element defines its external boundaries and relations.[339]

rights of women. These second wave feminists come from the backgrounds like journalism, the social sciences, linguistic, the media and the arts. Christa Knellwolf and Christopher Norris, *The Cambridge History of Literary Criticism: Twentieth-Century Historical, Philosophical and Psychological Perspectives*, (Cambridge: Cambridge University Press, 2007), 194-199.

[334] Elaine Graham, "What's Missing? op. cit., 244.

[335] Ibid., 245.

[336] Errol Miller, "Gender, Power and politics: An Alternative Perspective," op. cit., 81.

[337] Max Weber defined patriarchy as *women and younger men being ruled by older men, who were heads of household.* Errol Miller, "Gender, Power and politics: An Alternative Perspective," in *Gender, Peace and Conflict*, 81.

[338] Ibid., 82.

[339] Here Miller apparently means that genealogy of external boundaries and relation refers to the kinship outside the immediate circumstances of the household or family, by establishing links with other collectives through common ancestry. Sometimes it defines collectives which are not kin. He says that, conceptually and historically, patriarchy involves not only asymmetry in power between men and women, but also shared identity, group solidarity, common bonds and mutual obligations. He added on to say that, historically, patriarchal collectives had great difficulties with other collectives that fell outside the covenant of kinship. Suppose if the patriarchal collectives interacted outside boundaries where kinship could be established, then one group had to submit to the hegemony of the other. If they fail to do so, the end result will be compromised by violent

Miller brought out that the essence of patriarchy, does not affect only one part of the element such as the marginalisation of women within the kinship collective, but the effect is also upon the men of unrelated collectives over which dominance has been established. Therefore, he said that patriarchy must include the marginalisation of men of the unrelated collective, in one way or another. Gender operates in conjunction with other social criteria according to which societies are organised. Gender analysis is neither the asymmetry in power between men and women, nor of men's domination of women alone, nor about women's issues alone, and nor assume solidarity between men and women belonging to different groups in society alone.[340] It cannot be conveniently divided into segments related exclusively to gender, or class, or religion, or region, or generation, or race, or tribe or clan. When we look at gender inequality we cannot avoid confronting the other inequalities as well.[341]

From a redemption perspective, gender no longer privileges one over another—as well as race or class. In terms of redemption, Christ's mediation removes the privilege associated with one gender, and exalts the oppressed gender. In the Kingdom of God, there is no "gender"; however, there are sexes that uniquely honour God through diversity.[342]

2.4.3. Culture

It is revealed that in one of the six communication images of Paul A Soukup's reviewed essay it says that, communication cannot be separated from the overall culture-patterns of human thoughts, manifestations of that thought, and the construction of society. It says that communication is termed as an 'effects model' because it primarily considers the impact of communication and communication media on human culture.[343]

There are various ways of defining culture. It may be a person's way of life, one's own attitudes, customs and beliefs, art, social organisation of a particular country or group etc. Here, we particularly talk about the culture that is referring to certain customs or roles which people perform in society. And we go along with Gabriele Dietrich who puts inflexibility towards rethinking of cultural practices

---

means for their dominant establishment. For example, genocide, where one collective sought the physical elimination of another, the killing of male captives, enslavement of men, the castration of male captives. On the other hand, patriarchal collectives found it easier to incorporate women of non-kin groups than the men of such groups. Miller therefore, expressed that the external relations with men of hostile collectives is as much as element of patriarchy as are the internal relations with women of the kinship collective. Errol Miller, "Gender, Power and politics: op. cit., 82.

[340] Ibid., 83.

[341] Ibid,. 103.

[342] Thomas V. Frederick, "An Interpretation of Evangelical Gender Ideology: Implications for a Theology of Gender," in *Theology and Sexuality*, no 16. (May 12th 2010), 191.

[343] Paul A Soukup, *Communication and Theology: Introduction and Review of the Literature* (London: World Association for Christian Communication, 1983), 28.

and norms as arising from a feeling that "this is our culture, we are quite happy with it." Dietrich says that we normally hear such kinds of sentence when people try to explain the role of men and women in society, and the relationships between generations as well as between castes or other social groups, even though people are aware that such customs and roles are different from one society to the other and that they change within one society throughout history. But, the need for preservation of one's own tradition is advocated often, apparently because they give a certain sense of belonging and fulfilment to people which they don't wish to lose.[344]

To this sense of belonging, people often subordinate the question of right or wrong, good or evil. Whether a custom or a role oppresses people or hamper their development is either not asked or a rationalisation is found even if they may be a bit oppressive. The most striking examples for this understanding of "culture" can be found with respect to the family, male-female relationship, etc. In this case "culture" mainly refers to the regulation of social relationships. The other side of the coin is the rejection of the inherited social pattern.[345]

Wood has defined that culture is made up of structures, institutions, and practices that reflect and uphold a particular social order. This is usually done by defining certain social groups, values, expectations, meanings, and patterns of behaviour as natural and good and others as unnatural, bad, or wrong.[346]

Whenever one talks of culture, the gender element always gets appended to it. One of the major issues that remains ignored and unchallenged even today by our culture and tradition is the bias towards women. Sonia Bathla has rightly pointed out that women face unequal treatment in a democratic country like India as well as in other Asian countries particularly in relation to women's role and status. This is based on the so-called ancient civilisations in which traditional or cultural social structures and institutions are very strongly established. Although, the impact of modernisation on political administration, economic system, industrial and technological development, etc., are enormous, the traditional structures that suppress women's role and status remained the same.[347] As part of their fight against the external powers, the developing countries were often extremely protective of their culture and the responsibility to carry tradition mainly fell on women. Being the carriers of culture, women are expected to live up to the traditions, and hence retain the nation's identity against foreign culture.

---

[344] Gabriele Dietrich, *Culture, Religion and Development* (Bangalore: Centre for Contemporary Christianity, 1978), 5.

[345] Ibid.

[346] Julia T Wood, *Gendered Lives,* op. cit., 30.

[347] Sonia Bathla, *Women, Democracy and the Media: Cultural and Political Representations in the Indian Press.* (New Delhi, Thousand Oaks, London: SAGE Publications, 1998), 43.

Trapped within the complexities of a transitional society with a "modern face but traditional soul," the position of women in Indian society remains powerless.[348]

2.4.4. Communication

As gender is central to cultural life, communication too becomes a primary tool that structures society. Communication functions as an instrument to promote social, cultural, and political actions for change. Communication is to share with other cultural identities and not to dwell or preserve in isolation but to strengthen cultural identities. Communication is the articulation of social relation between human beings. It is, therefore, quite apt that communication is considered as the product and moulder of society.

One of the five main functions of communication, "Communication is socialisation" is which it plays an important role in the society. It facilitates the involvement of people in public life, both individually as well as collectively, it plays the role in decision-making, it participates actively in problem solving activities and it is also considered as an integral part of the process of the democratisation of public life.[349]

2.5. Dialogical Process of Communication

Dialogical process of communication becomes part and parcel in one's individual as well as among groups. "When as persons, the members enter into dialogue with one another and assume responsibility for their common life it becomes a community. The individuals and society are abstractions without dialogue."[350] Dialogue plays an important role in the society among the different social, cultural, religious, ethnic and gender groups in the community: "Dialogue is a commitment. The more one engages in it, the greater is the perspective and the goal."[351] Let us try to see what dialogue is and how it works.

2.5.1 What is Dialogue?

Reuel L. Howe in his book *The Miracle of Dialogue* wrote categorically about the nature and meaning of dialogue. For Howe, dialogue means:

> Address and response between persons in which there is a flow of meaning between them in spite of all the obstacles that normally would block the relationship. It is that interaction between persons in which one of them seeks to give himself [*sic*] as he [*sic*] is to the other,

[348] Ibid.

[349] Subrata Banerjee ed., *Culture and Communication* (New Delhi: Patriot Publishers, 1986), XIX.

[350] Reuel L. Howe, *The Miracle of Dialogue* (New York: The Seabury Press, 1963), 5.

[351] Maura O' Neill, *Women Speaking Women Listening: Women in interreligious Dialogue*, (Maryknoll: Orbis Books, 1990), 104.

> and seeks also to know the other as the other is. This means that he [*sic*] will not attempt to impose his [*sic*] own truth and view on the other. Such is the relationship which characterizes dialogue and is the precondition to dialogical communication.[352]

Lynne A de Silva also added that: "Dialogue seeks to break down moats of separation and build bridges of understanding."[353] Dialogue normally takes the other person seriously, that makes language to become the means of genuine meeting between persons and conversation becomes a tool of re-creation.

Dialogue is a long-range goal of the endeavour where both women and men would participate equally. If this dialogue could occur between the two parties, then it could be transformed and understanding could exist across religious and cultural lines as well as gender lines.[354] Communication is empowerment in any situation of dialogue either religious or cultural or gender etc. In the situation where we see the wide disparity between gender relationships in the society, communication through dialogue could be an agent of change. There must be a consistent dialogue upon love and unity, recognition and appreciation, reconciliation and trust, sharing and fellowship among human (male and female, etc.) community.

2.5.2. Gender and Dialogue

One of the main concerns of dialogue in communication is based on gender issues. How it should press towards liberation in the social, economic, political, cultural and religious circle. This is because society is generally controlled by patriarchal structures and mind-sets where the voice of a woman is ignored. It is "through dialogue and literature, that women will be able to communicate their growing consciousness of themselves and others and their experiences of similarities and differences with one another."[355] There is a growing concern that many need to expand their visions to include the woman, her voice, her story and her lessons. It is the need of the hour that women must join together in dialogue with their male partners so that together there exists a mutual relationship and co-operation that may genuinely grow and develop to its full potential here on earth. As it is said: "A complete description of a utopian community of men and women in dialogue is impossible…When men and women enter into an open dialogue as equal participants, the results could be revolutionizing."[356]

It is also observed that development commitment toward gender justice becomes a necessity. Through initiative for dialogue in development one may

---

[352] Reuel L. Howe, *The Miracle of Dialogue*, op. cit., 37.

[353] Lynne A de Silva, "Editorial," *Dialogue,* 1/1 (April, 1974), 2.

[354] Reuel L. Howe, *The Miracle of Dialogue*, op. cit., 44, 100.

[355] Ibid., 103.

[356] Ibid.,105-106.

be able to play an important role in increasing awareness of inequalities, in supporting a constructive search for solutions, and in enabling women to have an effective voice in this process.[357]

The fourth analogue for the communication process used in the theology and communication literature is interpersonal dialogue. Interpersonal dialogue allows for conversation and sees communication that links people or that builds up community as the perfection and goal of all communication.[358]

2.5.3. Church and Dialogue

Sometimes Church tends to withdraw from the world, is reluctant to communicate with it, and treats it as an enemy instead of the place of its life and mission. Reuel L. Howe writes: "The separation between the world and the Church also calls for the ministry of dialogue."[359] It is also true that "[t]he Gospel can only become real in the world of creation through dialogue in the medium of culture."[360]

Dialogue has the dynamic power to intervene between church and the world through which God acts in and through it to influence both the church and the world and to judge, purify, and transform both.[361] Michael Amaladoss once mentioned in one of his articles, "Culture and Dialogue" said that:

> We have to develop an integral approach not only in considering God's self-revelation but also in the response of the human community. In multi-religious situations we have to think of basic *human* communities rather than of basic Christian communities. Christians will find themselves together around the eucharistic table on the Lord's day. At other times their life will be structured by the other human communities to which they belong. It is in the midst of the human community that the eucharistic community becomes meaningful. It is in building up the world that the church is being built up. It may be helpful to formalize proclamation, dialogue and liberation for clearer understanding. But, they are mutually involved in each other as integral elements of evangelization.
>
> The convergent movement I have talked about will be carried by symbols that are capable of a certain polyvalence around a central core and whose concrete connotations are controlled by the context of usage. This is what makes possible not only common reading of

---

[357] "Culture," www.hhs.se/CASL/news/Documents/NFF%20romani.pdf? accessed on 10.5.2013.

[358] Paul A Soukup, *Communication and Theology*, op. cit., 28.

[359] Reuel L. Howe, *The Miracle of Dialogue*, 14.

[360] John B. Kariuki Wakareg, "Evangelization and Cultural Pluralism: A Call for Dialogue, Change and Renewal," *AFER*, 47/3 (2005), 231.

[361] Reuel L. Howe, *The Miracle of Dialogue*, op. cit., 15.

> scriptures, common prayer, common celebrations, etc., but also the use of other religio-cultural symbols in the self-expression of the word.[362]

As highlighted here by Amaladoss, we can understand that a wider concept of dialogical approach from mere Christian communities to human communities is the need of the hour. Converging towards a unified community is relevant today where everybody joins in, where they all will be able to participate in the conversation. The diverse individuals (inclusive of all), with diverse perspectives and challenges must be recognised. Howe continues that: "A word spoken in isolation cannot have the same meaning as the same word spoken in relation."[363] Therefore, where and when there is dialogue things change and gradually love, truth, peace and life strengthen and move towards better relationship among humankind.

2.5.4. Steps for Constructive Dialogue

In order to lead a fruitful dialogue, a long-term view and professionalism is required. From the beginning, the initiative must be contemplated; only then the constructive dialogue with the partners on gender equality issues is established. Another requirement is preparedness which is necessary. In this, one must be ready to make contribution to the discussion, allow for the time required to develop mutual trust and respect, and adhere to the long-term objective of gender equality. It must be followed by innovative ways of planning things. It also requires gender analysis: "A gender analysis is required for all initiatives as it ensures that planning is based on facts and analysis rather than assumptions."[364]

Silva has stated that openness which is penetrable or accessible to both the parties is required in genuine dialogue; it implies a willingness to subject oneself to a process of mutual correction and learning. It also involves critical appreciation and balanced judgement which should be based on sober criticisms pursued in a rational manner with modesty, respect and charity.[365]

Cees J. Hamelink says that "[t]he creation of security and empathy – vital to the defence of human rights – cannot come about by dictate, it needs to evolve through societal dialogue."[366] He claimed that to include a human right to communicate in the human right catalogue, one needs to ask whether people can

---

362 Michael Amaladoss, "Culture and Dialogue," *International Review of Mission*, 74/294 (April, 1985), 176.

363 Reuel L. Howe, *The Miracle of Dialogue*, op. cit., 14-15.

364 "Culture," www.hhs.se/CASL/news/Documents/NFF%20romani.pdf? accessed on 10.5. 2013.

365 Lynne A de Silva, "Editorial," *Dialogue*, op. cit., 2.

366 Cees J. Hamelink, "Grounding the human right to communicate," in *Many Voices, One Vision: Right to Communicate in Practice*, edited by, Philip Lee (Penang: Southbound, 2004), 27-29.

be deprived of the freedom to exercise this right. He would argue if this can be the case in the following situations.

Hamelink further asserted that in real life situations, the confidentiality of the conversational mode is not adequately secured; people (individuals or groups) are excluded from the public and/or private dialogue; people are not listened to; the positive dimension of the right to engage in the conversational mode is not secured.[367]

For Hamelink, a meaningful dialogue requires an internal dialogue. Internal dialogue implies that all participants question their own judgments and assumptions. Dialogue also requires the capacity to listen and to be silent. Above all, dialogue needs to acquire learning from the very beginning. As he says, "[T] he essence of dialogue could and should be taught in the early stages of people's lives in the school, at home, and through the media."[368]

2.6. A Network Approach

Sven Windahl, Benno Signitzer, and others brought Rogers and Kincaid communication networks based on a new model of communication, the convergence model, while at the same time comparing it with Schenk who emphasised the analysis of social networks in general, with communication networks being only a part of the earlier one. Later on it is realised that Schenk's approach become more sociological that is directly applicable to our purpose.

Rogers and Kincaid characterise a *communication network* as consisting of "interconnected individuals who are linked by patterned communication flows."[369] Sven Windahl, Benno Signitzer, et.al, mentioned that: "the interpersonal linkages created by the sharing of information in the interpersonal communication structures"[370] the network. Through this definition of communication network, we can know the persistent character of such networks, which means practically everyone in society, belongs to one or several communication networks. Through this it is clear that the significance of studying communication from a network perspective is a part of the study of human communication in general.[371]

Cees J. Hamelink as well as Rogers and Kincaid criticised on the S-M-C-R linear model of communication in this model the process cannot describe what happens in dynamic and complicated communication situations.[372] For

---

367 Cees J. Hamelink, "Grounding the human right to communicate," in *Many Voices, One Vision: Right to Communicate in Practice*, edited by, Philip Lee (Penang: Southbound, 2004), 27-29.

368 Ibid.

369 Sven Windahl, Benno Signitzer, et.al, *Using Communication Theory: An Introduction to Planned Communication* Second Edition (Los Angeles, London, New Delhi, Singapore, Washington DC: Sage Publications, 2009), 95-96.

370 Ibid.

371 Ibid.

372 Ibid., 96.

Hamelink, the linear model of Shannon and Weaver (1949) mathematical theory of communication is one-way process which is very limited. This model ignores the essence "to communicate" that refers to a process of sharing, making common or creating a community.[373] Example of traditional model study in Korea shows that the Korean women in a small village organised themselves to improve their general living conditions for themselves and their families. For that, they had developed its very essence – its interaction, mutuality, and constructions as an entire communication structures. That was due to the well maintaining communication process, the traditional model became so powerful in their cooperative effort.[374]

It is said that the role of communication in network is not limited only to the sender-receiver, interpersonal relationship and by ignoring communication as a property of groups. Because, group and network factors are often to blame when planned communication fails, they may equally well explain why it succeeds. Here, the classical information theory which is applied in the study of communication network has been brought in. These are:

> traffic: who does most of the talking and how much talking is done;
> closure: how open the group is to outsiders and ideas from the outside;
> convergence: whether members in group communication are on an equal footing or whether some are chiefly generators of communications while others are mainly passive receivers.[375]

Collective action, the act of sharing information is the origin of the process. Mutual understanding is a product of on-going interaction and communication is a key element of the convergence model.[376] In most communication model it is said that, the single individual is the unit of analysis; in the network model, the dyad, that are two elements – individuals, groups, etc., – linked together by communication, and the clique (groups within the groups) are studied. Two-way communication within these dyads or systems of dyads is more significant than one-way communication.[377] Here effects arise from a joint activity and affect all participants but not the common definitions of effects. In the network perspectives, sometimes it may be the source that is affected by the communication, not the receiver.[378]

Here the writers direct us saying that, the network model encourages communication planners and researchers to use new cause/effect variables in their

---

[373] Cees J. Hamelink, "Grounding the human right to communicate", in *Many Voices, One Vision: Right to Communicate in Practice*, 25. See also Sven Windahl, Benno Signitzer, et.al, *Using Communication Theory: An Introduction to Planned Communication* Second Edition, 96.

[374] Ibid.

[375] Sven Windahl, Benno Signitzer, et.al, *Using Communication Theory*, op. cit., 97.

[376] Ibid., 98-100.

[377] Ibid.

[378] Ibid.

analyses. They had cited with an example that properties of the very communication network, such as connectedness, integration, diversity, and openness, may prove to be important to comprehending a communication situation.[379]

A group of Swedish researchers had successfully developed the *spiral of interaction* affirming that communication is a means of empowerment for emancipation. It has been suggested that the less privileged can improve their situation by improving their communication potential. Not only have to make their voices heard but also brought about an interactional spiral, which originates in communication between people.

Windahl and others discussed the different functions of communication towards the empowerment. They had brought the functions mentioned by Thunberg and others which are as follows:

> *The expressive function.* Individuals express themselves effectively in order to create an identity for themselves (and their group).
>
> *The social functions.* By communicating together, people develop a sense of community.
>
> *The information function.* Through communication, individuals can share information and thereby increase their knowledge.
>
> *The control activation function.* Communication leads to join action, modifying the environment and improving the situation of individuals and their groups.[380]

There are threats to the spiral of communication. It may be threatened from above, below, and within a system. The above or top means societies, communities, and organisations all have their own goals, their organisational lifestyles and their developed structures. It means that there are little interests in making room for the activities of a small group. The spiral is threatened from below by its own participants. The spiral is threatened from within means bureaucratization, professionalization, and institutionalization are dangerous for successfully growing interaction spiral; they developed due to the size and complexity of the spiral. To bring solution to this problem is to revitalize the group often in order to recapture the dynamics that exists in smaller groups.[381]

2.7. Voice: An Emancipatory Approach

We must consider and admire women whose voice was powerfully raised and whose lives were dynamic and vibrant. There are many such women who have

---

[379] Sven Windahl, Benno Signitzer, et.al, *Using Communication Theory*, op. cit., 98-100.

[380] Ibid., 103-104. See also Rogers E.M. and Kincaid D.L., *Communication Networks: Toward a New Paradigm for Research* (New York: Free Press, 1981).

[381] Ibid.

been actively involved and playing prominent role for the noble cause of the community in many different ways all over the world. The voice of women has been quite vibrant in the community from time immemorial. Women's voice has been a guiding principle and the cradle of wisdom and knowledge during time of war,[382] for peace making, reconciliation, for economic stability and such other related social issues.

In the Ao Naga tribal community, *Watsu Mungdang* (women's organisation)[383] has been an active agent in the society, supporting and empowering women in the community. Among many other issues tackled by *watsu*, one example is the issue of rape cases perpetrated by Security Forces in 1994 and in 1997. In both the cases, *watsu* won the case and compensation was given to the victims by the Army authorities and the offenders were reprimanded.[384]

The voice of women reaches out again and again for peace negotiation, such as building up understanding between different factional groups in the region in the recent past. In some instances, it was women rather than men who stepped forward at a critical time when the situation becomes tense in the militant zones of north-east India. Women negotiated courageously, accomplishing the tough task of mediating between the government and the common people during the time when there was no one to handle such kind of tense situation. One of the most perilous incidents encountered by the Naga Mothers Association (NMA) in 2010 was when two young Nagas were shot dead by the army at Mao town on the Manipur border. For eight days, villagers refused to claim the bodies, tensions had intensified on both sides. The brave Naga mothers underwent so many tough times they were stopped by the army at every step. Nonetheless they could push through security cordons shrouded the bodies and took them to the boys families.[385] This shows that women have the capabilities to voice and exercise their God given talents for the good of the community. There are many instances where Naga Mother's Association (NMA) and the Naga Women's Union of Manipur (NWUM) joined together to negotiate informally with state and non-state actors to safeguard their communities, mobilise for reunion, sustain the cease-fire,

---

382 The stories of some legendary women, such as Akangla and others had been narrated in the third chapter.

383 *Watsu Mungdang* (women's organisation) which was formed in 1982 is the apex organization of Ao women. "The journey of *watsu Mungdang*", http://nagalandpost.com/SundayPost/ArticleShow.aspx?sid=UzEwMDAwMDIwNQ%3D%3D-01foIaISCCA%3D accessed on 27.4.15.

384 Ibid.

385 "TOI Social Impact Awards: Life Time Contribution- Naga Mother's Association," by Rukmini Shrinivasan, in http://timesofindia.indiatimes.com/india/TOI-Social-Impact-Awards-Lifetime-contribution-Naga-Mothers-Association/articleshow/17963150.cms accessed on 25.4.2015.

extend the official talks with seniors officials in the state government as well as with the Indian Military officers, and forge a more inclusive process.[386]

"Shed No More Blood campaign" was organised on August 4, 1994, when 3,000 mothers from various tribes came together in Kohima, the capital of Nagaland, to launch the initiative. There had been a lot of development due to the Naga women's intervention during conflict in the region. It had provided space for dialogue and created a greater desire for peace. Women had in the recent past gone forward representing and participating in the consultation (the third Bangkok Consultation in 2002), at an assembly (in Manipur in April 2003).[387]

The strength and willpower of women is expressed in the National Freedom Movement in India as well. A woman such as Rani Gaidinliu's[388] voice and action from north-east India had been expressed during the Indian freedom struggle. Another legendary lady Irom Chanu Sharmila who has been fasting for more than a decade fighting for rights against the Armed Force Special Powers Act in north-eastern part of India are seen as a role model for many and that have been witnessing by the world. [389] The achievements of women clearly show that woman's voice is powerful and that her emotion, abilities, intellectual, spiritual and physical strength must not be overlooked in any manner.

2.8. Cultural Network Approach

There is only one-way flow of communication in and through the decision-making bodies in the day-to-day functioning of the Ao Naga tribal community. The essential element of human "voice" of the female members of the community is blocked by the traditional socio-cultural set-up; that is, "male voice alone" concept is to be seen. Hence, it is glaringly noticeable how the voice of the female is often supressed and kept under total control.

---

[386] "Naga women making a difference: peace building in Northeastern India" By Rita Manchanda, (January, 2005): vii-ix, http://www.iiav.nl/epublications//2005/Naga_Women_Making_a_Difference.pdf accessed on 27.4.15.

[387] Ibid., ix.

[388] Rani Gaidinliu was born at the Nangkao village in Manipur. She was a fearless Indian freedom fighter who joined the agitation at the age of 13. She headed the movement against the British in the Manipur and Naga belts. She spearheaded an inspiring socio-political movement to cast the British out from the Manipur and Naga belts. It was in 1932 at the age of 16 Gaidinliu was arrested and imprisoned for life until India achieved independent in 1947. http://www.in.com/rani-gaidinliu/biography-229097.html, accessed on 1.5.15.

[389] On 2 November 2000, in Malom, a town in the Imphal Valley of Manipur, ten civilians were shot and killed while waiting at a bus stop. The incident, known as the "Malom Massacre", was allegedly committed by the Assam Rifles, one of the Indian Paramilitary forces operating in the state. Irom Sharmila's fast-to-death began in the aftermath of this incident. See, "AFSPA and Unsolved massacres in Manipur", Anjuman Ara Begum, http://twocircles.net/2010nov03/afspa_and_unsolved_massacres_manipur.html#.VTs9z1WSyPs, accessed on 25.4.15

In such a context, the two-way flow of communication, female–male relationship, interaction, and exchanging of ideas are completely missing. The corporate representation of human voice is absent. The other group of individuals, that is female members, are being deprived of participation in the socio-cultural, political, religious and economic spheres. The top-down communication of the dominant group of individuals (male members) controlling another group of individuals (female members) is to be seen. Mutual sharing is missing in this top-down communication and is exclusive by nature. In this perspectives Ao Naga tribal community, where women's voice is being controlled by men there is no balanced flow of communication. The voice which is one of the irrefutable gifts of God to humankind is blocked by the male dominated culture.

In such a situation, the study of culture in Ao Naga tribal community becomes a necessity. Through this cultural study we could identify the socio-cultural-religious and economic condition of the past and present Ao Naga tribal society. Therefore, this cultural study will direct us to grasp the distinct gender roles in the family, clan and society. This will help locate how these distinctive gender roles function and foster practices and transport ideas in the society privileging one gender over another. This will further help us to understand the similarities as well as the differences and disparities in social station between female and male, and also the way they behave and exercise their rights.

Basing on this context, in this study the researcher would like to bring and suggest a new theory that is, the **Cultural Network Approach** in communication. In the cultural network approach each individual, both female and male, plays equal role in communication. With each individual considered as a vital part of a network, the sharing of information and ideas from all corners are being accepted and accommodated. This cultural network approach is "gender inclusive" by nature. Both female and male members are already being integrated and are equal participants in communication. Individuals and groups involve in the interaction and it becomes realistic. Each individual female - male member are being connected and interconnected and the communication is being strengthened. This is deliberated as the two-way process of communication. A balanced and mutual consensus of communication among genders (female and male) is to be found in this cultural network approach. The decisions are being made through all the individuals' (female – male) collective voice.

Therefore, the study directs us to see how gender imbalance in the Ao Naga tribal decision-making bodies can be solved through the use of cultural network approach. By applying cultural network approach, it will develop towards female-male relation. And how through their relation enhances participation towards shaping life more meaningful existence in the environment they live.

The Ao Naga tribal community was by nature traditionally interactive yet due to the impact of the dominant model (flow) of communication the interactional nature has vanished. Therefore, the cultural network approach emerges from the depth of the Ao Naga tribal community, evolving as an alternative to resist the dividing nature of communication between women and men. The objective of the model is not to promote the dominance of women's voice; rather this approach suggests for a more interactive personal and instinctive way of communication.

The above-mentioned theories that have been discussed, direct us to engage innovatively observing them the strength of the elements and pointing us to apply into the field of study. These theories will be involving in the proceeding chapters of the research when we discuss the topic accordingly. In the next chapter, we shall discuss the "Cultural history of Ao Naga tribal community" in this; we will be relating the theory on 'Cultural Studies' which we now had been discussed.

Chapter 3

Cultural Studies of Ao Naga Tribal Women: Conceptualising "Voice"

Introduction

The Ao Naga tribal community today is tremendously suffused with and in its various walks of life enormously impacted upon by Christianity and modern education. Nevertheless, the practices and functions of the traditional system of administration and activities in the villages are still kept intact.[390] Each village unit continues to enjoy a high level of autonomy, and functions to a large extent as a republic in its own right with its own set of rules and regulations. Moreover, these verbal "legislations" are strictly enforced and equally binding on the members, the "citizens" of the village, irrespective of social status.

Aos are, by nature, communitarian, and no individual could thrive or even survive without the support of the other. One's existence, indeed one's identity, is always associated with family, clan, village and tribe. No individual is allowed to go his/her own way in accordance with his/her own wishes; on the contrary, it is obligatory for everyone in the community to abide by the aforementioned rules. The traditional customs of sharing and caring are still very common to the present day. Under the traditional set of governance, certain roles and responsibilities are laid down for female and male members respectively, and these norms and practices are expected from them. These traditional structures and functions are discussed below.

[390] Article 371-A of the Constitution of India practically guarantees special provisions, among others, for the perpetuation of "Naga customary law and procedure" and "administration of civil and criminal justice involving decisions according to Naga customary law" in spite of any Parliamentary legislation.

The focus of this chapter is on the Ao Naga tribal socio-cultural, religious, economic and political practices of the past and the present. We will see how traditional values and norms affect the individual and community life of the Aos. We will also attempt to unearth the different roles and responsibilities carried out by women and men in the past Ao society, locating the importance of "Voice" while they communicated with one another. Here it employs theory based on cultural studies which have been dealt with already in the previous chapter.

3.1. Socio-Cultural Functions in Ao Naga Tribal Community

The traditional socio-cultural practices in the Ao Naga tribal community can be seen in various ways. The participation, contribution and distinction of roles and responsibilities carried out by the community members will be seen.

3.1.1. The Importance of Ariju

The *Ariju*[391] (*Morung*) was the centre of traditional education for boys beginning at the age of 12-15 till the time of their marriage. To enter as a full member as citizen in the village a boy would begin all the formalities and duties required by tradition and culture. *Ariju* was an important place for all young boys who underwent all the training and learned all the social and political activities from the senior boys. Back in the days when headhunting was practised, all the boys learned how to be strong and bold, how to fight with the enemies, how to work hard without any complaint, how to respect the elders, what mannerisms to use, etc. The *Ariju* was also used as a watch tower for keeping vigilant watch day and night to guard from their enemies.

The aim and objective of the *Ariju* was to defend the village from enemies. Therefore, they required well-organised, trained personnel who "... have to perform multifarious functions covering a large area of societal needs ranging from social security, civil administration, manpower training, personal development, promotion and preservation of culture etc."[392]

The *Ariju* was exclusively for the men of a particular village, and was restricted for men of the other villages or strangers. Women too were considered as taboo, and it is mentioned that, "[E]ven the courtyard of this house is highly

---

[391] *Ariju* and *Arichu* denote the same meaning. *Ariju* was an educational centre, a building (*Ariju ki*) for young boys to stay in, normally from 12 years until marriage. They learnt and trained from the senior boys for the good of an individual as well as for the welfare of the community. *Ariju* is referred to by many as *Morung* which means bachelors' building.

[392] Lanunungsang, "Working System of Ariju in Traditional Ao Society: A Socio-cultural Institution," in *Naga Society: Continuity and Change,* edited by N. Venuh (Delhi: Shipra Publications, 2004), 77.

restricted to woman and if she comes near the vicinity, it is regarded as a bad omen."[393] However, the members of the *Ariju* used to visit *Tsuki*[394] constantly.

3.1.2. The Distinctions in the Ariju

The Arichujangr (M) /Arichununger (C)[395] who are inmates of the *Ariju* are composed of three groups namely – (1) *Chuzen,* the senior members in the *Ariju* and who exert power and authority upon the juniors; (2) *Tenapang*, the middle group; and (3) *Tzuir* (M)/ *Sungpur* (C), the youngest group who are newly enrolled in the *Ariju* and undergoing their training for duty, discipline and obedience. Though traditional institutions such as *Ariju* (bachelor's dormitory) have been discontinued, the work and practices are still continued by the village community.

3.1.3. Tzuir (M)/Sungpur (C)

The name *Tzuir* in *Mongsen* dialect means water carrier, and *Sungpur* in *Chungli* means wood carrier. Therefore, the names are derived from the work allotted to them, their duty being to bring water for bathing senior leaders every night and to collect firewood to burn in the *Ariju.*

There is a certain ceremony that is performed during the admission of young boys to the *Ariju.* The older boys help in this ceremony by procuring a cock and inviting the *Tir*[396] of *Ariju* to perform the ceremony. In the evening, all the young boys assemble and wait for the arrival of *Tir*, when they stand up in line in the first room of the *Ariju* called *Sama.* The *Tir* then performs a ceremony which involves taking up the cock and waving it over the boys, then killing it and predicting the future from its entrails. After this, the young boys are declared as

---

[393] Lanunungsang, "Working System of Ariju in Traditional Ao Society: A Socio-cultural Institution," in *Naga Society: Continuity and Change,* edited by N. Venuh (Delhi: Shipra Publications, 2004), 78.

[394] The *Tsüki* is the female learning institution looked after by a widow or an unmarried elder woman of the same clan. She is an elderly widow, chosen for having good conduct and high moral discipline. She can accommodate four or five girls in her house. A girl after attaining the age of around 12 years and when the tattooing process is done is considered as a full member of society and is allowed to go and stay at night with a widow or matron called *Tsukibutsüla.* The girl's mother will approach a *Tsukibutsüla* who is well experienced in all-round development in society and who has a high knowledge and skill to train and teach the girl and guard her every evening and morning under her care. The girls who stay in *Tsuki* are called *Tsükir.*

[395] The Ao Naga tribal community speaks two major dialects; *Chungli* and *Mongsen, Chungli* being spoken as a common language. Hereafter, the *Mongsen* Ao dialect will be written 'M' and *Chungli* Ao dialect 'C'.

[396] *Tir* is a recognised leader of the *Ariju.* He is considered as religious head of the *Ariju.* The *Tir* post cannot be held by any ordinary man, but someone is qualified only when he attains certain requirements in the community. These are such as both he and his wife should be healthy at the time of his appointment, should be a successful warrior who has conducted raids, fought battles with skill and vigour and brought an enemy's head. See Tajen Ao, *Ao Naga Customary Laws* (N.p.: Aowati Imchen, 1980).

Tzuir and they will work and sleep in the *Ariju* from that night onwards till their marriage.

3.1.4. Duties of Tzuir

Once he is enrolled as *Tzuir*, a boy is regarded as a full citizen in the village. His duty is to do all the manual work of the *Ariju* including all the community work for a number of years until the junior members take over. He has to obey and serve the seniors and follow all the duties assigned to him. It is customary for every male to undergo this stage without which he would not have any place to live in the community. He will be counted as a full-grown member who is able to work and give his physical labour. He will participate in all the community works, and his contribution will be considered as follows:

> If he is living with his widowed mother, he is regarded as a male householder in the house of his mother, and he gives his labour representing his mother's family. If he is living with his father he will represent his father though the father is the house holder in the family. He can always represent his father or family in work such as house construction, village sentry ... or other community work.[397]

A *Tzuir*'s duties include carrying urgent messages to faraway places about the sickness of a person to his/her relatives. They clean the surrounding areas of the *Ariju* and Log-drum house. The last and farthest part of the village path will be allotted to *Tzuirs* for cleaning and clearing. They carry carcasses like wild boars and tigers to the village which are killed during community hunting; they carry fish caught during community fishing. It is also the duty of the *Tzuir* to stay in the *Ariju* as sentry to watch the *Ariju* and the village. They also work in the *Tir's* farm.

3.1.5. Tzuir and Zünga/Yanga

In the village administrative structure, a group of people born within a given period of three years, inclusive of both female and male constitute a significant age-based group called *Zünga* in the *Chungli* dialect and *Yanga* in the *Mongsen* dialect. Boys first admitted to the *Ariju* are called *Tzuir*. And when the *Zünga* of this particular age-group is formed, girls enrol and join along with the boys as full members. However, the traditional social norms treat them differently[398] since patriarchal social structures dominate the entire system; male members are counted as permanent citizens dominating in all the important administrative

---

[397] Ibid., 22.

[398] A girl of the same age-group/*Zünga* will work in many of the community and group activities along with the boys of her same age-group, but she is not allowed to enter the *Ariju* which is considered as taboo for her. She is not given any share in the village functioning or administration. (Interview with Liden, 9 December 2013).

functions of a village whereas female members do not have any place in the village administrative systems.

The age-group *Zünga* is central to the cultural, political, social, and economic organisation of the Ao villages notwithstanding that in many situations the age-group *Zünga* plays an important role even in religious activities, and even after they were influenced by Christianity.[399] Once a person is enrolled as *Zünga* she/he will remain with that same age-group throughout her/his life. We will discuss the function of *Zünga* in detail in the latter part of the study.

3.1.6. Tenapang

Tenapang means "blooming period". This age-group is relieved from the menial duties taken up by the *Tzuirs*. However, they are not exempted completely from their duties but continue to perform other works under the supervision of their *Chuzen* seniors for the welfare and goodwill of the *Ariju*. Many people get married at this *Tenapang* stage. Unlike his junior *Tzuir*, who is dealt with leniently for offences committed by him, a member of the *Tenapang* age-group is liable to punishment for wrong acts committed by him.

3.1.7. Chuzen

Chuzen is the most senior group in *Ariju*. As and when the younger ones get admitted in *Ariju*, automatically the existing *Tzuir* get succeeded by the new age-group and the older ones are promoted to *Tenapang*; the existing *Tenapang* go to *Chuzen*.

The power and responsibility of *Chuzen* include the building and repairing of the *Ariju* under their supervision, taking up all the matters concerning or on behalf of the inmates of the *Ariju*, and also in organising feasts for the members of the *Ariju* in festivals such as *Moatsu*, etc.

Any outgoing member of *Chuzen* who is not married by the time the others leave the *Ariju* will remain in the *Ariju*, but he does not exercise his power as before since the younger group has already succeeded. He will leave the *Ariju* if his age-group's son or sons become *Tzuir* because he belongs to the generation of the son's father and the men of two generations should not remain in *Ariju* at the same time.[400]

---

[399] *Züngas*, both female and male, participate in singing competition during Christmas. They also render service whenever necessary, donating cash or other materials to use for the church. They even organise feasts during special occasions like Christmas etc. (Interview with Sunep, Yaden, Sunjemkaba, Limaba Mupongchuket village. 13 August 2013).

[400] The *Arichu* system or the division of stages as age-group, called *Zünga* (in *Chungli* dialect), *Yanga* (in *Mongsen* dialect), is still prevalent today in all Ao Naga tribal areas/villages. The *Arichu* (house) traditional institution of learning for young boys does not exist anymore. They no longer stay together in the *Arichu* with their age-group, junior or senior, but now stay in their own house with their parents till they are married. The old structure has changed in many ways, partly due to the coming of Christianity and the influence of modernization into Ao Naga society. However,

3.2. The Importance of Age-Group (*Zünga*) in Community Activities

As mentioned before, the age-group called *Zünga* is considered one of the key holders and performers of the entire system of administration in the Ao villages without which a village would not run smoothly. Girls and boys of the same age-group enjoy equal status. In the words of N. Talitemjen Jamir and A. Lanunungsang: "They can participate in any festival and manual works arranged by their age-group. From the household works to the field activities, they work together with their counterparts."[401] Once they enter this institution, they are recognised as responsible citizens in the society. They will be enlisted in all the community works that are done according to their age group, failing which they will be dealt with according to their established customs.[402]

3.2.1. Participation of Zünga in Field Works

Along with the community work organised by the village council, individual works are also initiated by the *Zünga*. For example, the *Zünga* rotate and take part in each of the parents' fields which is a kind of exchange of labour in the fields. The number of a working group of that particular age-group *Zünga* may be more than ten people at a time consisting of both girls and boys. For example, if they work in Mr A's field today, the next day they would be working in Miss X's and the following day with Mr or Miss so and so till everybody gets the facility. This will rotate in the same way till the works are completed. This is practised in the villages even today.

Mutual care and cooperation is the core responsibility of every age-group. As they work together in the field, they will help each other in many ways; for instance, the boys will sharpen the tools and implements of the girls, and the girls will carry all minor items from the village to the field. When they return home from the field, girls carry firewood that is arranged by the boys in advance.[403]

---

traditional social and cultural functioning is still very strong in the Ao Naga tribal villages even today. The majority of the population are settled in towns and cities, and people who have left their villages seem to observe the traditional set of roles and functions less. However, they cannot deny their identity from the village to which they belonged. Aos are very much attached to their village, which is called *Soyim* (their native village), and her/his identity as family, as clan, and as tribe is carried along wherever she/he may go. This set of rules cannot be ignored by any Ao citizens. (Interview with Manenba, Toshisangla, Mokokchung Town. 14 September 2013).

[401] N. Talitemjen Jamir, A. Lanunungsang, *Naga Society and Culture* (Mokokchung: Nagaland University Tribal Research Centre, Department of Sociology, 2005), 218.

[402] Some of the community based work allotted by the village council is binding only on men and not on women. Since male members become the village administrators, there are certain sets of rules which are done and performed only by men. (Interview with Sunep, Calcutta, 20 March 2013, Narosenla, Bengaluru.12 February 2013).

[403] Lanunungsang, "Working System of Ariju in Traditional Ao Society, op. cit., 76-7.

Lanunungsang adds that: "This is the time of making friendship, learning from each other through constant interaction."[404]

3.2.2. Participation of Zünga in Wild Boar Hunting

In the past, there were common activities in the community such as the trapping and hunting of wild boars in the Ao Naga tribal villages. In such activities, the age-group *Zünga* were the main initiators who played an active role in the process of hunting. In this venture, they divided the work according to the age-group including women of their same age-group who also took part along with the men. However, the share meat distributed among the members of the village was exclusively for male members and not for female.[405]

In whichever way the age-group was dealt, without recognising or questioning the weaknesses of the traditional socio-cultural structures, everybody enjoyed the friendship and relationship that was strengthened through the age-group *Zünga,* as we can see in the following lines:

> Every *Züngar* maintains a distinct demarcation of self-identity not only in terms of years but also at the level of social interactions, marriage, exchange of labour, contributions to family lives and societal concern and challenges ... one will notice a strong sense of 'we feeling' among themselves ... Aged people count the names of the living ones of their age group with sweet reminiscence. They maintain self-respect and self-pride among themselves. They feel as brothers and sisters whether they live in their village or away as '*Züngapur*' and '*Züngatsür*' or '*pur züngar*.'[406]

3.3. The Importance and Functions of *Tsüki*

The *Tsüki was* the traditional institution of learning for girls which was similar to the boys' dormitory or *Ariju,* and it was as old as the *Ariju.* The *Tsüki* was looked after by a well-experienced widow who had made a good impression on the society and gained recognition for being morally upright. A total number of four or five girls of her clan members would be accommodated by the matron. There were *Tsüki* for children of the rich families, accommodated by a matron

[404] Lanunungsang, "Working System of Ariju in Traditional Ao Society, op. cit., 76-7.

[405] Some age-groups among men would sometimes cut their ear of the animal and present it to female friends of their age-group. Again with certain restrictions, if while cutting the ear of a wild boar touched another portion of the body, than a fine would be imposed by the village council. Waromung village among the Ao community practised this community participation in wild boar hunting in the recent past.

[406] Ibid.

who is a rich widow of the same clan whose husband had already performed feast of merit or gained recognition as a warrior in his life time.[407]

3.3.1. The Role Played by Matron/Tsukibutsüla

In the *Tsüki*, the *Tsukibutsüla* carried a number of responsibilities for the girls. She was a guide, advisor, planner, matchmaker, beautician, technician, educator, priest, as well as a parent for the *Tsükir*. She acted as a time keeper for the girls, waking them up in the morning and sending them to their parents' houses on time; she also made sure that the girls returned to the *Tsüki* on time in the evening. It was the initiative of the *Tsukibutsüla* in *Tsüki* that led to the formation of the women's organisation known as *Elangtsür* (C) /*Patsalar* (M) (group of women of the same clan coming together in socio-cultural work force and other activities). N.Talitemjen Jamir, and A. Lanunungsang continue to say that: "They extend help and support to the family members of *Elangtsür/Patsalar* during the time of distress whatever they can contribute in terms of free labour, cash or any other means of support."[408] The relationship is still maintained and very much alive even today.

The main function of the *Tsüki* was similar to that of *Ariju* for boys, i.e., to train the girls into the ideal womanhood.[409] It was in the *Tsüki* that they learned the social graces and the art of industry. The practice of junior and senior was maintained even among girls in the *Tsüki*. It was the youngest member of the *Tsükir* who did all the petty works, such as making the fire, fetching water, cooking, sweeping the house, feeding the pigs and the chickens of a matron. Whenever the matron fell sick, the girl would take care of all the household work such as husking paddy as well as collecting fuel-wood, and also sometimes massaged her body. She would also on reaching home from the fields look after her siblings, complete the other household chores, and serve food to her parents before leaving for the *Tsüki*.[410]

Junior members of the *Tsuki* would go early in the evening and clean the house and arrange the cots and seats properly. They would fetch water and collect enough fuel-wood to be burnt through the night. The senior girls would arrive a little later with the work to be completed at night such as cotton for ginning or spinning, or to stitch and mend cloths. At the same time, some boys from the *Ariju* would come to visit them in the evening, and this time was used to share

---

[407] N. Talitemjen Jamir, *Ao-Naga Cultural Heritage* (Mokokchung: Author, 1997), 52.

[408] N.Talitemjen Jamir, A. Lanunungsang, *Naga Society and Culture*, op. cit., 110.

[409] Ideal womanhood denotes what and how a woman should do and should not do in Ao Society. A fixed notion was imposed upon both female and male members respectively.

[410] N. Talitemjen Jamir, A. Lanunungsang, *Naga Society and Culture,* op. cit., 103-4.

and interact by exchanging ideas through songs and narrating folklore.[411] It has been mentioned that:

> During Festivals, the boys of the Ariju visit this place for special purpose. This is known as *Tsükimak* ... On this evening they sit nearby the fireplace and go on singing, responding to each other in unison, the most melodious songs. On their own expenses, their *Züngatsur* (girls of same age-group) offer rice beer to their counterpart. They stay in each other's' company for hours together till late night singing songs, gossiping and joking with the most interesting humor.[412]

The gift exchange during the festivals like *Moatsü* among girls from the *Tsüki* and boys from the *Ariju* was well known. Girls received gifts of handicrafts like specially-designed mini baskets, smoking pipes, etc. In return, the girls would give woven dao-holder belts to the boys. This indicates the true nature of friendship that they developed in the traditional institution *Tsüki.*[413]

3.3.2. The Interaction between Tsükir and Arijumen/Arijusanger[414]

Although women were restricted from entering the *Ariju,* men used to visit the *Tsüki* in the evenings. The *Tsüki* became the centre of interaction and relationship building where both the parties *Tsükir* and *Arijumen* exchanged their ideas, shared their views, and spent their time together in laughter and merrymaking and in getting to know each other better. The members of the *Tsüki and Ariju* were both morally disciplined. These institutions helped to improve with efficiency.[415]

3.4. The Importance of Clans[416] in the Village Administration

In the patriarchal Ao Naga tribal community, the clan was considered as an important body inherited through birth. The identity of a person was determined by her/his own clan. The clan had its own share of responsibility in good times as well as during the troubled years. Sharing and caring among the clan members

---

[411] The visits of boys to the *Tsüki* and the relationship that they developed were highly valued but one should keep in mind that this relationship was not meant for sexual relation but for social interaction. Male folks visited the *Tsüki* at night but only in the presence of matron/*Tsükibutsüla.* It was normally in the *Tsüki* that boys and girls began to like each other and chose their life partner. The matron of the *Tsüki* played a great role in this, and she would consult with the girl's parents on her behalf.

[412] N. Talitemjen Jamir, A. Lanunungsang, *Naga Society and Culture,* op. cit., 107-8.

[413] Ibid., 107.

[414] *Tsükir* was the girl of the *Tsüki* and *Arijumen/ Arijujanger* was the boy of the *Ariju.*

[415] N. Talitemjen Jamir, A. Lanunungsang, *Naga Society and Culture,* op. cit., 110.

[416] In the Ao Naga tribal community, the formation of clan begins at the place called *Chungliyimti.* The tradition says that, three males and three females burst out of the six stones. These three pairs got married to each other leading to the emergence of the three main clans of the Aos.

was practised. The members of the clan shared their crops, seeds, vegetables, etc., if some members of the clan did not harvest enough.

In Ao tribal society, a person could exercise his/her power in village affairs only with the approval and consent of the clan. The clan members selected their own representative for the post in the village administration. Marrying within the same clan was considered taboo and whoever violated the rules would be treated with contempt and expelled from the village. In all the Ao villages there were common properties of a clan such as *jhumlands*, house-sites, forest land, bamboo groves, etc., which were used by the clan members with the permission of the oldest male member of the clan. Clan played many domineering roles in the village that extended even outside the village. Since women did not really have any say in the clan decisions and functions, they remained passive observers and submissive followers.

3.5. Land Owning System in Ao Naga Tribal Community

The land, which was the most valuable resource that provided livelihood and subsistence for the people, was owned by male members in the Ao community. The cultivable land is one of the symbolic and valued forms of property for its economic and political ground. It is a fruitful, wealth-creating and livelihood-sustaining asset. This land provides a sense of identity and belongingness because it has a longevity, which no other asset owns.[417] A woman could not inherit immovable property like land and she was not liable for debts of her ancestors or her heir.

> In Naga societies, at birth both boys and girls take their social identity from their father and are placed in his agnatic group and familial unit. A female child's membership of her father's agnatic unit is neither permanent nor complete. Gender differences in group membership and social identity are closely connected with the patterns of inheritance and resource distribution.[418]

The traditional system of ownership of land is still practised and regulated according to the traditional customs and practices. There are three types of landholdings in the village among the Ao Naga Tribal community. These are: the village land that is owned and regulated by the village (the Village Council or the elected representatives of elders regulate and control its resources); the clan land owned and managed by the clan members; and the private land owned by an individual.

The Village Council/*Putu Menden* will decide which site or plot cultivation will be done each year. The Council decides the site for cultivation after consulting

---

[417] Government of Nagaland, Department of Planning & Coordination, *Nagaland State Human Development Report,* 2004, 152.

[418] Ibid., 153.

the Unger Menden/Upper House and lays down the rules and regulation of the village. After the selection of a particular site, the villagers are informed and all the villagers are required to cultivate only in the selected site. No villager is allowed to cultivate in any other site or land even in his or her individual land. The decision of the Village Council is final and failure to abide by the Council's decision entails serious fines and penalty. The Village Council has the right to impose certain rules in the use of land in accordance with the traditional customs and laws.[419]

The communities that practise shifting cultivation, the distribution of land for cultivation, have strict customary laws and socio-political institutions to regulate it.[420] According to the customary laws, land is also owned only by male members, and women are simply victims in the name of the traditional socio-cultural system. We can clearly see in one of the illustrations given by Tajen Ao that women and men were treated differently by the Ao Naga Tribal customary laws with regard to land ownership.

> **In Mokokchung Case No. 20 of 1915, dt. 3. 3. 1915.**
> Aosatang & his guardian
> Vs
> Noksumilla, Bendangsingla, Takusinla,
> Noksenlula, Mirangmongla and Chongponginla.
> Aosatang was the last of his clan. The accused were related and [were ordered] to let Aosatang's guardian clear his field as usual. The G.B.s [Gaon Boras (village heads)] had decided in his favour but the accused refused to observe the decision.
> It is clearly contrary to custom for women to inherit land in the Ao country. The accused claimed that their father had left them the land. But, he could not do so to the prejudice of the customary heirs who were men [and who would have to be consulted, and who certainly never have agreed] to the breaking of what is virtually an entail. Land goes to the male heir, however distant he may be. Aosatang proves possession of 3 house sites and 18 jhums.[421]

A daughter has no right to inherit land; therefore, a woman is always looked upon as stranger at home. Land is one of the important sources of life, a symbol of unity and identity. The land "... holds not only the clan, village and tribes as one, but it also unites the Supreme Being, spirits, ancestors and creatures as one family ... A person who is not deeply rooted in the land is like a stranger without

[419] Jacob George, Khrietuo Yhome, "Community Forest Management: A Case Study of Nagaland, India," http://dlc.dlib.indiana.edu/dlc/bitstream/handle/10535/2185/George_211601.pdf?sequence=1, accessed on 27.4.13.

[420] Ibid.

[421] Tajen Ao, *Ao Naga Customary Laws*, op. cit., 65-6.

an identity and a home."[422] The land has a significant relationship to the Ao Naga tribal community and can be inherited only by men; therefore, "Ao Naga women are rendered valueless from this perspective."[423]

3.6. Woman During Headhunting

In the past the indiscriminate chopping of heads by the Ao Naga Tribal community did not spare even vulnerable people like the old, infirm, women and children who could not resist the ferocious and powerful invader. Headhunting was considered as a powerful game, and this was to show masculine superiority. It is said that women's heads were considered a more prized trophy, which may be due to several reasons. It is said that women were kept under special protection by the village fold, because "taking a [sic] woman's head meant penetrating deep into the adversary's ranks with all its concomitant risks." Taking women's heads could be possibly in order to reduce the enemy's population by killing their womenfolk. And another reason could be the desire for women's hair that was used for ornamental purposes.[424]

Wati Longchar pointed out some probable reasons why most tribal women in North East India are denied rights and privileges at home and in the society. Firstly, he asserts that it is due to the headhunting practices that exclude women from decision-making bodies, and the treatment of women as subordinate to men. He says:

> In the course of time, people became conscious of social status. Freedom of speech, rights, dignity and honour were won through success in headhunting. The village who brought the highest number of heads stood in the highest esteem ... The consciousness of social status brought subordination of women. For example ... headhunting involved tremendous risks. It was not possible for women to participate in such a risky adventure as man. This led men to treat women as inferior physically.[425]

Looking at the history of the Ao Naga Tribal community, one is hard pressed to gather evidence to prove that women and children were being protected by men all the time. Women had been moving around for their everyday needs without

---

[422] Narola Imchen, *Women in Church and Society: The Story of Ao Naga Women* (Jorhat: Eastern Theological College, 2001), 21.

[423] Atola Longkumer, "Not All is Well in My Ancestors' Home: An Indigenous Theology of Internal Critique," *Ecumenical Review* (December, 2010): 399-410.

[424] Sukhdev Singh Chib, *Caste, Tribes and Culture of India: North-Eastern India,* Vol. 8 (New Delhi: ESS Publications, 1984), 199-200.

[425] A. Wati Longchar, "Issues in Feminist Theology," in *Transforming Theology for Empowering Women: A Theological and Hermeneutical Reflection in the Context of North East India,* edited by R.L. Hnuni (ETC, Jorhat: Women's Studies, ETC, 1999), 20.

the protection of the male counterparts. It is recorded that, "women and children in groups brought wood from the jungles and water from the springs far down the hillsides, never going singly, as the lower springs were favourite lurking places for enemies seeking human heads."[426]

It is also true that in the past, women were not given any training skill like men for self-defence. Moreover, women had to face double risks to protect their whole families from the enemy's raid. Therefore, women and children become more vulnerable and easily victimised. It is recorded that an alarm was sounded at a village announcing that there were enemies ahead of them leading to "... mothers hurrying with their little ones in arms and dragging others after them."[427]

Women were left with all the major tasks beginning from child rearing and caring to the household chores with additional burdens such as physical labour in the field, fetching water, collecting firewood; these were all accepted norms and were considered as the duty of a woman. They managed all the significant affairs "except headhunting and decision-making which was denied for the women."

During the headhunting days, when all the Ao villages were being watched and guarded by the *Ariju* men for 24 hours from their furious enemies, we still see Ao women being assigned for risky jobs by the community. Acharongmang and Chaksüngnaro, two beautiful, eloquent and smart women from Longkhum village, were chosen by the villagers to sell and display the feathers of a hornbill to the entire Ao villages.[428] Therefore, it is observed that whenever the need arose women also were not spared from the duty-bound community's affairs. This can be seen in many instances, e.g. women being sold off as slaves either by parents for debt, or used for war indemnities.[429] There was a case reported that a eighteen year old woman who was deserted by her husband was enslaved by her father because her father had an enormous debt of two rupees and eight annas (about 3s. 6d.) for a pig.[430]

---

[426] Mary Mead Clark, *A Corner in India* (Philadelphia: American Baptist Publication Society, 1907), 46.

[427] Ibid., 75.

[428] The story clearly says that two ladies from Longkhum village were chosen to sell and display the feathers of a hornbill to the entire Ao warring villages. Finally, they accepted the decision made by the village and ventured for the mission that was assigned to them. The story also narrated that they had departed from their home looking back towards their home, missing the families and friends longing to be back soon. They seemed to have realised that there were impending dangers ahead of them. Unfortunately, they were killed in one of the Ao villages, since women's heads were also highly valued those days. See Kiremwati, L. Imti Longchar et. al, eds., *Nokranger Aser Nokrang*, (Nagaland Kohima: Waromung Yimten, 1993), 25-35.

[429] A woman who was not sold into slavery when young was tattooed in her body parts. See Mary Mead Clark, *A Corner in India*, op. cit., 53.

[430] William C. Smith, *The Ao-Naga Tribe Of Assam* (London: MacMillan & Co. Limited, 1925, reproduced in New Delhi: Mittal Publications, 2009), 54.

One can understand that Ao Naga tribal women in the past had played the major role in their 'community formation.' They had been involved in all the duties faithfully even to the extent of risking their own lives for the common good. Unfortunately, the Ao Naga tribal community did not give due recognition to women, but rather treated them as mere objects and as inferior to men.

3.7. Participation in Singing

One of the social features of the Ao Naga Tribal community that kept the community vibrant was maintained and communicated through songs. Songs were an important means of communication whereby both female and male voices achieved high regard. There were many songs that were sung reciprocally by male and female individually as well as collectively. Through songs they conveyed their messages of joy and sorrow. Through songs they entertained their partners on various occasions. While working in the paddy fields, in the religious and community festivals, etc., messages through songs played an important role among the Ao Naga Tribal community in the past.

Through these responsive voices we can gather that an individual male or female alone would not survive without their counterpart; both parties' presence was equally important in singing. The moments of support and cooperation, love and respect were the core responsibility of every individual in the community those days. The reciprocal songs sung by both male and female during farming in the field and during the festive seasons will be seen. An example of each type of song is given here:

3.7.1. Farming Song

Male: *Tayip zoni chokaku, sungtipangko yajonger, kumongjen wadang aingjanoa* (This morning the sun has risen, covered over the tree groves, my farmyard looks deserted).

Female: *Naro nula zoni meti, tonglongpangko jentakoshi, ningmen yusha nula teya,*

Nila menjenlaoa (Flowers cannot resist the sun, should have adorned the ear lobe, do not hear rumours, I will never decay).

3.7.2. Tug-of-war Song of Moatsü Festival

Male: *Ali lenden paiko; O medem yarra mongdine; Ngangpa mao zungtine* (In this valley; Oh stay dancing in unison; Counting the un-married one). **Female**: *O ozu zungapur ae; Nangka tsungpu teyimne; Nika ngangpa moaline; Jinang riju yaba nenungtemka sheta rotine* (Oh our counterpart boys; Do not enter into manhood; I will remain un-married; Come closer, you, the most handsome boy in *Ariju*).

Male: O zunga mulusale; O mongpu tarune (Oh our age group dance; Oh don't come the winter) **Female:** O ora tzutelang sungkong; Ni tezongzane; (Oh far away log drum, beyond the ocean; Do not think of me).[431]

One can gather that even during the not so distant past, each voice was considered as very important in the Ao community. Each person's own feelings were communicated through songs. There was no distinction between female and male in singing. The message could cut across to the receiver and the feedback instantly received through songs.

3.8. The Fate of a Woman after Marriage

In the Ao Naga Tribal community there are tremendous burdens on barren women. A childless woman shares her anger and disappointment over her husband blaming her for not being able to bear a child.[432] There are many such instances where a husband divorces his wife and marries another all because she did not bear a child. The reason behind all this, Mary Clark said, is because "Nagas are very fond of their children and depend much upon them for support in declining years"[433] and also because they had to depend largely on cultivation which was supported largely by their children as the work force. More importantly, the heir, a son, is most sought by the family in order to inherit the landed property.

Even when she is not literally divorced, a barren Ao woman is psychologically, emotionally, and mentally tortured by her husband or in-laws. Many a Ao woman who has borne only daughters has faced constant verbal abuse from her husband who lays full blame on her for her "inability" to produce a male child. In each conversation, the husband pours out derogatory remarks over her for the failure to have a male child. Sometimes relatives and family members take the initiative and encourage him to divorce her and get another woman.[434] One woman shared her bitter experience and humiliation from her husband before her son was born a few years back. Even though she had already borne four daughters, her husband continually poured out his dissatisfaction over her by glaring at her and saying "only daughters."[435] This negative attitude towards women in Ao Naga Tribal community is very common.

Even though marriage laws were strict in matters related with divorce in traditional Ao Naga Tribal community, said to have been very rare those days,[436]

[431] N. Talitemjen Jamir, A. Lanunungsang, *Naga Society and Culture* (Lumami, Mokokchung: Nagaland University Tribal Resources Centre, 2005), 282-4.

[432] Interview with Limasenla, Jongpongkumla, Sharon, Akumsungla, Tiajunla, Limatemsula, and Shilutemla. All the interviewees live in Mokokchung Town on 15.7.2012.

[433] Mary Mead Clark, *A Corner in India*, op. cit., 50.

[434] This may not be experienced by all mothers who have only daughters in the family, but we cannot deny the fact that it does not exist in the Ao Naga tribal Community.

[435] Interview with Maotula, Dimapur Town, 25 May 2013.

[436] I. Bendangangshi, I.T. Apok Aier, *The Religion of the Ao Nagas*, op. cit., 142-3.

the condition of women was precarious, and they were often victimised and treated as inferior to men. It has been indicated in the writing of Mary Mead Clark: "The usual cause of divorce is adultery, but failure on the part of the wife to become a mother is considered as justifiable reason for parting."[437] William C. Smith mentioned that, after a woman is married, at the first place she will not be at peace since her position is not essentially secure until she has borne a child to her husband, because if she cannot bear any child within five or six years, the husband is justified in setting her aside. In some cases, if there are only female children, a man may put aside his wife and marry another woman. Smith states that: "If there be no male children, the father's name will fade away, because his daughters must marry into other father-sibs."[438]

In the Ao Naga Tribal villages, once the husband is dead the condition of a widow becomes miserable in many ways. In most cases, she ceases to enjoy authority over property or land in the way she used to when her husband was alive. The possession (mostly land) is controlled by her husband's family members and relatives if her son is a minor. She will have to obey all that they command; for instance, if her in-laws or uncles prefer to build a house at the very site where she resides, she has no other choice but to shift her house to some other place.[439] The condition is even worse if she does not possess any male child.[440]

3.9. Folklore Focussing on Ao Naga Tribal Women

In the Ao Naga tribal community, folklore is considered a very rich cultural heritage that was handed down from generation to generation by word of mouth until many of these were put into written form recently.[441] It is a fact that:

> The Naga folk items, as it is usually, have a distinctive feature of their own. They reflect the mind, the character, the background, the belief, the religion and taboos, the superstitions, the tradition, the culture and everything ... which tells about the deeds of women and men, the tales of warriors, tales of cunningness, ill behaviour of the stepmother/ women, about animals and birds, stories offering morals, ethical values

---

437 Mary Mead Clark, *A Corner in India*, op. cit., 50.

438 William C. Smith, *The Ao-Naga Tribe of Assam*, op. cit., 56-58.

439 Interview with Toshila, Akangtula, Sentilemla, Pangerla, Limakumla. Mokokchung Town, 15 June 2013.

440 Interview with Limasenla, Taochila, Moanaro, Noksangla, Sünjemla, Kohima Town, 2 May 2013.

441 Folklore content consists of folk songs, ballads, folk music, folk stories, proverbs, riddles, fables, legends, and anecdotes that are verbally expressed/oral tradition/literature in a country or community. Nonverbal communication such as folk dance, folk games, folk art, folk festivals, folk medicine etc. can also be seen. See Felix Wilfred, "From the Dusty Soil," in *Asian Theological Search*, Vol.4. (Chennai: Department of Christian Studies, 1995), 234. James Theophilus Appavoo, *Folklore for Change* (Arasaradi, Madurai: Tamilnadu Theological Seminary, 1986), 8-9.

> etc. ... portrays a large variety of women and men and their role in society. In other words, this folklore provides a system of values.[442]

When we look at some of the folktales in Ao Naga society such as Ongangla the diviner, Akangla a great diplomat, and Yongyintemla a great musician, these were the women whose wisdom and knowledge brought success to the whole of the Ao Naga community in those early days.[443] We can also see the amazing tale of *Lijaba* and two Orphan sisters, and the story about Longkongla which one cannot simply ignore and erase from the minds of the Ao Nagas.

3.9.1. A Tale of Lijaba and Two Orphan Sisters

Through the story of *Lijaba*[444] and the two orphan sisters, we could gather how the Ao Naga tribal community in the past failed to recognise the shortcomings of socio-cultural structures and failed to maintain equal status to all humankind.[445] The compassion, love and respect that people often talk about in the Ao Naga Tribal community seem invisible in this regard, but merely lip-service. This is

[442] A. Asola Jamir, "The image of women in selected Naga folklore and its impact on Naga women today," in *Communication and Naga Culture* (Dimapur: Tribal Development and Communication Centre, 2008), 79.

[443] N. Limatula Longkumer, "Rediscovering Women's Role and Status in Society," in *Transforming Theology for Empowering Women: A Theological and Hermeneutical Reflection in the Context of North East India,* edited by R.L. Hnuni (ETC, Jorhat: Women's Studies, 1999), 35ff.

[444] *Lijaba* in the Ao Naga tribal community was considered as the creator of the world, the god of the fields and vegetation who appeared every year to every village in disguised forms.

[445] The story goes like this. Once there lived two orphan sisters on the outskirts of the village (normally they were considered as outsiders because no other villagers live in such isolated places) whose mother died and father remarried. In the course of time, their stepmother did not like them and finally with the consent of the father she managed to drive them away from their home.

It so happened that one day *Lijaba,* in the form of a beggar, turned up at the house of the two orphan sisters after he was turned away from their homes by every member of the village because his outward appearance was very poor and unattractive. The villagers gave him different versions of excuses and refused to let him in.

However, the two orphan sisters, despite their massive poverty, showed compassion towards him and allowed him to stay in their hut without knowing that *Lijaba* was the creator god. That very night *Lijaba* began to perform miracles. They had nothing to eat at home that night, but *Lijaba* sat near the oven and began to cook; both rice and curry were being cooked deliciously. After the meal, three of them sat on the back platform *(Sünglang)* of the house, and *Lijaba* started to ask the two sisters about all the fields of the villagers.

They named and explained to him all the villagers' fields and to whom they belonged, and finally when *Lijaba* pointed out the two sisters' field was as small as *likho* (a 3ft. square bamboo mat used for drying and cleaning rice) and asked them to whom it belonged. The elder sister was ashamed to tell him that this tiny field belonged to them but the younger sister disclosed to him secretly in the absence of her elder sister. On hearing this *Lijaba* blessed the two sisters' field and cursed all the others. See Tekatemjen, *Studies on Theology and Naga Culture* (Delhi: CTC, Aolijen, Mokokchung & ISPCK, 1998).

exemplified by the story of *Lijaba* and the two orphan sisters (the story is referred in footnote no. 406).

The two orphan sisters of the story were expelled from their home, becoming victims of the society in which nobody, not even their own father and relatives, dared to give them protection. They were denied a normal life which is as good as being dead. They were left with no mother, father, friends, and not much to eat. The story implies that they too did not have enough land to cultivate.

The story also reveals to us that poor people were neglected by society. Tekatemjen in his writing mentioned that: "The characters who are depicted as sisters (women) and not brothers (men) may indicate that women had their own share of problems in the tribal society of the bygone days."[446]

3.10. The Political Administration in the Ao Naga Tribal Community: Past and Present

In the Ao Naga tribal community, each village is an autonomous unit of administration. A council of elders called the *Tatar Putu Menden/Samen Menchen* oversees all matters of common interest, and nothing can be done without its approval or sanction.[447] The members of the *Tatar Putu Menden* exercise legislative, executive and judicial powers in a village. The *Tatar Putu Menden* – which roughly translates as "chosen leader/holder of shares in meat" (*Tatar),* "seat/government" *(Menden)*, "of a generation" *(Putu),* – is the federal assembly of elders representing different founding clans of the village. There are broadly five established *putus (generations)* amongst the Aos and each *putu* rules the village for 30 years in a cyclic pattern. Within each *putu* are seven to nine of age/peer group units called *Zünga.*[448] Each *Zünga* consists of people born within a three year period and this forms the order of precedence within each *Putu*. The elders hold forth over their juniors and accordingly, the work distribution and roles and responsibilities in each *Putu* is established. Within the time frame of 30 years governance of a *Putu*, different *züngas* succeed one another as and when the time arises. At the end of the allocated 30 years, all councillors of the outgoing *Putu* vacate their position and a new *Putu Menden* takes over.[449]

---

[446] Tekatemjen, *Studies on Theology and Naga Culture,* 59-60.

[447] The Ao Naga tribal community speaks two major dialects; *Chungli* and *Mongsen*. Among these two dialects *Chungli* is spoken as a common language. In *Chungli,* the system of government is called *Tatar Putu Menden* but in *Mongsen* it is called *Samen Menchen.*

[448] In all the age-groups female members enjoy all the same privileges as their male counterparts, but when it comes to village administration and functions female members are set-aside. Interview with Sosang, Shilu, Manen, Mokokchung Town 12 June 2013.

[449] Amba Jamir, "Understanding Local Self Governance in Nagaland–An essence of the institutions and their activities" http://www.scribd.com/doc/51638389/Local-Self-Governance-in-Nagaland-India?olddoc accessed on (23.2.12). See N. Talitemjen Jamir, *Ao-Naga Cultural Heritage, op.cit.,* 81.

The *Putu Menden* consists of six tiers,[450] the first three tiers being the important functionaries and the other three tiers forming the subsidiary bodies in the village administration. *Putu Menden* does not have a fixed number of members; selection is done depending upon the size and population of the village.

3.10.1. Ungr's Power and Functions

In every *Putu Menden,* an *Ungr* is nominated among his clan who is entitled to be a member of the *Tatar.* After being appointed, he is called *Tatar Ungr*. The post of *Ungr* cannot be held by any ordinary man; he should be from the clan which had held the priesthood at the time of the founding of the village. He is regarded as the head of the *Tatar Putu Menden*. Along with him, there is an assistant called *Tonglu* from another founder clan of the village who will assist the *Ungr* in times of emergency like the absence, sickness or sudden death of *Ungr*. During an emergency, meetings of *Tatar Putu Menden* will be held in the *Tonglu's* house.

To be an *Ungr* in the *Putu Menden* he has to have certain qualifications. The following guidelines for *Ungr* are:

> He should be from a clan that held priesthood at the time they formed a new village,
> He should be chosen and approved by his clan,
> He should possess high morality and commendable personality,
> He should be economically sound,
> He should not be an illegitimate son,
> He should not be insolvent, and
> He should not be a thief, murderer, or convict of any crime or offence.[451]

Once the *Ungr* is appointed, all the important political, social and cultural matters of the village are discussed in his house. He will act as an advisor and render suggestions, but he cannot impose on or object to the discussion nor be directly involved in the deliberation of the *Tatar*. All the matters discussed and agreed upon at the *Ungr*'s house become statutory in the village.[452]

3.10.2. The Distinction between Women and Men in Political Affairs

In Ao Naga Tribal community a boy, on the day he entered the *Ariju*, becomes a full member of his community. He has the right to participate and voice his

---

[450] These are namely: *Ung Menden, Tazung Menden, Tekong Menden, Lash, Tarsosang/Tarjung or Jamija and Sosanglak/Chindangondang.* See L. Sosang Jamir, *Ao Naga Customary Laws and Practices* (Dimapur: Heritage Publishing House, 2012),10.

[451] Ibid., 10-15.

[452] Ibid.

opinion in the affairs of his village governance. Thus, this civic set-up gave him a sense of belonging to his community.[453]

Morung was the place around which all the activities were centred and matters concerning civil or criminal cases were settled. The village council was the highest law-making body and all the village affairs are under their control. It is said that the alumni of the *Morung* acted as judges.[454]

In this regard, women are disqualified from becoming members or holding any office in the entire social and political affairs of the community. A serious discrimination done to women in most of the tribal society is in decision-making bodies; for women to raise their voice is out of question, even to listen silently in the public meeting is a taboo because it is strictly prohibited. N. Limatula Longkumer has rightly pointed out that: "It is a taboo for women to appear on a political platform or to participate in any village council or public meeting … Women's role is simply to follow and cooperate with the men's decision without any complaint."[455]

Normally in Ao Naga tribal villages, the council is administered by an elected body represented from each clan but women are not even members in the village council. Patriarchal society in tribal culture promotes male chauvinism but suppresses women by denying equal participation in the administrative circle and puts women subordinate to men. Therefore, a woman does not enjoy the same status and privileges as a man. She was given a very law status and is considered as an inferior sex even to this day. Her life is controlled by her father before marriage, and her husband will take over after the marriage. Her uncles, in-laws and her sons will take over if misfortune befalls her husband.

In the olden days, a woman, even though she might be the oldest person in the village, could not become a priest (*Patir* (M)/*Putir* (C)). Therefore, she was debarred from performing religious rites and sacrifices. She could not participate in debate and discussion of public interest. She was not even entitled to get honour, title and fame.[456]

The continual restriction of the voice and activities of Ao women in traditional socio-cultural and religious norms from the past until the present day Ao Naga tribal community are obvious. They are not allowed to participate in public debates or discussions or in any other citizen forums in the public gatherings like village public meetings, *yim mungdang*. Village council meetings, various citizens' forums, *senso* meetings, etc., where all the policy decisions are taken. If

---

[453] Tekatemjen, *Studies on Theology and Naga Culture* (Delhi: CTC, Aolijen, Mokokchung & ISPCK, 1998), 8.

[454] Ibid.

[455] N. Limatula Longkumer, "Christianity and Naga Women," in *Transforming Theology for Empowering Women: A Theological and Hermeneutical Reflection in the Context of North East India*, edited by R.L. Hnuni (Jorhat: Women's Studies, ETC, 1999), 56.

[456] Tajen Ao, *Ao Naga Customary Laws*, op. cit., 65.

needed, they can counsel and advise their husbands at home to a certain extent. In this way, women are left in a dark arena without knowing many pertinent issues around them. Rather, they have to obey the decisions made by their menfolk, by the clan members, village authorities and tribesmen.[457]

Women in the bygone days of Ao society were regarded as inferior beings. They were forced to live with the narrow understanding of superstitious beliefs and taboos in all their entire lives without being aware that all the traditional norms and believes are human/man–made.[458]

3.10.3. Village Administration: The Exclusion of an Illegitimate Son

In Ao Naga Tribal community a child born out of wedlock is called *Kita-chir*, and is counted as illegitimate and treated with contempt. Such a child is considered unfit for any leadership role in the village community even if the child's father accepts him as his own and has given him a name. In cases where a woman or a girl has a child out of wedlock having no father to claim the child as his own, such a child is called *Asangchi* and is never given a name by which to be called, no father, no clan, and no heritage; they are rejected totally by the community and are excluded from community affairs. In the past Ao Naga tribal community, they were very rigid in dealing with such cases, believing that even after death, their souls were never given permission to enter into heaven or *Tipuli* but lived between heaven and earth. Such was the treatment meted out by the traditional Ao custom in the community for an illegitimate child, and it is practised even now.[459]

It is believed by the Aos that to hold an administrative post such as membership of the village council, one has to have certain qualities and be acceptable before God and human beings. Therefore, an illegitimate man, liar, thief or a convicted person are said to have no place in the village administration system. "*Sobaliba*[460] always upholds the belief that the seat of administration is

---

[457] N. Talitemjen Jamir, A. Lanunungsang, *Naga Society and Culture*, op. cit., 218-220.

[458] In the past, women could not become the religious head of their family, clan, or village and were debarred from performing religious rites and sacrifices. Generally, women and children are not allowed to come to the village common altar, due to fear and superstition. However, she could assist her husband in household religious sacrifices. In the past, the Aos used to observe as many as 26 public ceremonies and 13 household ceremonies. In all these, women were not allowed to participate fully except in certain public ceremonies like *Moatsü* and *Tsüngrem mong*.

On all these occasions, the wife assisted her husband to enable him to perform the sacrifices successfully. A widow was entitled to perform sacrifices in her paddy field for good crops and rich harvest, But, they were not entitled to fame and title. For performing feasts of merit, both husband and wife received honour but the husband was rated higher than his wife in praises and honour. See, N.Talitemjen Jamir, A. Lanunungsang, *Naga Society and Culture*, op. cit., 218–220.

[459] I. Bendangangshi, I.T. Apok Aier, *The Religion of the Ao Nagas,* op. cit., 142.

[460] *Sobaliba* is the moral principle practised by an individual in the private and public life of the Aos, in their dealing or way of life, etc. It is an essence of humanity. For example, to respect elders, to extend help to needy, destitute, aged and strangers, willing to share their belonging with their neighbours and friends in need, sharing land with the landless for cultivation, hospitable etc.

God's given privilege, so it is holy as the divine and therefore, should maintain high moral standard in choosing the members of the *putu menden.*"[461]

Aos still hold firmly to the notion of *sobaliba*, that nobody can question its traditional understanding of 'holiness' when it comes to village administration where only a 'pure' and blameless remarkable man will be entitled to hold office. Therefore, an illegitimate son who, according to *sobaliba* is "impure", has no place for the seat of *putu menden.*[462]

While the Ao Naga tribal community tries to maintain sanctity in moral conduct in the civil and political administration, one can also notice the shortcomings in the traditional socio-cultural structures, such as the harsh reality that befalls an illegitimate child in Ao society. An illegitimate son is placed more or less in the same category as a thief, liar or convicted person in the society. He/she is made to feel insecure and treated with contempt. The traditional socio-cultural norms do not consider who is really to blame for the life of such an ill-fated innocent child. Through no fault of hers/his, she/he is stigmatised and ostracised in the name of "*Sobaliba.*"

3.10.4. The Integration of Present Ao Naga Tribal Organisation: Yimten,[463] *Senso and Ao Senden in the Ao Naga Tribal Community*

In the course of time if some important issue arises and it is thought that the *Tatar Putu Menden* will not be able to handle it by themselves, then the matter is taken

Sobaliba also mould a person to be a member of a cosmic community that means love of nature (the environment), Supreme Being, care and concern for fellow humankind. *Sobaliba* also teaches abstinence from all things that degrade human being like committing adultery, killing or torturing living beings, false witness, stealing and cheating. See Nungshitula, *The Naga Images of The Human Being* (Jorhat: Tribal Study Centre, 2001), 54-55.

Sobaliba implies the activities of a person from cradle to grave, *Sobaliba* entails having married and issuing offspring, involves in farming, learning to be expert in any kind of handy crafts, involving in the village politics for a better goal etc. Renthy Keitzar, "Church and Ao Culture," in *The Church in Ao Society* (Impur: ABAM, 1984), 12.

"If one administers well without any corruption one would say that he is a person of *Sobaliba* or if one do not eat greedily and selfishly one would say one is a *Sobaliba* person....if one wears decently one would say that one is the person of Sobaliba....*Sobaliba* permeate throughout a person's practical, spiritual and rational life.... *Sobaliba* can be understood in totality in a person's good life." Imsenperong, Menjiwapong Jamir, Walotemjen, *Mapping the Context: An Interdisciplinary Exploration* (Kohima: Author, 2011), 47.

Sobaliba taught to respect women as well at the same time imposes certain restriction on women. For example, to include women in the village administration/decision-making body is not *sobaliba.*

[461] Imsenperong, Menjiwapong Jamir, Walotemjen, *Mapping the Context: An Interdisciplinary Exploration* (Kohima: Author, 2011), 31.

[462] Interview with Marlepden, Shilokokba, Makenshilu, and Bendangtemjen, Mopungjuket Village, 13 August 2013.

[463] *Yimten* and *Yimden* are variant spellings of the same institution of the Ao Naga tribal community. Renthy Keitzar, *Ao Dictionary* (Impur: Ao Theological Literature Society, Ao Mungdang, 1999).

up to the larger body, and notice will be given to the general public (exclusively men) called *Yimten.*[464] *Yimten* is the highest body in a village circle. Above all, *Senso*[465] is the apex body of a village where every citizen of a village who is settled elsewhere in the country joins in *Senso*, and they are called *sensopur* (citizenry). A *Senso* meeting is held once every two or three years in a village, during which all the male members gather from different places to attend the meeting; it is a mandatory for them, and whoever fails to come will be penalised with a fine. J. Longkumer mentioned: "Despite the tremendous developmental changes, the villages remain the most important entity in the lives of the Aos."[466] *Yimten* and *Senso* are two connected bodies that are run under the parameters of a village.

Ao Senden[467] is considered the highest body among these three (*Yimten, Senso* and *Ao Senden*),[468] the apex body of the Ao community. A similar arrangement like that of the village council can be seen even in places such as Mokokchung Town, the urban centre of the Ao area which is also the seat of the *Ao Senden.* Though Mokokchung is declared a municipality, the *Senden* seems to have a place and role not dissimilar to that of the *Putu Menden* in the village(s). Therefore, women have no voice, even in urban areas like Mokokchung, a "modernised" urban centre where the administrative systems are quite different from that of the village.[469]

---

[464] *Yimten* is the apex body within a village jurisdiction where all the male members are the part of this *Yimten*, but in this women are not included. The office bearers are the *Tatar Putu Menden.*

[465] *Senso* means citizen. It includes all the members of a village irrespective of sex, status and clan of a village. They have separate office bearers selected from the community but *Tatar Putu Menden* render service to them whenever necessary. Women cannot participate in the affairs of a village but must just obey whatever decision is made.

[466] J. Longkumer, "The Ao Village Organisation: Origin to Present Day," in *Naga Society: Continuity and Change,* edited by N. Venuh (Delhi: Shipra Publications, 2004), 35.

[467] *Ao* is the name of a Tribe among the Nagas of Nagaland and *Senden* means to "assemble; to gather; to come together; service; assembly." Therefore, the meaning of *Ao Senden* is the assembly or gathering of Aos. See Renthy Keitzar, *Ao Dictionary* (Impur: Ao Theological Literature Society, Ao Mungdang, 1999).

[468] *Ao Senden* is the apex body of Ao socio-cultural organization that governs the entire Ao population. It was established in 1980 with the theme 'Unity and cooperation.' Mokokchung town is the headquarters of *Ao Senden.* It is administered and controlled by the male member under whose vested interest the decisions are being made and activities are being carried out by representing the whole of Ao Naga tribal community.

[469] Ao Women have their organisation *Watsü* Mungdang for women but even this is under the control of *Ao Senden.*

3.10.5. *Watsü Mungdang*[470] *in the Ao Naga Tribal Community*

Watsü Mungdang is the apex body of the Ao women's organisation working in all areas for the socio-cultural uplift of the Ao Naga tribal community. It was established on April 23, 1982 with its headquarters in Mokokchung Town, under the banner of *Unity and Progress*. It deals with many social issues mainly related with women. Like the other organisations, its membership and support lies at the grass roots level of Ao villages/ranges/towns. Since its inception, *Watsü Mungdang* has been doing tremendous work in the society for the benefit of the common people. There are innumerable initiatives undertaken by *Watsü Mungdang* along with the Naga Mother's Association for the liberation of women in Nagaland, including active participation in peace making processes among the underground factions that bravely stand in the war zones for negotiation, and prohibition of alcohol etc. in the State.

No matter how far Ao women contribute towards the betterment of society, the traditional socio-cultural mind-set of the Aos still lingers in their "flesh, blood and spirit." The comment of Anungla Aier on Naga culture is appropriate here when she said, "When the external layers of their modern culture is peeled off, we find that the cultural framework of their society have not been changed drastically as commonly assumed."[471]

The exceptional work that have been done by *Watsü Mungdang* for years has never been truly valued or appreciated by most of the Ao community. The only platform for Ao woman where she can voice her concerns, ideas, knowledge and her feelings is ignored by most irrational Ao men as was experienced with *Ao Senden* very recently.

3.10.6. *The Ao Naga Tribal Understanding of Democracy*

Ao society has a very rigid traditional understanding of "democracy" when it comes to the village administrative systems and decision-making bodies. The majority of writers and like-minded thinkers proudly proclaim that "Aos is a democratic society." In a real sense, the way Aos look at democracy is totally contradictory to the common understanding of the term.

Firstly, Aos **select/nominate**, and not **elect**, their clan representative in the village council. Secondly, in the selection, only male members are represented and not female members. Thirdly, all decisions made among the clan members, village community or tribe are done only by male members. Aos in general are still impressed with their traditional understanding of democracy which is, in reality, not democratic at all as commonly understood.

---

[470] *Watsü* Mungdang is purely a women's association, first initiated by the Ao Women Baptist Association Impur which functions under ABAM (Ao Baptist Arogo Mungdang).

[471] Anungla Aier, "Cultural Change Among the Nagas: Festivals and Dress" in *Naga Society: Continuity and Change,* edited by N. Venuh (Delhi: Shipra Publications, 2004), 59.

This belief system of democracy by Aos has to be questioned today. Democracy which is supposed to be equalitarian, egalitarian, emancipatory, suffragist, republican, common, and relating to freedom and justice, etc., is missing in these traditional Ao Naga tribal administrative systems.

3.11. Religious Belief of the Ao Naga Tribal Community: Past and Present

The traditional religious belief of the Aos has been replaced by Christianity. All the traditional religious rituals and practices were discarded when Christianity came to the Ao land. Let us see how the past and present religious practices differ and also how similar they are.

3.11.1. Participation in Religious Ceremonies: Installation of the Log Drum as a Community Matter[472]

One of the important means of communication in the Ao Naga Tribal community is the log drum. But, the log drum was meant not only for communication purposes; it also carries a sacred religious significance for the whole of the community. There were no villages without a log drum in early times. To install a log drum in a village requires the combined efforts of the entire community. The work load was allotted to every age group according to their own capacity. Equal responsibility was distributed to young and old, men and women, and to the rich as well as the poor. It mentioned:

---

[472] 'Log drum' (*Sungkong* in Chungli and *Tongden* in Mongsen Ao Naga Tribal dialect) was highly honoured and regarded as sacred among many Naga communities. Installing a log drum in a village required lots of time, human power and energy. It took months to perform the process, which involved searching for a suitable tree which is then cut, carved out, painted, brought to shape and pulled from the thick forest.

The size of the log drum is normally around 30 to 40 ft. long and 13 to 14 ft. wide, and its tail about 5–6 feet. When the drum is being beaten the sounds can reverberate to neighbouring villages too. "There is variety of differences in the style of beating the drum producing different sounds indicating different meanings or messages ... Everyone in the village understands the sound that carries the core meaning."

The main function of the log drum was originally a war drum used for sirening [*sic.*] the village inmates about an attack or instructing them to proceed for the planned attack. The log drum was also considered as a village deity. It also gave information to the villagers for public meetings, to announce the sign of impending danger when the enemy approached, and to convey the message of victory during the time of festivity and when the warriors' returned home with the head as trophy. They also beat the drum during the solar and lunar eclipses believing that they may appear again through the beating of the drum. They had believed that the log drum will protect, guide and bless its worshippers. Therefore, they considered the log drum as one of the village deities. See N. Talitemjen Jamir, A. Lanunungsang, *Naga Society and Culture,* and Sukhdev Singh Chib, *Caste, Tribes and Culture of India: North-Eastern India,* Vol. 8 (New Delhi: Sheel Sethi (Mrs.) ESS Publications, 1984).

> The adult male members of the *khel* or sector in the village do all the physical works, while the womenfolk prepare food and drink for the men who are engaged in heavy work. The young male members supply food and drink to the workers. This division of work is followed till the completion of the log drum.[473]

The villagers performed prayer and feasting ceremonies for pulling and placement of a log drum after the work was completed. This ceremony was considered as one of the most significant ceremonies for the Aos, where both men and women, attired with new clothes, participated in singing new songs in the function. While the older members guarded the village during that time, the remaining people in the village were divided into different age groups for pulling the log drum.[474]

When the male members pulled the log drum on the last day, the elderly people stayed at home and looked after the children. On the other hand, the womenfolk worked side by side with the male folk, carrying food and drinks as the entire village population went to the site. On reaching the site, one commander *Tir* performed rites to the log drum so that it should slide quickly and also to prevent and protect the villagers from any ailment or accident. After performing the ritual, they would utter loudly, "Oh…Hoi"; this was echoed by all the members, both women and men in unison. Elders normally addressed their songs in honour of the log drum.[475]

The whole day at intervals the village priest and the commander *Tir* would call out to the log drum, evoking it to glide as they pulled together, proclaiming *Oruru aten* saying "hü … e, hü … e." When the male group shouted together while pulling the drum "hoi, hoi, hoi," the women group would respond "auwang keri ri ri ri … hoi hoi." At the intervals, age-group girls would serve wine *Zü* (rice beer) to all the male members. This was a sign of encouragement to the male members to strengthen their efforts while they pulled the log drum.[476]

There were many occasions such as festivals, working in the field, installation of log drum, etc., where the whole village was engaged together in working hand in hand, expressing their ideas and feelings through songs, and supporting each other for their achievement and development of their village community.

As we heard about the tug-of-war song in the festivals, both young women and men participated reciprocally in singing which was the sign of mutual sharing and cooperation. Without the support of the other (female or male) party the song would not have come out beautifully. This shows us that the presence of

---

[473] N. Talitemjen Jamir, A. Lanunungsang, *Naga Society and Culture,* op. cit., 118–119.

[474] N. Talitemjen Jamir, A. Lanunungsang, *Naga Society and Culture,* op. cit., 119-200.

[475] Ibid.

[476] Ibid.

both the parties (female and male members) in the singing was significant and very meaningful.

The entire village community was involved in the whole process of the installation of the log drum from the beginning till the end. Each played her/his role according to her/his own capacities. Each person's contribution was counted as very important whether young or old; women or men all played a significant role. This gives us the idea that they depended on each other. Without the support of one group the other group would not have been achieved their goal.

As the Ao Naga tribal community is based on 'male-centred-ness,' even though a woman assists her husband at the household religious sacrifice, preparing all the necessary items such as food and new wine to be used in the sacrifice and worship, her participation in religious ceremonies was not visible, not recognized and not counted as important; she was considered as secondary member. The writing of Panger Imchen also states that: "The concept of sanctity of the altar was immense in ancient times. Women, children and persons under age were restricted from the holy altar where sacrifices and worship were conducted."[477] However, history reveals us that apart from her daily household chores, she was also indeed actively involved and played a massive role in community functions like the installation of the log drum and festivals like *Moats*ü and *Tsüngrem mong* along with the male counterpart.[478]

3.11.2. Women's Participation in the Feast of Merit[479]

The Ao Naga Tribal community in the past observed many religious ceremonies where everybody in the community participated in the functions. Such practices and ceremonies were common among the Ao Naga community. For example bull and Mithun sacrifices, found in private religious ceremonies, were considered some of the greatest and most expensive sacrifices that were offered to the most supreme deity known as ***Teroktsungba.*** It is said that his name was not pronounced because of his holiness and greatness, but often he was addressed as *Soba-Tiyaba* or *Tiyar* or sometimes as *Ita-Anu* (moon and sun). He was regarded as supreme over every human being, which means he was the creator of all living and non-living beings, destiner, and controller of the universe. The purpose of Mithun

---

[477] Panger Imchen, *Ancient Ao Naga Religion and Culture*, op. cit., 164.

[478] It is said that Ao women in the past were not allowed to participate fully in many public ceremonies: this was observed in as many as 26 public ceremonies and 13 household ceremonies among the Ao community; however, women had participated fully in ceremonies like *Moatsü* and *Tsüngrem mong* festivals. See N. Talitemjen Jamir, A. Lanunungsang, *Naga Society and Culture* (Mokokchung: Nagaland University Tribal Research Centre, Department of Sociology, 2005), 219.

[479] In this, a Mithun or Bull was sacrificed to the Supreme Being of the Aos. 'Through the Feasts of Merit a wealthy man transmits his own fertility, proof of which is his wealth, to the members of the community by offering meat, rice and rice-beer, and receiving in turn merit and social prestige.' "Feasts of Merit," http://www.angelfire.com/nm/nagalim/feast.htm accessed on 26.8.13.

sacrifice by the ancestors was to seek longevity of life, for riches and prosperity, for recovery from sickness, for bliss of children and for health. It is said that this sacrifice was also done by the poor people by taking loan from the rich.[480]

i. The Role of Husband and Wife in the Mithun Sacrifice

To sacrifice Mithun was not an easy task for any person because Mithun is considered as the son of heavenly being, and killing of Mithun causes great anger in heaven where angels take revenge on the killer of Mithun. One of the important roles to play in this sacrifice is the husband and wife: without them this could not be completed. Therefore, in this Mithun sacrifice it was the practice that both husband and wife were involved in all the rituals, and they had to observe taboo *genna* with utmost care and stricture for fear of revenge from the god. This sacrifice could not be made by any single human being, such as a single man or woman, widow or widower, or a young couple either, no matter how rich they were.[481]

ii. Women's Role in the Ceremony

Traditionally, Ao, women were also seen taking part and playing important roles in most of the religious ceremonies along with the menfolk. In the sacrifice called *elangtsur* all the womenfolk from the clan of the sacrifice called *elangtsur* cried out loudly in unison chanting, "Au-ang ghri-ri-ri auok, auok." This chanting was done in the beginning as well as at the end when all the work was done. It was the formal cry to god of victory and thanksgiving. The womenfolk then begin to perform other activities such as serving rice beer to all those who are in the house, replacing the fermented rice called *peya* to another basket woven of bamboo splints, followed by many such other related works that took elaborate processes which were all done for the preparation and distribution in the ceremony.

iii. Children and Elderly people in the Religious Ceremony

Children took part and were engaged in drawing and fetching water which was in required in large quantities for the feast. Even some of the elderly people were engaged in preparing a chain with ropes of sword-bean to be put around the neck of the bull and fastened to the post.

iv. Responsive Singing in the Ceremony

In this Mithun sacrifice religious ceremony, there were certain times when both womenfolk and menfolk gathered together feasting and drinking. At first, all the womenfolk of the *elangtsur* (a group of women of the same clan) cried out the same shout, chanting the same tune *"Au-ang ghri-ri-ri auok,"* to which the menfolk

[480] I. Bendangangshi, I.T. Apok Aier, *The Religion of the Ao Nagas,* op. cit., 97-8.

[481] Imsongunger Süiren, *Imsongunger: Brief History and Genealogy* (N.p: Imsongunger Kidong Telongjem, n.d), 85.

responded "*oh-ho-ho*"; it was the sign of expressing joy. It would be followed by all the *elangtsur* trilling their songs of praises both old and new, dancing around the hearth of the house. After this the rope was placed onto the neck of the bull or Mithun and tied to the post for sacrifice. All the *elangtsur* would go out of the house a little ahead of time before the dedication of the bull was made by the husband and the wife and repeat both the old and new songs as they stood by the bull. These old songs were connected with the riches and prosperity of their clansmen who had offered bull and Mithun sacrifices. The new songs were about the songs of praises upon the sacrificer for his riches, and the songs of praises to god for blessing their clansmen.[482]

The involvement of both the womenfolk and the menfolk from the start till the end of the ceremony was quite significant in the Ao Naga Tribal Community. Each day was observed and counted as very special during the time of the Mithun sacrifice; a number of procedures were followed, such as gathering both womenfolk and menfolk inside the house where they cried in loud voice in order to drive away the heavenly beings. Womenfolk used to sing continually the whole night till cock crow on the night the Mithun was killed or sacrificed. They sing songs of praise to god and to the husband and wife of the sacrifice.[483]

Upon completion of all the rituals in the Mithun sacrifice, on the last ceremony of the day both old and young, friends, relatives, clansmen, clanswomen, and priests all went together to the paddy field of the sacrifice. There they performed certain customary practices and ceremonies with feasting.[484]

In this religious ceremony of Feast of Merit, we can observe that a common platform was given to all the clan's members to participate. Young, old, female and male members of the clan took part in this Mithun sacrifice. It is significant that the sacrifice could be performed only by a couple, i.e. husband and wife. A bachelor, divorcee or widower could not perform it. This shows that one of the most important requirements to complete this religious ceremony was an equal participation of both female and male in the Ao Naga tribal community. It also shows that every member of the clan was important, and that equal participation in all the ceremony carried significant meaning.

Another important observable point is that the Mithun sacrifice was a ceremony that qualified the sacrifice on two grounds; they were for the religious purpose of the appeasement of the god and also for the recognition of social status. Anil Kumar Singh has observed and mentioned that: "The feast brings the donor honour and he can henceforth wear special clothes and ornaments, can decorate his house in a special way and thus obtain a high status in social life."[485]

---

[482] Imsongunger Süiren, *Imsongunger: Brief History and Genealogy* (N.p: Imsongunger Kidong Telongjem, n.d), 102-3.

[483] Ibid., 120

[484] Ibid., 132.

[485] Anil Kumar Singh, *Tribal Culture and Polity* (New Delhi: Sarup & Sons, 1994), 74–75.

Song was an important means of communication in all the activities, both private and public. One can meaningfully communicate messages through songs, and that was done in the religious festivals where both female and male responded to each other through songs. It was here that ideas were exchanged, feelings shared, and communication made with one another.

The traditional customs and practices of the Ao Naga tribal community, therefore, acknowledge that in a religious festival and ceremony like Mithun sacrifice, the female voice was heard, acknowledged and appreciated by the Ao community. Equal sharing of responsibility and participation which was all inclusive, that is, involving participation of both female and male, was quite visible in this respect.

3.11.3. Ao Naga Tribal Christians

Ao Baptist Arogo Mungdang (ABAM) is the apex organisation of the Ao Baptist Churches in Nagaland, which functions in cooperation with all the autonomous churches among the Aos community.[486] The Executive Secretary is the head of the Association;[487] under him there are various other departments that run simultaneously in ABAM, including Church, Mission, Education, Literature, Women,[488] Youth, Children, Sunday School and Resource Development. The Executive Committee functions under the leadership of the Executive Secretary who chairs all the decision-making bodies. There are thirty-four executive members out of which five are women. The executive committee sits thrice a year and discusses matters concerning the Ao Churches. There seems to have been slight progress made in the ABAM decision-making body, where five women are represented.

---

[486] Ao Baptist Arogo Mungdang (ABAM) is the largest Baptist convention affiliated to Nagaland Baptist Church Council. It has its functions in relation to all the independent churches, covering over 125 fully-fledged churches. It has its mission compound at Impur near Mokokchung.

[487] The Ao Baptist Church Association was organised in March 1897 which is one of the 20 Baptist Church Associations in Nagaland. The American Baptist Foreign Mission Society (presently called "International Ministries") first introduced Christianity among the Aos of Nagaland and spread to other tribes of Nagaland as well. See, "The History of the Introduction of "The Gospel" among Aos," http://www.abamimpur.com/history.asp accessed on 24.8.13.

[488] Women ministry in ABAM runs workshop programmes for Drop-out Young Girls, Ministry for the Old Age, Selp-help Groups, Ministry for Differently-abled Persons, Enriching Families, Hostel Ministry, Vocational Training-cum-Production Centre, and Quarterly Published Magazine called *Khristan Kibong* (Christian Home), which plays an important role in women's ministry. http://www.abamimpur.com/history.asp accessed on 24.8.13.

The ABAM Women Department initiative towards Mission and Ministry is immense. One such example will be seen in the 'Handful of Rice' collection by the Ao Women Church Association. In one year (that is, 2012) they had collected more than rupees twenty-seven lakhs for the Mission and ministry that goes through ABAM. Interview with Panger Ozukum, P.A. to Executive Secretary, ABAM Impur, 25th August 2013.

i. Local Church

In the Ao Churches the decision-making bodies consist of the Board of Deacons which is made up of deacons; the Pastor ex officio, and the Associate Pastors (in some larger churches); the Church secretary; and the Church treasurer. All decisions concerning the Church's affairs are made by them.[489] Moanaro Imchen Jamir has observed clearly that: "Though its decisions have to be theoretically approved by the congregation as a whole, that is simply routine."[490]

ii. Departments in the Local Church

In a Church, there are various departments that function together such as Women Department with a woman Pastor, Youth Department under the leadership of the Youth Director, and the Child Department led by the Child Director. All these leadership positions are full-time ministries, and appointments are made from among theologically trained persons. In all these departments, the pastor occupies the highest position. A pastor is usually a licensed or ordained minister who has the authority to give baptism and administer the Sacraments. Normally a male pastor is preferred, and there is hardly any woman pastor in the Ao Church. All the departments function under the umbrella of the 'local Church' but are parallel to each other in the sense that female Pastors, Youth and Child Directors have no voice in the decision-making body except 'the Pastor.'

iii. Deacons/Elders

According to Baptist polity, deacons/elders are regarded as the main bodies who have governing authority in the Church. For the deacons, as in the case of the pastor, male members are usually preferred. Therefore, one hardly finds any female deacons in the Ao Baptist Churches. Thus, it is observable that though Baptist churches in other places may have made tremendous reforms, in the Ao Naga tribal churches the traditional Church structures are still very much in place. Since deacons are almost always male, one hardly finds any female voice being represented in the decision-making body in the Ao Naga tribal Church so far. It is therefore very similar to the function of the village council (*Putu menden*) that continue around the Ao Naga tribal society today.

3.12. The Economic life: Its Impact on Women

The economic stability of the Ao Naga tribal community in the past was mainly counted in terms of material possessions, i.e. the amount of land, rice, cattle, ornaments, clothes, etc. a person possesses. The one who could acquire those

---

[489] In the annual general body meeting (local church) women too attend the meeting. The agendas are screened by the deacons and pastor. Interview with Tali Longkumer, Choir Master Dimapur Ao Baptist Arogo, 5th August 2013.

[490] Moanaro Imchen Jamir, "The Role of Ao Women in Church and Society" *Tribal Journal of Theology* www.biblicalstudies.org.uk/pdf/ijt/37-1_045.pdf accessed on 25.4.2013.

possessions was economically sound and was regarded as a rich man. If a person was rich then he got the highest level of recognition and was held in high esteem in the society.

3.12.1. The Distinction between the Rich and the Poor

Although Aos are from time immemorial known for the ethics of sharing and caring in the community, we also find a number of cases of economic instability among the Ao Naga tribal community in the past. There was a wide range of economic disparity and social distinction between the rich and the poor, due to which the common people in the community irrespective of gender and age suffered under these traditional structures.

As we see in the records, before the British intervention in the late nineteenth century, the Aos would even sell off their own children for debts, to a richer man.[491] The debts ranged all the way from a value of a pig, up to the value of six or seven cows.[492] The distinction between the rich and the poor was so great that it led to the development of socio-economic injustices, even to the extent of parents having to give away their own children in payment for debts. On the other hand, the rich men's power and pride were so vast that they even carried and showcased their personal status up to the grave. As we observed in the Ao Naga tribal custom, when a man died a symbol was erected and displayed on his grave showing that in his lifetime he possessed slaves. This was done in order to show how each slave added to the master's social prestige.[493] There were times when the rich exploited the poor by taking advantage of their miserable condition.[494]

As mentioned above, a glaring feature of the Ao Naga tribal community in the past was its social distinctions. The distinction between the rich, the common people (the poor) and the women in particular was highly visible. The rich people received high recognition in the society unlike the common people. They were put in the category of 'warriors and rulers'. Panger Imchen also wrote that: "The warriors, rulers, rich men and men of socio-political status put their medals and symbols printed on their shawls and ornaments. Ordinary men and women wear only *süpu* and *sürem* plain cloth and do not put such valued ornaments."[495] The

---

491 Bertil Lintner, *Great Game East: India, China and the Struggle for Asia's Most Volatile Frontier* (New Delhi: Harper Collins Publishers India, 2012), 46.

492 There was a case reported that an eighteen-year-old woman who was deserted by her husband was enslaved by her father because her father had an enormous debt of two rupees and eight annas (the equivalent of some more than ten thousand rupees today) for a pig. See William C. Smith, *The Ao-Naga Tribe of Assam,* op. cit., 54.

493 Bertil Lintner, *Great Game East: India, China and the Struggle for Asia's Most Volatile Frontier*, 46.

494 This may not be applicable to all the rich men but one cannot pretend that everything was smooth in the past Ao society.

495 Panger Imchen, *Ancient Ao Naga Religion and Culture* (New Delhi: Har-Anand Publications, 1993), 53.

rich men's voice carried a lot of weight in community affairs whereas the common people's voice, particularly that of women, were not heard at all.

3.12.2. Debts as Obligatory: Women Were Not Exempted

There were stringent laws practised by the traditional Ao Naga tribal community which were binding on all the individuals, as indicated by the writers like N. Talitemjen Jamir and A. Lanunungsang. One of the laws implied in the traditional Ao Naga society is the payment of debt, which was obligatory for all. It was the next of the kin who had the moral responsibility and duty to clear up all the parental debts, or else it was considered shameful for the family. This was carried out by the sons in the family because the sons get all the inherited property after the death of the father. This continued till the debt was discharged by an heir, either by his sons, grandsons or paternal uncles.[496] There was no customary rule which permitted automatic liquidation of the ancestral debt even after the lapse of a given generation or time.[497]

The unstable economic status in the Ao Naga Tribal community bears witness that there was increasing frailty of traditional socio-cultural structures allowing no room to develop mutual co-existence within their own community. Sharing and caring ethics were dissolved by the greed and might of the few rich people.

Above all, women were the worst affected people who were victimized by these traditional socio-cultural systems. It is also quite obvious that women were behind the curtain silently bearing the entire burden with their families without any social recognition. Although, they were not given any share of inheritance as men were, and were said to have no parental debts incurred upon them, they were still not free from all these family burdens. N.Talitemjen Jamir, A. Lanunungsang said that: "Today, many of the liabilities including debts are liquidated by women left by men but they are not entitled to inherit the landed property."[498] Women directly or indirectly helped to pay off the debts that were carried out by the family either in her parents' home or in her husband's home. Several women shared the same story, saying, "Before I got married, I helped my parents in the rice paddies, through which my father could repay the debt of my grandfather who had borrowed a few baskets of rice from others."[499]

[496] It was normally the older son who received the largest share of property, and he carried all the responsibilities. Even if there were debts owed by his parents or ancestors the eldest son tried to repay it, but if he could not manage this by himself he would get his younger siblings' help.

[497] N. Talitemjen Jamir, A. Lanunungsang, *Naga Society and Culture,* op. cit., 236.

[498] N.Talitemjen Jamir, A. Lanunungsang, *Naga Society and Culture* (Mokokchung: Nagaland University Tribal Research Centre, Department of Sociology, 2005), 220.

[499] Interview with Tsüpongla, Tinuyangla, Naromenla, Tiakala , Taochila , Chunbanungla , Dimapur Town. 30 May 2013.

One of the main ways in which people become rich is also due to the continuous industrious work done by women. It is a known fact that there were tremendous contributions made by Ao women towards the production of food and other means of production for the economic stability of the family. Women were counted as an invaluable asset in contributing towards the economic system in the society as well. William C. Smith, one of the few earliest writers on the Ao Naga tribal community, had very rightly mentioned that:

> A woman is valued by her ability to work, and consequently a pair of muscular calves far outweighs a handsome face. The young women are generally stocky and plump; but this does not last long, because the hard life of carrying wood from jungle, doing cultivation work, raising children and performing other hard tasks soon make old hags of them.[500]

Tajen Ao shares the same view with Smith that the contribution of Ao women to economic affairs in the past was enormous. It has said that:

> Those families consisting of more female members such as mother and daughter who are the working members in the cultivation become self-sufficient and also become rich in food grains. On the other hand, it is said, that the male members are the consuming members in the family as they do not engage themselves in the cultivation but to go out on the other works.[501]

A woman was never exempted from economic affairs. She had always been a part of it, continually producing and involved in all the social and economic processes for the stability and smooth functioning of the family and society. However, all the contribution made by her was unacknowledged in her family, clan, village and the entire Ao Naga tribal community, and any trace or sign of her existence was erased. N. Talitemjen Jamir, and A. Lanunungsang clearly proved in their writing that: "They get maximum customary bindings but less customary privileges."[502] Her physical strength, her voice, her creativity, her feeling and emotions were all set aside and unnoticed.

3.13. Women in the Past

Ao Naga society during the olden days had built up many taboos and superstitious beliefs. Those beliefs were seriously observed for many generations until the advent of Christianity. One of these was the restriction of food items for women.

---

[500] William C. Smith, *The Ao-Naga Tribe of Assam,* op. cit., 54.

[501] Tajen Ao, *Ao Naga Customary Laws,* (N.p: Aowati Imchen, 1980), 181.

[502] N. Talitemjen Jamir, A. Lanunungsang, *Naga Society and Culture,* op. cit., 220.

The roles played by Ao women as life giving beings, her sacrificial acts and the contribution made by her in the community were beyond measure.

The stories confirm that in the past there were women who were well known for their wisdom, bravery and strength. They brought success and glory to their community. These women are still remembered by the Ao Naga tribal community.

3.13.1. Food Restriction for Women in the Past

In the Ao society of the past, once a girl attained the age of 10, she started on the process for tattooing, following which she had to abstain from several food habits. L. Sosang Jamir mentioned that: "Tattooing was a rite of passage and perfection for an Ao woman. A woman must avoid all prohibited food in order to maintain a strict and clean life."[503] The idea behind all this was that women were the bearers of future generations; hence, the maintenance of purity of their body and minds became a necessity. The Ao Naga traditions and cultures demanded from women observance of abstinence and chastity. All these strict roles are being made to ensure that children born of them had no defects.[504]

Here, we would like to bring some examples of certain food items which women should not eat after the completion of the tattooing process. Mutton, chicken, meat of animals killed by other animals or killed in accidents etc. were not eaten by women. Jamir continue to say that: "Goats make unpleasant sound when they bleat. They are also considered as promiscuous animal ... Goats give birth two to three times a year ... Though goats drink less, discharge much urine. For these reasons, women abstained from eating mutton."[505]

Some of the aquatic animals which tattooed women should not eat included frog, catfish, dragonfly nymph, crab, fresh water eel, bagarine fish, tadpole, and snake headed fish. One of the examples is catfish, "it is very slippery fish because of which it is difficult to catch. To ensure that their children do not become insolvent in society, women abstained from eating catfish."[506]

Wild animals whose meat tattooed women were forbidden from eating included cliff antelope, porcupine, pangolin etc. One of the reasons why they should not eat cliff antelope is that "[i]t is believed to be the carrier of a form of disease called *Shio-ra* [bronchitis]. It is said that if a person feels detested by the sight of the animals or eats its flesh with some reservation, he/she contracts the disease ... Women therefore, abstained from eating the meat of this animal."[507]

---

[503] L. Sosang Jamir, *Ao Naga Customary Laws and Practices* (Dimapur: Heritage Publishing House, 2012), 78.

[504] Ibid.,1 49.

[505] Ibid.

[506] Ibid., 150-151.

[507] Ibid., 151-152.

Birds of various kinds were also forbidden for the tattooed women. These included dove, thrush, green magpie, imperial pigeon etc. For instance, the dove should not be eaten because "[i]t has an unpleasant voice and seeks its food among empty husks of grain. It is believed that eating its meat makes a person forgetful and has meaningless dreams. For fear that children born of women who had eaten its flesh may remain poor and unproductive, women abstained from eating it.[508]

When the warriors returned to the village with victory, it was the Ao custom to give a grand reception to the warriors at the village gate. On such occasions, meat and rice beer which was considered one of the richest foods in Ao Naga culture were served lavishly but that was meant for the men folk only.[509]

In the Ao Naga tribal community of the past, women were not even spared from free selection of nutritional food of their own. The traditional socio-cultural norms compelled women to refrain from certain kinds of food items in the name of protecting their progeny from abnormalities. With the passage of time, the domestic work carried out from dawn till dusk, child bearing and rearing, and the process of tattooing her body seems to have been considered as part of her normal way of life in the passage of time. This miserable condition of Ao women were dictated by the tradition and culture of the Ao Naga Tribal community in the name of protection and procreation.

In the Ao Naga tribal community, the patriarchal influence was so strong that a woman's body movements, her mind, her heart, her soul and her emotions, were all controlled by the rigid socio-cultural norms. Her life was directed by the narrow traditional structure determining how she should be, how she should behave, how she should live and what she should eat for the sustenance of her family and community.

3.13.2. Triumph Through Akangla

Akangla was a wise lady whose husband was the village head of Waromung village. It is said that the two villages named Longkhum and Waromung decided to raid a village named Nokrang. They made a number of attempts but failed. The main reason why they could not attack that village (Nokrang) was that the most difficult hurdle before them was the ferocious dogs of Nokrang village which were used as sentries to detect the coming of enemies. In the nick of time Akangla came up with a marvellous idea. She gave word to all the women in her village to bring three days' collection of hair they collected as they combed their hair after washing. On that very day when the time came for the men to go to war, she distributed two to three rice balls to each person advising him to throw the rice ball as the dog approached near him (it was a cooked sticky rice mixed with the hairs). She gave the same instruction to all the men. The warriors accordingly

[508] Ibid., 152-153.

[509] N. Limatula Longkumer, "Rediscovering Women's Role and Status in Society," op. cit., 35-37.

followed what Akangla said to them. On eating the rice balls, the dogs found it difficult to swallow them as their throats got choked by the hair that was mixed in the sticky rice. The men could kill all the dogs, one after the other and they could easily capture and kill the enemies.[510]

The story tells of the wisdom of a woman who through her intellect and acumen helped achieve victory. She did not keep quiet but rather raised her voice and shared her brilliant ideas. It is a story of how a woman, by her wisdom and knowledge brought success to her village as well as to the other village "Longkhum." It also tells of how the effort of women and men together makes the seemingly impossible possible, and turns failure to success.

3.13.3. The Role of Ongangla in the Religious Ceremony

The Ao Naga Tribal community is said to have first settled in a village named *Chungliyimti*. It is said that when Ao Nagas first settled there, the villagers did not know how to worship and offer sacrifice to the Supreme Being. However, they wanted to worship the spring well which was located near their village. Finally, the villagers decided to approach Ongangla, the diviner, to seek her advice on this matter. This was Ongangla, a woman who taught the people the manner and the ways of worshipping God. She is the mother of Ao Naga religion.[511]

The forebears of that time were said to acknowledge that Ongangla was the only person among all men and women who could communicate with the gods directly and immediately, and foretell the future; she was the messenger between gods and human beings. In a trance, she would meet her god in heaven and bring down their wishes to their relatives on earth. She communicated and made known the prayers and wishes of her community to the god *Teroktsungba* who was often named as *Soba-Tiyaba*, creator and destiner. She also approached the judge *Meyutsungba*, the only judge in heaven. Ongangla was named as prophetess, diviner and also as medicine woman. Through her gifted talents she had contributed to the whole of the Ao Naga Tribal community. Her power was said to be very great and it was beyond human comprehension.[512] The contribution of Ongangla was mentioned and described in one of the oldest Ao songs.

The song says that a pronouncement was given to all the villagers to assemble. After they had all assembled, the villagers decided to go to a woman named Ongangla to consult her about the suitability of the site for establishing a permanent village. She instructed the villagers to worship the well in the new

---

[510] This story is translated from vernacular language. Kiremwati, L. Imti Longchar et al. eds., *Nokranger Aser Nokrang* (N.p.: Waromung Yimten, 1993), 51-53.

[511] N. Limatula Longkumer, "Rediscovering Women's Role and Status in Society," in *Transforming Theology for Empowering Women: A Theological and Hermeneutical Reflection in the Context of North East India,* edited by R.L. Hnuni (ETC, Jorhat: Women's Studies, 1999), 35-37.

[512] I. Bendangangshi, I.T. Apok Aier, *The Religion of the Ao Nagas* (Bamunimaidan Guwahati: I. Bendangangshi, 1997), 154.

spring and then to establish a head-tree in the centre of the village to perform ceremonies and for placing the heads brought from war.[513]

It was indeed, a woman who with full of knowledge and wisdom, used to perform religious rituals and miracles. Her voice was heard, and her advice was meaningful for the whole villagers. Ongangla was "a woman" who was recognized and accepted and whose voice was heard and valued by the Ao Naga tribal community in the past.

3.13.4. Longkongla and Her Villagers

It is said that Longkongla, a daughter of Tongpok, was one of the greatest warriors (*nokinkettsür*) in Chungliyimti where, according to legend, the Ao Naga Tribal community was first settled. She was an extraordinarily gifted woman with numerous talents. She was said to be an *arasentzür,* a medicine lady who cared and cured many sick people. She was also well-equipped and skilled (*inyaksangshi nung tetangshi*) in various physical and social activities with many men unable to compete with her. Longkongla had a son who, like his mother, acquired many talents. He was active and handsome, and many married and unmarried ladies were attracted to him. Unfortunately, he met with a tragic end because some other men of the village began to develop jealousy and hatred towards him, and he was killed through a trap laid by the villagers while fishing.

The killing of Longkongla's son led to a blood feud between her and these villagers and led to a series of vengeful acts in the village. Finally, Longkongla was compelled to leave behind all her possessions, her talents, her home, her normal life in the village. Since she could no longer live in Chungliyimti (her village), she requested the heavenly beings to send down a thread from heaven so that she could come up. Longkongla was instructed by the heavenly beings not to look back or down while being transported to heaven but to cling on to the thread. However, misfortunate befell her when her domesticated animals screamed and began to cry. She so dearly missed them that she could no longer resist looking down. On looking down, she immediately fell down and died.[514]

The story of Longkongla seemingly shows that the Ao Naga tribal community of the past was beset with jealousy, vengeance, and even hatred towards successful women. As part of this study, the researcher asked a handful of people to share their impressions on Longkongla's story. Some did not know the detailed story about Longkongla but remembered only a part of the story. The illustrations given by various people are as follows:

---

[513] Anil Kumar Singh, *Tribal Culture and Polity* (New Delhi: Sarup & Sons, 1994), 74.

[514] This story was originally written in Ao Naga Tribal language. For a detailed study, one can refer to *Imsongunger Suiren, Imsongunger: Brief History and Genealogy*, op. cit., 76.

The older people said that "Longkongla had a vengeful heart, and so, she took revenge."[515] Longkongla is said to believe that she was a divine being and not fully human.[516] One of the youngsters knew only the selected portions of the story through which she learned that: "Longkongla, a woman killed all the children of her village when their parents had left for work to the field."[517] Another had heard of an interpretation which said that "she was an immoral woman who had illegitimate sons."[518] Another said that, "out of greediness, or lust for worldly things she looked down and she died."[519]

It is noteworthy that this kind of story-telling never seems to be challenged by the Ao society. Assuming that the telling of the story itself serves a purpose, one must question why and how such a story, whether it be true or apocryphal, came about? Why and how did the developments in the story happen? One must also ask why the main character had to die an untimely death. Who interrupted her prosperous and peaceful existence on earth? Doesn't the story speak about the jealousy and insecurity of some menfolk initially provoking her and giving rise to a blood feud? The main character in the story is a mother who possesses strength of character, was successful and blessed with bountiful talents. But, her blissful existence was shattered with the unjustifiable killing of her son, a son who would probably have gone to become as successful as she was. However, the Ao community has told and retold the story till it ultimately becomes a story about "a woman who is greedy, arrogant, immoral, and having a vengeful heart."

3.14. Words that Denigrate Women

There is folklore which adds meaning to one's life. However, there is folklore that is discriminately used resulting in denigrating people, especially women. The Folklore such as folk stories, folk songs, proverbs etc. do not always seem to provide good moral lessons for the common people. This can be witnessed through many personal encounters with family members and friends, in conversation and in interaction. The negative attitudes towards women linger on and this perpetuates in the people the feeling that women are wicked and inhuman. Even though we would like to assert that people's views and ways of life have moved on from the evils of the traditional practices, we can still see some of the traditional elements like folklore that tend to hamper the growth of the Ao Naga tribal society.

---

[515] Interview with Maongkala, Limayangla, Taochila, Aokokla, Sentilemla, Waromung village. 1 June 2013.

[516] Interview with Tekatemjen, Merangkokba, Lepdensangba, Lima, Katiba, Debua Village. 2 June 2013.

[517] Interview with Akangtula, Merensangla, Chubalemla, Yarsangla, Debua Village. 2 June 2013.

[518] Interview with Bendangsanen, Chuchuyimpang Village, 9 May 2013.

[519] Interview with Sakutemjen, Chuchuyimpang Village, 9 May 2013.

There are scholars who critique this negative attitude towards women portrayed in folklore. A. Asola Jamir mentioned:

> Their life activities are clearly projected in the various forms of folklore. Ao Naga folklore has a male dominated socio-religio, cultural and political background. Much of the folklore items flourished in the context of head hunting and wars where women were not allowed to participate. Therefore, Ao Naga folklore was developed with the notion of women's inferiority in the minds of the narrators, song composers and the like. Women are portrayed as weak, passive, inferior, sex object to men and also incapable in decision-makings ... Women as impure, quarrelsome, wicked and selfish with devilish attitude ... Such folklore items, which reflect the systematic discrimination of women, are deeply rooted in the minds of the Aos and are instilled in the societal structures providing the status and differentiation of role between women and men.[520]

The story of a *wicked stepmother*[521] tells about a woman who lacked compassion, a woman who daringly managed to banish her stepson from home. A. Asola Jamir writes: "In all the stories of stepmother the 'father figure' remains silent. It is he who brought the children to a new home where his wife was a

[520] A. Asola Jamir, "The image of women in selected Naga folklore and its impact on Naga women today," in *Communication and Naga Culture* edited by, L. Imsutoshi Jamir, C. Alitemjen Longkumer (Dimapur: Tribal Development and Communication Centre, 2007), 75.

[521] Once upon a time in a village called Rithu, lived a man who remarried after his wife's death. Unfortunately, his new wife started to dislike and mistreat his son who was from the first wife. One day the opportunity came to his wicked stepmother when their whole village had decided to move from the present village to another faraway place. All the men in the village were assigned to go to various directions for safety and security reasons while they proceeded on that day. The husband instructed his wife to go with the two children along with a group of the villagers. Before leaving the old village, she sent both the children to fetch water from the pond saying that they would need it on their journey to a new village. She decided to make a hole at the bottom of the bamboo hollow container, and gave it to her stepson, and gave another smaller bamboo container with no hole to her daughter. Then she whispered to her daughter secretly to come without waiting for her brother. As per her instruction they followed her. The half-sister filled her container and rushed back home but the boy's container was never filled as much as he tried because of the hole made by his stepmother. Sadly, as a small boy he realised very late that his container had a hole and desperately and fearfully when he returned home there was no one in the village. When the father came to know about the missing of his son Athiba from his wife, he went in search of his son to their old village; finally, he found his son roaming in the flower garden chasing butterflies. The father was so happy to see his son again and he called his son to come back to him but instead he ran farther and farther away from his father, and the son communicated to his father only through song that he was not returning to that new village with him. When the father returned home he narrated the story to his relatives about his son and the evil scheme of his wicked wife. See I. Bendangangshi, I.T. Apok Aier, *The Religion of the Ao Nagas* (Bamunimaidan Guwahati: I. Bendangangshi, 1997).

stranger to his children. In any kind of problem between his wife and his children he should be the communicator ..."[522]

The traditional folklore such as Wicked Stepmother, Kongrola and Her Slaves, and many other such related stories are being told and retold by the people even today. Unfortunately, new technological advancements have added to the spread of communicating wrong messages and perceptions about women to the audience. The stereotypical images, attitudes and stories about women portrayed through these new media are very common. A good example is that of a recently-released Nagamese video-film called "*Morom Na Thaka Amah*" (Mother Without Love),[523] whose intention was to promote traditional Naga folktales by trying to bring out moral lessons from past mistakes. What the makers of such films do not realise is that they convey a wrong message in perpetuating negative attitudes towards women.

The story about Kongrola and Her Slaves[524] is another that is told by people in the community. One can confidently say that the story is apocryphal. The Ao social and familial set-up would not give room even for the widow of a rich man to remain rich for long. Hence, in the real world, no one had ever come across or heard of any other Ao rich widow of the past.[525] Therefore, it is hard to imagine that such a thing ever existed. However, the telling and retelling of such a story must also have a purpose. This kind of story has long been used as a tool to subjugate and suppress the innocent widow by relating and reinforcing it as a 'moral lesson' to the society, saying that such is the character of a rich widow.

3.14.1. Derogatory Remarks About Women

Derogatory remarks made about Ao Naga tribal women can be seen in countless ways even today. Following are some of the common names given to women:

1. *Aningnoza* (the children of the sky).[526]

---

[522] A. Asola Jamir, "The image of women, op. cit., 83.

[523] Released on 31st January 2013, with the aim of promoting the folktales film in the society; it is also said to have encouraged people by passing the message of good culture down to the coming generations. Morung Express 2nd Feb, 2013. www.morungexpress.com/entertainment/91151.txt accessed on 10.7.13.

[524] The story says that there was a rich widow who owned many slaves; she used to mistreat the slaves by giving them very hard work. The slaves could not bear her cruelty any more, and one day they decided to run away from their mistress. They managed to escape from her, thinking never to return. Her slaves were all turned to apes, and since then apes have come into being. The slaves that turned into apes used to cry, Kongrola! Kongrola! See I. Bendangangshi, I.T. Apok Aier, *The Religion*, op. cit.

[525] Interview with Bendangsunep, Limanungla, Aotemjen and Lanusunep Molungkimong Village, 3, 4 July 2013.

[526] R.L. Hnuni, "Women in North East India: Vision For Tribes," in *Women and Society*, edited by Nirmala Jeyaraj (Madurai: Lady Doak College, 2001), 312.

2. *tetsur tanur* (women and children) which demotes women or ranks them of low status.[527]
3. *Azu chetentsur* meaning, like a female nursing dog with puppies.[528]
4. *Tepang mayip/Tsuklipang* meaning, a bird which has a pointed mouth. She is the queen of gossip, backbiting and has a loose mouth.[529]
5. *Pongla pongshiba tetsur* meaning, woman of unstable mind, not trustworthy.[530]
6. *Süngolang lep* (bundle of leaves), meaning, women are just as a bundle of leaves.

These kinds of derogatory remark gradually generate in women the development of an inferiority complex. Women themselves are socialised and accustomed to imbibe such notions and, in turn, subscribe to this already-existent mind-set which is already legitimised as a natural phenomenon.

3.14.2. Superior and Inferior Sex

In the Ao Naga tribal society women and men are termed differently. A man who failed to act as per the traditional norms and mores is looked down upon. There are certain sets of rules and roles which each female and male member in the community is expected to perform. A man in the community had to play certain roles, and likewise there are expectations of women too. For example, if a man goes against the said rules he will be branded with different names. In most of the Naga tribal society a woman, and not the husband, does all the domestic work because if he does it, he will be considered as an effeminate.[531] In the past, "men were dubbed women or cows until they had contributed to the village skull-house."[532] Imchen continued saying that: "Those who do not go to war and do not join in the regular activities are given the tittle as *laphi tesü* girlish ... looked down, but those men of social status are praised with nick names ... son of the land, horn bill, hero and male tiger etc."[533]

During the ancestral days, when headhunting game was very common and everybody valued manpower, they were kept in high esteem.

---

[527] Ibid.

[528] A. Asola Jamir, "The image of women, op. cit., 90.

[529] Ibid.

[530] Ibid.

[531] "Nagas: (Wild Tribes)" *Encyclopedia of Indian Tribes and Castes,* edited by S.M Channa, Vol. 16, (New Delhi: Cosmo Publications, 2004.): 4726.

[532] Mary Mead Clark, *A Corner in India,* op. cit., 47.

[533] Panger Imchen, *Ancient Ao Naga Religion and Culture,* 53.

Folksong sung by a father giving advice to his son goes like this:

My son, sharpen your daos and spears
For a man's duty is to hunt heads,
For if not, you will be called a coward.[534]

Song sung at the birth of a son:

Oh! The maker of the universe,
Bless me with many sons,
Let them be all strong warriors,
May they bring heads in dozens.[535]

The socio-cultural tradition encourages men to be rough, tough, strong, powerful, successful, passionate about head hunting, and not to behave like a woman. "The favour of a son in the Ao Naga community is so strong that there are also songs sung in want of sons."[536] This favouritism about sons continues even today in the community. However, for a daughters and wife the song goes like this:

Song sung to daughters:

May my daughter live a life,
Which the entire village will envy;
May she meet a wealthy man.[537]

Value of a girl:

Girls delay not to get married,
Because when your hair grows long, you will grow old,
When that cometh your life is at end.

Song sung to wife:

My wife is the most beautiful woman in the world,
She prepares the best food for me;
She washes and cleans the house;
She welcomes me with rice beer when I come from the field.[538]

---

[534] A. Asola Jamir, "The image of women, op. cit., 87.

[535] Ibid.

[536] A. Asola Jamir, "The image of women, op. cit., 87.

[537] Ibid., 88.

[538] Ibid.

These songs depict the value of a woman who is to win a man's heart and to please him. The only good fortune that she could hope for is of marrying a wealthy man.[539] A woman is also expected, encouraged and compelled to have early marriage so that she can produce more children. The song also conveys the message that a wife/woman is beautiful and praiseworthy only when she does all the household chores.

In the name of preserving generation-old traditional "cultural values," she has to follow and play a certain set of roles. Women often remember grandmothers and mothers who often say, "serve your husband well," "respect him," "shame on your part to let your husband work at home," "be obedient to him," "honour him," "bear the burden," "you are a woman, be silent," etc. All these show how traditional and cultural norms nurtured a woman's mind, heart and soul. A woman's mind is preoccupied with words like, "what to do," "how to behave," "how to live" and "how I should be." Submissiveness is regarded as the virtue of an ideal woman. Therefore, a woman who stands against the family traditions, a woman who raises her voice and shares her concerns is treated with scorn and contempt and rejected both within the family circle as well as in the society.

The concept about women in the Ao Naga tribal community was that women are considered as an inferior sex to men; therefore, they are incapable to speak in public gatherings, and are regarded as the weaker sex. Nungshitula proclaimed: "They had no inheritance, no history, no political power but were expected to serve menfolk as the superior sex. The females took the male as rulers, head of the family and defenders."[540]

3.15. Ao Women's Voice: A Forgotten Story

Ao women's involvement and participation in the family and community activities can be seen in the past as well as at present. The traditional socio-cultural, political, economic and religious structures of the Aos are still followed even today. No matter how much a woman achieves, she remains voiceless and unacknowledged in many ways. There follows a description of the lot of Ao women:

3.15.1. Silenced Voice of Ao Women

The present position of a Ao woman:

i. For women to listen, to speak and to take part in private or public meetings is prohibited even in the urban areas. In the Clan decisions and functions, women remain passive observers and submissive followers. They are left in the dark without knowing many pertinent

---

539 Ibid.

540 Nungshitula, *The Naga Images of the Human Being*, (Jorhart: Assam, Tribal Study Centre, 2001), 92.

issues around them. Rather, they have to obey the decisions made by their menfolk, by the clan member, village authorities and tribesmen.

ii. Women have been silenced in the name of protecting customary laws, and are therefore still bound under the traditional model of submission and obedience, a tactic carried out by men even in this modernised generation.

iii. A woman was debarred from performing religious rites and sacrifices though she may be the oldest person in the village; she cannot become a priest (*Patir* (M)/*Putir* (C)).

iv. A daughter has no right to inherit land; therefore, a woman is always looked upon as a stranger at home.

v. In the Ao Naga Tribal villages, if a husband dies, the condition of his widow becomes miserable in many ways. Her possessions (mostly land) are controlled by her husband's family members and relatives. She will have to obey all that they command.

vi. Women were not even spared from free selection of the nutritional food of their own. The traditional socio-cultural norms compel women to refrain from certain kind of foods items in the name of protecting their progeny from abnormalities.

vii. Derogatory remarks made about women cause them to development an inferiority complex. Women themselves are socialised and accustomed to imbibe such notions and, in turn, subscribe to this already-existent mind-set which is already legitimised as a natural phenomenon.

viii. Women were/are left with all the major works beginning from child rearing and attending to the household chores with additional burdens such as physical labour in the field, fetching water, collecting firewood; these were all accepted norms which were considered as the duty of a woman. Her contributions for the Ao nation as mother, wife, and sister and as daughter were ignored but rather controlled.

ix. We can see the myth of a successful woman, told and retold by the community till it ultimately becomes a story about "a woman who is greedy, arrogant, immoral, and a vengeful heart."

x. In the Church, too, women are discriminated against, since deacons are almost always male. It is therefore, very similar to that of the function of the village council (*Putu Menden*) that continues in the Ao Naga tribal society today.

3.15.2. The Forgotten Histories of Successful Women

The story revealed to us that it was indeed a woman who with full of knowledge and wisdom performed religious rituals and miracles in the past. Her voice was heard and her advice was meaningful for all the villagers, but these memories are all erased and forgotten by the Aos.

As we have noted before, the traditional customs and practices of the Ao Naga tribal community acknowledge that in a religious festival and ceremony like Mithun sacrifice, the female voice was heard, acknowledged and appreciated by the Ao community. Equal sharing of responsibility and participation which was all inclusive, that is, involving participation of both female and male, was quite visible in this respect.

However, the contribution made by the female was unacknowledged in her family, clan, and village and by the entire Ao Naga tribal community, and any trace or sign of her existence was erased. Her physical strength, her voice, her creativity, her feelings and emotions were all set aside and unnoticed.

The story tells of the wisdom of a woman who through her intellect and acumen helped her achieve victory over enemies. Women even risked their lives for the common good as we hear in the narrative story. One can understand that Ao Naga tribal women in the past had played the major role in their "community formation."

Ao Naga tribal women are enormous contributors when it comes to the economic sustainability as well. The woman is also the bread winner at home who toiled from morning till dusk for the life sustenance of her family. She not only contributes to the life of her family but she extends beyond her home and contributes to the life of her community too.

3.16. Reclaiming "Voice" Rights

We might well question tribes like the Aos who claim 100% uncritical Christian acceptance and at the same give more importance to moral system of *Sobaliba* than to Jesus Christ.

The belief system of democracy by Aos must be questioned today. Democracy is supposed to be egalitarian and emancipatory, ensuring suffrage, freedom, justice, liberation, and so on. However, all these elements are missing in the traditional Ao Naga tribal administrative system.

The question for us now is how to recover the long-forgotten voice of Ao women. How do we devise and erect a common platform for voice? Fundamentally voice is not merely an utterance by the mouth alone but is attached with multiple layers of meaning. One's own voice is vivacious, and nobody can break down its distinctiveness attached to a person.

How do we make women's voice relevant and authentic in the decision-making bodies? Tony Dundon rightly says: "Voice is about having opinions and observations heard. How voice is realised, recognised and acted upon is what matters. There is no 'real' voice if it is not listened to."[541] How can communities be made more inclusive, and women and their voices incorporated as collective

---

[541] Tony Dundon, *The Management of Voice in Non-Union Organisations: Managers' Perspectives*. 21. http://www98.griffith.edu.au/dspace/bitstream/handle/10072/16840/34192_1.pdf;jsessionid=3026F2041F678121E6075450A99B22E2?sequence=1 accessed on 4.4.2015.

participants and an essential part of the central core instead of being treated in isolation? It is asserted that "... collective voice achieves what the lone voice could never do: it humanises and civilises the workplace."[542] How do we correct the exclusivist nature of weaker/stronger attitudes between women and men? How could we see women's voices as valuable depositories of knowledge? It is in this situation that this study strives to advocate a better alternative, that is an urgent need for the rights of women in the decision-making bodies, and to ensure that women also have their say.

Reclaiming Voice's Rights in relation to various natures that form part and parcel of a woman's life experiences. The strength of a woman itself is her voice. Her voice is the energy which she possesses and contributes towards the development of family and society. Her physical strength that contributes towards economic life, at home as well as in society is considered as part of her voice. Therefore, it is ethically and theologically right to recognise her voice in various practices, whether in physical, mental, emotional, or spiritual spheres, which is counted as the greatest gift of God.

Women's voice is considered vital and powerful in every aspect. Now is an appropriate time to reconstruct and remodel past history by dismantling the discriminatory frame of mind that overlooked women and their voice for centuries in the Ao Naga tribal community. It is our right and our ardent sense of duty to allow women's voices the right to mould their confidence and to make them feel a sense of belonging in their everyday life and existence within and outside the community.

It is in this condition that the study uses the sharing-caring metaphors as an accepted norm to link with what was missing for centuries. Hence, we ask, can we not apply the traditional ethos such as the reciprocal interaction of female-male communication in decision-making as well? By nature, the Ao Naga tribal community in the past as well as the present does value the role played by both females and males in many instances: mutual understanding and sharing of responsibilities are being carried out among female and male members in the community. But, the real challenge is to consider whether we can relate and incorporate such values in the decision-making bodies as well.

We must consider the optimistic motive of women's voice that resonates with contemporary discussions about effectiveness as well as democracy. The submissiveness and stigmatization attached to a woman – restriction, control, adverse comment, and domination – none of these have significance any longer in this contemporary society. In place of those mentioned above, the collective voice needs to be legalised. Voice is diverse and transparent, and this needs to be established and strengthened.

Reclaiming Voice's Rights questions preconceived notions about women's voice that seeks to perpetuate predetermined conclusions. All value judgments

[542] Ibid., 28.

about a woman that do not take her potentialities into consideration, but continue seeing and conceptualising her as irrational, inconsistent, inferior, and the weaker sex, must be challenged and ultimately rejected and revoked. Women in Ao Naga tribal community are not aware of how much information is disseminated in the council. The practice of dismissing women's voice without any deliberation in all the communication processes is to be questioned.

A call for attention must be made and a platform be instituted to legitimise voice for women as well as men. The optimistic voice is to be encouraged which will boost opinions, dynamic and constructive. Authentic voice will be reckoned when the collective (female and male) participation is enhanced. This study advocates the implementation of inclusive policy, theory and practice of voice in decision-making bodies. The agenda of common human rights grounded on diversity, equality of opportunity and practical justice is needed today.

In order to progress, to be a part of God's people in the reign of God, a community must seek the common ground where it can find mutual sharing, participation and understanding. Some of the communitarian ethos which was equally shared in the Ao Naga tribal community must be reinstituted. The word *aruk*, meaning 'for all,' 'togetherness,' can also be interpreted as 'common'. *Aruk ola* ('collective voice') is to be instituted in the decision-making bodies. *Aruk meyung* in the Ao Naga tribal language meaning 'belongs to everyone.' It does not talk in terms of individuality but in terms of collectivism.

Reclaiming Voice's Rights reinvent some of the exemplary practices of Aos in the community. These practices include the participation of the Zünga age-group (both female and male) in the work place (farm) and in other social activities, participation in festivities, etc., the interaction between Tsükir and Arijumen/Arijusanger (group interaction among females-males), and so on. These practices must be brought into in the decision-making bodies too. A common platform must be created, for sharing, exchanging, valuing, accepting and celebrating life together. A "voice" that must be spoken, heard **by, for** and **with** all should be encouraged.

This chapter has highlighted the influence of voice in the past and present Ao Naga tribal community, focussing on the socio-cultural, religious, political and economic spheres. It has sought to generate and conceptualise the voice which was not realised earlier. It has conveyed that there are many gender-based interactional elements waiting to be excavated and implemented for meaningful communication in the decision-making bodies. The fourth chapter will move further in investigating women's voice in the Ao Naga tribal community.

Chapter 4

Ao Women's Voice: Field Study Analysis

Introduction

This chapter deals with an introduction of various methods which the researcher employed to gather and analyse findings of the field research. These methods are employed as guiding principles in this research so as to make it meaningful. In the first part of this chapter, we will see the importance of the use of ethnography, qualitative, quantitative, textual analysis, etc. For instance, how the use of ethnographical tools helped the research, how these tools made it possible to observe people's attitudes, behaviour, etc., and how with the help of quantitative tools the study was able to collect data within a large area etc. The second part of this chapter will deal with the field research, analysis, evaluation and application.

Steps were taken to observe carefully how people talk, how they answer back, and the manner in which they behave while talking. Through this, it was observed how people perceive women and women's voice in the decision-making bodies in the Ao Naga tribal community. The study also involved meeting several people, female and male, young and old and from different backgrounds and places, individually and collectively among the Ao Naga tribal community. In order to carry out the study meaningfully, it applies two main methods – ethnography and quantitative method.

4.1. Research Sample

In order to acquire a more profound understanding of how the Ao Naga tribal community considers women's role and her voice particularly in the decision-making bodies, the researcher applied different types of methods in the field research. One was ethnography, which includes an empirical and theoretical approach. In this connection, both quantitative and qualitative research methods were employed. The qualitative research method included personal interviews and focus group discussions. Questionnaires were distributed in applying the quantitative research method.

4.2. Methods Used in the Research

4.2.1. Ethnography

One of the methods of study employed by the researcher in the research is ethnography. As Hammersley and Atkinson mentioned, "ethnographer participates in people's lives for an extended period of time, watching what happens, listening to what is said, asking questions."[543] It includes verbal and non-verbal, "taken-for-granted assumptions that operate within cultural life."[544] In connection with that, Berger endorses some of the points made by Garfinkel on ethnomethodology: "[t]he ethnomethodologist's concern with people's understanding of things which suggests that ethnomethodologists do not offer their interpretations of the meanings of people's activities but search for the way *they* make sense of things and find meaning in things – especially conversations people have and things people do."[545] Its focus is on people's "common-sense" knowledge of society.[546]

Ethnography involves the qualitative exploration of values and meanings in the context of a "whole way of life." The researcher penetrates deep inside the socio-cultural and religious practices of the people and tries to observe how those practices affect the society, especially women and their status, and their voice in the decision-making bodies. Qualitative research in ethnography study explores questions about cultures, identities and life-worlds. Ethnography becomes a code-word in the media-oriented cultural studies, too; it requires qualitative methods such as **participant observation**, **in-depth interviews** and **focus groups.**[547] Although, the use of ethnography in research methods faces criticism, it has its own epistemology and that is applied in this research.

---

[543] Ethnography comes from anthropology which includes an empirical and theoretical approach. It involves field work, detailed holistic description and analysis of cultures. See, M. Hammersley and Atkinson, P, *Ethnography: Principles and Practice* (London: Tavistock Books, 1983), 2.

[544] Chris Barker, *Cultural Studies: Theory and Practice,* third edition, (Los Angeles, London, New Delhi, Singapore: Sage Publications, 2008), 32.

[545] Arthur Asa Berger, *Media and Communication Research Methods: An Introduction to Qualitative and Quantitative Approaches,* second edition (Los Angeles, London, New Delhi, Singapore, Washington DC: Sage Publications, 2011), 174.

[546] Ibid.

[547] "According to Kitzinger, "focus groups are group discussions organised to explore a people's views and experiences on a specific set of issues." M. Peter Singh, *Cyber theology* (Delhi: ISPCK, 2009), 162. See also, Chris Barker, op. cit., 32.

4.2.2. Qualitative Research Methods

The second method that the researcher has employed in the study is the qualitative method. Qualitative research normally results from the intensive analysis of a single case, or perhaps a few cases. For instance, the intimate knowledge gained of individual families, subcultures, organisations, communities, or individuals is written up in a way that discloses the author's insights.[548] Qualitative research methods are distinguished from quantitative methods because quantitative methods rest their evidence on the logic of mathematics, the principle of numbers, or the methods of statistical analysis. In qualitative methods, according to Lindlof, "actual talk, gesture, and other social action are the raw materials of analysis." The qualitative method is based mostly on interview data. It has a great deal in common with both ethnography and naturalistic inquiry and has a broader concept.[549] Qualitative research converges on issues of how humans articulate and interpret their social interests. It also includes several approaches such as case study, action research, collaborative research, phenomenological research, field study, and interpretive interactionism, among many others.[550]

In this qualitative method, the researcher carefully chooses to apply various kinds of interview in the study. These interviews are *Informal Interviews, Unstructured Interviews, Structured Interviews and Semistructured Interviews* in order to make the research more complete.[551] *Participant observation* is another qualitative research method that is also used in the study. It is a qualitative research technique that provides the opportunity to study people in real-life situations.[552]

---

[548] This analysis is called idiographic. In qualitative research one does generalise, but not in a way that tries to attain the scope of a universal law. See, Sven Windahl, Benno Signitzer, et.al., *Using Communication Theory: An Introduction to Planned Communication,* second edition, op. cit., 57.

[549] Meyer T. P., Anderson J.A., *Mediated Communication: A Social Action Perspective* (Newbury Park, CA: Sage Publications, 1988), 247. Qualitative research converges on issues of how humans articulate and interpret their social interests. It also includes several approaches such as case study, action research, collaborative research, phenomenological research, field study, and interpretive interactionism, among many others.

[550] Thomas R. Lindlof, *Qualitative Communication Research Methods,* op. cit., 21.

[551] There are four kinds of research interview. *Informal Interviews, Unstructured Interviews, Semistructured Interviews* (normally the interviewer has a written list of questions to ask the informant but tries, to the extent possible, to maintain the casual quality found in unstructured interviews. Focus groups are considered to be semistructured interviews. Focus groups are usually between 6 and 12 individuals, led by moderator, designed to obtain information about some topic. They are free-form discussions by a group of people) and *Structured Interviews,* where the researcher uses an interview schedule – a specific set of instructions that guide those who ask respondents for answers to questions. Questionnaires that are self-administered are also classified as structured interviews. See, Arthur Asa Berger, *Media and Communication Research Methods: An Introduction to Qualitative and Quantitative Approaches,* op. cit., 136-137.

[552] It is a form of "field research" which includes observations that are carried out in real settings and where there is a lack of the kind of control and structure you have in experiments. In this, researchers have to balance two roles, that is that of being participants and that of being

i. Personal Interviews

One of the methods employed by the researcher in this study is the qualitative research method in which personal interview was chosen as one of the research methods. In the qualitative research the researcher used *informal* and *unstructured* interviews. *Informal Interviews* are not organised or focused, and are generally used to introduce researchers to those being studied. Informal interviews are, in essence, conversations that serve the purpose of helping the researcher gain the confidence of his or her informant. The researcher also engaged in *Unstructured Interviews*. In this the researcher is focused and trying to gain information, but he or she exercises relatively little control over the responses of the informant.[553]

Here, the researcher asked questions and tried to catch the tenets of people's understanding on women's voice by meeting various individuals (both women and men) who are involved in various organisations in different settings. The researcher also met people of different age groups, regions, family (single, married, widow), professions (farmers, lay people, educated, employed, church leaders and pastors) in order to connect and recognise the respondents' views. A total number of fifty interviewees were contacted for the study.

There are two very important motives for choosing personal interviews in this research. Firstly, this method was chosen to get to know the detailed life situation of the present day Ao Naga tribal community in relation to women's voice in the decision-making bodies. Secondly, it was chosen in order to know how the mythical stories and histories of Aos are handed down and carried forward especially in relation to Ao Naga tribal women.

In employing the qualitative research method through personal interviews, the researcher conducted in-depth interviews with fifty persons. The researcher carefully selected the interviewees, and made enquiries from them with well-planned questions. As much as possible, the researcher attempted to include ordinary/common people both female and male members in equal numbers. The interviewees in the personal interviews were selected from elderly people who acquired a lot of knowledge about Ao myths, stories and histories, and who also had gone through many personal experiences as they passed through life.

ii. Focus Groups

Under the qualitative research methods, the researcher conducted four focus groups with well-planned questions. These focus groups were conducted among female and male members, and in rural and urban centres respectively.

---

observers. And researchers have to avoid "going native," that means becoming so identified with the group that they lose their objectivity.

See, Arthur Asa Berger, *Media and Communication Research Methods: An Introduction to Qualitative and Quantitative Approaches*, op. cit., 189-190.

[553] Ibid.

Before going into a detailed study, we would like to discuss the nature and function of focus groups in the study. We find many definitions of focus groups in the literature. However, features like organised discussion (Kitzinger 1994), collective activity (Powell et al. 1996), social events (Goss & Leinbach 1996) and interaction (Kitzinger 1995) had been identified as the contributions that focus groups make to social research which will be used in the study.[554] Focus group means a small-group that is guided by a trained leader in the discussion which used to learn more about opinions on a chosen topic, and then to guide future action.[555] A clear definition of the focus group has been given by Powell and Morgan:

- A group of individuals selected and assembled by researchers to discuss and comment on, from personal experience, the topic that is the subject of the research.
- Focus groups are a form of group interviewing but it is important to distinguish between the two. Group interviewing involves interviewing a number of people at the same time, the emphasis being on questions and responses between the researcher and participants. Focus groups however rely on interaction within the group based on topics that are supplied by the researcher.[556]

In a focus group discussion, the group's arrangement and the dialogue should be carefully planned to create a non-threatening environment, so that participants feel free to talk openly and give honest opinions.[557] Following are some points mentioned about the nature in which focus groups have functioned and are considered as important in the study:

- Focus group involves organised discussion with a selected group of individuals to gain information about their views and experiences of a topic.
- Focus group interviewing is particularly suited for obtaining several perspectives about the same topic.
- The benefits of focus group research include gaining insights into people's shared understandings of everyday life and the ways in which individuals are influenced by others in a group situation. [558]

---

[554] Anita Gibbs, "Focus Groups," in Social Research Update, http://sru.soc.surrey.ac.uk/SRU19.html accessed on (27.5.2015), 1.

[555] "Conducting Focus Groups," http://ctb.ku.edu/en/tableofcontents/assessment/assessing communityneedsandresources/conductfocusgroups/main accessed on (27.5.15).

[556] Anita Gibbs, "Focus Groups," in Social Research Update, op. cit., 1-2.

[557] "Conducting Focus Groups,"

[558] Anita Gibbs, "Focus Groups," in Social Research Update, op. cit., 1-2.

Morgan and Kreuger have given an explanation why focus groups are useful in social research:

> The main purpose of focus group research is to draw upon respondents' attitudes, feelings, beliefs, experiences and reactions in a way in which would not be realistic using other methods, for example observation, one to one interviewing, or questionnaire surveys. These attitudes, feelings and beliefs may be partially independent of a group or its social setting, but are more likely to be revealed via the social gathering and the interaction which being in a focus group entails. Compared to individual interviews, which aim to obtain individual attitudes, beliefs and feelings, focus groups elicit a multiplicity of views and emotional processes within a group context. The individual interview is easier for the researcher to control than a focus group in which participants may take the initiative. Compared to observation, a focus group enables the researcher to gain a larger amount of information in a shorter period of time. Observational methods tend to depend on waiting for things to happen, whereas the researcher follows an interview guide in a focus group. In this sense focus groups are not natural but organised events. Focus groups are particularly useful when there are power differences between the participants and decision makers or professionals, when the everyday use of language and culture of particular groups is of interest, and when one wants to explore the degree of consensus on a given topic.[559]

In the focus group discussion, the role of the moderator becomes essential and crucial too. She/he may be called as group facilitator especially in terms of providing clear explanations of the purpose of the group, helping the participants feel at ease and enabling interaction between the group members. The moderator in the meeting will need to promote debate, possibly by asking open questions. The moderator may also need to stir the participants, mainly to draw out people's differences, and tease out a diverse range of meanings on the topic under discussion. Sometimes moderators will need to probe for details, or move things forward when the conversation is drifting. Moderators also have to ensure that everyone participates and gets a chance to speak. At the same time a moderator is encouraged not to show too much approval, must avoid giving personal opinions, so as to avoid favouring particular participants. Moderators need to possess good interpersonal skills and personal qualities, being good listeners, non-judgmental and adaptable.[560]

---

[559] Anita Gibbs, "Focus Groups," in Social Research Update, op. cit., 1-2.

[560] Ibid.

The researcher conducted four focus groups for the present study. The manner in which the focus group was conducted was of two types. One type of focus group conducted consisted of female members and another group consisted of male members with both being dealt with separately. The participants were selected from different age groups with multiple backgrounds and provisions from the rural and urban areas. Each group consisted of eight to fifteen members. The participants in the rural areas included farmers, school teachers, church leaders, widows, students, elders/deacons, and lay people. Senior citizens, members of the village council, and educated members holding high posts in government offices were also included.

The researcher established some important questions in the focus group discussion. The same questions were asked in both groups, that is, among the female and male participants.

1. Do you think Customary Law can be revised and allow women to participate in the decision-making bodies?
2. Do you still believe in the traditional functioning of decision-making bodies that do not allow women?
3. Are you willing to change the systems and allow accommodating women in the decision-making bodies?
4. Are you satisfied with the present society that is functioning without a woman's voice?
5. Do you know the meaning of democracy?
6. Do you consider voice as an important means of communication in one's life?
7. Do you still believe that women and men must not mix together when it comes to the decision-making bodies?
8. Today in the government administrative offices women and men carry equal responsibilities; how do you view this?
9. Do you think that the Church also must play a role for transforming society especially when we talk about women's voice in the decision-making bodies?

The above questions were asked and discussed in the focus group discussions. Both the rural and urban participants were actively involved in the discussions. The opinions shared and the understandings they acquired were collective and common although female and male members frequently differed in most cases. It was observed from the statements made by both the rural and urban female participants that they had the same pattern of understanding in the views they expressed. In the mixed group (both female and male) discussion, the participants at various points agreed with each other, but there were contradicting views between female and male members at certain times.

The focus groups were formed of eight to fifteen participants in a group along with the moderator. The researcher herself was the moderator who moderated the discussion. The moderator opened the discussion and interaction among the group members. The questions were monitored by the moderator one at a time, followed by the subsequent question. Although, the moderator led the group, all the participants in the focus group could freely express their opinions and exchanged their feelings with one another. The researcher played the role of moderator hinting some questions for discussion and opinion while involved in listening and observing to the interaction and discussion in the meantime. The researcher carefully observed the participants' body language and facial expressions in gauging how they agreed or disagreed with the set questions.

When the focus group interacted, and discussed the topic given, the majority of the female members agreed with the topic of the questions discussed. The general comments made by female members in focus group discussions[561] are as follows:

- The participants believed that customary Law can be revised, they strongly believed that such system which hinders women's voice do not relate in the present context anymore.
- Denying women in the decision-making bodies/process is a major setback in the march towards a progressive, egalitarian society.
- Failure in decision-making bodies is due to the lack of responsibility and rationality on the part of men making coercive decisions without proper understanding.
- With the passage of time and change of attitudes, Ao society must also change. Decision-making processes must be followed by both women and men according to their wisdom and knowledge, talent and understanding if they want to go forward in life.
- Since only male members attend the meetings and make decisions, the voices and concerns of the majority of community members, namely that of children and women especially widows, go unheard. Moreover, the issues discussed and decisions made were often not adequately communicated to all.

In the interaction, some of the female members expressed their dissatisfaction with women who are not open and feel themselves inferior to men. They say that:

[561] The majority of the women participants in the focus group discussions were in the age group of 46 above followed by age group 36-45, 26-35 and a very few in the age group 15-25. The names of the female participants are Ajungla Lily, Sungjemla, Tajenla, Alula, Achala, yajenla, Narola, Asenla, and Ajunla. Mokokchung Town, interview, 27 January, 2013.

- On the part of women whenever opportunity comes they often feel reluctant and hesitant to come forward; this attitude must be changed and they must be emboldened enough to overcome it.
- In order to bring the issue of gender discrimination to light and to raise awareness among the common people, there is a need to provide proper education and direction.
- It is to recognise the value of wholeness of humankind, not just a woman or a man but by recognising both female and male as God's unique creation so as to fulfil God's purpose.
- On the part of the women, they must act upon their willingness to breach the restrictions of the patriarchal socio-cultural systems.

One woman in the discussion expressed that women must not interfere with men in certain matters. She said that it would not be prudent to attend and participate in all the decision-making bodies as there are some sensitive matters which should be avoided by women. But, the rest of the participants in the discussion did not agree with her statements. They expressed that:

- If half of the population in a community is voiceless, that community is seriously sick. No matter how educated or healthy we think we (the Aos) are, we are still very sick and unrefined.
- Hoping and longing to see changes among our community for women's voice in the decision-making bodies.
- We want to participate and take part in all the decision-making bodies but are hampered by our tradition and culture. To my knowledge it will not change now.
- We Ao women are highly educated and have all the potentialities to thrive under every challenging circumstance. In spite of all these, we have a general weakness, lack of co-operation and low self-esteem to voice out in public. It is high time for us to take the matter into consideration.

When the question about the role of the Church for transforming society, such as enabling women's voice in the decision-making bodies, was brought up the majority of the female participants said that:

- To bring changes in the society, the issues should be first conveyed and discussed in the Church since the Church becomes the model for the Ao Naga tribal community.
- If instead of men alone but also women are allowed to attend and participate in the decision-making bodies, it will be immensely beneficial for all.

- In the name of tradition and culture, women are denied rights to participation in most of the decision-making bodies, including church bodies.
- Women's organisations, either church or state women's group, must initiate and co-ordinate efforts for women to stand up confidently for their rights.
- Generally, women by nature can come up with more innovative ideas than men who are normally very simple and random. Therefore, if both contribute together in the decision-making, it will bring better results.
- Some of the ancient socio-cultural traditions which were relevant in the past have become irrelevant today. Earlier, the word of an older man was highly regarded and valued, and a younger man's word was not valued much in the decision-making bodies. Today those cultural practices are still perpetuated in the community. The suggestions brought by younger men are not recognized even today.

4.3. Appraisal of the Above Statements

The above comments made by female respondents confirm that gender imbalance in the decision-making bodies brings undesirable results in development. Inclusion of both genders in the decision-making bodies will yield good results in the society. It has been pointed out how women are devalued by being considered in more or less the same category as children. On the other hand, some of the women felt that there are exceptional cases in the decision-making bodies in which women must not interfere and which must be dealt with by men only. Other women shared their view that the creativity and innovativeness of women are being ignored. It was also mentioned that the negative impact of the age-old traditional, social and cultural mind-set and practices continues to be imbibed not only through socio-political institutions but also through the Church. It was also mentioned that a community is considered as sick and unrefined if women's voices are not being heard in the decision-making bodies. It is suggested that in line with the passage of time and change of attitudes, systems need to be changed. This will ensure equal participation of and mutual respect for both women and men in all walks of life.

However, there are others who also observed that though women are educated and capable, due to their lack of co-operation and low self-esteem they are not yet able to stand up firmly for their rights. Women's organisations in the Church as well as in the State bodies require self-confidence and co-ordination. It was also suggested that the Church's involvement becomes a necessity to sensitize the people towards gender justice and bring changes since the Church provides the archetype on whose lines the Ao Naga tribal community is built.

In the study, the researcher noticed a great disparity between female and male participants. The female members in the discussion expressed their shared opinion and anticipation towards reform of traditional socio-cultural structures. However, the majority of the male participants in the focus group discussions expressed negative comments when asked about reform. These negative comments were mostly expressed by the older group, whereas younger groups felt that both male and female members must participate equally in the decision-making bodies.

Among the male participants in the focus group discussion, the comments made by the older member participants[562] are markedly different from those made by the younger ones. When comparing the rural and urban participants in the discussion, the researcher noticed that the understandings were much the same apart from one or two in a group who differed. The comments made by the older groups in the discussion expressed that:

- It is normal that women do not have voice in the state decision-making bodies; they have voice in the church matters.
- The strength of women and men cannot be compared as equal, for example, women will never be able to play football like men.
- In all the decisions men take, women accept and follow accordingly without any objection. Therefore, I believe that what we are should be continued as it is.
- Women do not have any rights and have no value in themselves; this tradition has been followed since time immemorial. The Ao Naga tribal community is aware of democracy and has continued to practise it even now.
- Woman was created from the rib of a man. She is weaker than man. Due to modern advancement women should also be given some of the rights in the community but not equal voting rights with men.
- It is good that both women and men take part in the church concerns; but women must not interfere in the state affairs among the Ao Naga tribal community.
- The traditional socio-cultural systems of functioning by Aos, specially the decision-making bodies, will remain the same and will not change instantly. Church and State's functioning are different, but they go hand in hand with mutual co-operation and understanding by respecting one other.
- By nature, women are flowers and men are swords; there are big differences between these two. Flower fades away but sword has won many battles in the past and will continue to do so. God did not give

[562] These are some of the common comments made by the male respondents in the focus group. There were equal number in the age groups of 46 above, 36-45, 26-35 who had commented along with a very few members of the age group 15-25.

talent to women like men neither in the past nor in the present, nor would he in the future.

- Though it is a blessing to have wise women around, they are not gifted for administration. Women are created by God as helper for men. Just like hens never crow, till the end of time it will remain the same.

In the group discussion, the researcher noticed some of the pastors' attitudes towards change. In two different focus group discussions, two pastors were obstinate against social change and rather reaffirmed the present situation by saying that:

- If women and men are capable, it is good to sit together and make decisions. But, since culture has brought us up and taught us in the way that is practised, I think it will not be possible to change the system immediately.
- There are times when women and men come together, so also there are times when they meet separately. Therefore, we should not change the system and it should remain as it is now.
- Our culture and tradition do not permit letting women to come and attend and to participate in the decision-making bodies; therefore, it will take time to change.
- It is impossible to change the age old traditional practices which are considered valuable.

The younger male members were very positive about changing the old traditional structures and concerned about women's participation in the decision-making bodies. The comments made by them are such as:

- In our Ao country up until now people are still not willing to listen to women's concerns and refused to understand the condition of women's issues. Unless and until people recognize and change this attitude towards women, the Ao Naga tribal community will never go forward. Therefore, it is very important to educate the common people.
- While I feel that women can play a good role in every field, women themselves do not come forward to participate actively. They alienate themselves and stay behind. They should also take initiatives to break the stereotype.
- In our village, as far as I know, we have not discussed women's concerns deeply in any of the gatherings. It will be helpful and people will be more aware if we convey the message to the common people.
- In my opinion, the composition and functioning of decision-making bodies is very primitive. They do not function according to the rule of law which, in my opinion, is quite necessary. Though decisions made are meant for the welfare of all, I have learnt through experience that

> it is mostly at the direction of a single influential leader and sometimes can be very narrow. Also, because there is no code to ensure that differing voices are heard, some effective voices go unheard.

There were younger respondents in the focus group discussions who were open and felt that women's voice is essential in the decision-making bodies. They said that due to the lack of social awareness with regard to the issues (women's voice), common people do not consider it very seriously. It was also said that women themselves do not come forward and challenge the traditional socio-cultural structures, thereby hampering their voice.

The majority of the male respondents considered having and hearing women's voice in the decision-making bodies highly undesirable. They are aware that there is no women's participation in the socio-cultural structure and that women's voice goes unheard in the decision-making bodies. However, they felt that the age old traditional practices are valuable and that the structures and systems must not be changed. They felt that God created men and not women to rule and that women's role is to take care of the family and not to be an administrator. They understood that the main reason for women not given prospects in the decision-making bodies is based on culture which cannot be broken down instantly.

4.4. Quantitative Research Methods

The researcher in this study uses quantitative research methods as well. This was required because with a large area of research among the Ao Naga tribal community to cover, the researcher felt that one would be able to collect sufficient target audience for the study through questionnaires. According to Marianne Dainton and Elaine D. Zelley, quantitative methods rely on numbers or statistics as the source of data which are generally explanatory and comprehensive in nature; they seek to predict what will happen for large groups of people. To accomplish this, researchers control the study by identifying the variables of interest before data collection takes place and trying to prevent extraneous influences from affecting the data. These commitments allow social scientists to make generalizations.[563]

---

[563] Dainton and Zelley also contend that social scientists are also more inclined to use quantitative surveys or textual analyses. For example, they will collect data about how many people prefer a new formulation of a product versus a previous formulation of a product, or how frequently a manager uses a particular communication strategy in interaction. In the meantime, humanists tend to use qualitative surveys and textual analyses. They ask participants to respond at length to questions in their own words about a particular product or they identify various communication themes evident in a corporate brochure.

Both academic traditions point out that communication is social scientific as well as humanistic. Therefore, we should not regard these distinctions as dichotomies, but as continua. It is said that individual theories may be more or less social scientific or humanistic (not either-or), with elements borrowed from both traditions. See Marianne Dainton, Elaine D. Zelley, *Applying*

Under quantitative research methods, Berger listed various kinds of methods such as content analysis, surveys, experiments, and a primer on descriptive statistics.

i. Surveys

Survey research normally seeks to provide empirical data collected from a population of respondents on a whole number of topics or issues. Sometimes, the data is used to lend support to, or to negate, hypotheses or propositions, but at other times it can simply provide basic information on existing or changing patterns of behaviour.[564] Surveys can be used to collect data about current attitudes and opinions as well. They are not simply restricted to the collection of information about things, and this makes them a useful method to finding out about individual opinions, attitudes, behaviour and so on towards a whole range of topics and issues.[565] The questionnaire is the basic tool in this research. Here, identical or very similar questions can be asked of a large number of people. A questionnaire can be used in a face-to face situation either in the home or in some public space.[566] There are *descriptive* surveys and *analytic (or explanatory)* surveys in the study[567] along with *Experiments*[568] and *descriptive statistics.*[569]

Communication Theory for Professional Life: A Practical Introduction (Thousand Oaks, London, New Delhi: Sage Publications, 2005), 17-18.

[564] Anders Hansen, Simon Cottle, et al., *Mass Communication Research Methods* (London: Macmillan Press, 2006), 225.

[565] Ibid.

[566] There are different types of questionnaire that can be used. There are those that seek out factual information and then others that seek out opinions or attitudes. Hence, different types of questions may be needed: closed questions for the factual data and open-ended questions for those instances when the respondents' opinions are sought at length. See, Anders Hansen, Simon Cottle, op. cit., 226.

[567] In short, descriptive surveys describe the population being studied. These surveys seek to obtain information about demographic factors such as age, gender, marital status, occupation, race or ethnicity, income and religion, and to relate this information to opinions, beliefs, values, and behaviour of some groups of people. For instance, broadcasters use surveys to find out how popular their programmes are, and manufacturers use surveys to determine who uses their products.

Analytical surveys seek to find out why people behave the way they do. Researchers often use data from descriptive surveys to develop hypotheses and use analytical surveys to test their hypotheses about what causes certain kinds of behaviour. Analytical surveys attempt to determine whether there are causal relationships between certain kinds of behaviour and various social and demographic characteristics of people. See, Arthur Asa Berger, *Media and Communication,* op. cit., 222–223.

[568] An experiment is said to be a procedure or kind of test that demonstrates that something is true, examines the validity of a hypothesis or theory, or attempts to discover new information. See, Arthur Asa Berger, *Media and Communication,* op. cit., 222–223.

[569] Statisticians differentiate between four different kinds of data, depending on the various levels of measurement used. There are also two kinds of statistics: descriptive and inferential. Descriptive statistics refer to methods that we use to obtain, from raw data, information that characterizes or summarizes the whole set of data. Inferential statistics allow us to generalize from

ii. Questionnaire

The study also made use of the quantitative research method. The purpose of applying a questionnaire in this study was to obtain information from large areas of the Ao region. In order to cover all the areas/ranges of Ao country, three-hundred questionnaires were distributed. The way the questionnaires were disseminated was such that two villages were selected from each range (each area/range consists of at least nine to twelve villages, and altogether there are six ranges). Along with the rural set ups, three urban areas were chosen, namely, Mokokchung, Kohima and Dimapur. Some selected individuals from the cities were also included.

The respondents were carefully selected from different sections of society (young, middle and older groups, farmers, government employees, students, educated lay people, church leaders, rich and poor people) with the aim of getting the information accurately. Equal numbers of female and male respondents were represented. We shall see in the following section how the field research was executed and the result it produced.

The present study makes an attempt at applying the aforementioned methods and methodology in a variety of ways. This is done in order to help foster a multi-disciplinary approach towards the chosen area of research and with the expectation that it would help in undertaking a thorough examination and analysis of the research topic. The next section will present to us the findings, analysis, suggestions and implications.

4.5. Presentation of the Field Research

1. Age-wise and Gender-wise Classification

The respondents were classified into four groups according to their age groups. Both female and male members were represented in all the classified age groups. The total number of female respondents was 129, and the total number of male respondents was 171. Among the respondents, the age group of '46 and above' outnumber the other age groups, followed by age group of 26-35 and 36-45.

2. Classification of Profession by Gender

The respondents were chosen from various professions. These included farmers, government employees, students, church leaders/Deacons[570] (including both full time and part time workers), Pastors,[571] Associate Pastors (women), and others.

the data collected to the general populations they were taken from. See, Arthur Asa Berger, *Media and Communication,* op. cit., 259–261.

[570] 'Church leaders/Deacons' in Ao Naga Baptist churches are predominantly male. Women normally hold leadership roles among women's group in the 'Women's Fellowship'. Some theologically trained women hold the post of Child Directors, Youth Directors and Associate Pastor Women (Associate Pastor Women are pastors only in women's fellowships).

[571] In the whole of the Ao Naga tribal community, Pastors are males; however, there are altogether five women pastors so far who have served and who are still in office. These are

This will enable us to see how all these varied occupational groups of respondents contribute towards the formation of the Ao Naga tribal community today.

3. Organisation by Gender

Here we bring out the important organisations of the Ao Naga tribal community. The respondents include both females and males. Organisations like *Ao Senden* and Village Council are composed of male members only; similarly, the organisation *Watsü Mungdang* is made up of female members only. *Ao Baptist Arogo Mungdang* (ABAM) and *Ao Baptist Tetsür Mungdang* (ABTM) are religious organisations. Both female and male members are represented in the 'youth' organisation Student Council.

4. Locations of the Studies

The majority of the respondents were from rural areas. The total number of respondents from rural areas was 187, of which 82 were female and 95 male. The total number of respondents from the towns was 83 respondents; altogether there were 32 female respondents and 51 male respondents. Some of the respondents were from among the Ao Naga tribal community who reside in different parts of the cities. The total number of respondents from the cities was 40, among whom 15 were female and 25 were male.

5. Area/Range

Area/Range	Female	Male	Total
Ongpangkong	17	18	35
Asetkong	15	16	31
Langpangkong	13	16	29
Changkikong	15	16	31
Japukong	11	14	25
Tsürangkong	11	15	26
Urban Areas	47	76	123
Total	**129**	**171**	**300**

The above data show the areas/ranges inhabited by the Ao Naga tribal community. Each range consists of at least nine to twelve villages. There are six ranges in the Ao Naga Tribal area. The respondents here represent all the six ranges; two villages from each range in the Ao country were selected. The respondents

Tongpangla, assumed to be the first woman pastor among the Ao tribe, Sennangshila Longchar, Talijungla, Imzangyula and Katila.

were chosen from these villages as well as three major towns in Nagaland and from different cities in India. It is hoped that highlighting the views of these respondents, hailing from different backgrounds and different locations among the Ao Naga tribal community, will contribute towards understanding the present condition, lifestyle and understanding of Ao Naga tribal society, particularly attitudes towards/about Ao Naga tribal women.

6. Importance of Voice

Do you think "Voice" is important for speaking, sharing and responding to each other?

Regarding this question, 124 out of 129 female respondents (96.12%) and 164 out of 171 male respondents (95.9%) consider voice as an important means for speaking, sharing and responding while 5 (3.88%) females and 7 (4.1%) males do not. This means that a large majority of the respondents regard "voice" as an intrinsic part of one's own life in relation to others.

7. Voice Debarred

What if one's "Voice" is debarred from speaking?

It was noticed that there were varying attitudes towards someone being debarred from giving 'voice.' Sixty-one (47.28%) female and 77 (45.02%) male respondents felt that such a person is practically dead. 58 (44.96%) females and 78 (45.61%) males felt that she/he is not a complete being. 6 (4.65%) females and 9 (5.26%) males are of the opinion that it does not pose any problem, while 4 (3.1%) females and 7 (4.09%) males did not give any response to this question and left it blank.

Through the above answers, it can be seen that majority of both female and male respondents agreed that one's own voice is vital in a person's life. If voice is debarred from speaking than she/he is equivalent to dead and she/he considered as an incomplete being.

8. Relevance/Irrelevance of Traditional Structures

Do you think the traditional structures that do not allow women to participate in the decision-making bodies are still relevant today?

In response to this question, 34 (26.35%) females and 92 (53.8%) males affirmed that the traditional structures that do not allow women to participate in the decision-making bodies are relevant even today. Seventy-six (58.91%) females and 66 (38.59%) males did not agree with the traditional set of structures, while 19 (14.72%) females and 13 (7.6%) males could not say whether it is still relevant or not.

The responses show that even though more than half of the male respondents still believed in the relevance of the traditional system of decision-making bodies that do not allow women, a significant number of males disagreed with this old system. This also shows that there are male members who disagree with depriving equal opportunity to female members and who, in all likelihoods, are open to the idea of allowing both female and male members to take part and raise their concerns in the decision-making bodies. On the other hand, there are quite a significant number of women who still believe in the relevance of the traditional structures of decision-making bodies.

There are also both female and male respondents who could not say whether they agreed or disagreed. In this matter one may safely assume that there are people who are not fully aware of the importance of decision-making making bodies in the community.

9. Reasons for Denying Women in Decision-making Bodies

What are the reasons behind denying women's participation in decision-making bodies?

Sixty-four (49.61%) females and 85 (49.70%) males agreed that the reasons behind denying women participation in decision-making bodies are due to the traditional socio-cultural practices that must not be changed. Twenty-one females (16.27%) and 31 males (18.12%) held that it is because decision-making must be done only by men. There were 14 females (10.85%) and 10 males (5.84%) who held that due to other responsibilities taken by them, such as child rearing, caring etc., women are denied participation in decision-making bodies. Twenty females (15.5%) and 40 males (23.39%) held that there are other reasons. Ten females (7.75%) and 5 males (2.92%) did not give any response.

The majority of the female and male respondents agreed that the reasons behind denying women participation in decision-making bodies are due to the traditional socio-cultural practices which promulgate the idea that only men must be involved in the decision-making bodies.

Any other reason

The following are some of the comments given by respondents who understand that women's participation in the decision-making bodies is important. There were 142 respondents altogether who agreed with this:[572]

- Everybody, whether male or female, has the right to participate and make decisions for a good cause.
- There should be sharing and exchanging of ideas, and the community must look forward for change.

---

[572] Among the respondents who had expressed their opinions stating that women's participation in the decision-making bodies is possible and is important, the common comments made and shared by them are mentioned below. These include all the age groups, both female and male.

However, among female respondents the age group of 36-45 and the age group of 46 and above had the most comments. Among the male respondents, the age groups of 26-35, 36-45 and 46 and above had the most comments.

- Though age-old practices have come down to us through tradition, the time has come to change.
- If the community over-emphasises the age old culture which gives no room to voice for women in the decision-making bodies, Ao Naga tribal society will never go forward.
- In order to bring changes, firstly there should be co-operation among women's bodies.
- If we want to bring changes, firstly it is imperative to educate (influence) the older men in this regard.
- There is no way that the tradition and culture should not be changed; there are possibilities for change.
- One must not be fixated on holding on to the age old culture and tradition which do not allow them to progress; they must be changed according to the change of time and context.
- Women have potential; therefore in today's generation women must be included in all the decision-making bodies.
- Equal opportunity must be given to women too.
- Women should come forward to participate.
- Sharing ideas together (female and male) will be far better.
- Unless and until both the parties (female and male) come to realise and understand the importance of each individual towards the development of society, change will never happen.

126 respondents disagreed about the participation of women in the decision-making bodies. The comments made by them were as follows:[573]

- Women are generally unstable by nature, which means that if they are good they are very good, but if bad very bad; women do not have deep thinking minds like men who make decisions carefully.
- It will take time to bring changes among the Ao Naga tribal community.
- It is impossible to change.
- In short, no matter how intelligent and active and wise a woman is, she is insolvably troublesome by nature.
- The strength of women and men are different, therefore women should not compete with men and should not interfere with men in all the affairs such as decision-making bodies.
- We cannot avoid the direction of the Constitution of India which has already stated in Article 374 (A).
- One must preserve one's own socio-cultural and traditional practices; the most significant and guiding principle of all the Ao Naga tribal

[573] This includes both female and male members. In this, the majority who gave negative comments were male respondents.

community where 'men only' can do this and they are the decision makers in all the affairs.

- Women are the best source of wisdom and knowledge for men at home but not in decision-making, indeed the best supporter but not a decision maker.
- Men never attend women's fellowship; hence, women also should not participate in men's affairs.
- It will take time.
- The time is yet to come
- Women can participate in other state or government programmes but not in the socio-cultural and traditional set-ups such as decision-making bodies.

The comments mentioned above show that there were both female and male respondents who were open and supportive of women in the decision-making bodies. There were also female and male respondents who were hesitant and had an aversion to including women in the decision-making bodies. However, male respondents were more adamant in their refusal to include women in the decision-making bodies. There are plain excuses brought forth by many male members saying that it will take time, not yet ready to accept, tradition and culture do not permit, etc. It is noticeable that many of the male respondents believed that decision-making is to be done only by men.

Some male respondents reaffirmed their stand on the direction of the Constitution of India stated in Article 374 (A) which gives certain 'freedom' to the community to exercise one's own cultural and traditional practices. Basing on this, the traditional socio-cultural practices which were already male centred are once again invigorated by this provision leaving the position of women further pushed aside.

Some of the drawbacks found and shared by female respondents were that they see the lack of co-operation among women's groups in the society, bringing failure in implementing women's participation in the decision-making bodies. It was also mentioned that the need to motivate and convince older men in the community by making them aware of the recent context becomes an important concern to bring changes in the decision-making bodies.

The study also shows that the majority of the female respondents wished to come out of the old socio-cultural systems that hamper the progress of women in the community, especially women's voice in the decision-making bodies. The majority of the women felt that they have the ability and capability to involve and raise voice in the decision-making bodies.

10. Denial of Rights to Women

Are you aware of the denial of rights to women in the decision-making bodies in our community?

123 females (95.34%) and 156 males (91.22%) affirm that they are aware of the denial of rights to women in the decision-making bodies in the community. 3 females (2.32%) and 15 males (8.77%) assert that they are not aware. 3 females (2.32%) did not give any response.

This shows that majority of both female and male respondents are aware of the denial of rights to women in the decision-making bodies. Through this study we can understand that the traditional socio-cultural set-up has remained unchallenged. The common belief is that this is an accepted norm. Therefore, even though people are aware of the denial of rights to women in the decision-making bodies, it is never questioned by anyone.

11. Willingness to Accept Women in the Decision-making Bodies

Would you be willing to change the traditional system of decision-making in the village council, Yimten, Senso, *etc., and allow women to participate?*

94 females (72.86%) and 91 males (53.21%) asserted their willingness to change the traditional system of decision-making bodies in the Village Council, *Yimten, Senso*, etc., and to allow women to participate. But 20 females (15.5%) and 60 males (35.08%) did not agree. 15 females (11.62%) and 20 males (11.69%) did not say anything or give any comment in this regard.

Thus, the majority of the female respondents were willing to change the traditional system of decision-making process where women are not allowed to attend and participate. More than half of the male respondents also asserted their willingness to change the traditional system of decision-making process, although a significant number of male respondents were reluctant to change and allow women to participate in the decision-making in the village council, *Yimten, Senso* etc.

The above data is a clear indication that most of the respondents understand the lack of female voice in the decision-making bodies. They apparently felt that women's participation would be better and beneficial for the community. The data also indicates that majority of the women are willing to participate in the decision-making bodies.

Any other reason

Following are comments given by the respondents in addition to the data shown above:[574]

Female respondents:

1. If a person is capable, why should we deny such rights especially in a democratic country like India?

[574] The respondents who gave their opinions are both female and male respondents; this includes the Associate Pastors and Pastors. Several of them expressed the same opinion on this question.

2. Women have their understanding and reasoning power. Therefore, in order to dismantle the unjust social set-ups and traditional structures and to allow women to raise their voice, I feel that the church also has a role to play to bringing transformation in the community.

Male respondents:

1. There will be chaos in the community if women attend.
   It is not possible to change the old traditional system but women attending in the decision-making bodies would be good.
2. We do not know the future but our culture does not allow.
   In some intellectual societies, if there are people who have more knowledge they can come and attend, and this is already happening.
3. It is good if women come and attend the meetings; but they should not be included in the decision-making.
4. There are various activities in which women can be involved, but not in the decision-making bodies.
5. Woman is physically weaker than man. Women are exempted from hard work in the village. On the other hand it will be good to let her attend or contest in the election.

Female respondents were very positive. They believed that women should also be given equal opportunity with men to participate in the decision-making bodies in this present age. There were male respondents too who were open to accommodate women in the decision-making bodies, suggesting that if women are willing and are capable they must be allowed.

Among the male respondents, some strongly believed that decision-making bodies must be held by men only. Some of them still believe that women are physically weaker than men and therefore must not participate alongside men in the decision-making bodies. Some of the pastors too among the respondents are still very conservative; they agreed that women should not interfere with men especially in the decision-making bodies. It was observed that there were often no sign of initiatives being taken by pastors towards bringing changes in the community. They (pastors) rather validate the traditional socio-cultural structures.

12. Resistance to Decision-making Bodies

Do women resist and challenge the traditional functioning of decision-making bodies which does not give voice to women?

Ninety-four females (72.86%) and 91 males (53.21%) agreed that women resist and challenge the traditional functioning of decision-making bodies which does not give voice to women. 20 females (15.5%) and 61 males (35.67%) disagreed. Fifteen females (11.62%) and 19 males (11.11%) did not give any comment as to whether they agreed or disagreed.

Even though the majority of both female and male respondents agreed that women do resist and challenge the traditional functioning of decision-making bodies,[575] a few females and almost one-third of male respondents believed that women do not resist and challenge the traditional functioning of decision-making bodies. Through this data we can understand that, even though women themselves want to transform and come out of the traditional systems, they have not often tried to resist in the public arena.

However, it is also observed that though women do not announce outright in public, the data above clearly shows that women too wanted to come out of the traditional structures that do not allow them to raise their voice in the decision-making bodies.

13. Women and Men in the Decision-making Bodies

Do you think both women and men sharing and exchanging ideas in the decision-making bodies would be better?

One-hundred and fifteen (89.14%) females and 113 (66.08%) males agreed that women and men sharing and exchanging ideas in the decision-making bodies would be better. While there was no female respondent who disagreed, 40 (23.39%) of male respondents disagreed. Fourteen (10.85%) females and 10 (5.84%) males did not say anything in this regard. Eight (4.67%) of male respondents did not give any response.

The data clearly show that the majority of the female and male respondents were willing and agreed that it would be better if both women and men shared and exchanged their ideas in the decision-making bodies.

On the other hand, it is noticeable that there were quite a number of male respondents who do not agree that women and men sharing and exchanging ideas in the decision-making bodies would be ideal. There are a few respondents who strongly oppose females and males coming together and sharing ideas. A comment made by a male respondent was, "good, but she may have a forceful personality who may want to win over every matter because she thinks only of herself."[576] Another comment was that, "There would be breakdown of the family structure because she will neglect child rearing, caring and many more domestic tasks if she attends."[577]

---

[575] The researcher presumed that women would like to resist and challenge traditional functioning of the decision-making bodies. However, in practice they have not expressed this view yet in public.

[576] This comment was made by a respondent in the questionnaire.

[577] This is a comment made by a respondent in the questionnaire.

14. If Option is given to Men and Women

a. *Would you still willingly participate in the decision-making bodies if you have an option to do otherwise?* (for men only)

Out of 171 male respondents, 102 (59.64%) asserted that they would continue to participate willingly in the decision-making bodies, while 53 (30.99%) were not willing to attend if they were given an option. Ten (5.84%) could not decide and 6 (3.5%) declined to respond.

The majority of the male respondents were willing to participate in the decision-making bodies. At the same time there were many respondents who did not wish to attend if they were given the option. They attend the meeting only because, being 'male' by birth, tradition has compelled them to participate in the decision-making bodies.

b. *Would you willingly participate in the decision-making bodies if you have an option to do so?* (for women only)

One-hundred and five (81.39%) females asserted their willingness to participate in the decision-making bodies if they were given a chance. Nine (6.97%) would not want to attend and 15 (11.62%) were unable to decide.

This clearly indicates that the majority of the female respondents were willing to participate in the decision-making bodies. The above data indicated that the traditional set of structures hampers women from expressing their views and to attend in all the affairs in the decision-making bodies. Being born as women, they are debarred from participation. Women's voice, which is one of the important means of communication, is not only controlled but even suppressed.

15. Awareness of Principles of Christian Communication

Are you aware that denial of a person's voice amounts to a negation of the basic principles of Christian communication, i.e., the right to participate and the right to information?

One-hundred and six (82.17%) female and 140 (81.87%) male respondents claimed to have awareness about the basic principles of Christian communication, i.e. the right to participation and right to information. Fourteen (10.85%) female and 24 (14.03%) male respondents did not know about it, and 9 (6.97%) females and 7 male (4.09%) could not comment on this.

The majority of female and male respondents are aware that the denial of a person's own voice amounts to a negation of the basic principles of Christian communication. However, it also indicates that no matter how much people know and learn about the accomplishments and changes that abound in contemporary society, it does not seem to carry any significant effect or change on Ao Naga traditional society. Discrimination on the basis of gender can still be seen in the decision-making bodies.

16. Awareness of Democratic Systems

Are you aware that democracy and the democratic process should include everyone?

One-hundred and nine (84.49%) female and 134 (78.36%) male respondents answered that they are aware of democracy and that the democratic process should include everyone. Thirteen (10.07%) female and 22 (12.86%) male respondents were not aware of this, and 7 (5.42%) female and 15 (8.77%) male respondents could not comment on this question.

This clearly shows that the majority of the respondents were well aware of the democratic process whereby freedom of expression and opinion is of primary importance for all citizens of India. However, in spite of knowing that in detail, one finds that the Ao Naga tribal community ignores the rights of the citizenry but rather lays emphasis on the age old traditional structures which are anti-democratic in nature.

17. Traditional Belief about Women

Do you believe that, because men in general are stronger than women, women cannot and should not join in any of the socio-cultural, religious and political affairs?

A majority of the respondents both female (84.49%) and male (62.57%) do not believe in the statement that men are stronger than women and that therefore they cannot and should not join in any of the socio-cultural, religious and political affairs. On the other hand there were a significant number of respondents, especially men, who believed the statement strongly. Through this we can identify clearly that the present generation generally believe that both females and males must have equal roles to play.

18. Traditional belief about Child born out of Wedlock

Do you still hold on to the traditional belief that a child born out of wedlock is impure and hence does not have any share (to hold office) in the Village Council?

The majority of both female (75.19%) and male (66.08%) respondents still strongly hold on to the traditional belief that a child born out of wedlock is impure and hence does not have any share (to hold office) in the Village Council. On the other hand, we also see that quite a few numbers of respondents both female (15.5%) and male (22.22%) disagree with the traditional understanding that a child born out of wedlock is impure and has no share (to hold office) in the Village Council. There was also a group of respondents who could not say whether it is right or wrong.

Through this study, we can also understand that the traditional notion of impurity imposed on a child born out of wedlock is still kept intact by the Ao community.

19. Success of Ao Women's Association (Watsü Mungdang)

Do you consider the achievements made by the Ao Women's Association for the community praiseworthy?

Majority of the respondents, both female (76.74%) and male (60.81%), accept and agreed on the achievements brought by the Ao Women's Association for the community praiseworthy. There were respondents both female (13.17%) and male (15.78%) who do not agree with the above statement. There were also some respondents especially male (23.39%) who could not say anything about Ao women's achievements.

20. Value of Women's Voice

Do you value women's (your wife's, mother's, sister's, and daughter's) voice when they give you advice or suggest some innovative ideas at home?

Majority of both female (78.29%) and male (81.87%) respondents agreed that they value women's (wife's, mother's, sister's, and daughter's) voice when they give advice or suggest some innovative ideas at home. Only a few of them do not value women's voice even at home. There were also few respondents who could not say whether they valued women's voice at home or not.

According to the study shown above, it can be observed that women's voice is highly regarded, respected and accepted in the private spheres. It is only when it comes to the public arena that traditional socio-cultural practises do not permit women to speak and voice their concerns.

21. Value of Women's Voice among the Age-group (*zünga*)

Do you value the voice of women from your age-group whenever they advise or suggest some innovative ideas in the social gatherings? (for male respondents only)

	Male	**%**
Yes	119	69.59
No	8	4.67
Can't say	35	20.46
No response	9	5.26
Total	**171**	

The data show that the majority of the males value the voice of women from their age-group whenever they give advice or suggest some innovative ideas in their age-group gatherings. Quite a few of them do not agree and could not say on this, and some of the respondents did not give any response.

This study shows that even among the age-group social gatherings which consist of both female and male members, woman's voice is being accepted whenever she advises or suggests some innovative ideas.

It is a clear indication that respect and concern for women's voice are valued and cherished by male counterparts when it comes to the age-group social gathering. It is therefore noticed that the only obstacle against women being allowed to attend and raise their voice in the decision-making bodies is due to the traditional socio-cultural structures that stops them from participating.

22. Co-operation between Church and State

Do you agree with the statement "Church andm state cannot be separated from one another but must complement each other"?

It has been indicated that 50.38% of females agreed with the statement regarding inter-relation between Church and state, 41.86% of the females disagreed and 7.75% could not really make up their minds. Among the male respondents, 52.63% agreed, 29.82% disagreed and 17.54% were not sure.

It shows that within the Ao Naga community, there is no definite and/or clear cut understanding about the Church and the state, whether they should be separate from one another or complement each other.

23. Decision-making Bodies in the Local Church

Does your local church provide a platform for both women and men in the decision-making bodies?

A majority of both female respondents (62.01%) and male respondents (61.4%) agreed that their local church provides a platform for both women and men in the decision-making bodies. At the same time, there were a number of respondents (31.78% of females and 28.07% of males) who did not agree that the local church provided a platform for both women and men in the decision-making bodies. A handful of respondents were not able to comment.

Through the answers given above, the we can come to know that there is no clear understanding about women being given a platform in the decision-making bodies at the local church. More than half of the respondents agreed that women are provided a platform whereas another half disagreed. As a result one is left with no definite answer in this regard.

24. Female Deacons/Elders in the Church

Do you think that we need female Deacons/Elders in the church today?

The majority of both female respondents (76.74%) and male respondents (61.4%) agreed that they need women deacons/elders in the church today. Twenty-one females (16.27%) and 40 males (23.39%) did not agree to having women deacons/elders in the church today. Nine females (6.97%) and 26 males (15.2%) could not say whether they needed women deacons/ elders in the church today.

Through this finding, one can also know that even though the majority were willing to accept and thought that we need women deacons/elders in the church today, there were a few respondents including female respondents who disagreed. However, in spite of this, the inclinations towards gender equality as female deacons/elders in the Church are positive signs.

24 a. *If yes, why do we need women deacons/elders in the church?*

There were 99 females who affirmed the need for female deacons/elders. Twenty-three (23.23%) did so because they believed that "women and men together would achieve more." Twenty-two (22.22%) believed that "women's contribution would make a difference." Seventeen (17.17%) did so because they believed that "God created both female and male in God's likeness." While 13 (13.13%) felt that all the previous reasons applied, 24 (24.24%) did not give any response.

One-hundred and five male respondents agreed that there was a need for female deacons/elders in the church. Sixteen (15.23%) did so because they believed that "women and men together would achieve more." Fifteen (14.28%) believed that "women's contribution would make a difference." Ten (9.52%) did so because they believed that 'God created both female and male in God's likeness." While 24 (22.85%) felt that all the previous reasons applied, 40 (38.09%) did not give any response.

24 b. *If no, why don't we need female deacons/elders in the church?*

There were 21 female respondents who felt that there was no need for female deacons/elders in the church. Three (14.28%) did so because they believed that 'the Bible does not allow' having female deacons/elders in the church. None of the women believed that women would be unwilling to take up the post. Eight (38.09%) did so because the church has not tried implementing it before, while 10 (47.61%) did not choose any of the plausible reasons given.

There were 40 male respondents who contend that there is no need for female deacons/elders in the church. Ten (25%) did so because they believed that 'the Bible does not allow it'. Five (12.5%) felt that women would be unwilling to take up the post, 9 (22.5%) did so because the church has not tried implementing it before, while 16 (40%) did not give any response.

25. No Room for Women's Voice in the Village Councils

Are you aware that there is no room for women to lend voice and participate in the decision-making process of village councils?

One-hundred and fifteen (89.14%) female respondents and 152 (89.47%) male respondents agreed that there is no place for women in the decision-making bodies at the village level. Five (3.87%) females and 10 (5.84%) males did not agree with this, while 9 (6.97%) females and 8 (4.67%) males did not give any response.

This indicates to us that a majority of both the female and male respondents are aware that there is no women participation in the decision-making bodies of the village council. Only a few of them did not know or made no comment. This shows that even though the community members are aware that only men make decisions through the decision-making bodies and the absence of women participation is noticed, it appears as a normal practice and is more or less considered acceptable by the Ao Naga tribal community.

26. Women in Village Development Board (VDBs)

Are you aware that 25% of the Management Committee of the Village Development Board (VDBs) should be composed of women?

Eighty-one (62.79%) females and 101 (59.06%) males affirmed awareness of the requirement for 25% women's representation on the Management committee of the Village Development Boards (VDBs). Forty (31%) females and 49 (28.65%) males were not aware of this. Eight (6.2%) females and 21 (12.28%) males did not give any comment.

It shows that half of both the female and male respondents were aware that the 25% of the Management Committee of the Village Development Boards (VDBs) should be composed of women, and that another half were not aware. Through this one can see that even though most of the respondents are aware of the female representation in the VDBs another half of the respondents are ignorant about this, which means that there is a lack of information and awareness among the general public.

27. Cooperation between Village Council and Village Development Board

How would you rate the level of cooperation between these two bodies, the Village Council and the Village Development Board (VDB), in your village?

35 (27.13%) females and 58 (33.91%) male respondents rated the level of cooperation between the Village Council and the Village Development Board (VDB) in their village as very good, 48 (37.20%) females and 49 (28.65%) males considered it good, and 27 (20.93%) females and 35 (20.46%) males considered it acceptable. While 7 (5.42%) females and 10 (5.84%) males say that it was not good at all, 12 (9.30%) females and 19 (11.11%) males did not give any response.

The Village Council is the continuation of the traditional set of structures or system which is incorporated with the Village Development Board (VDB), an initiative of the government that functions and provides funds for the village development where 25% seats are reserved for women. As it had indicated these two are intertwined and seemingly accepted and appreciated by the majority of the respondents. This means that the Ao Naga tribal community is willing to adapt the modern developmental programme, that is, the non-traditional structures in their own village.

4.5.1. Suggestions Made by Respondents towards the Improvement of Decision-Making Bodies in Ao Naga Tribal Community

i. Comments made by female respondents:[578]

- Denying women in the decision-making bodies/process is a major setback in the march towards a progressive, egalitarian society.
- In our land, the failure in decision-making bodies is due to the lack of responsibility and rationality. Coercive decision without proper realisation will be disastrous.
- With the passage of time and change of attitudes, Ao society must also change. The decision-making process must be followed by both women and men according to their wisdom and knowledge, talent and understanding if they want to go forward in life.
- Since only male members attend the meetings and decide, the voices and concerns of the majority of community members, namely that of children and women especially widows, go unheard. Moreover, the issues discussed and decisions made were often not adequately communicated to all.
- On the part of women whenever opportunity comes they frequently feel reluctant and hesitant to come forward; this attitude must be changed and they must be emboldened enough to overcome it.
- In order to bring the issue of gender discrimination to light and to raise awareness among the common people, there is a need to provide proper education and direction.
- We must recognise the value of the wholeness of humankind, not just a woman or a man, by recognising both female and male as God's unique creation so as to fulfil God's purpose.
- On the part of the women, they must act upon their willingness to breach the restrictions of the patriarchal socio-cultural systems.
- It would not be prudent to attend and participate in all the decision-making bodies as there are some sensitive matters which should be avoided by women.
- If half of the population in a community is voiceless, that community is seriously sick. No matter how educated or healthy we think we (the Aos) are, we are still very sick and unrefined.
- Hoping and longing to see changes among our community for women's voice in the decision-making bodies.

---

[578] These are some of the common comments made by female respondents through the questionnaires. The majority of the women were in the age group 46 and above followed by the age groups 36-45 and 26-35 and a very few in the age group 15-25.

- We want to participate and take part in all the decision-making bodies but are hampered due to our tradition and culture. To my knowledge it will not change now.
- We Ao women are highly educated and have all the potential to thrive under every challenging circumstance. In spite of all these, we have a general weakness, lack of co-operation and low self-esteem to speak out in public. It is high time for us to take the matter into consideration.
- Women's organisations, either church or state women groups, must initiate and co-ordinate efforts for women to stand confidently for their rights.
- Generally women by nature can come up with more innovative ideas than men who are normally very simple and random. Therefore, if both contribute together in the decision-making, it will bring better results.
- Some of the ancient socio-cultural traditions which were relevant in the past have become irrelevant today. Earlier, the word of an older man was highly regarded and valued, and a younger man's word was not valued much in the decision-making bodies. Today those cultural practices are still perpetuated in the community. The suggestions brought by younger men are not recognized even today.
- In Ao Naga society, women are usually considered as having mental capabilities equivalent to that of a girl child or children, meaning that Ao Naga culture does not value and regard a woman as a normal adult. Therefore, women are not included in the decision-making body which, in turn, is the reason why such bodies are incomplete in many ways and serious mistakes are often made.
- One very important thing is that in order to bring changes in the society, the issues should be first conveyed and discussed in the Church since the Church becomes the model for the Ao Naga tribal community.
- If instead of men alone also women are allowed to attend and participate in the decision-making bodies, it will be immensely beneficial for all.
- In the name of tradition and culture, women are denied rights to participation in most of the decision-making bodies, including church bodies.

The above comments made by female respondents confirm that gender imbalance in the decision-making bodies brings undesirable results in development. Inclusion of both genders in the decision-making bodies will yield good results in society. It has been pointed out that women are devalued by being considered in more or less the same category as children. On the other hand, some of the women felt that there are exceptional cases in the decision-making bodies in which women must not interfere and which must be dealt with by men only. Other women felt that creativity and innovativeness of women are being ignored.

It should also be mentioned that the negative impact of age old traditional, social and cultural mind-set and practices continues to be imbibed not only through socio-political institutions but also through the Church. It was also mentioned that a community is considered as sick and unrefined if women's voice is not being heard in the decision-making bodies. It is suggested that in line with the passage of time and change of attitudes, systems need to be changed. This will ensure equal participation of and mutual respect for both women and men in all walks of life.

However, there are others who also observed that though women are educated and capable, due to their lack of co-operation and low self-esteem they are yet unable to stand firm for their rights. Women's organisations in the Church as well as in the State bodies require self-confidence and co-ordination. It was also suggested that the Church's involvement becomes a necessity to sensitize the people towards gender justice and bring changes since the Church becomes the archetype on whose lines the Ao Naga tribal community is built.

ii. Comments made by male respondents:[579]

- It is normal that women do not have a voice in the state decision-making bodies; they have a voice in the church matters.
- The strength of women and men cannot be compared as equal, for example women will never be able to play football like men.
- In our village as far as I know we have not discussed women's concerns deeply in any of the gatherings. It will be helpful and people will be more aware if we convey the message to the common people.
- In my opinion, the composition and functioning of decision-making bodies is very primitive. They do not function according to the rule of law which, in my opinion, is very necessary. Though decisions made are meant for the welfare of all, I have learnt through experience that it is mostly at the direction of a single influential leader and sometimes can be very narrow. Also, because there is no code to ensure that differing voices are heard, some effective voices go unheard.
- In all the decisions men take, women accept and follow accordingly without any problem. Therefore, I believe that what we are should continue as it is.
- Women do not have any rights and have no value in themselves; this tradition has been followed since time immemorial. The Ao Naga tribal community is aware of democracy and has continued to practise it even now.

---

[579] These are some of the common comments made by the male respondents in the questionnaires. There were equal numbers in the age groups of 46 and above, 36-45 and 26-35 who had commented along with a very few the age group 15-25.

- Woman was created from the rib of a man. She is weaker than man. Due to modern advancements women should also be given greater rights in the community but not equal voting rights with men.
- In our Ao country up until now people are still not willing to listen to women's concerns and refused to understand the condition of women's issues. Unless and until people recognize and change this attitude towards women, Ao Naga tribal community will never go forward. Therefore, it is very important to educate the common people.
- While I feel that women can play a good role in every field, women themselves do not come forward to participate actively. They alienate themselves and stay behind. They should also take initiatives to break the stereotype.
- It is good that both women and men take part in the church concerns; but women must not interfere in the state affairs in the Ao Naga tribal community.
- The traditional socio-cultural systems of functioning by Aos specially the decision-making bodies will remain the same and will not change instantly. Church and State's functioning are different, but they go hand in hand with mutual co-operation and understanding by respecting one other.
- By nature, women are flowers and men are swords; there are big differences between these two. Flower fades away but sword has won many battles in the past and will continue to do so. God did not give talent to women like men, either in the past or in the present, nor would he in the future.
- If women and men are capable, it is good to sit together and make decisions. But, since culture has brought us up and taught us in the way that is practised, I think it will not be possible to change the system immediately.
- There are times when women and men come together, so also there are times when they meet separately. Therefore, we should not change the systems and things should remain as they are now.
- Our culture and tradition do not permit to allow women to come and attend and to participate in the decision-making bodies; therefore, it will take time to change.
- Though it is a blessing to have wise women around, they are not gifted for administration. Women are created by God as helpers for men. Just like hens never crow, till the end of time it will remain the same.
- It is impossible to change the age old traditional practices which are considered valuable.

There were a few male respondents who were open to reconsider and felt that women's voice is essential in the decision-making bodies. They said that due to the lack of social awareness with regard to the issues (women's voice), common people do not consider it very seriously. It was also said that women themselves do not come forward and challenge the traditional socio-cultural structures, thereby hindering their voice.

The majority of the male respondents considered having and hearing women's voice in the decision-making bodies highly undesirable. They are aware that there is no women's participation in the socio-cultural structure and that women's voice go unheard in the decision-making bodies. However, they felt that the age old traditional practices are valuable and that the structures and systems must not be changed. They felt that God created men and not women to rule, and that women's role is to take care of the family and not to be an administrator. They understood that the main hindrance for women not being given opportunities in the decision-making bodies is based on culture which cannot be broken down instantly.

4.6. Analysis of the Field Research

This study brought to us the gender-wise classification of respondents from various age groups in order to know their various aspirations and inclinations about women's voice in the decision-making bodies. Among the respondents the age group of '46 and above' outnumber the other age groups followed by age group of 26-35 and 36-45. Through this one can assume that this 46 and above age group have more knowledge and experience about such concerns to share confidently (see no.1).

In this study, the researcher has brought in both female and male respondents from various professions. These are farmers, government employees, students, church leaders, pastors/associate pastors and others. The aim was to get each of their opinions more clearly and to understand their attitudes and opinions about women's voice in the decision-making bodies (see no. 2). The members of various other important institutional organisations actively functioning at Ao Naga tribal community at present were also included. Through these, the researcher will recognise the importance of an individual's contribution towards church as well as towards community (see no .3).

For this study, the researcher has chosen respondents from various locations such as rural and urban: towns and cities respectively. The reason for choosing these areas was to study more clearly their understanding of the voice of women in the decision-making bodies from their point of view and to see how they differ, or relate to or support one another (see no. 4). As mentioned earlier, the common Ao Naga tribal community is settled in six major ranges apart from towns and cities. Though they are of the same tribe, unusually they also differ in language, mannerism, habits, attitudes, concepts etc. Therefore, bringing all these differing viewpoints the researcher hoped to get more insight into how they consider women, and particularly women's voice, in the decision-making bodies (see no. 5).

A study shows that 'voice' is considered as an intrinsic part of one's life. Both female and male respondents unquestionably agreed that without communicating with people through one's own voice a person's life is equivalent to being dead. The sharing or exchanging of ideas, feelings, emotions with one another emulate the essence of life This shows that the Ao Naga tribal community accepts that one's own voice is valuable and essential in life (see no. 6 and 7).

The study brings out the relevance/irrelevance of traditional structures that restrain women from participation in the decision-making bodies in the Ao Naga tribal community. The researcher had observed that even though many answered positively that one's own voice is undeniably important, it is disheartening to hear that more than half of the respondents, mostly male, say that traditional structures that do not include women in the decision-making bodies are still relevant. There were however significant numbers of respondents including males who believe that the old systems need to be changed. Regrettably, the traditional socio-cultural structures prevail over everything no matter how much one may talk or say that voice is as an important means of communication in one's own life (see no. 8).

A considerable number of female and male respondents believed and agreed that the traditional structure of decision-making bodies must not be changed. According to them, one of the reasons behind denying women's participation in the decision-making bodies is her responsibility towards rearing and caring for a child. Another reason was that the decision-making must be done only by men. These points hold firm among 126 respondents out of three-hundred, which means that almost half of the respondents agreed with this. There is no alternative reason to reconsider women's voice in such a context, no reason for integration and intervention to include women. It is fixed and therefore held that this must be strictly followed (see no 9).

The comments made in *Any other reason* (see no.9) include the taunting remark which the researcher observed was that the reaffirmation of Article 374 (A), where male respondents reaffirmed it and stated that it should be followed strictly because it gives certain "freedom" to the community to exercise its own cultural and traditional practices. However, we will notice the lop-sidedness in this where women have no voice in the cultural and traditional practices in the Ao Naga tribal community, as only males get ample opportunity in all this. This is another drawback for Ao Naga tribal women, in that even Article 374 (A) benefits 'men' disproportionately who receive maximum opportunities in all the socio-cultural, economic, religious and political functions.

The study clearly shows that about ninety-five per cent of both female and male respondents agreed that they are aware of the denial of rights to women in the community decision-making bodies. However, even among those who are aware of the denial of rights to women, a considerable number of people are not ready to accept or include women. This indicates that even though they are well aware of the disparity between female and male roles in the community's decision-making bodies, nobody is ready to challenge this inconsistency (see no. 10 and 11).

In addition to the information shown, some comments were made by the respondents. Here, some male respondents commented that they still believe that women are physically weaker and that therefore they are exempted from hard work done in the village or community life; therefore, women must not interfere with men, especially in the decision-making bodies. Thus, we will see women being excluded just because they are physically weaker, exempted from hard work and therefore excluded from the decision-making bodies.

Another very uneven attitude of the pastors towards women's voice was widely visible. The lack of pastors' initiatives towards bringing changes in the community was very evident. Pastors' voices, which are unconditionally accepted and respected by the people, do not show her/his desirable response towards women's voice in the decision-making bodies. (See no. 10 and 11).

It shows that the majority of the respondents, both female and male, agreed that women do resist and challenge the traditional functioning of the decision-making process. However, it was also noticed that there is a lack of women taking initiatives for their right to voice in the community (see no. 12).

A majority of the respondents agreed upon the mutual sharing and exchanging of ideas (female-male) in the decision-making. However, there were a few male respondents who had negative opinions about women attending and participating in the decision-making bodies. According to them, women are forceful personalities by nature, dominative and opportunist. They were afraid that if a woman joined and participated, tension and problems would arise. They also thought that family foundations would be loosened and collapse if mothers joined in the decision-making bodies. This shows that the gender role in the society is already divided, so the society norm and the task assigned to men (in public affairs) and women (in private affairs) must be followed as it is (see no. 13).

This shows us that only sixty per cent of the male respondents agreed to attend in the decision-making bodies if an option is given. It shows that even though men are not willing to attend, it is obligatory for every man to be present in the meeting. In contrary to this, eighty per cent of women were willing to participate in the decision-making bodies. In such a case, the universal, basic human rights of "freedom of expression and thought" are blocked and denied for women. There is therefore a socio-cultural set of norms forced on them (either female or male) to remain fixed and true to their social norms and roles without allowing any progress (see no. 14).

When asked about whether they are aware that the denial of a person's voice amounts to a negation of the basic principles of Christian communication, that is the right to participation and the right to information, eighty-two per cent of both female and male respondents agreed that they are aware (see no. 15). When asked about whether they were aware that democracy and the democratic process should include everyone in the decision-making bodies, the majority of the respondents both female and male agreed that they were aware of it (see no. 16). They were well aware that an individual's voice is an essential part in life, and the right to participation and the right to information are the basic principles of Christian communication, since democracy and the democratic process include everyone. However, despite these rights being recognised, we observed that women's voice is unwelcome in the decision-making bodies. Culture-bound structures supersede all these qualities.

The study shows that the majority of the respondents, both female and male, disagreed with the traditional belief systems about women who are debarred from socio-cultural, religious and political affairs because they are weaker than men. Even though many respondents, mostly male, who supported traditional belief systems, one can also perceive that the old belief systems are gradually disappearing from the minds of the common people (see no. 17).

It shows that the majority of the respondents, both female and male, still consider that traditional beliefs that a child born out of wedlock is impure and does not have any share (to hold office) in the village council (see no.18). It is still strongly believed that the office of the *putu menden*[580] must be "pure" and "holy," and that therefore office bearers must be pure and holy; and so, men born out of wedlock are considered as "impure" and "unholy."

It indicates that the majority of the respondents, both female and male, considered as important and agreed on the achievements of the Ao Women Association (*Watsü Mungdang*) (see no. 19). The data show that both female and male members agreed that they value and appreciate women's voice (wife, mother, sister, and daughter) whenever she gives advice or suggests some innovative ideas at home (see no. 20). The data also show that even among the age-group (*zünga*) female-male gatherings, the majority of the male respondents agreed that they greatly value their age-group women's voice in their social gatherings (see no. 21). In the Ao Naga tribal community, it is observed that the respect and concern and the acceptance of women by men is visible in this regard. Women's innovative ideas and suggestion were acknowledged highly. However, even though men value the voice of the women in domestic affairs such as the home, among their age-group gatherings, church functions etc., the male members act differently when it comes to women's voice in the decision-making bodies.

The it shows that 50 per cent of female and 41 per cent of male respondents disagreed with the statement "church and state cannot be separated from one another but must complement each other"; but on the other hand, half of both female and male respondents agreed that the church and state are separate from each other (see no. 22). Another question was whether the local church provided a platform for both women and men in the decision-making bodies. 61 per cent

[580] Generation seat in the village council in the Ao Naga tribal language. The meaning is clearly explained in chapter three.

of both female and male respondents agreed that they do provide a platform for women (see no. 23).

Considering all these findings, the researcher observed that there are no proper guidelines or parameters to show where exactly to draw the line between state and church in the Ao Naga tribal community. Again, one cannot simply say that women are given a platform in the local church decision-making bodies because the deacons/elders in the church are all normally males. Major decisions are made among the deacons/elders in a local church where they meet almost every week or so. There are hardly any meetings except the general body meeting once at the end of the year where all the departments (both female and male) participate.

Recently in one of the Ao churches in Nagaland all the women were asked to leave at the end of the church service, after which all male members sat and took decisions on church related matters.[581] This kind of attitude and mentality of Ao men show that they still strongly carry around their patriarchal mind-set, undermining and controlling women and their voice, not only in matters of state but even in those of the church.

The study showed that when asked about whether they needed female Deacons/Elders in the church, the majority of both female and male respondents agreed that they were needed (see no. 24*)*. Those who agreed with this said that both women and men together would achieve more. They said that women's contribution would make a difference. They also agreed that God created both female and male in God's likeness (see no. 24. a).

In this regard, it is observed that there is a sign of hope shown through the response of the respondents for women Deacons/Elders in the church. There is a belief that females' presence in church decision-making bodies would be valuable. The respondents also understood that accountability and respect with mutual sharing (female-male) of ideas would benefit the people more and advance the reign of God.

Among those respondents who disagreed on the above, both female and male respondents said that the bible does not allow it. A few male respondents said that women are not willing to take up the post. Most of the respondents said that their church has not tried implementing this before (see no. 24. b).

It is observed that there are church members who still cling to the literal understanding of the scripture believing that "'the bible does not allow it." This shows the lack of biblical teaching among the congregation in the church. The researcher also noticed that some male respondents blamed women for not accepting positions as Deacons/Elders in the church as if the church was already open for women Deacons/Elders. Realistically, there will be hardly any church who had opened up for women deacons/elders as it was found that most of the respondents agreed that their church had not tried implementing this before.

---

[581] Interview with Chubalemla, Pangerchila, Sademkala Dimapur, 12 February, 2015.

When asked whether they are aware of the absence of women's voice and participation in the decision-making process of the village council, the majority of both female and male respondents agreed and were aware of it (see no. 25). Despite knowing all this, people still do not question much on this imbalance in the decision-making process, but it appears as a normal practice and is more or less considered acceptable by the Ao Naga tribal community.

When asked whether they are aware about 25% of the Management Committee of the Village Development Board (VDBs) being composed of women, the majority of the respondents, both female and male members, affirmed that they are aware of this. Furthermore, we see several respondents, both female and male members, who were not aware of this (see no. 26). Here, the researcher observed two things: firstly, even though people are aware of this, nobody dares to question or challenge the partiality or unjust functioning of the administrative systems in the village council if women are not included.[582] Secondly, due to the lack of information or lack of awareness given to the general public, the position of women, their potentiality, contribution and participation are laid to waste in the Ao Naga tribal community.

The question was asked of the respondents how they would rate the level of cooperation between the two bodies, the village council and the village development board, in their community. The majority of the respondents, both female and male, accepted and agreed to this positively (see no. 27). The researcher in this regard observed that even though people are opposed to the change of traditional structures or systems in the community such as the inclusion of women's voice in decision-making bodies, on the contrary, the researcher observed that the double standard adopted by the Ao Naga tribal community is evident as they willingly accommodated and adopted the non-traditional/alien culture (VDB). It was also noticed that when they meet together (village council and village development board), women are being ignored or side-lined in the decision-making bodies (VDB).

4.7. Key Findings in the Research

1. Some of the basic points noticeable in the personal interviews were the importance and functions of *Zünga* (age-group) and the distinctions maintained between girls and boys. The researcher observed that *Zünga* plays a significant role in the cultural, political, social, and economic life of the Ao villages. The key role played by women towards 'community formation' in Ao Naga tribal society in the past, the gradual alienation and elimination of women's contributions, the songs that were reciprocally communicated between women and men, the derogatory remarks made about women and the gender distinction

[582] At present the village council which is the continuation of the traditional set of structures or system is incorporated with the village development board.

were all discussed. Also the concept of *sobaliba* and its drawbacks were observed.

2. The findings show that the reasons behind denying women participation in the decision-making bodies are due to the traditional socio-cultural practices. The study also shows that the majority of the female respondents wish to come out of the old socio-cultural systems that hamper the progress of women in the community decision-making bodies.
3. The study shows that both female and male respondents agreed that the denial of a person's voice amounts to a negation of the basic principles of Christian communication. An unwavering faith in the traditional institutions and allegiance to their norms is however still kept intact among the Ao Naga tribal community. The traditional socio-cultural practices do not permit women to speak and voice their concerns. The main obstacles and challenges are the traditional socio-cultural practices which do not allow women's voice in the decision-making bodies.
4. It has been noticed that the function of the Village Development Board (VDB) is known by many, but from the findings we see that many are still ignorant about it. It is also indicated that the Village Council and the Village Development Board (VDB) are intertwined and accepted and appreciated by the majority of the respondents. This shows that the Ao Naga tribal community is willing to adapt to modern development programmes, namely non-traditional structures, within the traditional village setup.
5. It is observed that there is willingness to adopt and blend non-traditional structures in the community; however when it comes to the inclusion of women in the decision-making bodies the majority of the male respondents were obstinate in their refusal to accept women.
6. In the focus group discussion, the study revealed that there were younger group participants who were open and felt that women's voice is essential in the decision-making bodies. However, the majority of the male respondents did not agree with the inclusion of women in the decision-making bodies.

4.8. Implications

The theories used in this study have been discussed in the earlier chapter. These theories will support, validate and strengthen the already analysed data in this research. Theories such as, *"Feminist Communication Theories," "the Concept of "Voice," "Transnational Feminism," "Cultural Approach to Communication," and "Network Approach"*[583] have been applied in this study. These theories in

[583] The theories that have been applied here in this research findings and application have already been described in chapter two.

communication might direct us to ponder over the traditional norms and to open up the possibility towards the restoration of women's voice which has been ignored for generations in the decision-making bodies.

Here, the feminist theories bring to light to identify, question, and seek to reform patriarchal ideologies that give rise to oppression, as well as the asymmetrical rights, opportunities, roles, etc. In the case of the Ao Naga tribal community, due to the traditional socio-cultural structures, only the male is the privilege one, especially in the decision-making bodies. Therefore, in order to bring mutual participation and representation among female and male members, the researcher feels that it might be appropriate to apply in this study feminist communication theories "which point the way toward alternatives that promote more egalitarian possibilities for individuals, relationships, groups, and societies."[584]

Another theory brought in this study is on "Voice" propounded by Lana F. Rakow and Laura A. Wackwitz, which is one of the essential elements in this study. The concept of voice in communication asserts and challenges us to "reclaim," "discover," and "give voice to" those who have not been heard in public discourse, and is an important phase of the work on voice.[585]

Transnational Feminism which is used in communication studies is relevant here in this study. Transnational feminism and communication studies maintain and question the lack of attention to the culture and economic inequalities of globalization in any interrogations of gender itself which is implicated in, and reinforcing of, global inequalities.[586]

It is observed that there must be a total change in the traditional structures of the Ao Naga tribal community where there is no recognition of and no voice for women in the decision-making bodies. The cultural approach to communication theory by James W. Carey is of relevance to our study. One of the concepts in the cultural approach is the ritual view of communication, which conveys to us that communication is linked to terms such as "sharing," "participation," "association," "fellowship," and the "possession of a common faith." Here, "a ritual view of communication is directed not toward the extension of messages in space but toward the maintenance of society in time; not the act of imparting information but the representation of shared beliefs."[587] The cultural approach to communication directs every individual to share and participate by voicing together towards community formation.

In the context of the female-male dichotomies in a society such as the Ao Naga tribal community, where women's voice is not heard in the decision-making bodies, the *Network Approach* in communication studies seems to have

---

[584] Ramona R. Rush, "Ten Tenets for Deeper Communications, op. cit., 201-202.

[585] Lana F. Rakow, Laura A. Wackwitz, "Voice in Feminist Communication Theory," op. cit., 95.

[586] Ibid.

[587] Ibid.

relevance in this research. The network model of communication encourages planners and researchers to use new cause/effect variables in their analyses. The network approach, such as connectedness, integration, diversity, and openness, may prove to be an important component to include in redesigning Ao Naga tribal community.[588]

The findings of the study demand democratising of decision-making process, and facilitating the agency of voice against kyriarchy, 'the rule of the 'man.' Therefore, theological articulation is required for the reconstruction of an inclusive and participatory Ao Naga tribal community.

---

[588] Lana F. Rakow, Laura A. Wackwitz, "Voice in Feminist Communication Theory," op. cit., 95.

Chapter 5

Ao Women's Voice: A Paradigm of Communication Theology

Introduction

Over the past centuries, whether in Ancient Israelite Judaism, during the Christian era, the Reformation period, or in the present Ao Naga tribal community, women had to undergo multifaceted challenges in all aspects of socio-cultural, religious, economic and political life. They had to face similar struggles alongside men as members of their communities. They have often raised their voices for freedom from domination and subjugation, and have indeed led to the emancipation of entire communities in many ways.

In spite of women being ignored in many areas, one cannot simply ignore their participation and the work that they have carried out in various parts of the globe. Women's voice has been reckoned as a powerful element and has been manifested in various walks of life. There are many historic events that shaped the entire society through women's voice. History has witnessed the struggles endured and the success stories in the socio-cultural-economic-political and religious field in their own community and at their own time.

This chapter explores and highlights the importance of women's "voice" in Judaism in Ancient Israel, in Jesus' time, early Christianity, the Reformation era and contemporary Ao Naga Tribal Community. It also deals with the gradual diminishing of the voice of women in the patriarchal socio-cultural, political and religious structures. Along with this, we shall also try to locate the significance of women's voice in history. Lastly, we will see how voice is an effective means of communication that operates through various conduits, and which conveys the clear message that each individual has her/his own right to communicate and to participate as an equal member in all spheres of life.

5.1. Women in Judaism and Ancient Israel

It is imperative to highlight in our study a brief background of women in Judaism and Ancient Israel. By observing the way in which the Ancient Israelite society functioned, one might be able to grasp the voice of women in the Israelite society of the past. In addition, by basing itself on this aspect, this study might be able to examine and compare if there are similar characteristics between the Ancient Israelite society and the Ao Naga tribal community on the roles and responsibilities of women in their day-to-day lives and experiences.

Another aspect of bringing in biblical study in this research is that the Ao Naga tribal community is already impressed and infused with Christianity, and literally believes what the scripture says. However, reliance on the literal texts of scripture might cultivate misinterpretation and misimpression about women and their voice. For that reason, it is necessary to discuss the nature and condition of women in Judaism and Ancient Israel.

It is agreed that the bible, which we believe dearly, has its own limitations. It has its biases in its own content, subject, and authorship, and since it has been written down from patriarchal perspectives the bible as a whole is androcentric or male-centred in nature. Ivy mentioned that: "The main focus of the bible is on the public and communal life of the people dominated by men-king, warriors, priests, prophets and others. Women's appearance in the public sphere and their private and domestic daily life are limited and constrained."[589] Therefore it is not surprising to see one-sided male-centred interpretation and writing in the bible. The biblical narratives are based and written mostly with the vested interest of men's knowledge as the norm. Therefore, women are in most cases invisible, and are generally portrayed from the perspective of male authors. Bearing all this in mind, we would like to discover how we understand the position of women's voice – how and where it has been located in the past. Did women really have voice in the Ancient Israelite society? Is there a similar situation with the present Ao Naga tribal women regarding women's voice in the community? In this study, we will observe the *Social, Legal* and *Religious life* of the people of Ancient Israelite society.

i. Social Life

In the Hebrew Scriptures, it is clearly mentioned that family is considered one of the basic social units in ancient Israel. Gen. 24:38 talks about the "father's house" or the 'household,' which was the basic unit of kinship in Israel. Gen. 38:11 and Lev. 22:13 reveal the frequent phrase used for "family" that means "house of one's father."[590] The role of the father begins at home and extends to the wider community.

---

[589] Ivy, *Voices from Narmada: Doing Ecofeminist Theology* (Delhi: ISPCK, 2009), 232.

[590] Shobana Kingson, "Forgetting the Father's House Vs. Honoring the Parents in the Hebrew Scriptures: Implications for Modern Families in India," in *Religion and Society*, 58/1&2 (March-June, 2013): 71-72.

The Hebrew family consisted of relatives or ancestors, above all the lineage. For them, the "father's house" was an extended family which comprised all the descendants of a single living ancestor which included the head of the house and his wife.[591] W.A. Visser't Hooft in his book explained:

> The father's role was monarchal, and the principal duty of the children was to honour and obey him ... the father was also the judge and priest of the household, holding social and religious sway over his wife or wives, his children and his slaves. His power was absolute, and he could, if he so desired, sell his daughter into slavery.[592]

A woman after marriage became her husband's property. As payment for a debt a female child could be sold by her father (Exod. 21:7).[593] The birth of a female child was less desirable than the birth of a son.[594] All a woman had to do was to submit herself to her father before marriage, and after marriage to her husband. She had no other option but to capitulate under the control of these males (husband or father) even if she was mistreated and abused. This was visible when Lot was ready to offer his daughters as substitute: "Look, I have two daughters who have not known a man; let me bring them out to you, and do to them as you please; only do nothing to these men, for they have come under the shelter of my roof" (Gen.19:8).

The wife's main task was to bear a (male) child (Gen. 16:1–2). Upon the death of her husband if he left her without a child; the wife of a deceased assumed power over her by marrying her to one of her husband's brothers or to the nearest kin (Gen. 38).[595] Keci Siang continued: "Barrenness was viewed as the ultimate dishonour, understood as a sign of divine disfavour (Gen. 30:23; 2 Sam. 6:20–23)."[596] Her status in Judaism was always regarded as "other" (inferior, or unclean or sinful).[597] She was subordinate to her husband.

---

591 Shobana Kingson, "Forgetting the Father's House Vs. Honoring the Parents in the Hebrew Scriptures: Implications for Modern Families in India," in *Religion and Society*, 58/1&2 (March-June, 2013): 71-72.

592 W. A. Visser't Hooft, *The Fatherhood of God in an Age of Emancipation* (Geneva: World Council of Churches, 1982), 5.

593 Gail B. Shulman, "View from the Back of the Synagogue: Women in Judaism," in *Sexist Religion and Women in the Church: No More Silence!*, edited by Alice L. Hageman (New York: Association Press, 1974), 150.

594 Vincent Emmanuel Hannon, *The Question of Women and the Priesthood* (London: Geoffrey Chapman, 1967), 63.

595 Keci Siang, *Paul, Women and Female Imagery: Approaching Difficult Passages* (Aizawl: Research and Development Department, Academy of Integrated Christian Studies, 2010), 22.

596 Ibid,. 23.

597 Gail B. Shulman, "View from the Back of the Synagogue, op.cit.,145.

In the Hebrew Scriptures, the husband was his wife's *baal*, that is, lord. "The forms of address used by husband and wife underscore the patriarchal structure of the Jewish family in Talmudic times. Whereas she called him "Rabbi," the term a slave or student used to mean "my master," he called her "my daughter."[598] In the rabbinic period the age of marriage for a woman was twelve and a half years, whereas a man's age compared to her was late teens or early twenties. The reason why she was counted as inferior and unequal to man may be due to the lack of education as well as marrying immaturely.[599]

It is mentioned that one of the most patriarchal influences in the Mediterranean crescent was the Palestinian Jewish culture. Women's roles and functions were restricted greatly, women being denied: (1) "their rights of inheritance; (2) their choice of relationships; (3) their ability to pursue a religious education or fully participate in the synagogue; and (4) their freedom of movement."[600]

Hans Küng adds that: "Husbands are advised not to talk much even with their own wives, far less with the wives of others. Women withdrew from public life as much as possible. In the temple, they had access only to the Court of Women. And their duties in offering prayer were identical to those of slaves."[601] This has been reflected even in the code of law where women are dealt unjustly and ignored by the judiciary.

ii. Legal life – the Judiciary

The testimony of women bore very little weight in court. A woman could not initiate divorce, but only a man could do so, which was referred to as "putting his wife away." When divorcing his wife, he must return the dowry which she had brought him during their marriage. However, divorces could be made without the return of the dowry if a wife had broken the Mosaic Law. Violation of the Mosaic law by a woman is, for instance, serving untithed food, having intercourse with her husband during her menstrual period, failing to set aside a dough offering, failing the vows; by breaking the law of Jewish customs such as a woman going out with loosened hair, spinning wool in the street, speaking with any man or by cursing the parents of her husband in his presence. According to some rabbis, the only claim on which a man could divorce his wife was due to her unchastity (Deut. 24:1). For others it could be anything including indecent cooking by his wife, and the husband preferring to have another woman. A wife could seek divorce only on one condition, that is, her husband's denial of cohabitation. Even then, it was also

---

[598] Gail B. Shulman, "View from the Back of the Synagogue, op.cit.,150.

[599] Ibid., 150.

[600] Amy-Jill Levine, "Second Temple Judaism, Jesus, and Women: Yeast of Eden," *Biblical Interpretation*, 2/1, (March, 1994): 8-33.

[601] Hans Küng, *Women in Christianity*, translated by John Bowden (London: Continuum, 2005), 2.

possible only on a personal and informal basis between her and her husband. Here again, she could set down the condition of the bill of divorce, but it was valid only if her husband signed the bill of divorce. The situation was worse and even more pathetic for a woman whose husband had deserted her and disappeared, because in a Jewish court, it was he who must initiate divorce proceedings. This ancient Jewish tradition remained the same even in the religious community.[602]

Women had the right to bear witness only in exceptional cases, such as the re-marriage of a widow, or the witness regarding the death of her husband which is similar to the witness of a Gentile slave.[603] Gail B. Shulman writes: "The rabbi repeatedly classed her with children and slaves in legal formulae, deemed her 'light' (flighty), and did not permit her to take oaths or give formal testimony."[604]

iii. Religious Life

There was wide disparity between women and men when it came to religious matters. Women were regarded as inferior beings with regard to the Torah; she was forbidden to study the Torah and was not allowed to recite the daily *shema*. Conservative Jews became more uncompromising in their interpretation of the Torah during the period of Hellenization. Many more regulations were added to God's Laws, thereby becoming more rigid, exclusive and male-biased, and the oral law prohibited speaking to a woman in public. The Jewish male prejudice over against females is quite evident in the morning prayer of the Jewish male, which goes like this, "Blessed art thou, O Lord our God, King of the Universe who has not made me a woman."[605]

Women, slaves and minors were exempted from *sukkah* and are also prohibited from living in the booth. Prema Vakayil writes: "The rabbis quoted a series of commandments from which wife was exempted: to make pilgrimages to Jerusalem on the feast of the Passover, Pentecost and Tabernacles."[606] It is recorded that deaf, mutes and women were not allowed to go to the Temple Mount. In the public prayer sessions women were grossly set aside. Women were not considered qualified to form a quorum in the worship community. In other rabbinic literature too, women were classified with children and slaves who similarly did not qualify.[607]

The Hebrew Scriptures are dominated by male heroes: Abraham, Moses, Joshua, David. The judges and prophets are exclusively or predominantly males:

---

[602] Hans Küng, *Women in Christianity*, translated by John Bowden (London: Continuum, 2005), 151.

[603] Prema Vakayil CSST, *Women Shall Prophesy: Anna, The Prophetess (Lk 2:36-38): A Study in Luke's Feminine Perspective* (Bangalore: Asian Trading Corporation, 2007), 53.

[604] Gail B. Shulman, "View from the Back of the Synagogue, op. cit., 150.

[605] Ibid., 145.

[606] Prema Vakayil, *Women Shall Prophesy, op.cit.*, 51-52.

[607] Ibid., 51-2.

Samson, Jephthah, Isaiah, Jeremiah etc., and even the teachers of the rabbinic period were all male.[608] The rabbinic literature did not make any attempt or to require study of the Torah for female children. It was the Rabbis who opposed female education very strongly. The result was that due to the unequal treatment among males and females in education, the inferior status of women in rabbinic literature developed.[609] Men fulfilled their *mitzvah* (divine commandment, good deed, merit) of the Torah (the teachings, the law, the Hebrew Scriptures, the entire body of Jewish wisdom; also the scrolls containing the Pentateuch), excelling in their studies, whereas their wives were confined in their own homes just to excel in their household chores.[610] Therefore, women not being permitted the study of the Torah naturally led to the belief that they were inferior in the eyes of God.[611]

It is obvious that the condition of women in Ancient Israelite Judaism was one of lived misery. Their entire existence on earth was full of hardship, and there was no room for them to voice their rights both in the family and society, either in religious life or in legal matters. Women were confined, tied-up and ruled by the staunch patriarchal norms in all spheres. Amy-Jill Levine also pointed out the socio-cultural and religious background of women in Judaism. Women were kept in subordinate position, where misogyny was profoundly and intimately bound up with Judaism in that formative period. Women were regarded as "weak-willed, wanton, and, in general, worthless."[612] Therefore, one can safely assume that the lot of a woman in Judaism in Ancient Israel was to be considered as an inferior being. The voice of women and their life existence seems to have had no meaning at all. As Elizabeth Candy Stanton once wrote:

> The canon and civil law; church and state; priests and legislators; all political parties and religious denominations have alike taught that woman was made after man, of man, and for man, an inferior being, subject to man.[613]

The voice of women was minimal in the ancient Israelite community in the socio-cultural, religious-political and economic domains. When this is juxtaposed with the similarities in the present Ao Naga tribal community, there is a noticeable absence of women's voice in the decision-making bodies in both societies that are millennia apart.

---

[608] Gail B. Shulman, "View from the Back of the Synagogue, op. cit.,145.

[609] Ibid., 147-8.

[610] Ibid., 145.

[611] Ibid., 149.

[612] Amy-Jill Levine, "Second Temple Judaism, Jesus, and Women: Yeast of Eden," *Biblical Interpretation*, 2/1, (March, 1994): 8-33.

[613] Elizabeth Candy Stanton, (et al.), *The Women's Bible, Part I, Comments on Genesis, Exodus, Leviticus, Numbers and Deuteronomy, Part II, Judges, Kings, Prophets and Apostles* (6th Reprint) New York: European Publishing Company, 1898), 7.

5.2. Customary Law and the Voice of Ao Naga Tribal Women

Although, women's emancipation has gained momentum everywhere in the world, it is ironic that woman's voices are still debarred from all the decision-making bodies in communities like that of the Ao Naga tribals in Northeast India. Ao society, like that of various other Naga tribes, is considered to have "developed a rudimentary but effective form of democracy" which has been practised from time immemorial.[614] However, based on the traditional socio-cultural ground, "the customary laws" have been placed above everything else in the Ao Naga tribal society today. When it comes to women's voice in the decision-making bodies, women do not have any voice at all. This is similar to the condition of Ancient Israelite women in their socio-cultural, religious and political settings, women who have no voice in the day to day affairs of the community.

Customary laws are a vital set of laws both for the Ao Naga tribal community in past and in present day Ao society. Though new legal systems have been introduced and reinforced in all the regions, the traditional customary law has gained more importance in Ao Naga tribal community. It has become intrinsic to their identity, and part and parcel of their culture and tradition.[615] Since the traditional socio-cultural, economic, religious and political systems of Ao Naga tribal community are all controlled by males with the customary law strengthening their hand, women do not have place to gain their voice.

The nature and function of customary law in the Ao Naga tribal community is disadvantageous to women in many areas. Rosemary Dzuvichu has rightly observed that the customary laws and practices have turned out to be the biggest stumbling blocks for women's empowerment, both politically and socially, in the state. They do not enjoy any privileges, and their status is inferior to men.[616] The customary laws restrict women from inheriting land and property specifically in

---

[614] Sanjoy Hazarika, *Strangers of the Mist: Tales of War and Peace from India's Northeast, Revised Edition* (New Delhi: Penguin Books India, 2011), 93.

[615] Customary law is defined as habits that grew into customs through imitation and acquiescence in the values they symbolise. Gradually a norm becomes a law when the community members respect and adhere to it as integral to their heritage. It is an unwritten law and usage regulating the human behaviour of individuals. Such laws maintain social order and are a stabilising factor in that society. Customary Law can thus be defined as a set of rules because a society observes them continuously and uniformly for a long time and that it becomes a force of law. These customs had been handed down from one generation to the next, providing rules, enforcement procedures and punishment for violations. Thus, a customary law is the habitual course of conduct of a society containing dos and don'ts based on its norms, practices and usages, mechanisms such as taboos, sanctions, social rituals, culture, public opinion and ethics of each individual, and thus restrains their patterns of behaviour. See Walter Fernandes, Melville Pereira, Vizalenu Khatso, *Customary Laws in North East India: Impact on Women* (New Delhi: National Commission for Women, n.d.), 24.

[616] Quoted in Prasanta Mazumdar, "Standing her ground in patriarchal Naga society," 8 March 2013, Guwahati http://www.dnaindia.com/india/report-standing-her-ground-in-patriarchal-naga-society-1808598 accessed on 12.10.13.

the rural setups. Asangla Lemtur Paul, expresses the present condition of the Ao Naga tribal community where women are given a subordinate status in society:

> In the economic sphere women's freedom to work is dominated by men and women are compelled to remain dependent on men ... In the political sphere, women's suffrage did not bring an equal distribution of political power. Women's participation in political decision-making is null and void. A woman entering a career gives up her femininity or family. A woman talking about violation of her rights means she has gone insane. In the ideological realm, women are still considered as lower beings and objects of sexual desire.[617]

Even the provision given by the Constitution of India which was implemented for the benefit of the people of Nagaland, the 1963 amendment of Article 371-A which had been introduced to bring civil affairs in Nagaland under the tribal customary laws, does not seem to have met the needs and purposes of all citizens. This is especially true for women in Nagaland in general and the women of Ao Naga tribal society in particular. The constitutional rights have rather been used to strengthen the patriarchal manoeuvres in the Naga tribal society based on the "customary law." There is no room for women's rights and privileges in Ao society under the customary laws. This leads to denial of land rights, denial of equal participation in decision-making bodies, etc. Women are just expected to obey, follow and subscribe to the decisions of men.

Article 371-A of the Constitution of India says,

> Notwithstanding anything in this Constitution –
> (a) no Act of Parliament in respect of -
> (i) religious or social practices of the Nagas,
> (ii) Naga customary law and procedure,
> (iii) administration of civil and criminal justice involving decisions according to Naga customary law,
> (iv) ownership and transfer of land and its resources,
>
> shall apply to the state of Nagaland unless the Legislative Assembly of Nagaland by a resolution so decides;[618]

All these provisions are apparently meant to safeguard the rights of the Nagas as a tribal community as well as to grant them a certain level of autonomy within the larger framework of Indian democracy. However, they have so far been used only to safeguard the privileges of male Nagas, who have utilised this Act

617 Asangla Lemtur Paul, "Naga Women or Women in Nagaland?: Denied Identity" in *Women's Issues and Reflections* edited by, Christina Manohar (Delhi: ISPCK, 2012), 87.

618 *The Constitution of India*, 1st edition (Lucknow: Eastern Book Company, 2009), 315.

to maintain the status quo in order to consolidate and exercise their power. M. Parwez, in his writing brought out: "Article 371-A of the Constitution provided them immunity from Parliamentary legislation in almost all their affairs unless the local bodies adopt it."[619] One example can be seen in the developments in the recent past that followed parliamentary decisions and governmental initiatives for the empowerment of Indian women, inclusive of Naga women.[620] The Naga Hohos (men) of different tribes of Nagaland, along with the Legislative Assembly of Nagaland, all males, turned down and rejected implementation of 33% reservation for women in the Town Councils and Municipality elections. One of the prominent Naga men said: "It was not a question of either curtailing the rights of Naga women or the murder of democracy as women had to stay within certain limits according to customary and traditional practices."[621] Another member of the *Ao Senden* said that he opposed reservation – for women, that is, and not necessarily reservation *per se* – because "reservation is against the customary laws and also against the Constitution's provisions of Article 371-(A)."[622] This is a clear indication of how the male majority in the Naga tribal community of Nagaland exercises power and control over women by misinterpreting and misappropriating the Constitutional rights in the name of protecting "customary law." N. Janbemo Humtsoe has rightly expressed that:

> Resurgence of resistance from prominent male dominated Naga civil organizations to the proposed implementation of women's reservation in the Nagaland State Municipal and Town Councils elections on grounds of Naga customary laws and traditions doesn't seem to qualify as a valid argument for the opposition of the Act. Rather, it appears

---

[619] M. Parwez, "Searching Space: Women in The Customary Laws and Practices of the Tribal Societies in North East India," *Indian Journal of Applied Research*, 2/3 (March, 2013): 175-177.

[620] The problem began when the Municipal Committee Elections in the municipal area called Mokokchung Municipal Council (MMC), among the Ao tribe of Nagaland, which was supposed to be held in October 2008, was cancelled. This was due to the issues surrounding the Women Reservation Bill which stipulated that 33% of seats to all elected bodies be reserved for women. The reason was that a number of men opposed and resented the amendment made by the state government (2006-7 Acts). They felt that it went against their customary law. According to the customary law, female members have no right to hold any office, or participate in public meetings which function as decision-making bodies. I. Lanusenla, "Called To Communicate The Words of Prophecy, Reconciliation and Healing." Paper presented at a theological workshop in Chennai organized by Christian Conference of Asia (CCA) in 2009.

[621] Daily Newspaper, "*The Telegraph*: Calcutta India" http://www.telegraphindia.com/1121001/jsp/northeast/story_16036726.jsp#.UaYCVNKnoSt, accessed on 29.6.2013.

[622] Jitendra, "Naga women approach Supreme Court for reservation of seats in local bodies" *Down To Earth*. http://www.downtoearth.org.in/content/naga-women-approach-supreme-court-reservation-seats-local-bodies accessed on 20.9.13.

> that the article 371(A) is again misused and abused with so many politically hidden agendas and socially flagitious intention.[623]

Indeed, "the strengthening of patriarchal modes of control has legitimized the processes of exclusion or marginalization of women from decision-making and political power."[624] Sano Vamuzo also says that:

> One should not misunderstand the objective of reservation – this 33 percent will not infringe upon the basic rights of men in our society. Even though the existing Naga customary law is gender biased in favour of the men folk, the proposed 33 percent reservation in Nagaland is in no way going to challenge or change the existing customary law on property rights, inheritance, etc.[625]

In September 2012, Naga women, under the aegis of the Joint Action Committee on Women Reservation, decided to organise a rally in protest against the resolution of the Nagaland State Assembly not to implement 33 per cent reservation for women in the municipal and town councils. Male-only organisations like the *Ao Senden*, the apex Naga organisation in Mokokchung district, warned women not to come out on the streets, and directed all units to stop women from organising protests.[626] The incident highlights the misogyny that often undergirds this type of male-only organisation, even one which claims to stand on behalf of the community as a whole. It is also a reminder that the traditional patriarchal Ao Naga tribal mentality which formed part and parcel of the ordinary Ao male psyche, and which ratified discrimination against women, still remains firm. This patriarchal mind-set that segregates women was widely visible in Ao society before. One such example is seen in a woman's personal experience that happened years ago:

> In 1957, out of the six Naga students who appeared [at] the matric exams from Namti Ali Government aided high school … she was the only one who passed. That also made her the first woman matriculate from her village … she decided to join the Eastern Theological

[623] N. Janbemo Humtsoe, "Naga Customary Laws and Women Reservation," *Morung Express* 20 June 2012.

[624] Jitendra, "Naga women approach Supreme Court for reservation of seats in local bodies."

[625] Sano Vamuzo, "Naga Women and the need for 33% reservation," http://www.morungexpress.com/frontpage/78468.html accessed on 1.12.13

[626] The Eastern Nagaland People's Organisation banned the rally in the four districts of Kiphire, Mon, Longleng and Tuensang, where it has considerable influence. It directed its members residing outside these four districts to abstain from the rally and warned that anyone participating would be doing so on their own responsibility. See, "Naga Groups 'Ban' Women Quota Rally". http://www.telegraphindia.com/1121001/jsp/northeast/story_16036726.jsp#.UaYCVNKnoSt, accessed on 29.6.2013.

> College, Jorhat … Co-incidentally, the same year her village celebrated its Golden Jubilee and presented her with the then generous sum of rupees two hundred for her success in the exams. She was first ecstatic to receive such an unexpected and large hearted gesture from her church. But, later on she learnt that the village church had actually planned to sponsor the first person from the village for theological studies presuming that the person would be a male. As she happened to be a female they decided not to sponsor her but give her a sum of money instead. Disappointed deeply at the realisation that the generous amount received so happily from the church was an afterthought and a substitution …[627]

Still today, negative attitudes towards women, and the ignoring and devaluing of a woman's achievements is the harsh reality in Naga tribal communities. In the case mentioned above, which is the real-life experience of an Ao Naga woman, she had been downgraded and side-lined by her community even though she surpassed every one among her tribe in her class, all because she was just a woman. There was no one to raise their voice for her and tell that she was a capable, intelligent and determined person, all because only men and no women were represented in the decision-making bodies. Today many such negative attitudes have changed, but they have not yet been removed completely, both in the church as well as in the society.

Nagas have gained an amendment to the Constitutional right to follow their customary laws. However, instead of reforming their imbalanced traditional socio-cultural structures which give no room to develop gender justice, Naga men have not moved even an inch to accommodate others, particularly women. This is particularly true of the Ao Naga tribal community. According to Temsula Ao: "Hardened by centuries of being bred in a system in which the inferiority of women in matters of social significance in society was accepted as a fact of life, Naga men find it extremely difficult to liberate themselves from this handicap."[628] One of the renowned women in Nagaland said that the need for women's reservation would not arise had there been true Christian spirit and true democracy. Hence, the need for reservation or quota has come up as a measure to ensure women's participation in decision-making bodies.[629] The suppression of Ao Naga tribal women in the community continues. They are being denied, in the name of "tradition and

[627] Sennangshila Longchar, "The Pioneering Pastor with Foresight and Determination," Unpublished Manuscript received on January. 2014.

[628] Temsula Ao, "'Benevolent Subordination': Social Status of Naga Women," in *The Peripheral Centre: Voices from India's Northeast,* edited by Preeti Gill (New Delhi: Zubaan, 2010), 104.

[629] Sano Vamuzo, "Naga Women and the need for 33% reservation" http://www.morungexpress.com/frontpage/78468.html accessed on 1.12. 2013.

culture," the freedom to exercise fundamental human rights, i.e. "the freedom of expression and the freedom of speech." As it is remarked:

> The women believed that the biased interpretation of the Customary Law promote[s] hierarchy, disempowerment and oppressive and is discriminatory for the women. Even in present time the Naga women are deprived of any participation in indigenous community institutions of the Hoho and Gaonboras."[630]

The statement made by Sonia Bathla decades ago when expressing the position of Indian women still holds relevance among the Ao Naga tribal community. She said that women are considered the carriers of culture, expected to live up to the traditions, and to retain the nation's identity against foreign cultures. Women are trapped in within the complexities of a transitional society with a "modern face but traditional soul", in spite of its being the largest democracy in the world, the condition of women in Indian society remains powerless.[631]

As Melville Pereira has rightly observed, in the process of change, some of the elements of customary laws can also stagnate amid their evolution, and give people a rigid interpretation especially if the customs continue when their social base has changed.[632] Pereira mentioned that: "A community may justify their continuance or avoidance by stating that its forefathers have ordained them."[633] This is true of the situation in Nagaland, where women have made tremendous progress in many spheres such as education, but men resist change on the basis of tradition.[634] It is said: "Nagas instead of using our customary practices as a step forward are using it as an obstacle."[635] One of the primary excuses Naga men often made is based on the customary laws and practices that exclude women in all spheres thus violating their rights. The major tragedy of women in Nagaland is that over the years there has not been the slightest change in their position in

---

[630] M. Parwez, "Searching Space: Women in The Customary Laws and Practices of the Tribal Societies in North East India", *Indian Journal of Applied Research*, 176.

[631] Sonia Bathla, *Women, Democracy and the Media: Cultural and political representations in the Indian Press* (New Delhi: SAGE Publications, 1998), 43

[632] Melville Pereira, "Modernisation of Customary Laws as Constraint to Development in the Northeast" *National Conference on Institutional Barriers to Development in the Northeast,* (Kohima: Nagaland University and Omeo Kumar Das Institute of Social Change and Development, 29-30th March, 2004). onlineministries.creighton.edu/.../NESRC/.../MELINSTBARRIERS.do..., accessed on 12.10.13

[633] Ibid.

[634] Ibid.

[635] "Nagas need to do away with outstanding customary practices" http://www.morungexpress.com/local/104624.html accessed on 8.10.13

the society.[636] Samuel May, a Unitarian clergyman once advocated equal rights for women:

> No! Woman is not the creature, the dependent of man but of God. We may with no more propriety assume to govern women than they might assume to govern us. And never will the nations of the earth be well-governed until both sexes, as well as all parties, are fairly represented and have an influence, a voice, and, if they wish, a hand in the enactment and administration of the laws.[637]

It is foolhardy for any community to cling on to a fixed traditional mind-set and unjust irrational belief systems while at the same time trying to fit in to the modern world. Global society is increasingly becoming a vast network of interconnected societies and interlinked communities. This network increasingly facilitates the vital flow of information, thereby ensuring that issues and concerns are communicated and awareness created through the sharing of ideals. To hold its own among such societies and communities, each society or community must ensure that there is vital flow of information to all sections – sex, class, culture, etc., and at all levels – local, state, national and international. Hence, contemporary Ao Naga tribal community needs to question and reconsider its age-old customary laws and traditional norms that do not allow half of its population to communicate and voice their concerns. Tissa Balasuriya has rightly expressed that:

> The pluralist worldview would not consider one people or their own values as necessarily more important than those of others. Historically, most humans have not had a pluralist worldview in that they have not recognised or respected many other aspects of this diversity, as they lived within their own narrow confines and knew or thought little of others. They often considered their own community as the main reality on earth. Others were less important or were considered alien or even subordinate to them.[638]

Genuine communication takes place when everybody joins in sharing their own views; expresses their own feelings, listens, and understands by equally participating regardless of frontiers. Balasuriya continued that: "We are all called

---

636 Prasanta Mazumdar, "Standing her ground in patriarchal Naga society", http://www.dnaindia.com/india/report-standing-her-ground-in-patriarchal-naga-society-1808598, accessed on 12.6.13

637 "Women's Suffrage," http://www.spartacus.schoolnet.co.uk/USAsuffrage.htm, accessed on 2.8.13.

638 Tissa Balasuriya O.M.I, "Communication Ethics with a Pluralist Worldview," in *Communication and Reconciliation: Challenges Facing the 21st Century*, edited by Philip Lee (London: WCC publications, Geneva, World Association for Christian Communication, 2001), 33.

to transcend our narrow particularities in order to arrive at a higher, wider and deeper level of sharing among all. This call demands a transformation of ourselves from within our innermost being, to accept all others as sisters and brothers."[639] As R.L. Hnuni once said, women need to have their hold which is imperative for empowerment and they need support in all social organisations, village level/town/municipal levels administration and in politics. If they are trusted, supported and given opportunities in decision-making bodies where they have never been before, they will surely do well.[640]

5.3. The Reformed Traditions and Culture[641]

Unlike Ao Nagas, other tribes in this regard seem to be more open and progressive when it comes to reviewing their customary laws towards more gender equality. It has been noticed that many customary laws have been reformed and are being transformed according to the change of time and situation. We can find in North-east India itself like that of Mizos in Mizoram, Paite in Manipur and Semas in Nagaland. This is noticeable in changes in the content, interpretation and enforcement.[642] They have led to the undoing of a few historical wrongs against women. One such example can be seen here:

> For instance, the Paite tradition did not allow parental property to be passed to the daughter even in the absence of a son. The Paite Tribal Council in a 2004 amendment to this law introduced provisions in favour of daughters, widows, illegitimate or adopted and other disinherited sons. They allow the father to appoint one of his daughters to inherit property if he does not have a son.[643]

Pereira, in his subtitle *Search for Solution* has given an important suggestion regarding the growth and development among the tribal customary laws. He said that if one were to think back only on the community's past history and try to retain the community as it was without looking forward, then it would be a romantic approach. On the other hand, if one looks only from the modern inputs without taking any precautionary measures to prevent impoverishment,

---

[639] Tissa Balasuriya O.M.I, "Communication Ethics with a Pluralist Worldview," in *Communication and Reconciliation: Challenges Facing the 21st Century*, edited by Philip Lee (London: WCC publications, Geneva, World Association for Christian Communication, 2001), 44.

[640] R.L. Hnuni, *Vision for Women in India: Perspectives from the Bible, Church and Society* (Bangalore: Asian Trading Corporation, 2009), 93.

[641] Here, the "Reformed Traditions and Culture" refers to the community who had already changed the old socio-cultural practices, norms and tradition that hampers the smooth functioning and growth of the common people mainly women.

[642] Melville Pereira, "Modernisation of Customary Laws, op. cit.

[643] Walter Fernandes, Melville Pereira, Vizalenu Khatso, *Customary Laws in North East India: Impact on Women* (New Delhi: National Commission for Women, n.d.), 4.

class formation and marginalisation it can be counterproductive. Therefore, he brought an example from *Nehru's Panchsheel for Tribal Development*, and said that tribal community ethos and values system should be the starting point and that one should attempt the type of development that combines the traditional with modern. Blending of these two seems to be the best way of ensuring development with class and gender equity.[644]

In Nagaland, particularly among the Ao Naga tribal community, it is clearly noticeable that based on the customary laws, the entire socio-cultural, economic and political structures are being laid, controlled and interpreted in the interests of the dominant males. This further leads to the creation of a few elite classes who are, quite naturally, not prepared to accept and talk about gender equity. Therefore, it is vital that people in the community really look for an alternative solution to the problem, if development and progress is to take place within the community as well as the in entire state. Pereira's statement made one to agree when he mentions: "So for equity based development to be real, one has to create a social environment aimed at motivating the men controlling their village councils and interpreting their customary law, to reinterpret their tradition in a more democratic form."[645] It is high time for the community to move on from a regressive mind-set that takes obsessive pride in its "rudimentary form of democracy,"[646] and to strive towards building a fully democratic society that ensures democratic participation and democratic decision-making.

Walter Fernandes and others have expressed concerns over customary laws. They believe that customary laws need to be recognised fully, but also contend that while recognising them formally, they have to be amended to ensure that women are equal participants in the village councils and other traditional bodies. If they fail to accommodate women in their socio-cultural and political setups, it would be the visible face of injustice.[647] Temsula Ao says that, "if there is going to be any meaningful reform in the society based on gender equality, it has to start from the grassroots level: the village polity."[648] It is also evident that the relationship between religion and society in the Ao Naga tribal community is intertwined. One such example is seen in a statement by Narola Imchen:

> If the church is to be restructured in such a way that discrimination against women is removed, so that the community of believers, composed of both women and men, can live and love in harmony with one another, and can thus be more effective agents of God's mission in

[644] Melville Pereira, "Modernisation of Customary Laws, op. cit.

[645] Ibid.

[646] Hazarika, Sanjoy. *Strangers of the Mist,* op. cit., 93.

[647] Walter Fernandes, Melville Pereira, Vizalenu Khatso, *Customary Laws in North East India: Impact on Women* (New Delhi: National Commission for Women, n.d.), 211-212.

[648] Temsula Ao, "'Benevolent Subordination', op. cit., 106.

> the world, it is necessary to recognize that the origins of the problem lie in the conditioning and continuance of traditional socio-cultural attitudes rather than in theological or biblical questions.[649]

Today, the entire Ao Naga tribe considers itself a Christian community where every individual is automatically registered Christian by birth.[650] As such, one might presume that the social, cultural, economic, religious, and political systems function according to Christian principles, in that they are managed and controlled by Christians. However, the Ao Christian community has a very unique characteristic which, in all likelihood, is an outcome of the Christianisation and accompanying process of modernisation initiated by American Baptist missionaries. The self-perception of the community is that of a tribe that enjoyed autonomy and independence till the advent of colonialism. These aspirations did not die out with the advent of colonialism, but the floodgates were opened for the influx of new teachings, ideas and principles, which have left imprints that lingered long afterwards. One of these is a peculiar understanding of the principle of separation of church and state which the community inculcated. The state, for the average Ao, is to be identified primarily with Ao society that functions in accordance with its customary laws alongside but not necessarily in direct relationship with the church.[651] Thus, there is an Ao society on one side, and an Ao church on the other.

However, the memberships of both institutions are drawn from the same populace. Having a foot in both realms, the community thus has to juggle its traditional understanding of customary laws and the Christian teachings of the Church, without any serious theological investigation so far into how these two could function together and complement each other. Moreover, there is the understanding that the ministrations of church and society should not overlap. Hence, there are instances of lay leaders leaving leadership positions in the church in order to take up their seats in the Village Council. The separation of church and state, as understood and practised by the Ao Christian community, further leads to a very unique situation. Some of the most progressive attitudes towards women – at least in comparison with some other Naga tribes – as well as regressive ones co-exist within the same community. For instance, the Aos as a community have a very good record in encouraging female education, both secular and theological. Rev. Sennangshila Longchar, whose experience at the beginning of her theological journey was recounted earlier, was the first female church leader to receive

[649] Narola Imchen, *Women in the History of Christianity* (N. p.: Tribal Development and Communication Centre, 2010), 199.

[650] The majority of Ao Christians belong to the Baptist tradition.

[651] There are instances when the two overlap, for instance, in the enforcement of exogamous marriage.

ordination and then be appointed Pastor.[652] And every local Ao Baptist church has a female Associate Pastor whose responsibilities include, but are not limited to, facilitating the ministry of the women's fellowship. Nevertheless, we have also seen how the *Ao Senden*, an all-male non-ecclesiastical organisation that aspires to speak for the community, reacted to the efforts to implement reservations for women in elections to local councils. It was a knee-jerk reaction, triggered by a deep-rooted understanding that only men should handle affairs of the society, and, by extension, the state. The average Ao male would readily accept a woman as a minister of the church. But, he has no compunction about protesting against any piece of legislation that could elevate her even to the position of a local councillor, let alone a minister in the state machinery.

Each individual, particularly male, member participates directly in the church as well as in the society, the state. Therefore, if they recognize the presence of God in them, that God dwells in them, and if they believe that every human being both female and male is made in the likeness of God and honour God above all, it is the individual that needs to be reformed first. In the writing of Imsenperong, Menjiwapong Jamir and Walotemjen it says: "Holding rigidly the traditional practice and custom without giving a place for re-interpretation in accordance to the flow of time is not *sobaliba* at all rather there is enough room for re-construction and re-interpretation in *sobaliba* for it is a science of human living."[653] The wholeness of life which is central to the Christian witness of faith cannot be accomplished without challenging political and social systems at present which make such fullness of life impossible.[654]

The church and society both need reform, to be converted into institutions that allow equal opportunity to voice in all the decision-making bodies without any discrimination based on gender. If people have genuine intention for change nobody will question it. It is only the mind, heart and attitude of the people that need to decide for the community either to bring transformation for the society without discriminating between genders or to remain adamant and static. Philip Potter once said: "The heart of God's revelation of humanity was male and female. In that he indicated to us that there is no homogeneous, uniform way by which

---

[652] Ordination is not a prerequisite for Pastoral Ministry in the Ao Baptist churches; local deacon boards select individual Pastors and Associate Pastors who are then licensed by ABAM (Ao Baptist Arogo Mungdang, the Association of Ao Baptist Churches) to perform the sacraments. Ordination is an honour bestowed upon the most respected Pastors and church leaders.

[653] Imsenperong, Menjiwapong Jamir, Walotemjen, *Mapping the Context: An Interdisciplinary Exploration* (Kohima: Authors, 2011), 46.

[654] Pamela Dickey Young, "Encountering Jesus through the earliest witnesses" *Theological Studies*, 57/3, (September, 1996): 520.

God wills that we should live, but rather in full recognition of our diversities and through those diversities we find our unity and community."[655]

5.4. Jesus's Movement a Voice for All

One of the mandates fulfilled through Jesus Christ is the "Salvation" and "Voice" conveyed for women. Jesus managed to elevate women by transforming old unjust structures and bringing them new life. The Jesus movement was against all the oppressive structures that had existed in the socio-cultural, religious, economic and political life of the people in Israelite society. Elisabeth Schüssler Fiorenza opined that Jesus's movements are to be understood as inner Jewish emancipatory movements that proclaimed the goodness of the Sophia-Creator God who wills the well-being of everyone without exception. It is indeed an inclusive ethos of Jesus movements which allow all that are, wo/men, the poor, the rich, and the cultically unclean as well as strict observers of Torah to become disciples.[656] S. Kappen commented on how Jesus showed objection through his word and deeds on this unjust state of affairs. Among his generation, Jesus was the first to have seen that man and woman are equal partners in the pursuit of fuller humanity.[657]

The call of women by Jesus and his allowing of women to follow him was unconventional in that it undermined the existing patriarchal structures.[658] Amy-Jill Levine writes: "Oppressed, repressed, suppressed, and therefore depressed by patriarchal socio-cultural controls, Jewish women of course were attracted to the "community of equals" of the Sophia - Christ."[659] In Hans Küng's writing, it is mentioned that:

> Jesus dissociated himself from the customary exclusion of women. Not only does Jesus show no contempt for women; he is amazingly open towards them. Women accompany him and his disciples from Galilee to Jerusalem. ... Joanna, Susanna, Mary the mother of James and Joses, Salome and 'many other women', first and foremost Mary of Magdala. Jesus showed personal affection towards women. The group of disciples, which travelled around without possessions and had no fixed abode, was given effective support by women and the families of sympathizers, like those of Martha and Mary.[660]

---

[655] Philip Potter, "A Chance to Change," in *The Community of Women and Men in the Church: The Sheffield Report,* edited by, F. Parvey (Geneva: World Council of Churches, 1983), 28.

[656] Elisabeth Schüssler Fiorenza, *Sharing Her Word: Feminist Biblical Interpretation in Context* (Edinburgh: T&T Clark, 1998), 114.

[657] S. Kappen (ed.), *Jesus Today* (Madras: AICUF, 1985), 51.

[658] Hans Küng, *Women in Christianity*, translated by John Bowden (London: Continuum, 2005), 2.

[659] Amy-Jill Levine, "Second Temple Judaism, Jesus, and Women: Yeast of Eden," in *Biblical Interpretation,* 2/1, (March 1994): 8-33.

[660] Hans Küng, *Women in Christianity*, op. cit., 2.

The entire gospel accounts record that women were faithful followers of Christ.

> Soon afterwards he went on through cities and villages, proclaiming and bringing the good news of the kingdom of God. The twelve were with him, as well as some women who had been cured of evil spirits and infirmities: Mary, called Magdalene, from whom seven demons had gone out, and Joanna, the wife of Herod's steward Chuza, and Susanna, and many others, who provided for them out of their resources. (Lk. 8:1-3; Mk. 15. 40-41; Mt. 27. 55-56.) Mary Magdalene went and announced to the disciples, "I have seen the Lord"; and she told them that he had said these things to her (Jn. 23:18, NRSV).

W. A. Visser't Hooft also writes that: "Jesus in his frequent encounters with women proved to be wholly free from any prejudice which allocated a subordinate role to women, and reflection upon this fact opens up even wider horizons."[661] As it is said:

> Jesus' attitude towards women was truly revolutionary because, in the way he treated them, he broke with Jewish as well as Roman custom. His disciples were surprised by his empathic attitude towards women, as when he spoke with a Samaritan woman (John 4:27) and when he shocked the Pharisees by rescuing a young woman from being stoned to death for adultery (John 8:3-11). Women surrounded Jesus during his ministry; invited him into their houses and, generally, seem to have been welcomed by him as disciples and friends.[662]

In the first chapter, the work and ministry of Jesus among women in public and his attitudes towards women was mentioned. Following from that, we shall now highlight how Jesus encountered women by questioning some of the Jewish tradition, how women were made visible before everyone, and that they are no longer subservient to the dominant socio-cultural-religious structures but rather included as Disciples of Christ. Some of the examples are as follows:

5.4.1. Jesus Communicated with the Bent-Over Woman on the Sabbath Day

Luke 13:1-17; 14 contains another liberating statement made about women by Jesus to the public. Susan McLeod-Harrison writes: "Jesus not only speaks with authority to evil beings, he also uses his voice to speak powerfully for those to whom no one listens. On a Sabbath, while he is in the respected and powerful position of speaking in the synagogue, Jesus notices a bent-over woman who

[661] W. A. Visser't Hooft, *The Fatherhood of God in an Age of Emancipation* (Geneva: World Council of Churches, 1982), 54.

[662] "Misogyny: The Origin and Effects of the Oppression of Woman" http://www.annebaring.com/anbar20_bk_dreamwater_08.htm, accessed on 18.10.13

can barely return his gaze."[663] Jesus' intervention with the bent-over woman on the Sabbath day is an exceptional one, transforming religious as well as cultural barriers and implementing new law, bringing hope to the distressed and lowly by revealing God's abundant grace upon women. Susan McLeod-Harrison, has described it this way:

> He discerns her poverty of spirit, and the kingdom that is truly hers. Calling her forth, he blesses her with the freedom, dignity, and beauty of a tall stature. Then, when the synagogue leader rebukes her implicitly for receiving healing on a Sabbath, Jesus defends her right to be healed as a "Daughter of Abraham." The title "Son of Abraham" would normally describe male Jews, so Jesus radically includes the woman, and all women, in God's kingdom.[664]

Healing on the Sabbath day, according to Jewish tradition, would constitute a violation of the Torah (Mt.12:9 – 14). In fact, Jesus' action was criticized, and the Pharisees consulted with one another as to how they might destroy Jesus. However, implicit in Jesus' action, according to Ted Newell, is an alternative, generous view of Israel's God and an apparently liberal, non-legal response to God. Jesus' main mission is to teach an interpretation of the Scriptures by precept and example toward a fuller picture of God. Ted Newell writes: "You are wrong, because you know neither the scriptures nor the power of God" (Mt. 22:29). According to Jesus, the dominant worldview was corrupt.[665]

5.4.2. The True Disciples of Christ

It has been witnessed in the gospel writings that women were faithful followers and true Disciples of Christ. One example can be seen in Luke 10:38-42. Here we see a clear indication of women whose characters have proved that they are undeniable Disciples of Christ.

In Luke 10:38-42, Jesus advocated for Mary to Martha. Martha's mind seems to have been preoccupied with the same old tradition where women's normal duty was nothing but to work at home. Having that same old concept in mind, she might have complained about Mary, who was sitting near Jesus listening attentively along with the male disciples uninterrupted by domestic works. Here, in this story the unusual practice of Mary "a woman," who went against her tradition, has been the main highlight in the gospel of Luke. J. Lyle Story, in "*The Discipleship of Women – From Jesus' Birth to the Empty Tomb*" posits that:

---

663 Susan McLeod-Harrison, "Good News for the Poor in Spirit: The Ways of Jesus and Power," *Mutuality*, 18/4 (winter, 2011): 7-9.

664 Ibid.

665 Ted Newell, "Worldviews in Collision: Jesus as Critical Educator," *Journal of Education & Christian Belief*, 13/2 (autumn, 2009), 141-154.

> Luke intends that his readers understand that Mary is a disciple whose activity is to be imitated. The setting itself is extraordinary in that it was unheard that a Jewish rabbi would enter and "teach" in the household of women who were not relatives. Jesus defies what is expected of a man and a woman. Jesus does not provide the answer that Martha expected. He does not devalue Martha's role of hospitality, nor does he question women's "traditional role." Instead, he focuses upon Mary's choice of discipleship, i.e., learning from him. This is the main issue of discipleship for both women and men. ...The response of faith and listening to Jesus are universal in nature and provide the common and equal ground between women and men. ... are summoned by Jesus to responsive "discipleship" to Jesus' words.[666]

Another example is seen in the "widow's offering" when she, with all her heart, could bring to God the most precious gift, i.e., everything she has.

> He looked up and saw rich people putting their gifts into the treasury; he also saw a poor widow put in two small copper coins. He said, "Truly I tell you, this poor widow has put in more than all of them; for all of them have contributed out of their abundance, but she out of her poverty has put in all she had to live on" (Lk. 21:1-4).

Susan McLeod-Harrison, in "Good News for the Poor in Spirit: The Ways of Jesus and Power," says, "Jesus also sees authentic discipleship in a woman, this time in a widow with clearly very little money ... Jesus commemorates her generous, faith filled act not only to the male disciples but also, through Luke, to Bible-readers throughout time."[667]

In Luke's gospel, Mary the mother of Jesus and Elizabeth the mother of John the Baptist are considered as the two intertwining annunciation stories of two women of faith who shared to each other their wondrous events from God which have to be fulfilled through them. "As "model disciples," the two women voice their heartfelt joy and acceptance of their new roles" (Lk. 1:39- 45ff.). J. Lyle Story wrote that:

> Discipleship also expresses itself through the confession by both women; Elizabeth is the first to confess Jesus as "my Lord,"... Her committed discipleship is all the more remarkable in that Mary says nothing at the moment about her own impending miracle birth, as though to say in response to Elizabeth, "He is not only your Lord, He

[666] J. Lyle Story, "The Discipleship of Women – From Jesus' Birth to the Empty Tomb," *Priscilla Papers*, 21/1 (Winter, 2007), 14-20.

[667] Susan McLeod-Harrison, "Good News For The Poor In Spirit, op. cit., 7-9.

is my Savior." In boldest relief, discipleship is linked to the miraculous activity of the Holy Spirit.[668]

In Luke's gospel we find two contrasting personalities, namely, Mary who believed in the signs of God's revelation, and Zechariah who doubted God's revelation on him that comes through the angel Gabriel. Zechariah said to the angel, "How will I know that this is so? (Lk. 1:18). God answered back to Zechariah's disbelieving word, but in a negative manner: "... you did not believe my words, which will be fulfilled in their time, you will become mute, unable to speak, until the day these things occur." (Lk. 1:20). J. Lyle Story mentioned that: "Both the young Mary and the aged Zechariah receive promises of a birth in impossible circumstances, and they respond with similar words; however, one is noted as believing and the other as unbelieving."[669]

Unlike Zechariah, a disbelieving husband, Elizabeth is also a believing woman like Mary. When she conceives, she expresses her thanks: "This is what the Lord has done for me when he looked favourably on me and took away the disgrace I have endured among my people" (Lk. 1:25). Since in the Hebrew Scriptures (cf. 1 Sam. 1: 7, 11) women were considered to be the faulty ones in the case of barrenness, it was an exciting and joyous moment of her life for Elizabeth. Hence, she states that the Lord has taken away her reproach, i.e., her barrenness.[670] Elizabeth and Mary could cling on to what the angle of the Lord revealed to them and believed without any doubt and they became the true Disciples of Christ. Pamela Dickey Young expressed that:

> The early Jesus movement did include women and men and was addressed to all as interpreters and experiencers, not just to some. As the movement recalled and passed on by its earliest followers, it manifested no signs of following an established order of domination and subordination.[671]

It is clear that Jesus accepts and includes everybody equally without barrier i.e. both female and male in his movement.

5.5. Women's Voice in the Early Church

It has been said that in the first two centuries after the death of Jesus, the contribution of women and the role they played was valued in the early Church. It is assumed that in the Greco-Roman world, of both the New Testament and the early Church, there was no social discrimination regarding the status and rights of women. In some parts of the Roman Empire, women were involved

---

[668] J. Lyle Story, "The Discipleship of Women, op. cit., 15.

[669] Ibid.

[670] Ibid.

[671] Pamela Dickey Young, "Encountering Jesus, op. cit., 520-521.

in business, social life, theatre, music, sports, travelling, with or without their husbands and as equals with men.[672] It is said that, the religious movements of the first, second and third centuries, which had influenced largely in the fourth century, had encouraged women to act independently of and/or equally with men in public life, especially in religious practices.[673]

There were many wealthy and distinguished women who were well respected in their community at that time. When they accepted Christianity, their whole households including slaves were baptised with them. In the early Christian community women preached, taught, baptised and performed healing and exorcisms. Women were impressed with Christianity because it gave them a freedom and respect that they were not accorded either in the Jewish, Greek or Roman culture.[674]

The Apostle Paul proclaimed the message of liberation to the believers by telling them to follow the footsteps of Christ and to adopt that which Christ has taught them. Unfortunately, among the young churches "this new freedom was misconstrued as an invitation to unlimited self-indulgence and the denial of moral standards and social conventions."[675] But, we also have reason to believe that were strong negative attitudes about women at work within Christian culture, not least because of Paul himself and his teachings.

Paul was brought up in the Jewish faith and the early Christian fathers. This is indicated in his writings to various churches. The instructions for women are such as to keep their heads covered, not to teach or speak in church and to be subject to their husbands in all things (1 Tim. 2:8–14, Eph. 5:22–4, 1 Cor. 14:34–5, 1 Cor. 11:7–9).[676] Therefore Paul, responding to some misconduct, instead of restoring them it had rather brought a more devastating result which placed greater emphasis on the need to follow the rules and norms of a rigid patriarchal society. Thus, the young churches lived in a dilemma between the old patriarchal ethics and the claims of the new faith.[677]

One is also led to believe that when it comes to the position of women, the Greco-Roman world of the early Church witnessed much variety and is quite difficult to assess. Therefore, we cannot simply generalise Jewish society as a single entity because there are exceptions that fall outside a normal framework; some of the Jewish women were 'free and married' in the first-century Greco-

[672] Louis A. Brighton, "The Ordination of Women: A Twentieth-Century Gnostic Heresy?" *Concordia Journal*, 8/1 (January, 1982), 12-18.

[673] Ibid.

[674] "Misogyny: The Origin and Effects of the Oppression of Woman" http://www.annebaring.com/anbar20_bk_dreamwater_08.htm, accessed on 18.10.13

[675] W. A. Visser't Hooft, *The Fatherhood of God in an Age of Emancipation,* op. cit., 7.

[676] "Misogyny: The Origin and Effects of the Oppression of Woman," http://www.annebaring.com/anbar20_bk_dreamwater_08.htm, accessed on 18.10.13

[677] W. A. Visser't Hooft, *The Fatherhood of God in an Age of Emancipation,* op.cit., 7.

Roman Palestine. It has been said that the Second Temple Jewish society was a heterogeneous one. Different groups lived by different versions of Jewish law, and Jesus and/or the gospel writers were a part of that community.[678]

Glenna Jackson has brought the study of many scholars including Ross Shepard Kraemer who argues about the omission of women's roles in public lives in the rabbinic literature within first century Judaism. It is said that, in the rabbinic writings, only the social realities of a handful of Jewish communities are highlighted, and at worst may reflect the utopian visions of a relative handful of Jewish men. In reality, when one looks carefully at the other epigraphical, archaeological and non-rabbinic writings as Kraemer has studied, some Jewish women seemed to have played active religious, social, economic, and even political roles in the community.[679] Bernadette J. Brooten claims that the inscriptional evidence indicates clearly shows that there were many early Jewish Christian women leaders in the community who hold leadership positions where one cannot simply ignore. The three such noted women were: the apostle Junia (Rom.1.7), the teacher and missionary Prisca (Acts 18.2, 18, 26; Rom. 16.3-4; I Cor. 16.19; 2 Tim. 4.19), and Miriam of Rom. 16.6).[680] It conveys to us this vital piece of information, that woman's voice was powerful, acknowledged, recognised and accepted among the early Christian community.

5.6. The Concept of Women in Philosophy and Religion

In the Christian era, male domination over females gradually becomes the norm in the minds and works of the great philosophers and religious thinkers. Negative views and concepts about women were to be seen in society both in the biblical and non-biblical worlds. Male chauvinistic views had extended across religious leaders' and the philosophers' minds. And it cannot be denied that this male-female dichotomy had crept in and was widely visible in its functioning in the entire socio-cultural, religious and political framework in any given society. The gender stereotypes of male as superior and dominating agent and female as an inferior being have been the norm based on the teachings of the early thinkers, reformers and religious leaders.

Some of the prominent nations of the ancient world, such as Greeks, Romans and Jews, whose notions were also based on patriarchal setups, failed to recognise the value of women in all spheres of life. This can be discerned in numerous writings. The Greek philosopher Socrates allegedly said that 'all the pursuits of men are the pursuits of women also, but in all of them a woman is inferior to a man.' Plato recorded Socrates' teachings and passed them on to his

[678] Glenna Jackson, "Jesus as First-Century Feminist: Christian Anti-Judaism?," *Feminist Theology: The Journal of the Britain & Ireland School of Feminist Theology*. Issue 19, (September, 98): 90-9.

[679] Ibid.

[680] Ibid., 92.

pupil, Aristotle. For Aristotle, reality is dynamic. But, growth and development are nowhere random. Either an animal or a plant, each own growth is determined by its final cause, that is, by what it is to become ultimately.[681] Chandrakala Padia mentioned the expression of Aristotle that:

> A seed necessarily tends to develop into a tree and a child into grown-up human beings. Likewise, a girl realizes her full significance as a female in becoming a mother, that is, by participating in the function of reproduction. But, in so doing (according to Aristotle), she is only a passive participant; she only provides matter to the process of reproduction, and the father provides the imprint of human personality (or the human form) on this matter: Man is thus the active agent and so may be regarded as superior to woman.[682]

For Aristotle, a man has the reasoning ability but not a woman. Even for Plato, women are considered as creatures of sheer passion. Even philosophers such as Rousseau and Hegel are not free from condemning women as an inferior sex.

Karen Jo Torjesen in her exploration highlights the impact of the Greek theory about human self which divides humanity into two aspects, the masculine self and feminine self. This belief had considerable influence, and the negative beliefs about woman's nature were communicated uncontrollably into Christianity through the philosophers. Men are considered as superior, masculine self-rational, virile, masterful and noble, and women are termed as an inferior aspect of humanity that is irrational, sexual, animal, and potentially dangerous.[683]

The patriarchal philosophical influence of the ancient cultures, namely the Greek (and Roman), combined with the Jewish (patriarchal) beliefs of Hebrew Scriptures such as the myth in the creation story about the sin of the Fall and the shame of sexuality, making a disastrous impact on women's psyche and women's lives in Christian culture.[684] Early Church fathers like Tertullian, who spoke against women's participation in the public act of worship, have had an immense negative impact on Christian believers. Tertullian claims that: "It is not permitted for a woman to speak in the church, nor is it permitted for her to teach, nor to baptize, nor to offer the Eucharist, nor to claim for herself a share in any masculine function – not to mention any priestly office."[685]

Even for thinkers closer to our times, such as Karl Barth, woman is ontologically subordinate to man, and Dietrich Bonhoeffer insisted that "women

---

[681] Chandrakala Padia, *Theorizing Feminism* (Jaipur: Rawat Publications, 2011), 27.

[682] Ibid.

[683] "Misogyny: The Origin and Effects of the Oppression of Woman," op. cit.

[684] Ibid.

[685] Louis A. Brighton, "The Ordination of Women: A Twentieth-Century Gnostic Heresy?," *Concordia Journal*, 8/1 (January, 1982), 12-18.

should be subordinate to their husbands."[686] Renowned religious leaders like Augustine, Thomas Aquinas, and the great religious reformers like Martin Luther were also no exception; they are all guilty of considering women as inferior beings.[687] As Mary Daly observed, "… the system and the entire conceptual apparatus of Christian theology, developed under the conditions of patriarchy, have been the products of males and that in large measure these serve the interests of sexist society."[688] It is therefore, logical to conclude that patriarchal religion supports and perpetuates patriarchy.[689]

5.6.1. Voice in Christian History

In the religious sphere, especially among the Christian community, women have worked hard in the formation of the Church, and have helped to lay a firm foundation for it. One such example is found in the early Baptist church history. Harry Leon McBeth, years ago presented his papers on "The changing role of women in Baptist history" it goes like this:

> In 1929 when a woman addressed the Southern Baptist Convention, several men used every effort to prevent her from speaking. In 1978 it was a woman who drew the largest crowd and the most publicity as she addressed the Pastors' Conference before the Convention.
>
> In 1885 women were excluded from the Southern Baptist Convention and the constitution changed to prevent women from being messengers; in 1963 a woman was elected vice-president of the Convention.
>
> In 1901 a few women were allowed to sit in the back of the classroom at Southern Baptists' only seminary, but they could not raise questions or write exams, and they could not receive degrees. In 1978 every SBC seminary has women students, women trustees, and women faculty, including at least two ordained ministers.[690]

The statement above shows that in the early years, women had shown their strength and zeal of moving forward in the midst of dominated male counterpart even in the churches.

---

[686] Mary Daly, "Theology After the Demise of God the Father: A Call for the Castration of Sexist Religion," in *Sexist Religion and Women in the Church: No More Silence!, edited by, Alice L. Hageman (New York*: Association press, 1974), 125-6.

[687] Robert Runcie, "1354 Years from that Easter Day," in *The Community of Women and Men in the Church: The Sheffield Report*, edited by, Constance F. Parvey (Geneva: World Council of Churches, 1983), 20-21.

[688] Mary Daly, "Theology After the Demise of God the Father, op. cit., 127.

[689] Ibid., 126.

[690] Harry Leon McBeth, "The changing role of women in Baptist history," *Southwestern Journal of Theology*, 22/1 (1979), 84-96.

John Smyth's writing is often considered as the earliest recorded comment on the role of Baptist[691] women in 1609. In Smyth's record, it is written that, the Church hath power to elect, approve, and ordain her own Elders and Deacons of both men and women.[692] Thomas Helwys issued a Baptist confession of faith in 1611, in which Article 20 says: "That the Officers off everie Church or congregation are either Elders, who by their office do especially feed the flock concerning their souls ... or Deacons Men, and Women who by their office releave the necessities off the Poor."[693]

Time and again there was opposition to women's active roles in Baptist polity. This is found in the writing of Thomas Edwards, a leading English churchman who, in 1646, wrote a book against Baptists entitled *Gangraena*. With great resentment, he accused Baptists of tolerating women who preach and who also baptise in their time.[694] Though there were troubles and hardships as a result of opposition from their male counterparts, one cannot simple erase the work and ministry of women as found in early Baptist history. Leon McBeth narrated a story about Dorothy Hazzard, a young widow from a Baptist church in England back in the late 1630s.[695]

Hazzard was not a Baptist at the beginning, but was a devoted Christian who valued the Bible and was opposed to infant baptism. She had often met with and gathered a band of dissenters, men and women, at her house for Bible study and prayer. When John Canne, a Baptist preacher, came to Bristol in early 1640, Dorothy Hazzard sought him out and heard him preach.[696] It was said to believe that Dorothy Hazzard had led them to accept believer's baptism and form themselves into a Baptist church. She had been a teacher, preacher, Bible study leader, and personal soul-winner. [697]

Nineteenth century Southern Baptist women in America, Lottie Moon and WMU, were renowned members who made their greatest impact in missions. It is also mentioned that apart from missions, Southern Baptist women made their greatest contribution in the area of stewardship. The Southern Baptist Convention adopted major statements on stewardship in 1873, 1884, and 1888, but none of them mentioned tithing. It is mentioned that most Southern Baptists had never

---

[691] The Baptist tradition, as far as we know, originated in England in the early 17th century, See Harry Leon McBeth, "The changing role of women in Baptist history," op. cit., 85- 6.

[692] William T. Whitley, ed. *The Works of John Smyth,* Vol. II (Cambridge: University Press, 1915), 509.

[693] William L. Lumpkin, ed. *Baptist Confessions of Faith* (Philadelphia: The Judson Press, 1959), 121-22, quoted in Harry Leon McBeth, "The Changing Role of Women in Baptist History," 85-6.

[694] Harry Leon McBeth, "The Changing Role of Women in Baptist History," op. cit., 86.

[695] Ibid.

[696] Ibid.

[697] Ibid., 87.

heard of tithing due to many reasons.[698] However, Southern Baptist women had taught and practised tithing for years which owes much of its inspiration and methods to the women.[699]

In addition to enormous amounts of contribution towards the church by women, another area of their contribution in development was in the forming of churches. Like Dorothy Hazzard who led in forming the Baptist church more than a century ago, many Southern Baptist churches in America too owe their origin and existence to faithful women who never gave up.

In ministerial formation, too, it has been mentioned that in the earliest Baptist history, male deacons and women deacons basically had the same status.[700] But, regrettably, the woman deacons became deaconesses, which put women into a non-ordained status, distinctly inferior to the deacons for decades. But, then that was not the case always, the church had remerged again. It is said that, in the early twentieth century, women deacons had the same election, ordination, and duties as men deacons.[701] We have heard that Baptist women preached in England and early America, but without formal ordination. It is believed that Addie Davis was the first Southern Baptist woman formally ordained to ministry in 1964. Since then more women have been ordained. Most of them serve as chaplains and counsellors, several of them in pastoral roles, and others as professors.

Another example is found in the early twentieth-century Christian and Missionary Alliance. Throughout the decades of the twenties, thirties, and forties, women served as pastors, evangelists and teachers.[702] There were by that time 140 women in 200 citations called pastors, as mentioned in Alliance periodicals. Some women served as pastors for many years, such as Mary B. Peacock who served as pastor, Sheraden, Pennsylvania, for 17 years, and there were women pastoring more than one church. There were women elders too. Churches like

---

698 "One of the reasons why they opposed was because it sounded too much like the hated church tax Baptists had been forced to pay in colonial days." See Harry Leon McBeth, "The changing role of women in Baptist history", op. cit.

699 "Women stressed the importance of regular giving each week, even if the amount was small. This was quite contrary to earlier Baptist practice, where churches often had only one or two offerings a year, largely by outside subscription rather than at church." See Harry Leon McBeth, "The changing role of women in Baptist history", op. cit.

700 From the time of the Bristol days in England, the church regularly ordained women deacons.

701 "The Wake Forest Baptist Church in North Carolina has had women deacons since 1924. The Danville Baptist Church in Georgia ordained a woman deacon in 1931. The present chairman of deacons at the First Baptist Church, Decatur, Georgia, is a woman, who was first ordained back in 1952. However, this practice has mushroomed in the past decade. Though numbers are not to be had, today some hundreds of Southern Baptist churches ordain women deacons, and the total number of such deacons probably runs into the thousands." See Harry Leon McBeth, "The changing role of women in Baptist history", op. cit.

702 Paul L. King, "Women as pastors in the early twentieth-century Christian and Missionary Alliance," *Wesleyan Theological Journal,* 43/2 (fall, 2008), 68-86.

the African-American Alliance Church in Cleveland, Ohio had eleven elders, ten of whom were women and a church in Western Pennsylvania too had a woman elder. Although the title "Reverend" has usually been reserved in the Alliance only for ordained male ministers, in at least three instances women pastors in the Alliance were referred to as "Reverend."[703]

Anna Kay Scott, a widow with three children, was a renowned missionary of Assam, India, whose work is recorded in the fifth-sixth annual report of the ABMU (1870). After her husband's death, Scott was left in sole charge of the station, with the additional care of the three children. She looked after the Church and school, helped the native people and handled financial matters successfully.[704] Similarly, Ingalls continued the Burma mission more than 30 years after her husband's death.[705] Jebdakla, an Ao Naga tribal woman with ten children, served in the mission field in various capacities for 59 years beginning from 1925.[706]

Back in the fourth century, the first missionary to Georgia was St. Nina.[707] She had preached and converted many Jews and pagans.[708] She witnessed the spread of Christianity throughout Georgia before her death. Through her preaching, Queen Sophia of Kakhetian was moved and she and her kingdom were converted to Christianity. The church built by St. Nina's grave was dedicated to St. George and became the Bodbi metropolitanate.[709]

Another influential woman was Queen Bertha (539 – c. 612). She was the Queen of Kent whose influence led to the introduction of Christianity into Anglo-Saxon England. Her husband king Aethelberht was the first English king to convert to Christianity.[710] It is said that towards the end of the seventh century

---

[703] Paul L. King, "Women as pastors in the early twentieth-century Christian and Missionary Alliance," *Wesleyan Theological Journal,* 43/2 (fall, 2008): 78-83.

[704] Narola Imchen, *Remembering Our Fore Mothers: The Influence of the American Women's Movement on America Baptist Women Missionaries in North East India* (Jorhat: Women's Study Department, 2003), 157.

[705] Ibid., 80.

[706] Jepdakla, "Kor Nung Mener Waromungi Aruba Bilemteter," in *Waromung Baptist Arogotsur Centenary: 1897-1997 Nüngo Kake* (Mokokchung: Waromung Baptist Arogotsür Nagaland, 1997), 48-52.

[707] Philip Potter, "A Chance to Change," in *The Community of Women and Men in the Church: The Sheffield Report,* edited by, F. Parvey (Geneva: World Council of Churches, 1983), 26.

[708] St. Nina was the only daughter of Roman general Zabulon and his wife Susanna, and was born in Cappadocia in the late third century. Nina became the foster child of Nianfora, a pious elderly woman under whom Nina quickly learned the rules of faith and piety. See "Bertha and Ethelbert: Queen and King of Kent, 616," http://satucket.com/lectionary/Bertha_Ethelbert.htm, accessed on 28.4.14.

[709] Karen Keck "The Life of St. Nina," in O*rthodoxy and the World: Russian Orthodox Church* website 27.1.2009, http://www.pravmir.com/article_488.html, accessed on 28.4.14.

[710] Bertha was the daughter of Charibert I, Merovingian King of Paris. When she married the pagan King Aethelberht of Kent, she brought Liudhard , a bishop with her to England. She restored

there were many mixed religious houses, and that five of them in Kent were governed by women.[711] At one point in time, there were movements and groups after the Reformation in the Christian history that maintained equality between men and women. Quakers, Moravians and even some Methodists all maintained equal status among women and men.[712]

5.6.2. Voice in Social Movement

History will speak of how women's movement took momentum seeking rights on various levels based on unjust socio-cultural, political and religious set-ups. In the United States of America during the 19th and early 20th centuries, women's legal rights, such as the right to vote, along with other rights that had been sought and fought successfully. The Chinese Revolution stands out among the socio-cultural reforms of the recent past in world history. A tremendous change took place in Chinese society in the first half of the 20th century. When the Chinese Communist Party led the Chinese people to wage a great and profound national democratic revolution on the ancient soil, one of its features was the liberation and emancipation of women that won worldwide attention.[713] Chinese women had been under the 'culture of silence' for thousands of years. The feudal patriarchal system incurred grave injustice upon Chinese women. The entire nation supposedly stood firm with Chinese women demanding their rights in national struggles and movements for a century, as shown by this statement:

> The Taiping Heavenly Kingdom enacted and promulgated a series of policies on sexual equality. The Reform Movement of 1898 advocated and ignited the wave to ban feet binding and establish schools for women. The 1911 Revolution kindled a feminist movement which focused on equal rights for men and women and participation by women in political affairs.[714]

---

a Christian church in Canterbury, which dated from Roman times. Augustine of Canterbury, whose mission was sent by Pope Gregory I to preach the Gospel in England in 596, owed much of his favourable reception to the influence of Bertha. See "Bertha and Ethelbert: Queen and King of Kent, 616", op. cit.

711 Philip Potter, "A Chance to Change", op. cit., 26.

712 Ibid.

713 Women were considered as inferior to men in all aspects of their lives. In socio-political, cultural-economic, and in family life women did not have any rights. They had no independent source of income, no property and inheritance rights. Therefore, no social status, no personal dignity or independent status, but were forced to obey their fathers before marriage, their husbands after marriage and their sons if they become widowed. Women were not allowed to remarry if her spouse died. "... being harassed by systems of polygamy and prostitution, the overwhelming majority of them forced to bind their feet from childhood. For centuries, 'women with bound feet' was a synonym for the female gender in China." See "Historic Liberation" http://www.china.org.cn/e-white/chinesewoman/11-2.htm, accessed on 26.4.14.

714 Ibid.

The Chinese Communist Party set the achievement of female emancipation and equality between men and women as one of its goals. Thus, women could be mobilised and organised to form a united front with working women in industry and agriculture as the main body under the leadership of the party.[715] All women of different ethnic groups united to stage women's liberation movements closely tied to the Chinese revolution. And the outcome, at least in the opinion of one writer, "[t]he revolutionary political powers issued a series of decrees and regulations to ensure the rights of women and raise their status. This brought light and hope to women throughout the country in China."[716]

Another achievement for women was the 'land reform movement' in the early days of the People's Republic. Like their male counterparts, rural women obtained land and became masters of their piece of soil which was distributed on the basis of the number of members in a family.[717] In the new China, various laws for the emancipation of women were implemented. Among them marriage laws, equal voting rights and women candidacy for election as men were carried out. For the same writer whose views we have seen earlier mentioned that: "This indicates that ever since the founding of the People's Republic, the participation of women of all ethnic groups in state administration has been not only written into the law but also an actual practice."[718]

China took only a few years to clear the old traditional practices left over from a feudal society that had lasted for thousands of years. This purportedly brought fundamental emancipation for women in all aspects of their lives that signified an important transformation in the history of contemporary social development that China can be proud of. This is a great model and key contribution made by the Chinese revolution to the worldwide movement for women's liberation.[719]

5.7. Patriarchy and Christianity

In order to understand the concept of patriarchy in Christianity, one must strive to get into a deeper understanding of how patriarchy is linked to or functions within any given culture or society. 'Patriarchy' literally means the rule of

---

[715] Women were considered as inferior to men in all aspects of their lives. In socio-political, cultural-economic, and in family life women did not have any rights. They had no independent source of income, no property and inheritance rights. Therefore, no social status, no personal dignity or independent status, but were forced to obey their fathers before marriage, their husbands after marriage and their sons if they become widowed. Women were not allowed to remarry if her spouse died. "... being harassed by systems of polygamy and prostitution, the overwhelming majority of them forced to bind their feet from childhood. For centuries, 'women with bound feet' was a synonym for the female gender in China." See "Historic Liberation" http://www.china.org.cn/e-white/chinesewoman/11-2.htm, accessed on 26.4.14.

[716] Ibid.

[717] Ibid.

[718] Ibid.

[719] Ibid.

fathers. As Elisabeth Moltmann-Wendel said, it is vital to know and understand that patriarchy is not to be blamed on men. Patriarchy is a cultural form dating back thousands of years which has indeed facilitated cultural and economic achievements of the world. However, in the last eighteenth and nineteenth centuries devastating association with colonialism and racism, capitalism and sexism, have developed out of patriarchy and these have been sustained, justified, and even religiously adored by a patriarchal Christianity.[720]

Thus, closely connected with, and which in fact may be considered intrinsic to, patriarchy is the attitude known as misogyny. Shefali Moitra mentioned that the three general forms of misogyny or woman-hating denoted by feminists are *sexism, patriarchy* and *phallocentrism.* In this, the first is *sexism.* Moitra continued that: "Any visible act or speech or attitude or theory which treats women as inferior to men, which disadvantages women to men, and thus subjugates women and when subsequently the subjugation is thought to be legitimate, then it is a form of sexism."[721] Examples of such sexist references are found in the texts written by the most revered philosophers and theologians like Plato, Aristotle, Augustine and others. Sexism has its origin in a deeper and more pernicious form of misogyny, namely, patriarchy.[722]

Patriarchy is identified as another manifestation of misogyny. Under patriarchy, all institutions and customs are advantageous to male supremacy. It is said that patriarchy has specific roles assigned to men and to women. In reality, women are objectified in this social mode in various ways that varies from society to society and from one period of time to another. In all these, the common form of patriarchy is male supremacy which is related to power. It works on the principle that 'superiority justifies domination' because it directs that those who have power have the right to control the fate of those who are powerless.[723] Moitra continued by saying that,

> In patriarchy, man is born with a male gender privilege. This advantage is not gained by choice. Even though one cannot be held responsible for having such a privilege one can be held personally responsible for not doing anything to stall the perpetuation of male gender privilege. An accomplice in patriarchy is thus guilty of a sin of inaction. He is collaborating by ignoring woman's rightful participation in social engineering by perpetuating the status quo which ignores the status of

---

[720] Elisabeth Moltmann-Wendel, Jürgen Moltmann, "Becoming Human in New Community," in *The Community of Women and Men in the Church: The Sheffield Report,* edited by F. Parvey (Geneva: World Council of Churches, 1983), 30.

[721] Shefali Moitra, *Feminist Thought: Androcentrism, Communication and Objectivity* (Kolkata: Munshiram Manoharlal Publishers Pvt, Ltd. in association with Centre of Advanced Study in Philosophy, Jadavpur University, 2002), 89.

[722] Ibid.

[723] Ibid., 9.

> women. One could be guilty on either count – by committing sexist act or by not resisting sexist acts.[724]

The third is *Phallocentrism*, which is a form of discrimination against women at the conceptual level. Moitra said that if sexism discriminates at the level of speech and action, and patriarchy is structural oppression, then phallocentrism is a form of conceptual male domination.[725] But, patriarchy enslaves not only women but also men. It is mentioned that:

> The liberation of women and then of men from patriarchy goes hand in hand, therefore, with the rediscovery of the freedom of Jesus and of the energies of the Holy Spirit. Leaving the monotheistic God of rulers and males behind us, we shall discover from the sources of Christianity the God who is in relationship, the God who can suffer, the uniting God, the God of fellowship and community. This is the living God, the God of life, who was distorted through a patriarchal system with its idols of power and domination. In this living God the male too will experience deliverance from the distortions which he himself has suffered and still suffers under patriarchy.[726]

We can observe that the patriarchal tradition which was followed for centuries in the pre-Christian era continued to persist and was not done away with. In fact, it has gradually evolved and ultimately morphed into something akin to a foundational tenet of Christianity: The God of patriarchy is often portrayed through Christian forms in terms of the head and the body. The man is the head of the woman, Christ is the head of the man, God is the head of Christ (1 Cor. 2).[727]

This was effectively used to promote a graded understanding of the relative places of women, men, Christ and the Godhead. However, it also has undesirable consequences, at least with regard to elevating God to such a high level that it promoted an understanding of God as an isolated supernatural being:

---

[724] Shefali Moitra, *Feminist Thought: Androcentrism, Communication and Objectivity* (Kolkata: Munshiram Manoharlal Publishers Pvt, Ltd. in association with Centre of Advanced Study in Philosophy, Jadavpur University, 2002), 9.

[725] One of the examples cited by Shefali Moitra shows that Aristotle refers to man as a rational being. For him reason is a monolithic category which excludes emotion and context and by implication woman's 'lived' experience. For Aristotle woman is referred as 'deformed man.' Here, in this, women, children and slaves are disqualified from the same kind of reason and virtues available to men. Therefore, in a phallocentric conceptual scheme woman is always related to a subordinate position. See Shefali Moitra, Feminist Thought: Androcentrism, Communication and Objectivity, op. cit.,10 ff.

[726] Elisabeth Moltmann-Wendel, Jürgen Moltmann, "Becoming Human in New Community," op. cit., 3

[727] Ibid., 33.

> The distress of the male Ruler-God lies in his lack of a name and his loneliness. He is defined only by his function as ruler and proprietor of the world. Who he himself is remains unknown. Thus patriarchy divides, separates, and isolates God. A God who is no more than "the Almighty" is not a God but a monster. Any man who emulates this God becomes a hapless beast; he is no more than an expression of the will to power ... Patriarchy has ceased to be source of order and protection and has instead become a source of destruction and fear.[728]

Another point of contention is that, when Christianity gained acceptance in the Roman Empire under Constantine the Great in the fourth century AD, it moved from being a persecuted minority to an official religion. In the meantime, Christianity grew so rapidly that the Church did not get enough time to work out a new and coherent social system inspired by the Christian faith. Therefore, the line of least resistance was chosen, and the church had accepted the existing social framework, so that ultimately and inevitably the patriarchal system remained in force.[729] Yet again, the patriarchal tradition was spread to Western civilization through three main channels. Instead of affirming Christian insight, it was, however, reinforced and modified with Roman code of law which is now been an influence of life to the present day.[730]

The incorporation of Hebrew Scriptures in the Christian teaching was another channel of igniting the patriarchal norm as a moral lesson: "In spite of attempts made by Marcion and certain gnostic sects to present the Christian faith as opposed to, rather than rooted in, the revelation of Israel, the church defended the validity of the old Testament."[731] Elisabeth Moltmann-Wendel writes that:

> The Bible was written, or at least given its final form, in a predominantly patriarchal culture. It contains a number of sexist remarks, i.e. remarks which suppress women, e.g. in the Old Testament, which sees the wife as her husband's personal property. In the late writings even in the New Testament she is once again burdened with 'Eve's sin'. In a patriarchal society, preference is given to this patriarchal superstructure, and it is used for the political suppression of women.[732]

The patriarchal ethos was extolled by the Church itself which became an ever-increasing motif of a typical patriarchal institution. Finally, the bishop

---

728 Elisabeth Moltmann-Wendel, Jürgen Moltmann, "Becoming Human in New Community," op. cit., 33

729 W. A. Visser't Hooft, *The Fatherhood of God in an Age of Emancipation,* op. cit., 7.

730 Ibid., 7-8.

731 Ibid.

732 Elisabeth Moltmann-Wendel, *The Women Around Jesus: Reflections on Authentic Personhood,* (London: SCM Press Ltd, 1982), 7-8.

became the central figure in church organisation and the father figure for his community. Unfortunately, women in this case once again remain subservient to men. The Church had reaffirmed and re-established the patriarchal line where women had no voice in church affairs. The pope became the supreme authority whose hierarchical superiority became one of the main virtues.[733]

Thus, Russell D. Moore expresses observations on the "softness" of patriarchy in the Church,[734] visibly impressed with the writing of W. Bradford, *Soft Patriarchs, New Men: How Christianity Shapes Fathers and Husbands*. In soft patriarchy, male headship is not about male privilege but it is all about protecting women and children by calling men to take up the responsibility. This mandate, all things in Christ (Eph. 1:10) is all about "a loving, sacrificial, protective patriarchy in which the archetypal Fatherhood of God is reflected in the leadership of human fathers, in the home and in the church (Eph. 3:14-15; Matt. 7:9-11; Heb. 12:5-11)."[735] But gradually, it had turned into the opposite by failing their responsibility given by God. Russell therefore asks, "Patriarchy is good for women, good for children, and good for families. But it should also remind us that the question for us is not whether we will have patriarchy, but what kind."[736]

However, as Maria Mies said, it has gone beyond its limit, meaning that it has incorporated the male dominance over female by consolidating the "'rule of fathers' [that] includes the rule of husbands, of male bosses, of ruling men in most societal institutions, in politics and economics, in short what has been called 'the men's league' or 'men's house.'"[737]

Philip Potter writes about the dissection between women being considered as inferior beings and men as superior beings which need to be addressed. It says:

> First of all, our whole understanding of sexuality is challenged ... The whole division between flesh and spirit, often putting flesh as woman and assuming spirit implicitly in terms of man, has been a heresy, even worse than a heresy in the life of the church; or again the dualism of private and public – women being private, men public – keeping men with the mentality in which the ordinary human virtues were private while in public it was the survival of the fittest which reigned. This dualism is also challenged by our new understanding of what it is be human. And the third dualism which is being challenged is that of meekness over against power – that meekness belongs to women and

---

733 W. A. Visser't Hooft, *The Fatherhood of God in an Age of Emancipation,* op. cit., 8.

734 Russell D. Moore, "After Patriarchy, What? Why Egalitarians are winning the Gender Debate," *Journal of the Evangelical Theological Society*, 49/3 (September, 2006): 569-576.

735 Ibid.

736 Ibid.

737 Maria Mies, *Patriachy and Accumulation on a World Scale: Women in the International Division of Labour* (London: Zed Books Ltd., 1986), 37.

> power to man. Because of the inability to relate these two things, our humanity has been brutalized, and we are in this pursuit of death by rearmament and war.[738]

Above all, in the true sense, the earthly privileges and powers associated with one gender over against another are removed by Jesus Christ and redeemed by the power of Christ's sacrificial act on the Cross. The domineering patriarchal structures have been suffocated and subdued under the power of Christ. Thomas V. Frederick also mentioned that: "In the Kingdom [sic] of God, there is no "gender"; however, there are sexes that uniquely honor God through diversity."[739]

5.8. The *Ekklesia* of Women: Against Kyriarchy[740]

Church is understood in patriarchal terms. This has led to the thinking of men as masters and women as subordinates, and that has made to the formation of an empire in every aspects of life. Women theological scholars such as Elisabeth Schüssler Fiorenza have questioned this understanding.

In classical Greek "*ekklesia*" meant "an assembly of citizens summoned by the crier, the legislative assembly."[741] Therefore, an understanding of the word "church" as *ekklesia* could mean a political, religious, social, economic and cultural assembly where every citizen is accorded the right to voice. Elisabeth Schüssler Fiorenza has said:

> If the vision of the ekklēsia of wo/men – understood as the congress of full decision-making citizens – is to articulate a sociopolitical religious horizon for biblical interpretation, it must be spelled out both in sociopolitical and cultural-religious terms. Ekklēsia is not just a Christian religious notion; rather it expresses a sociopolitical radical democratic vision. The expression does not refer primarily to "church" but seeks to convey the notion of radical democracy.[742]

---

738 Philip Potter, "A Chance to Change," in *The Community of Women and Men in the Church: The Sheffield Report,* edited by, F. Parvey (Geneva: World Council of Churches, 1983), 27-28.

739 Thomas V. Frederick, "An Interpretation of Evangelical Gender Ideology: Implications for a Theology of Gender," *Theology and Sexuality*, 16/2 (May, 2010): 180-192.

740 Kyriarchy is defined by Elisabeth Schüssler Fiorenza as "the rule of emperor/master/lord/ father/ husband over his subordinates" It is also mentioned in chapter two. See *Jesus Miriam's Child, Sophia's Prophet: Critical Issues in Feminist Christology* (New York: Continuum, 1994), 14.

741 A careful examination of word *ekklesia* in Greek shows that it comes from two words 'ek' meaning 'out' and 'kaleo' meaning to 'call.' Used for a community rather than an individual, an *ekklesia* or 'calling out' was not just an assembly. "The Church, the ekklesia" http://www.hisholychurch.net/ekklesia.php, accessed on 8.2.14.

742 Elisabeth Schüssler Fiorenza, *Sharing Her Word: Feminist Biblical Interpretation in Context* (Edinburgh: T&T Clark, 1998), 112.

Elisabeth Schüssler Fiorenza in her another writings on the topic, "Discipleship of Equals: Reality and Vision," mentioned that: "The radical democratic belief that all are created equal and the notion of the ekklesia as the decision-making congress/assembly of all citizens stand in conflictive tension with the reality of classical and modern Kyriarchy."[743] The radical democracy becomes embodied and realised continually in the emancipatory struggles to change relations of domination, exploitation and marginalisation; hence it is an alternative to kyriarchy.[744]

For Fiorenza, *ekklesia* is rendered as "democratic assembly/congress of full citizens." She held that, in the translation process *ekklesia*/democratic assembly was transformed into *Kyriak/church* which directs a historical development that has privileged the kyriarchal/hierarchical form of church against that of a democratic congress or discipleship of equals.[745]

Therefore, it must be affirmed that the *ekklesia* which will allow women to join as congress of full citizens to share and join with one another in democratic manner in all the decision-making bodies is the true *ekklesia* of God. Philip Potter also asserted an understanding of the church as the "whole people of God."[746] In this, both female and male can participate and voice: "If there is a fellowship, a real sharing of life with life in which we are all in council together, then it means both women and men are in council together, that decisions are made together, and that decisions are made by those who have the gifts required without regard to sex and culture."[747]

5.9. Women Theologies as Powerful Voice

Women's voice in the theological field gains momentum, challenging the patriarchal-kyriarchal structures in all the socio-religious-cultural-political spheres

---

[743] "There is a tension between radical democracy and 'malestream' Kyriarchal socio-religious vision where the problem itself lies in the linguistic notion of the word 'church.' 'The Greek word 'ekklesia' is usually translated as 'church,' although the English word 'church' derives from the Greek word 'Kyriak' (i.e. belonging to the lord/master/father/husband). Accordingly, the translation of ekklesia as 'church' is misleading." Elisabeth Schüssler Fiorenza, "Discipleship of Equals: Reality and Vision," in *In search of a Round Table: Gender, Theology and Church Leadership,* ed. Musimbi R.A. Kanyoro (Geneva: WCC Publications, 1996), 3.

[744] Ibid.

[745] The same word "church" in English involves two contradictory meanings. One is the derivative of the patri-kyriarchal household in antiquity that was ruled by the lord/master/husband/ father of the house to whom freeborn women, freeborn dependents, clients, workers and slaves, both women and men, were subordinated. The other meaning of church – *ekklesia* – understands all members as equal citizens and friends. See, Elisabeth Schüssler Fiorenza, "Discipleship of Equals: Reality and Vision, op. cit., 3.

[746] Philip Potter, "A Chance to Change," in *The Community of Women and Men in the Church: The Sheffield Report,* edited by, F. Parvey (Geneva: World Council of Churches, 1983), 26.

[747] Ibid.

around the world. Theologians from the West, Asia, India, Northeast India and the Ao Naga tribal community raise their vibrant voice which is clear and loud against all the evil structures that exist on earth. Some theologian's voices are expressed in our study. Elisabeth Schüssler Fiorenza states that:

> Wo/men are not ladies, wives, handmaids, seductresses, or beasts of burden but full citizens. This definition alludes to the democratic motto "We, the people" and positions feminism within radical democratic discourses that argue for the rights of all the people. It evokes memories of radical democratic struggles for equal citizenship and decision-making powers in society and religion. Theologically, it understands the death-dealing powers of oppression as structural sin and life-destroying evil. It focuses on the rights and dignity of wo/men living on the bottom of the kyriarchal pyramid of exploitation and understands their courage and survival with integrity as the visible presence of G*d at work in our midst.[748]

Fiorenza stressed that feminist theology must probe how the malestream economic, institutional, and ideological structures of kyriarchal exploitation control its institutional structures. It has to study how cultural gender assumptions and "feminine" ideals affect theological language and Christian values that internalize and withstand women's exploitation. It must investigate into the structural interconnections between the gendered economic system of kyriarchal capitalism, its racist underpinnings, and women's global poverty.[749] Theology and ministry will be changed into social institutions that cease to produce one-sided malestream knowledge only if they allow for the full intellectual participation and decision-making citizenship of wo/men.[750] What women need is to share and live together by building a new inclusive community – a community of men and women that supports the sense of belonging, inter-connectedness and interrelationships of all people, inter-dependence, fostering harmony and mutual growth in faith, hope and love.[751] When applied to traditionalistic tribal communities like the Aos, "this calls for a paradigm shift in formulating a relevant

---

[748] Elisabeth Schüssler Fiorenza, "Feminist Liberation Theology as Critical Sophialogy," in *The Power of Naming: A Concilium Reader in Feminist Liberation Theology*, Concilium Series, ed. Elisabeth Schüssler Fiorenza (New York: Maryknoll, 1996). Xvii.

[749] Ibid., Xxiii.

[750] Ibid., Xxvii.

[751] Limatula Longkumer, "Feminist Theology and Local Congregation: A Search for Common and Relevant Ministry," in *Tribal Theology: A Search for Quality Theological Education & Relevant Ministry*, Tribal Study Series No. 17, edited by Yangkahao Vashum (Jorhat: Tribal Study Centre, Eastern Theological College, 2009), 85.

tribal theology from tribal perspectives." And in doing so will women's role and status be recognised.[752]

Women have always been great contributors in the economic spheres as well. Gabriele Dietrich has mentioned the formulation summed up in a South Asian workshop on Women and Development which says that women are the "production of life" rather than production for profit which means that "Production of life" includes not only the bearing and rearing of children but also the basic sustenance of life in subsistence production, household labour, informal sector, basic ecological activities which preserve forest cover, water systems, energy and ozone layer."[753]

It has been made apparent that the feminist practices of theological education try to motivate the traditionally silenced and the disadvantaged ones who are being denied participation in the making of culture.[754] It is asserted that if women are called precious jewels they should be treated with respect and care and not treated more like property of the male.[755] "Woman cannot accept being named by man as if she is extension of the plant, bird and animal kingdom. She will not be named and controlled by man; she will only be named like man by God as a "co-equal" and a "partner" with him."[756]

Another challenge ahead of women in general and Ao Naga tribal women in particular is the question whether the Church can be obedient to repentance and faith in Jesus Christ, including relocating itself in response to women in the New Creation, which will help towards building an inclusive community.[757] To this end, a woman has raised her voice thus:

---

[752] Limatula Longkumer, "Feminist Theology and Local Congregation: A Search for Common and Relevant Ministry," in *Tribal Theology: A Search for Quality Theological Education & Relevant Ministry*, Tribal Study Series No. 17, edited by Yangkahao Vashum (Jorhat: Tribal Study Centre, Eastern Theological College, 2009), 87.

[753] Gabriele Dietrich, "South Asian Feminist Theory and Its Significance for Feminist Theology," in *The Power of Naming: A Concilium Reader in Feminist Liberation Theology*, Concilium Series, edited by Elisabeth Schüssler Fiorenza (New York: Maryknoll, 1996), 49.

[754] Limatula Longkumer, "Naga Women in Theological Education: Problems and Prospects," in *Side by Side: Naga Women Doing Theology in Search of Justice and Partnership*, edited by Limatula Longkumer and Talijunla Longkumer (CCA-EgY Unit & Naga Women Theological Forum, 2004), 28.

[755] Zakali Shohe, "Protest with a Cause: A Study of the Temple Act of Jesus for Empowering Naga Women in their Struggles," in *Side by Side: Naga Women Doing Theology in Search of Justice and Partnership*, edited by Limatula Longkumer and Talijunla Longkumer (CCA-EgY Unit & Naga Women Theological Forum, 2004), 136-7.

[756] Sathianathan Clarke, "Analysis and reflection of a case study on "Gender Discrimination: A Barrier for Identity," in *Lived Realities: Faith Reflections on Gender Justice*, edited by Elizabeth Joy (Bangalore: CISRC Publications Trust, 1999), 30.

[757] Narola Imchen, "Re-Reading the Bible through New Eyes to Build Up an Inclusive Community," in *Side by Side: Naga Women Doing Theology in Search of Justice and Partnership*,

> If and when women are denied equality with men due to culture, that culture must be countered with the Gospel. The cultural practice of relegating women secondary status in the church amounts to denying them justice, and denying them justice is violence against them, it means silencing them and denying them their fundamental rights, as humans created equal and in God's image, to live and develop as God intend them to live.[758]

Asangla Lemtur has expressed the methodology of re-reading and re-interpreting Bible from a Naga tribal women's as well as other women's perspective the 'contextual liberative hermeneutics.'[759] She expressed that it should be an inclusive method for the entire human family for partnership' and not domination, for liberation and life affirming not bondage and life demeaning that will direct us into a praxis-oriented approach to the bible.[760] Women have been voicing that "Naga Christian women today should be courageous enough to raise issues of identity, subordination, domination and stereotyped male-role."[761] In line with this, male tribal theologians like Zhodi Angami also expressed the need to add a new element, that is, tribal feminism, to be woven into the tapestry of feminist hermeneutics in order to mould it from the view of tribal women.[762] He expressed that:

> Tribal worldview affirmed community building since men and women shared equally in the struggle for survival. ... Women were honoured through the idea of collective motherhood. ...Women gain knowledge from a wisdom tradition passed down the centuries through women

edited by Limatula Longkumer and Talijunla Longkumer (N.p.: CCA-EGY Unit & Naga Women Theological Forum, 2004), 148.

758 Aphuno Chase Roy, "Gospel and Culture: Women's Empowerment," in *Side by Side: Naga Women Doing Theology in Search of Justice and Partnership*, edited by Limatula Longkumer and Talijunla Longkumer (N.p.: CCA-EGY Unit & Naga Women Theological Forum, 2004), 4.

759 Asangla Lemtur, "Reading the Bible From Naga Women's Context," in *Side by Side: Naga Women Doing Theology in Search of Justice and Partnership*, edited by Limatula Longkumer and Talijunla Longkumer (N.p.: CCA-EGY Unit & Naga Women Theological Forum, 2004), 85.

760 Ibid., 87.

761 Abeni Lotha, "A Challenge for Courage," in *Side by Side: Naga Women Doing Theology in Search of Justice and Partnership*, edited by Limatula Longkumer and Talijunla Longkumer (N.p.: CCA-EGY Unit & Naga Women Theological Forum, 2004), 152.

762 Zhodi Angami explains, "What is tribal feminism? Although, this term has not been used before, it may be defined as the tribal woman's affirmation of her identity, and celebration of it, as a tribal woman with her tribal way of life. It is the substance of her root in tribal history and culture spanning the history and culture of her foremothers and the milieu in which she finds herself today. It allows her to celebrate life in music and dance with her foremother in contemporaneity." Zhodi Angami, "Constructing Tribal Feminist Hermeneutics," in *Weaving New Patterns of Ministry for Women in North East India*, Women Study Series No. 3, edited by Narola Imchen (Jorhat: Women Study Department Eastern Theological College, 2004), 13-14.

> elders in the institution of the girls' dormitory. Tribal folk tales abound with stories of courageous women who came to be regarded as the heroines of the village. Their songs address women with respect and clothe her with dignity. Therefore, a hermeneutic of tribal feminism must draw its resources from meanings and values embedded in tribal cultural codes and traditions. As we read the Bible from the perspective of tribal women, we need to be informed by our own heritage of feminism. We need to use tribal women history, culture, and religious experience as clues for biblical interpretation.[763]

Angami suggested four elements for the construction of tribal feminist hermeneutics. These are (1) a critique of patriarchy in the Bible, (2) an application of scientific tools of investigation fuelled by a genuine desire for women's liberation, (3) a hermeneutic of tribal women's experiences, and (4) an application of a hermeneutic of tribal feminism.[764]

It is also point towards intercultural reading of the Bible, an attempt to be authentic, contextual, and relevant, bringing into context in an inclusive way and also not overlooking the context of the other.[765]

It is said that Naga Christian theology today must address the living realities of Nagaland such as the determination of the people; their pains and sufferings; the problems of peace, justice and human rights; the unity of the people, etc.[766] At the same time, we must also continually strive towards raising awareness so that the issue of cultural rights of women in the decision bodies may be addressed. For women's concerns and their rights is one of the burning issues in Naga tribal society.

Corinne Scott raises concerns over the frequent assertion about women's status in North East India, which proclaims NE women as having higher status than other women in "mainland India." She said that such statement raises more questions than it answers, and said that nowhere is women's status equal with men's.

---

[763] Zhodi Angami explains, "What is tribal feminism? Although, this term has not been used before, it may be defined as the tribal woman's affirmation of her identity, and celebration of it, as a tribal woman with her tribal way of life. It is the substance of her root in tribal history and culture spanning the history and culture of her foremothers and the milieu in which she finds herself today. It allows her to celebrate life in music and dance with her foremother in contemporaneity." Zhodi Angami, "Constructing Tribal Feminist Hermeneutics," in *Weaving New Patterns of Ministry for Women in North East India*, Women Study Series No. 3, edited by Narola Imchen (Jorhat: Women Study Department Eastern Theological College, 2004), 13-14.

[764] Ibid., 16.

[765] Akhrieno Savi, "'Listening to the Other Side of The Story': An Intercultural Bible Reading" in *Tribal Theology and The Bible: A Search for Contextual Relevance*, Tribal Study Series No. 19, ed. Yangkahao Vashum (Jorhat: Tribal Study Centre/Eastern Theological College, 2011), 165.

[766] Mar Pongener, *Morung Speaks: Cultural Values and Elements for the Enrichment of Naga Christian Community* (Mokokchung: Clark Theological College and Tribal Development and Communication Centre, 2011), 117.

She states that, "in your [Naga] societies there may not be discrimination against the girl child, within the household, or in education, but there is M/F inequality in the society and especially in the church, in positions and job opportunities, and in customary law."[767] Along with other hindrances there are a variety of forces occurring presently such as modernization, commercialization, and economic development in the course of individualism, all of which may be disadvantageous to the interest of the majority of women. However, some women are awakening regarding their rights and equipping themselves and others to challenge both traditional discrimination and the new forms that have been taking place. Scott proposes that women be informed about these trends, and mobilize women to gain self-confidence and work for the welfare of women in general.[768]

5.10. Communication: The Fundamental Human Right[769]

5.10.1. Right to Communicate

The right to communicate is a basic human right. Every individual is entitled to voice her/his opinion and participate in sharing, listening, expressing and dialogue with one another. It has no age, sex, caste, class or culture bar. One is free to communicate either within one's own community, local, national or internationally. One understands that communication represents an essential human need, and a basic human right. No individual, community, group or any other institution would be able to exist, or prosper without having the possibility to communicate and talk to each individual.[770] The World Association for Christian Communication aims to strive for the communication rights which undergird the ethical framework of life and work of the association.[771]

---

[767] Corinne Scott, "Changing the Stream: Women Engage Issues of Church and Society," in *Weaving New Patterns of Ministry for Women in North East India*, Women Study Series No. 3, edited by Narola Imchen (Jorhat: Women Study Department Eastern Theological College, 2004), 41-42.

[768] Ibid.

[769] Civil or freedom rights can be said to be the first generation of human rights. The second generation of human rights is said to include the right to work, education, shelter, and the right to participate in cultural life. These were formulated as binding international law in two conventions that were adopted in 1966 and in 1976: the International Covenant on Civil and Political Rights. See Jan Servaes, "Human rights, participatory communication and cultural freedom," in *Many Voices, One Vision: Right to Communicate in Practice,* edited by Philip Lee (Penang: Southbound (London: WACC), 2004), 149.

[770] "Communication-An essential human need",www.crisinfo.org accessed on 2.4.15.

[771] The World Association for Christian Communication was founded in the wake of the 1939-45 World War. Since then WACC has promoted the democratization of communication, freedom of expression, and the right to communicate. WACC has given a special focus on women, indigenous peoples, refugees, and people on the margins of society. See Philip Lee, "Introduction," in *Many Voices, One Vision: Right to Communicate in Practice,* edited by Philip Lee (Penang: Southbound (London: WACC), 2004), 8.

In honest communication there is no barrier between high or low status, privileged or underprivileged, male or female, young or old, literate or illiterate etc. On the contrary, it extends to all humanity. In communication, control and manipulation has no room to breed. If it does exist, the end result will be distortion and failure. Genuine communication accommodates not only the socio-cultural, political-economic, and religiously advantaged people but includes disadvantaged humankind too.

Freedom of expression has been declared and mentioned in the United Nations' Universal Declaration of Human Rights Article 19, which says, "Everyone has the right to freedom of opinion and expression; this right includes freedom to hold opinions without interference and to seek, receive and impart information and ideas through any media and regardless of frontiers."[772] Andrés Cañizález has mentioned that, "[...] the effective respect for the freedom of expression is a basic tool for the inclusion of those who, because of poverty, are marginalised from information and all dialogue."[773] Freedom of expression must also be extended to all, i.e. regardless of sex, age, class, caste and race. Cañizález said that:

> It is the state's duty to guarantee equal opportunities for all with respect to the receiving, seeking, and sharing of information through any communication channel whatsoever, eliminating all measures that discriminate against the equal and full participation of individuals or groups in their countries' political, economic, and social life. This right guarantees an informed voice for all people, which is an indispensable requirement for the subsistence of democracy.[774]

In communities like that of the Ao Naga tribal community in the Northeastern part of India, when it comes to freedom of expression or right to communicate, women are curtailed by the traditional socio-cultural norms in the community. Women's voice is completely ignored and left unheard in the decision-making bodies. Women are not allowed to speak, listen, or have any representative in the village councils. In this regard, culture and tradition has made a mockery of democracy which is supposed to safeguard every individual.

Genuine communication takes place where there is love, peace, justice, freedom, and equality. Philip Lee in once wrote that: "Equality does not demand homogeneity or uniformity, neither does it contradict the special roles that societies confer on individuals or groups of people. Yet equality does imply the right not to be discriminated against because of race, ethnicity, religion, sex or

---

[772] "The Universal Declaration of Human Rights" 3/19/2014.

[773] *Andrés Cañizález* , "Serving justice in a world of inequality," *Media Development* edited by Philip Lee, vol. LVIII (1/2011), 49-50.

[774] Ibid.

age, etc."[775] In the family, among groups or in the larger society, relationships will be strengthened and communities will make progress only when they are willing to listen, share and include everyone. Lee continues to write that: "People cannot communicate with other people if they consider them "inferior" in any sense. Communicative freedom presupposes the recognition that all human beings are of equal worth."[776] In 1789 it is stated in the French *Les Droits de l'Homme et du Citoyen* that, "the free expression of ideas and opinions is one of the most precious human rights; every citizen should be able to speak, write, and print freely; this freedom can only be restricted in those cases determined by law."[777] But, in social practice, that does not always happen.

Jan Servaes has rightly said that the policymakers can enshrine cultural freedom as one of the pillars but they cannot legislate respect, nor can they coerce people to behave respectfully:[778] Servaes mentioned that individual freedom must be the first and foremost priority among other freedoms. It says:

> First, most freedoms refer to the individual. Cultural freedom, in contrast, is a collective freedom. It is the condition for individual freedom to flourish. Second, cultural freedom, properly interpreted, is a guarantee of freedom as a whole. It protects not only the collectivity but also the rights of every individual within it. Thirdly, cultural freedom, by protecting alternative ways of living, encourages creativity, experimentation and diversity, the very essentials of human development. Finally freedom is central to culture, and in particular the freedom to decide what we have reason to value, and what lives we have reason to seek.[779]

5.11. Voice is Being Personhood and Reconciliation

In communication ethics, personhood transcends all creatures as has been brought out in the debate about ethics and culture. Personhood is the ground of ethics. Michael Traber in his writing mentions that: "Personhood implies the capacity of free choice, the ability to reflect and argue rationally, and the endowment of its inner and intrinsic worth. Personhood thus brings together freedom, rationality,

---

[775] Philip Lee, "Introduction," in *Many Voices, One Vision: Right to Communicate in Practice,* ed. Philip Lee (Penang: Southbound (London: WACC), 2004), 5.

[776] Ibid.

[777] Jan Servaes, "Human rights, participatory communication and cultural freedom," in *Many Voices, One Vision: Right to Communicate in Practice,* edited by Philip Lee Penang: Southbound (London: WACC), 2004), 149.

[778] Ibid., 151.

[779] Ibid.

and equality in dignity."[780] Therefore, personhood is voice, meaning that it is a person's ability to think, speak and listen which makes her/him to participate with her/his whole being.

One of the important features of the Christian ethos is reconciliation. Communicators communicate the message of hope, peace and love so that communities become life affirming, assuring, and healing for the well-being of the people. And that is to be achieved by engaging in and embodying genuine reconciliation. As it is said, "[W]e are in need of communication that humanizes; that speaks of persons, not numbers; that speaks of people's needs, their sufferings and their dreams. When communication acquires such a human face, it will become a force for reconciliation."[781]

5.12. Voice is Democracy

To be a full citizen of any given community, we need to identify with people. We need others to provide us with feedback on our thoughts, to talk back to us, and to respond to our questions. Thus, we do not attain our identity in a solidary condition. So also, our voices need to be heard by others. It is only then that we become an integral part of a human rights culture where people are taken seriously and treated with respect. Thus, the central part of democracy is accomplished only when there is interaction and the freedom to participate in it.[782] Cees J. Hamelink rightly pointed out that: "Therefore, the key question to pose is not whether one is for or against a right to communicate, but whether one is for or against the realization of communication in the conversational mode as essential to the overall defense of human rights!"[783]

By way of concluding, I would like to cite from Leon McBeth who said this decades ago in his talk:

> In the nineteenth century most interpreted Scripture in such a way as to keep women in silence and subjection. However, in recent years many are reading the same passages in a different light. They discover in both testaments an emphasis upon human dignity and equality. Even the most restrictive biblical statements about women take on

---

[780] Michael Traber, "An Ethics of Communication Worthy of Human Beings", in *Communication Ethics and Universal Values,* edited by Clifford G. Christian and Michael Traber (Thousand Oaks, CA: Sage Publications, 1997), 337.

[781] Carlos A. Valle, "Breaking the Chains of Inhumanity: Stories on the Way to Reconciliation," in *Communication and Reconciliation: Challenges Facing the 21st Century*, edited by, Philip Lee (London: WCC Publications, Geneva, World Association for Christian Communication, 2001), Xii.

[782] Cees J. Hamelink, "Grounding the human right to communicate", in *Many Voices, One Vision: Right to Communicate in Practice,* edited by Philip Lee Penang: Southbound (London: WACC), 2004, 25.

[783] Ibid., 31.

> a new dimension when interpreted in context, and in light of the teachings and practices of Jesus. It is a fact of far-reaching import that a growing number of... scholars, pastors, and laypeople alike, no longer interpret the Bible as excluding modern women from an active role in religion.
>
> We know that women were not silent for twenty centuries, they were not always on the sidelines in the early church, the middle ages, and the Reformation. Modern women insist they are but reasserting some of their historic precedents and prerogatives.[784]

Having dealt with various perspectives on voice from different arenas, we shall now move on to the final chapter which will be a discussion on the outcome of the field research. An attempt will be made to connect the findings with their implication for unearthing and giving voice to the aspirations of Ao Naga women towards a more inclusive and participatory community.

5.13. Ao Women's Voice: A Paradigm of Communication Theology

Voice in totality is not about being silent, so also in today's context, silencing a woman's voice due to socio-cultural and traditional norms and practices in the community is a challenge and can be term as an imprudent act.

In the context of Ao Naga tribal women, we bring "voice as a paradigm," that demands mutual sharing, equal rights, and equal participation in all the decision-making bodies. It is to be pronounced as right to voice is right to life. A paradigm of communication theology denounces the exclusion of voice among genders which is a form of violence. It also denounces the marginalisation and silencing of women in the name of culture and tradition. Communication theology demands realistic acts and practices in order to bring transformation. This paradigm of communication theology demands voice as praxis oriented. Voice must be followed with "doing" rather than "thinking" in communication theology.

784 Harry Leon McBeth, "The changing role of women in Baptist history", op. cit., 95.

Conclusion

If we want to progress, and be a part of God's people in the reign of God we must seek the common ground where we can find mutual sharing and understanding through raising our voice. Some of the communitarian ethos which was equally shared in the Ao Naga tribal community must be reinstituted. This Study concludes by making three crucial concerns of voice as a human right.

i. Reclaiming Women's Rights to "Voice"

Communication studies challenge the loss of women's identity. The loss of identity results from not being able to have direct access to the information discussed in the meetings. The loss of women's identity results from not being permitted to listen and attend. The loss of identity comes from being excluded from all the decision-making bodies, either in the family decision-making, in the clan or in the larger community decision-making bodies in Ao Naga tribal community. This study has clearly brought out the power of women's voice and hence is an appeal to re-examine the age old traditional socio-cultural practices where women's voice had been side-lined for centuries.

The study in this research suggests giving renewed importance to some of the exemplary practices of Aos in the community. These are practices such as participation of Zünga (age-group both female and male) in the work place (farm) and in the other social activities, participation in the festivities, the involvement of both husband and wife in religious ceremonies, etc., the interaction between Tsükir and Arijumen/Arijusanger (group interaction among female-male). These practices and concepts might be developed and applied in the decision-making bodies too. Building up a common platform for all, with female and male sharing and exchanging ideas and accepting each other could lead to a celebration of life together. This could lead to a genuine corporate "Voice" which will be spoken and heard **by, for** and **with** all.

The uncritical claim by the Ao Naga tribal community, which claims to be 100% Christian and the continuation of a non-Christian moral system of ***Sobaliba*** being kept in a position higher than Jesus Christ is something which needs to be questioned. The traditional socio-cultural mind-set which discriminated women's voice from that of men needs to be challenged and corrected. The irrational romanticising of socio-cultural mores and norms raise serious questions today. While there is nothing wrong in valuing *Sobaliba*, placing high emphasis on it without any serious consideration and reflection upon its drawbacks needs to be questioned.

The beliefs held by Aos about their traditional "democratic" system also needs to be questioned today. Democracy is supposed to be egalitarian and emancipatory, ensuring universal suffrage, freedom, justice, liberation etc. However, all these are missing in the traditional Ao Naga tribal administrative systems. It is wrong to assume that women's voice is being communicated through the other person (i.e., father, husband, brother or friends) on her behalf. Such voice cannot be claimed as significant voice.

One often hears the assertion that women's voice has been heard through preaching in the church and seminaries. However, the researcher finds fault with this claim. Preaching and teaching are, to some extent a part of the extension of voice. Nevertheless, the non-inclusion of women's voice in the decision-making bodies cannot be compensated by giving them opportunities elsewhere, i.e. engaging in preaching and teaching.

Through this study, the researcher also disproves the widespread notion that women's role is to be involved in child rearing and caring for the family and that she must not aspire to a place in the decision-making process. It is only the patriarchal notion about women and men that leads to assumptions and conclusions, and labels women as fragile, feeble, illogical and emotional. Such biased attitudes towards women's voice must be denounced, and such traditional patriarchal concepts must be corrected and tested.

The name *Ao Senden* itself is to be questioned. *Ao Senden* is not a singular noun; it is never a "male alone." The literal meaning itself, properly interpreted, is "Ao Council" which means it denotes both female and male. Therefore, one needs to question the very existence of the name *Ao Senden* that excludes and dehumanises Ao women's voice.

Senso, which means citizens, is also divided according to gender. There are two categories, namely women *senso* and men *senso*, with each having separate functions. However, the women do not have ultimate voice on any matter; their decision is to be taken up to the council, and the decision to either approve or reject is in the hands of the men in the "men's council." The dichotomies in gender role in the Ao Naga tribal community, such as women being considered inferior beings and men performing as superior beings, is to be confronted. The Ao Naga tribal community must accept multiple gender assortments as God-given talents to humankind from the God of diversity and seek to make room for unique voices to be heard.

ii. Re-fashioning Gender Dialogue

Communication studies call people to enter into gender dialogue. The researcher recognises that cultural barriers might be removed through honest dialogue. Through dialogue, each individual might develop to recognise the importance of one's voice. Through dialogue the relationship between two parties, i.e. female and male, may be strengthened and bridges built between the female and male dichotomy in the decision-making bodies. Through dialogue one party will begin to recognize the other party's wishes and aspirations. Mutual respect and sharing between genders will be enhanced through dialogue.

Giving "voice" to women was a transformation brought by Jesus Christ. Women who were once enslaved by patriarchal socio-cultural, religious, political and economic norms were liberated and emancipated through Jesus Christ.

In the ***ritual view of communication***, communication is linked to terms such as "sharing," "participation," "association," "fellowship," and the "position of a common faith."[785] In the case of the Ao Naga tribal community, the adaptation of the ritual view of communication may be applied in relation to gender roles such as the sharing and participation of both the female and male members in the decision-making bodies. Common faith and fellowship will be strengthened through this.

Another theory such as a ***Network Approach***[786] theory in communication studies seems relevant in our research. The network approach, such as connectedness, integration, diversity, and openness, may prove to be an important component to comprehending a communication situation. The Ao Naga tribal community must integrate women rather than constricting them with old concepts. And in order to achieve this, it must look through diverse perspectives with an open mind.

The **Reciprocal** concept of communication also seems appropriate in this study. In the reciprocal model, individuals compliment "each other" and "one another."[787] Mutual "reciprocal respect" is given or felt by each toward the other.[788] Reciprocity of communication is required if it is to achieve its goal in the community. For female-male interaction their "Voice" either in the interpersonal communication, group communication or in the mass communication needs to be achieved. Then and there the community will experience the fullness of life which means the full and complete fellowship of related beings.

---

[785] James W. Carey, "A Cultural Approach To Communication," in *Theorizing Communication: Readings Across Traditions,* 38ff.

[786] Sven Windahl, Benno Signitzer, et.al, *Using Communication Theory: An Introduction to Planned Communication,* Second Edition, 97 ff.

[787] The Reciprocal model is a researcher's view expressed in this study. See, dictionary.reference.com/browse/reciprocal accessed on 17.3.2015.

[788] Ibid.

The use and choice of the medium might also help disseminate the message among the community members. The best possible suggestion might be the local television channel, radio station etc., which the community members watch and/or listen to every day. Through this, community members might be conscientised, strengthened, and encouraged to cultivate optimistic thinking about gender and such related issues for social transformation.

The researcher suggests embracing a new perspective, that is, the "incorporation of women's voice" in the Ao Naga tribal decision-making bodies. As Brightstar Jones Syiemlieh, one of the tribal theologians says, the tribal perspective is highly patriarchal and parochial, and unless the tribal perspective is blended with the women/feminist perspectives and other perspectives in order to help tone down its patriarchal and close-minded natures, such problems can never be overcome or reduced. Thus, we need to be controlled and balanced by the use of other perspectives.[789]

The Church is the most influential socialising agent. Today, the Ao Naga tribal community as a whole (pastors, church leaders, and educated lay people) needs to re-examine the prevalent perceptions about theology and the traditional understanding of socio-culture structures which is insulated from change for the better by a narrow primitive mind-set that needs to be replaced by inclusive thought patterns. It is said:

> Today's 'Tribal theology' which is enthusiastically researched, propagated and discussed in the academic circle has to be tested further to prove its usability in the local Churches. The much discussed and debated issue on Feminist Theology or Gender Issue is still yet to face the challenges posed by traditions, status-quo, cultures and context of the people and place.[790]

The Church is a centre stage to communicate a genuine message of hope. The researcher felt the local church might be the ideal place to talk about and mediate gender justice. The following words from Elisabeth Schüssler Fiorenza remain genuine and relevant, and hold tremendous promise for communities everywhere:

> Equality, freedom and democracy cannot be realised if women's voices are not raised or not heard and heeded in the struggle for justice and liberation for everyone, regardless of sex, class, race, nationality or region. If our varied struggles for the drastic democratic equality,

---

[789] Brightstar Jones Syiemlieh, "The Future of Tribal Christian Theology In Northeast India: Possible Directions," in *Tribal Theology On The Move,* edited by Shimreingam Shimray, Limatula Longkumer (Jorhat: Tribal/Women Studies Centres, Eastern Theological College, 2006), 42-43.

[790] Akheto Sema, "Contextual Theology in the Changing Context," in *Tribal Theology On The Move,* edited by Shimreingam Shimray, Limatula Longkumer (Jorhat: Tribal/Women Studies Centres, Eastern Theological College, 2006),111.

dignity and well-being of all in society and church continue this feminist tradition of struggle, the discipleship of equals becomes an ever-expanding reality.[791]

iii. Re-visioning Solidarity Voice

Ola (voice) encompasses and surpasses all barriers that prevent the building up of a sharing community in the socio-cultural, political, religious, and economic realms. *Ola* is universal, myriad, liberating and empowering and has no gender or age frontier. *Ola* allows for the expression of personal feelings, bringing innovative ideas, being open for critiquing, and promotes interactions of one individual with the other individual.

Ola accommodates both peripheral and central artists in the interaction. It is reckoned as an integral part of our being. It connects with people and allows one's own emotion to flow out. It is not limited to a single entity, but has multiple variables which involve openness and acceptance for conversation with all. The **cherished elements of *ola*** consist of empowerment, equality, attainment, achievement, integration, diversity, connectedness, and liberation.

The interaction between female and male members was already existent in the Ao Naga tribal community in the past. The valuable elements of voice can be seen in many instances such as participation in reciprocal singing between women and men during religious ceremonies, during festivities, during the Feast of Merit (Bull and Mithun sacrifices), during occasional gathering of the age-group (*zünga*) etc.

The power of women's *ola* has been manifested several times in history in general and in the Ao Naga tribal community in particular. Success and honour was brought into the community in the past through the wisdom and knowledge of women's *ola*. At the physical level or from the economic aspect, women have always been great contributors in the family. Women's voice and role has always been visible in the community formation of Ao Naga tribal society. Therefore, *ola* which is the universal form of every individual must be recognised and open for all without any gender, clan, class and such related distinction in the decision-making bodies of the Ao Naga tribal community.

In conclusion, this study wishes to achieve an objective re-visioning. This, in effect, means a voice that affirms solidarity in all the decision-making bodies which accommodates and accepts the personhood of every individual in the Ao Naga tribal community.

---

791 Elisabeth Schüssler Fiorenza, "Discipleship of Equals: Reality and vision," in *In Search of a Round Table: Gender, Theology and Church Leadership,* edited by Musimbi. R.A. Kanyoro (Geneva: WCC Publications, 1996), 11.

Bibliography

Adler, Ronald B., George Rodman. *Understanding Human Communication.* Third Edition. New York: Holt, Rinehart And Winston, INC.,1988.

Aier, Anungla. "Cultural Change Among the Nagas: Festivals and Dress." In *Naga Society: Continuity and Change.* Edited by N. Venuh. Delhi: Shipra Publications, 2004.

Aitchison, Jean. "Defining language." In *Communication Studies: an Introductory Reader*. Edited by John Corner, Jeremy Hawthorn. London: Edward Arnold Pty Ltd, 1983.

Akang, M. "Akidang Ao Yimli Nung Tetzurtem Jenjang Meyiba Reprarigshiba." In *Shisa Lemsa Kaket.* Edited by Ruth and Chubala, N.p.: n.p., 1989.

Anderson-Rajkumar, Evangeline. "Decoding 'Silence-Voice-Speech' as an Epistemological Tool for a Theology of Engagement," in *God of Life, Lead us to Justice and Peace: A Theological Reflection in the Context of India Today*. Edited by H. Vanlalauva. Serampore: Department of Research/SATHRI, 2012.

Angami, Zhodi. "Constructing Tribal Feminist Hermeneutics." In *Weaving New Patterns of Ministry for Women in North East India*, Women Study Series No. 3. Edited by Narola Imchen. Jorhat: Women Study Department, Eastern Theological College, 2004.

Appavoo, James Theophilus. *Folklore for Change.* Arasaradi, Madurai: Tamilnadu Theological Seminary, 1986.

Ao, Tajen. *Ao Naga Customary Laws.* N.p.: n.p., 1980.

Ariarajah, S.Wesley. "Creating a "Culture of Dialogue" in a *Multicultural and Pluralist Society," in Communication Reconciliation: Challenges Facing the 21st Century.* Edited by, Philip Lee. Geneva: World Council of churches, 2001.

Aristotle. *Politics*. Harmondsworth: Penguin, 1992.

Arndt, William F., F. Wilbur Gingrich. *A Greek-English Lexicon of the New Testament and Other Early Christian Literature*. Chicago: The University of Chicago Press, 1957.

Balasuriya, Tissa. "Communication Ethics with a Pluralist Worldview." In *Communication and Reconciliation: Challenges facing the 21st Century.* Edited by Philip Lee. London: WCC publications, Geneva, World Association for Christian Communication, 2001.

Barker, Chris *Cultural Studies: Theory and Practice.* 3rd ed. Los Angeles, London, New Delhi, Singapore: Sage Publications, 2008.

Barthes, Roland. "Language and Speech (langue and parole)." In *Communication Studies: An Introductory Reader.* Edited by John Corner, Jeremy Hawthorn. London: Edward Arnold Pty Ltd, 1983.

Bathla, Sonia *Women, Democracy and the Media: Cultural and Political Representations in the Indian Press.* New Delhi, Thousand Oaks, London: SAGE Publications, 1998.

Baumert, Norbert. *Woman and Man in Paul: Overcoming a Misunderstanding.* Minnesota: The Liturgical Press, 1996.

Belenky, Mary Field, Blythe McVicker Clinchy, et.al., *Women's Ways of Knowing: The Development of Self, Voice, and Mind* Tenth ed. New York: Basic Books, A Member of the Perseus Books Groups, 1997.

Bendangangshi, I., I.T. Apok Aier. *The Religion of the Ao Nagas.* Bamunimaidan Guwahati: n.p., 1997.

Berge, Erling. "Language and Culture: On the Possibility of an Emerging Cartoon-based Language." In *Communication and Society: The Emerging Human Concerns.* Edited by, Kamlesh Mahajan. New Delhi: Classical Publishing Company, 1990.

Berger, Arthur Asa *Media and Communication Research Methods: An Introduction to Qualitative and Quantitative Approaches* 2nd ed. Los Angeles, London, New Delhi, Singapore, Washington DC: Sage Publications, 2011.

Boomershine, Thomas E. *Story Journey: An Invitation to the Gospel as Storytelling.* Nashville: Abingdon Press, 1988.

Buzzanell, Patrice M. *Rethinking Organizational and Managerial Communication from Feminist Perspectives.* New Delhi: Sage Publications, 200.

Capes, David. "Where did the title 'The Voice' come from?" (7 December 2012). Personal letter to the author (15 December 2012).

Carey, James W. "A Cultural Approach To Communication," in *Theorizing Communication: Readings Across Traditions.* Edited by Robert T. Craig, Heidi L. Muller. Los Angeles, London, New Delhi, Singapore: SAGE Publications, 2007.

Changkija, Monalisa. "*Ariju:* The Traditional Seat of Learning in Ao Society." In *Glimpses from the North-East.* Shillong: National Knowledge Commission, 2009.

Chib, Sukhdev Singh. *Caste, Tribes and Culture of India: North-Eastern India.* Vol. 8. New Delhi: Sheel Sethi ESS ESS Publications, 1984.

Clark, Mary Mead. *A Corner in India*. Philadelphia: American Baptist Publication Society, 1907.

Clarke, Sathianathan. "Analysis and reflection of a case study on Gender Discrimination: A Barrier for Identity." In *Lived Realities: Faith Reflections on Gender Justice*. Edited by Elizabeth Joy. Bangalore: CISRC Publications Trust,1999.

Cohen, Sylvie I. "Mobilizing Communities for Participation and Empowerment." In *Communication and Human Values: Participatory Communication for Social Change.* Edited by Jan Servaes, Thomas L Jacobson and Shirley A White. Thousands Oaks, London, New Delhi: SAGE Publications, 2002.

Dainton, Marianne, Elaine D. Zelley. *Applying Communication Theory for Professional Life: A Pratical Introduction.* Thousand Oaks, London, New Delhi: Sage Publications, 2005.

Daly, Mary "Theology After the Demise of God the Father: A Call for the Castration of Sexist Religion," in *Sexist Religion and Women in the Church: No More Silence!.* Edited by, Alice L. Hageman *(New York*: Association press, 1974.

DeConick, April D. *Holy Misogyny: Why the Sex and Gender Conflicts in the Early church Still Matter.* New York: The Continuum International Publishing Group, 2011.

Dietrich, Gabriele *Culture, Religion and Development.* Banglore: Centre for Contemporary Christianity, 1978.

Dietrich, Gabriele. *A New Thing On Earth: Hopes and Fears facing Feminist Theology*. Delhi: ISPCK, 2004.

Dyrness, William. *Themes in Old Testament Theology*. UK: Paternoster Press, 1979.

E.M., Rogers and Kincaid D.L. *Communication Networks: Toward a New Paradigm for Research*. New York: Free Press, 1981.

Elliott, Neil. *Liberating Paul: The Justice of God and the Politics of Apostle.* Bangalore: Theological Publications In India, 2006.

Evans, Mary. *Gender and Social Theory.* Berkshire: Open University press, 2003.

Fernandes, Walter, Melville Pereira, Vizalenu Khatso. *Customary Laws in North East India: Impact on Women*. New Delhi: National Commission for Women, n.d..

Fiorenza, Elisabeth Schüssler. "Discipleship of Equals: Reality and Vision." In *In Search of a Round Table: Gender, Theology and Church Leadership.* Edited by Musimbi R.A. Kanyoro. Geneva: WCC Publications, 1997.

Fiorenza, Elisabeth Schüssler. "Feminist Liberation Theology as Critical Sophialogy." in *The Power of Naming: A Concilium Reader in Feminist Liberation Theology*. Edited by Elisabeth Schüssler Fiorenza. New York: Orbis Books, 1996.

Fiorenza, Elisabeth Schussler. *In Memory of Her: A Feminist Theological Reconstruction of Christian Origins*. New York: Crossroad, 1988.

Fiorenza, Elisabeth Schüssler. *Sharing Her Word: Feminist Biblical Interpretation in Context*. Edinburgh: T&T Clark, 1998.

Firestone, Shulamith. *The Dialectic of Sex: The Case for Feminist Revolution*, New York: William Morrow and Company, Inc., 1970.

Flack, Elmer E. "The Approach to the Word of God." *In Old Testament Commentary: A General Introduction to and A Commentary on the Books Of The Old Testament.* Edited by Herbert C. Alleman, Elmer E. Flack. Pennsylvania: The Muhlenberg Press Philadelphia, 1949.

Freire, Paulo *Cultural Action for Freedom*. Cambridge, Massachussets: Penguin Books, 1972.

Freire, Paulo. *Education for Critical Consciousness*. London: Sheed and Ward, 1979.

Freire, Paulo. *Pedagogy of the Oppressed*. New York: The Continuum Publishing Corporation, 1982.

Gabriele Dietrich, "Wise Like Snakes, Innocent Like Doves: Thirty Biblical Reflections." In *Feminist Perspective.* Delhi: ISPCK, 2011.

Greed, Clara. "A Feminist Critique of the Post-secular City: God and Gender." In *Post-Secular Cities: Space, Theory and Practice.* Edited by Justin Beaumont and Christopher R. Baker. London: Ashgate, 2011.

Guha, Ranajit ed. *South Asian History and Society*. Delhi: Oxford University Press, 1985-1994.

Hamelink, Cees J. "Grounding the human right to communicate." In *Many Voices, One Vision: Right to Communicate in Practice*. Edited by Philip Lee. Penang: Southbound (London: WACC), 2004.

Hammersley, M., Atkinson P. *Ethnography: Principles and Practice*. London: Tavistock Books, 1983.

Hannon, Vincent Emmanuel. *The Question of Women and the Priesthood.* London: Geoffrey Chapman, 1967.

Hazarika, Sanjoy. *Strangers of the Mist: Tales of War and Peace From India's Northeast.* Revised Edition. New Delhi: Penguin Books India, 2011.

Hnuni, R.L. "Women in North East India: Vision For Tribes." In *Women and Society*. Edited by Nirmala Jeyaraj. Madurai: Lady Doak College, 2001.

Hnuni, R.L. *Vision for Women in India: Perspectives from the Bible, Church and Society*. Bangalore: Asian Trading Corporation, 2009.

Hooft, W. A. Visser't. *The Fatherhood of God in an Age of Emancipation*. Geneva: World Council of Churches, 1982.

Hosken, Fran P. "Women and International Communication." In *Women Transforming Communications: Global Intersections*. Edited by Donna Allen, Ramona R. Rush and Susan J. Kaufman. Thousands Oaks, London, New Delhi: SAGE Publications, 1996.

Howe, Reuel L. *The Miracle of Dialogue*. New York: The Seabury Press, 1963.

Imchen, Narola. *Remembering Our Fore Mothers: The Influence of the American Women's Movement on America Baptist Women Missionaries in North East India*. Jorhat: Women's Study Department, 2003.

Imchen, Narola. "Re-Reading the Bible through New Eyes to Build Up an Inclusive

Community." In *Side by Side: Naga Women Doing Theology in Search of Justice and Partnership*. Edited by Limatula Longkumer and Talijunla Longkumer. N.p.: CCA-EGY Unit & Naga Women Theological Forum, 2004.

Imchen, Narola. *Women in Church and Society: The Story of Ao Naga Women*. Jorhat: Eastern Theological College, 2001.

Imchen, Narola. *Women in the History of Christianity*. N.p.: Tribal Development and Communication Centre, 2010.

Imchen, Panger. *Ancient Ao Naga Religion and Culture*. New Delhi: Har-Anand Publications, 1993.

Imsenperong, Menjiwapong Jamir, Walotemjen. *Mapping the Context: An Interdisciplinary Exploration*. Kohima: Authors, 2011.

Ivy. *Voices from Narmada: Doing Ecofeminist Theology*. Delhi: ISPCK, 2009.

Jackson, B.F. "Spoken Communication: A Medium," in *You And Communication In The Church: Skills And Techniques* by, B. F. Jackson. Waco, Texas: Word Books, Publisher, 1974.

Jamir, A. Asola. "The Image of Women in Selected Naga folklore and its Impact on Naga Women Today." In *Communication and Naga Culture*. Edited by, L. Imsutoshi Jamir, C. Alitemjen Longkumer. Dimapur: Tribal Development and Communication Centre, 2007.

Jamir, A. Asola. "Nagas: A General Introduction." In *Encyclopedia of Indian Tribes and Castes*. Edited by S.M Channa. Vol.16. New Delhi: Cosmo Publications, 2004.

Jamir, L. Sosang. *Ao Naga Customary Laws and Practices*. Dimapur: Heritage Publishing House, 2012.

Jamir, N. Talitemjen, A. Lanunungsang. *Naga Society and Culture*. Mokokchung: Nagaland University Tribal Research Centre, Department of Sociology, 2005.

Jamir, N. Talitemjen. *Ao-Naga Cultural Heritage*. Mokokchung: n.p., 1997.

Jepdakla. "Kor Nung Mener Waromungi Aruba Bilemteter." In *Waromung Baptist Arogotsur Centenary: 1897-1997 Nüngo Kake*. Mokokchung: Waromung Baptist Arogotsür Nagaland, 1997.

Jones, Rufus M. *Studies in Mystical Religion*. London: Macmillan and Company, 1909.

Keitzar, Renthy "Church and Ao Culture." In *The Church in Ao Society*. Impur: ABAM, 1984.

Keitzar, Renthy. *Ao Dictionary*. Impur: Ao Theological Literature Society, Ao Mungdang, 1999.

Kiremwati, L. Imti Longchar et al., eds. *Nokranger Aser Nokrang* (N.p. : Waromung Yimten, 1993.

Kiremwati, L. Imti Longchar et. al, eds., *Nokranger Aser Nokrang*. N.p.: n.d.

Knellwolf, Christa, Christopher Norris. *The Cambridge History of Literary Criticism Volume 9: Twentieth-Century Historical, Philosophical and Psychological Perspectives*. Cambridge: Cambridge University Press, 2007.

Koshy, Ninan. "Introduction to Paulo Freire." In *Education for Liberation: Addresses by Paulo Freire and Critical Reflections on Indian Education*. Whitefield, Bangalore: Ecumenical Christian Centre, 1983.

Küng, Hans. *Women in Christianity*. Translated by John Bowden. London: Continuum, 2005.

Lanunungsang. "Working System of Ariju in Traditional Ao Society: A Socio-cultural Institution." In *Naga Society: Continuity and Change*. Edited by N. Venuh. Delhi: Shipra Publications, 2004.

Lee, Philip. "Introduction," in *Many Voices, One Vision: Right to Communicate in Practice*. Edited by Philip Lee. Penang: Southbound (London: WACC), 2004.

Lindlof, Thomas R. *Qualitative Communication Reaserch Methods*. Thousand Oaks, London, New Delhi: Sage Publications, 1995.

Lintner, Bertil *Great Game East: India, China and the Struggle for Asia's Most Volatile Frontier*. New Delhi: Harper Collins Publishers India, 2012.

Lemtur, Asangla. "Reading the Bible From Naga Women's Context." In *Side by Side: Naga Women Doing Theology in Search of Justice and Partnership*. Edited by Limatula Longkumer and Talijunla Longkumer (N.p.: CCA-EGY Unit & Naga Women Theological Forum, 2004.

Longchar, A. Wati. "Issues in Feminist Theology." In *Transforming Theology for Empowering Women: A theological and Hermeneutical Reflection in the Context of North East India.* Edited by R.L. Hnuni. Jorhat: Women's Studies, ETC, 1999.

Longkumer, J. "The Ao Village Organisation: origin to Present Day." In *Naga Society: Continuity and Change.* Edited by N. Venuh. Delhi: Shipra Publications, 2004.

Longkumer, N. Limatula. "Christianity and Naga Women." In *Transforming Theology for Empowering Women: A Theological and Hermeneutical Reflection in the Context of North East India.* Edited by R.L. Hnuni. Jorhat: Women's Studies, ETC, 1999.

Longkumer, Limatula, ed. *No More Sorrow in God's Garden of Justice: Tribal Women Doing Theology,* Women Studies Series 4. Eastern Theological College, Jorhat: Women's Study centre, 2007.

Longkumer, N. Limatula. "Rediscovering Women's Role and Status in Society." In *Transforming Theology for Empowering Women: A theological and Hermeneutical Reflection in the Context of North East India.* Edited by R.L. Hnuni. ETC, Jorhat: Women's Studies, 1999.

Lotha, Abeni. "A Challenge for Courage." In *Side by Side: Naga Women Doing Theology in Search of Justice and Partnership.* Edited by Limatula Longkumer and Talijunla Longkumer. N.p.: CCA-EGY Unit & Naga Women Theological Forum, 2004.

Maisch, Ingridl. *Between Contempt and Veneration...Mary Magdalene: Image of a Woman through the Centuries.* Minnesota: The Litergical Press Collegeville, 1998.

Mehta, Vera. "The Human Communications Support Environment." In *Woman's Image Making and Shaping.* Edited by Peter Fernando, Frances Maria Yasas. Pune: Ishvani Kendra, 1985.

Menon, Krishna. *Research Methods for Media and Cultural Studies.* Delhi: Manglam Publications, 2010.

Mies, Maria, Vandana Shiva. *Ecofeminism.* Jaipur: Rawat Publications, 2010.

Mies, Maria. *Patriachy and Accumulation on a World Scale: Women in the International Division of Labour.* London: Zed Books Ltd., 1986.

Miller, Errol. "Gender, Power and Politics: An Alternative Perspective." In *Gender, Peace and Conflict.* Edited by Inger Skjelsbaek, Dan Smith. Delhi: SAGE Publications, 2001.

Millett, Kate. *Sexual Politics,* New York: Doubleday, 1970.

Minh-Ha, Trinh T. "Writing Postcoloniality and Feminism." In *Post-Colonial Studies Reader.* Edited by Bill Ashcroft, Gareth Griffiths and Helen Tiffin. London: Routledge, 1995.

Moitra, Shefali. *Feminist Thought: Androcentrism, Communication and Objectivity* (Kolkata: Munshiram Manoharlal Pubilshers Pvt, Ltd., 2008.

Moitra, Shefali. *Feminist Thought: Androcentrism, Communication and Objectivity.* Kolkata: Munshiram Manoharlal Pubilshers Pvt, Ltd. In association with Centre of Advanced Study in Philosophy Jadavpur University, 2002.

Moltmann-Wendel, Elisabeth, Jürgen Moltmann. "Becoming Human in New Community." In *The Community of Women and Men in the Church: The Sheffield Report.* Edited by F. Parvey. Geneva: World Council of Churches, 1983.

Moltmann-Wendel, Elisabeth. *The Women around Jesus: Reflections on Authentic Personhood.* London: SCM Press Ltd, 1982.

Myers, Gail E., Michele Tolela Myers. *The Dynamics of Human Communication: A Laboratory Approach 5th ed.* New York: McGraw-Hill Book Company, 1988.

Nayar, Pramod K. *Reading Culture: Theory, praxis, Politics.* New Delhi: SAGE Publications, 2006.

Neill, Maura O.' *Women Speaking Women Listening: Women in Interreligious Dialogue.* Maryknoll: Orbis Books, 1990.

Nungshitula. *The Naga Images of the Human Being.* Jorhart: Assam, Tribal Study Centre, 2001.

O'Brien, Peter T. "God as the Speaking God: "Theology" in the Letter to the Hebrews." In *Understanding the Times: New Testament Studies in the 21st Century.* Edited by Andreas J. Kostenberger, Robert W. Yarbrough. Nottingham: Crossway Books, 2011.

O'Day, Gail R. "Surprised By Faith: Jesus And The Canaanite Women." In *A Feminist Companion to Mathew.* Edited by Amy-Jill Levine, Marianne Blickenstaff. Cleveland: The Pilgrim Press, 2001.

Other Early Christian Literature. Chicago: The University of Chicago Press, 1957.

Padia, Chandrakala. *Theorizing Feminism.* Jaipur: Rawat Publications, 2011. Paul, Asangla Lemtur. "Naga Women or Women in Nagaland?: Denied Identity." In *Women's Issues and Reflections.* Edited by Christina Manohar. Delhi: ISPCK, 2012.

Paul, Asangla Lemtur. "Naga Women or Women in Nagaland?: Denied Identity." In *Women's Issues and Reflections.* Edited by Christina Manohar. Delhi: ISPCK, 2012.

Pertti, Alasuutari *Researching Culture: Qualitative Method and Cultural Studies.* New Delhi: SAGE Publications, 1995.

Pongener, Mar. *Morung Speaks: Cultural Values and Elements for the Enrichment of Naga Christian Community.* Mokokchung: Clark Theological College and Tribal Development and Communication Centre, 2011.

Porras, Luz Estella and H. Leslie Steeves. "Feminism in a Post-Development Age." In *Development Communication: Reframing the Role of the Media.* Edited by Thomas L. McPhail. Chichester, United Kingdom: Blackwell Publishing Ltd, 2009.

Potter, Philip. "A Chance to Change." In *The Community of Women and Men in the Church: The Sheffield Report.* Edited by F. Parvey. Geneva: World Council of Churches, 1983.

Rajkumar, Evangeline Anderson. "Decoding 'Silence-Voice-Speech' as an epistemological tool for a theology of engagement," in *God of Life, Lead us to Justice and peace: A Theological Reflection in the Context of India today*. Edited by H. Vanlalauva. Serampore: Department of Research/SATHRI, 2012.

Rakow, Lana F., Laura A. Wackwitz. "Voice in Feminist Communication Theory." In *Feminist Communication Theory.* Edited by Lana F. Rakow and Laura A. Wackwitz. Thousand Oaks, London, New Delhi: SAGE Publications, 2004.

Ramazanoglu, Caroline, Janet Holland. *Feminist Methodology: Challenges and Choices.* New Delhi: SAGE Publications, 2002.

Reid, Clyde H. "Spoken Communication in Small Groups," in *You and Communication in the Church: Skills And Techniques.* B. F. Jackson, Jr., Waco, Texas: Word Books, Publisher, 1974.

Rowbotham, Sheila. *Hidden From History: 300 Years of Women's Oppression and the Fight Against It*, London: Pluto Press, 1973.

Roy, Aphuno Chase. "Gospel and Culture: Women's Empowerment." In *Side by Side: Naga Women Doing Theology in Search of Justice and Partnership.* Edited by Limatula Longkumer and Talijunla Longkumer (N.p.: CCA-EGY Unit & Naga Women Theological Forum, 2004.

Roy, Aphuno Chase. *Women in Transition: Angami Naga Women From 1878 to the Present.* Kohima: Published by the Author, 2004.

Runcie, Robert. "1354 Years from that Easter Day." In *The Community of Women and Men in the Church: The Sheffield Report.* Edited by Constance F. Parvey. Geneva: World Council of Churches, 1983.

Rush, Ramona R. "Ten Tenets for Deeper Communications: Transforming Communications Theory and Research." In *Women Transforming Communications: Global Intersections.* Edited by Donna Allen, Ramona R. Rush and Susan J. Kaufman. Thousands Oaks, London, New Delhi: SAGE Publications, 1996.

Savi, Akhrieno. "'Listening to the Other Side of The Story': An Intercultural Bible Reading." In *Tribal Theology and The Bible: A Search for Contextual Relevance*, Tribal Study Series No. 19. Edited by Yangkahao Vashum. Jorhat: Tribal Study Centre/Eastern Theological College, 2011.

Schaberg, Jane, Melanie Johnson-Debaufre. *Marry Magdalene Understood.* New York, London: The Continuum International Publishing Group Inc, 2006.

Schmidt, Werner H. *The Faith of the Old Testament.* Translated by John Sturdy. Oxford: Basil Blackwell, 1986.

Scott, Corinne. "Changing the Stream: Women Engage Issues of Church and Society." In *Weaving New Patterns of Ministry for Women in North East India,* Women Study Series No. 3. Edited by Narola Imchen. Jorhat: Women Study Department Eastern Theological College, 2004.

Sema, Akheto. "Contextual Theology in the Changing Context." In *Tribal Theology On The Move.* Edited by Shimreingam Shimray, Limatula Longkumer. Jorhat: Tribal/Women Studies Centres, Eastern Theological College, 2006.

Sen, G., C. Crown, *Development Crises and Alternative Visions: Third World Women's Perspectives.* New York: Monthly Review Press, 1987.

Servaes, Jan. "Human rights, Participatory communication and cultural freedom." In *Many Voices, One Vision: Right to Communicate in Practice.* Edited by Philip Lee. Penang: Southbound (London: WACC), 2004.

Shome, Raka "Transnational Feminism and Communication Studies." In the Communication Review 9. Routledge: Taylor & Francis Group, 2006.

Shulman, Gail B. "View from the Back of the Synagogue: Women in Judaism." In *Sexist Religion and Women in the Church: No More Silence!.* Edited by Alice L. Hageman. New York: Association Press, 1974.

Siang, Keci. *Paul, Women and Female Imagery: Approaching Difficult Passages.* Aizawl: Research and Development Department, Academy of Integrated Christian Studies, 2010.

Simon Cottle, Anders Hansen, et.al., *Mass Communication Research Methods.* Houndmills, Basingstoke, Hampshire RG21 6XS, London: Macmillan Press LTD, 2006.

Singh, Anil Kumar. *Tribal Culture and Polity.* New Delhi: Sarup & Sons, 1994.

Singh, K. S., ed. *Tribal Ethnography Customary Law and Change.* New Delhi: Concept Publishing Company, 1993.

Singh, M. Peter *Cybertheology.* New Delhi: ISPCK, 2009.

Smith, William C. *The Ao-Naga Tribe of Assam.* London: MacMillan& Co. Limited, 1925, reproduced in New Delhi: Mittal Publications, 2009.

Soukup, Paul A. *Communication and Theology: Introduction and Review of the Literature.* London: World Association for Christian Communication, 1983.

Spivak, Gayatri Chakravorty. "Subaltern Studies: Deconstructing Historiography." In *Subaltern Studies IV: Writings on C. I. David Joy, Hermeneutics: Foundations and New Trends: A Postcolonial Reading of John 4.* Delhi: ISPCK, 2012.

Stanton, Elizabeth Candy (et al). *The Women's Bible, Part I, Comments on Genesis, Exodus, Leviticus, Numbers and Deuteronomy, Part II, Judges, Kings, Prophets and Apostles* (6th Reprint). New York: European Publishing Company, 1898.

Stromquist, Nelly P. "Voice, Harmony and Fugue in Global Feminism," in *A feminist Critique of Education: 15 Years of Gender education*. Edited by Christine Skelton and Becky Francis. London/New York: Routledge Taylor and Francis Group, n.d.

Subrata, Banerjee ed. *Culture and Communication*. New Delhi: Patriot Publishers, 1986.

Süiren, Imsongunger. *Imsongunger: Brief History and Genealogy*. N.p.: Imsongunger Kidong Telongjem, n.d.

Swamy, Muthuraj. "Women's Work and Sexual Division of Labour: Critiques from Feminist Perspectives." In *Women's Issues and Reflections*. Edited by Christina Manohar. Delhi: ISPCK, 2012.

Syiemlieh, Brightstar Jones. "The Future of Tribal Christian Theology in Northeast India: Possible Directions." In *Tribal Theology On The Move*. Edited by Shimreingam Shimray, Limatula Longkumer. Jorhat: Tribal/Women Studies Centres, Eastern Theological College, 2006).

T. P, Meyer, Anderson J.A. *Mediated Communication: A Social Action Perspective*. Newbury Park, CA: Sage publications, 1988.

Tekatemjen. *Studies on Theology and Naga Culture*. Delhi: CTC, Aolijen, Mokokchung & ISPCK, 1998.

Tekatemjen. *Studies on Theology and Naga Culture*. Delhi: CTC, Aolijen, Mokokchung & ISPCK, 1998.

Traber, Michael. "An Ethics of Communication Worthy of Human Beings." In *Communication Ethics and Universal Values*. Edited by Clifford G. Christian and Michael Traber. Thousand Oaks, CA: Sage Publications, 1997.

Traber, Michael. "why communication studies in theological education." In *communication in theological Education: New Directions*. Edited by, Michael Traber. Delhi: ISPCK, 2005.

Turner, Mary Donovan Mary Lin Hudson. *Saved from Silence: Finding Women's Voice in Preaching*. Denver: Mary Donovan Turner and Mary Lin Hudson, 1999.

Turner, Mary Donovan, Mary Lin Hudson. *Saved from silence: Finding Women's Voice in Preaching*. Danver: Mary Donovan Turner and Mary Lin Hudson, 1999.

Vakayil, Prema. *Women Shall Prophesy: Anna, The Prophetess (Lk 2:36-38): A Study in Luke's Feminine Perspective*. Bangalore: Asian Trading Corporation, 2007.

Valle, Carlos A. "Breaking the Chains of Inhumanity: Stories on the Way to reconciliation." In *Communication and Reconciliation: Challenges facing the 21st Century*. Edited by Philip Lee. London: WCC publications, Geneva, World Association for Christian Communication, 2001.

Vitso, Adino. *Customary Law and Women. The Chakhesang Nagas*. New Delhi: Regency Publications, 2003.

Walton, David. *Introducing Cultural Studies: Learning through Practice*. New Delhi: SAGE Publications, 2008.

Wilfred, Felix. "From the Dusty Soil." *Asian Theological Search*. Vol. 4. Chennai: Department of Christian Studies, 1995.

William T. Whitley. Ed. *The Works of John Smyth*. Vol. II. Cambridge: University Press, 1915.

Williams, Noel. *How to get a 2:1 in Media, Communication and Cultural Studies*. London, Thousand Oaks, New Delhi: SAGE Publications, 2004.

Windahl, Sven, Benno Signitzer, et.al., *Using Communication Theory: An Introduction to Planned Communication* 2nd ed. Los Angeles, London, New Delhi, Singapore, Washington DC: Sage Publications, 2009.

Wolf, Virginia. "Woman and Fiction," in *The Feminist Critique of Language: A Reader, 2nd Edition*. Edited by Deborah Cameron. London/Newyork: Routledge Taylor & Francis group, 1998.

Wood, Julia T. "Critical Feminist Theories: A Provocative Perspective on Families." In *Engaging Theories in Family Communication: Multiple Perspectives.* Edited by Dawn O. Braithwaite, Leslie A. Baxter. Thousand Oaks, London, New Delhi: SAGE Publications, 2006.

Wood, Julia T. *Gendered Lives: Communication, Gender, and Culture.* 8th ed. Boston: Wadsworth Cengage Learning, 2009.

Young, Robert C. *Postcolonialism*. London: Blackwell, 2001.

"New Revised Standard Version Catholic Edition for India." Bangalore: Thomas Nelson, 1993.

Articles

Amaladoss, Michael. "Culture and Dialogue," *International Review of Mission.* 74/294 (April, 1985): 169-177.

Brueggemann, Walter. "Voice as Counter to Violence." In *Calvin Theological Journal* 36 (2001): 22-23.

Brighton, Louis A. "The ordination of Women: A Twentieth-Century Gnostic Heresy?"

Concordia Journal 8/1 (January, 1982): 12-18.

Cañizález, Andrés. "Serving justice in a world of inequality." *Media Development* Edited by Philip Lee. Vol. LVIII (1/2011): 49-50.

Capes, David. "Where did the title "The Voice" come from?" Letter to the author 12 Nov. 2012.

Chappuis, Jean-Marc. "Jesus and the Samaritan Woman: The Variable Geometry of Communication." *Ecumenical review* (January 1, 1982): 8-34.

Chung, Paul S. "God's Mission as Word Event in an Age of World Christianity: An Asian Linguistic-Transcultural Model." *International Review of Mission* 8/2 (November 2009): 328-341.

Frederick, Thomas V. "An Interpretation of Evangelical Gender Ideology: Implications for a Theology of Gender." *Theology and sexuality* 16/2 (May, 2010): 180-192.

Graham, Elaine. "What's missing? gender, reason and the post-secular." *Political Theology.* 13/2 (April, 2012): 233-245.

Greenbury, James. "1 Corinthians 14:34-35: Evaluation Of Prophecy Revisited." *Journal of the Evangelical Theological Society* 51/4 (December 2008): 721-731.

"God's Voice You Have Never Heard, God's Form You Have Never Seen": The Characterization of God. The Gospel Of John." *Semeia* (January 1, 1993): 177-204.

Government of Nagaland, Department of Planning & Coordination. *Nagaland State Human Development Report,* 2004.

Harder, Lydia Neufeld. "The witness of women: Dying to Sin and rising to life." *Vision* (Spring, 2006): 19.

Harrison, Susan McLeod. "Good News for the Poor in Spirit: The Ways of Jesus and Power." *Mutuality* 18/4 (winter, 2011): 7-9.

Heidebrecht, Doug. "Distinction and Function in the Church: Reading Gal. 3:28 in Context." *Direction* 34/2 (Fall 2005): 181-193.

Hollingsworth, Andrea "Spirit and voice: toward a feminist Pentecostal pneumatology." *Pneuma* 29/2 (2007): 189-213.

Ivy, "Engendering Women Power Towards the Reign of God" Paper presented in Pre-Governing Council Seminar at Tamilnadu Theological Seminary, 7.8.12.

Jackson, Glenna. "Jesus as First-Century Feminist: Christian Anti-Judaism?" *Feminist Theology: The Journal of the Britain & Ireland School of Feminist Theology* Issue 19 (September, 98): 90-9.

Jervis, L. Ann. "1 Corinthians 14:34-35 A Reconsideration of Paul's Limitation of The Free Speech of Some Corinthian Women." *Journal for the Study of the New Testament* No. 58 (June 1995): 51-74.

Jamir, L. Imsutoshi. "Morality of Inter-subjectivity: Toward Inclusive Tribal Community," Journal of Tribal Studies, XVI/1 (Jan-June, 2010): 16-31.

King, Paul L. "Women as pastors in the early twentieth-century Christian and Missionary Alliance." *Wesleyan Theological Journal* 43/ 2 (fall 2008): 68-86.

Kingson, Shobana. "Forgetting the Father's House Vs. Honoring the Parents in the Hebrew Scriptures: Implications for Modern Families in India." In *Religion and Society* 58/1&2 (March-June 2013): 71-72.

Lanusenla, I. "Called To Communicate The Words of Prophecy, Reconciliation and Healing." Paper presented at the theological workshop in Chennai organized by Christian Conference of Asia (CCA) in 2009.

Levine, Amy-Jill. "Second Temple Judaism, Jesus, and Women: Yeast of Eden." *Biblical Interpretation* 2/1 (March 1994): 8-33.

Longchar, Sennangshila. "The Pioneering Pastor with Foresight and Determination." Unpublished Manuscript received on Jan. 2014.

Longkumer, Atola. "Not All is Well in My Ancestors' Home: An Indigenous Theology of Internal Critique." *Ecumenical Review* (December, 2010): 399-410.

Malick, David E. "An Examination of Jesus's View of Women through Three Intercalations in the Gospel of Mark." *Priscilla Papers* 27/3 (Summer 2013): 4-15.

McBeth, Harry Leon. "The changing role of women in Baptist history." *Southwestern Journal of Theology* 22/1 (1979): 84-96.

McDougall, Joy Ann. "Rising with Mary: Re-visioning a Feminist Theology of the Cross and Resurrection." *Theology Today* 69/2 (July, 2012): 166-176.

Mel, Deb Beatty "Jesus and the Canaanite Woman: An Exception for Exceptional Faith." *Priscilla Papers* 23/4 (Autumn, 2009):8-12.

Meru, K. "The rule of women before and now." *Highlander,* 1978.

Moore, Russell D. "After Patriarchy, What? Why Egalitarians are winning the Gender Debate." *Journal of the Evangelical Theological society* 49/3 (September 2006): 569-576.

Morgan, Timothy C. "Learning from Widow." *Christianity Today* 53/5 (May, 2009): 7.

Newell, Ted. "Worldviews in Collision: Jesus as Critical Educator." *Journal of Education & Christian Belief* 13/2 (autumn, 2009):141-154.

Okure, Teresa. "Jesus and the Samaritan Woman (JN4:1-42) in Africa." *Theological Studies* 70/2 (January, 2009): 9-108.

Parwez, M. "Searching Space: Women in the Customary Laws and Practices of the Tribal Societies in North East India." *Indian Journal of Applied Research* 2/3 (March, 2013): 175-177.

Perry, Gregory R. "Phoebe of Cenchreae and "Women" of Ephesus: "Deacons" in the Earliest Churches." *Presbyterion* No. 36 (Spring I): 12-20.

Polaski, G Sandra Hack. "Paul and Real Women." *Word & World* 30/4 (Fall 2010): 391-398.

Sánchez, Patricia Datchuck. "The Word Scripted for Life." *National Catholic Reporter* 50/1 (25th October, 2013): 27-27.

Singh, M. Peter "Methodological Issues in Communication Research" Paper presented at the D.Th. Methodology, Organised by SATHRI at United Theological College, Bangalore, 9 May, 2009.

Story, J. Lyle. "The Discipleship of Women-From Jesus' Birth to the Empty Tomb." *Priscilla Papers* 21/1 (Winter, 2007): 14-20.

Skilton, John H. "The Voice of God's Word." *Westminster Theological Journal* 2/60 (1 September, 1998): 185-195.

The Constitution of India 1st ed. Lucknow: Eastern Book Company, 2009.

Thompson, Marianne. "God's Voice You Have Never Heard, God's Form You Have Never Seen": The Characterization of God in the Gospel of John." *Semeia* No. 63 (January 1, 1993): 177-204.

Wakarega, John B. Kariuki. "Evangelization and Cultural Pluralism: A Call for Dialogue, Change and Renewal." *AFER*, 47/3 (2005): 219- 238.

Young, Pamela Dickey. "Encountering Jesus through the earliest witnesses." *Theological Studies* 57/3 (September 1996): 520-521.

Theses and Manuscripts

Ao, Lanuyanger. "Women's Relation to Property in Ao-Naga Customary Law of Inheritance." M.Th. dissertation, Tamilnadu Theological Seminary, 1995.

James, Lovely Awomi. "A Womanist Theological Critique on the Naga Traditional Worldview." D.Th. dissertation, Federated faculty for Research in Religion and Culture, 2010.

LKR, Imnuksungla. "Tradition of Tsuki (Girl's Dormitory) and Its Contribution to Ao Naga Women's Solidarity." M.Th. dissertation, Tamilnadu Theological Seminary, 2007.

Longchar, Sennangshila. "The Pioneering Pastor with Foresight and Determination," Unpublished Manuscript Received on 25 January, 2014.

Internet Resources

Ashba, Aaron. "Postmodern feminism." (24th January, 2008). feminism-gender.blogspot.com accessed on 19.3.2015.

Ashby, Christine. "Whose "Voice" is it anyway?: Giving voice and qualitative research involving individuals that type to communicate." *Disability Studies Quarterly* dsq-sds.org/article/view/1723/1771 accessed on 31.10.2012.

"Are dreams real?" http://www.angelfire.com/nt/theology/theology/02rev.html, accessed on 13.10.2012.

"*Bat kol.*" http://www.jewishencyclopedia.com/articles/2651-bat-kol accessed on 12.3.12.

"Bertha and Ethelbert: Queen and King of Kent, 616." http://satucket.com/lectionary/Bertha_Ethelbert.htm, accessed on 28.4.2014.

Begum, Anjuman Ara. "AFSPA and Unsolved massacres in Manipur." http://twocircles.net/2010nov03/afspa_and_unsolved_massacres_manipur.html#.VTs9z1WSyPs accessed on 25.4.2015.

Casaregola, Vincent. "The 'Exact Location' of the Voice: Walter Ong and the 'Embodiment' of Discourse." http://www.media-ecology.org/publications/MEA_proceedings/v10/7_exact_location.pdf accessed on 15.1.15.

Casey, Sarah. "For You Are All One in Christ (Gal 3:28): The Role of Women in the Pauline Churches" (2010). *Honors Projects*. http://digitalcommons.iwu.edu/religion_honproj/18, accessed on 10.9.2012.

"Communication – An essential human need." www.crisinfo.org accessed on 2.4.15.

"Culture." www.hhs.se/CASL/news/Documents/NFF%20romani.pdf? accessed on 10.5.2013.

Dundon, Tony. "*The Management of Voice in Non-Union Organisations: Managers' Perspectives.*" http://www98.griffith.edu.au/dspace/bitstream/handle/10072/16840/34192_1.pdf accessed on 4.4.2015.

Ferguson, Sian. "kyriarchy 101: We're Not Just Fighting the patriarchy Anymore." 23 April, 2014. everydayfeminism.com/2014/04/kyri…accessed on 6.2.2015.

"Feasts of Merit," http://www.angelfire.com/nm/nagalim/feast.htm accessed on 26.8.2013.

"Feminist Perspectives on Class and Work." First published 1st October, 2004, revised on 12th October, 2010, plato.stanford.edu/entries/feminism-class, accessed on 19.3.2015.

Freire, Paulo. *Pedagogy of the Oppressed*. http://www.sonoma.edu/users/d/daniels/Freire_summary.html accessed on 11.9.2013.

George, Jacob, Khrietuo Yhome. "Community Forest Management: A Case Study of Nagaland, India." http://dlc.dlib.indiana.edu/dlc/bitstream/handle/10535/2185/George_211601.pdf?sequence=1, accessed 27.4.2013.

Ilan,Tal. "Huldah, the Deuteronomic Prophetess of the Book of Kings." http://www.lectio.unibe.ch/10_1/ilan.html accessed on 19.2.2013.

Jamir, Amba. "Understanding Local Self Governance in Nagaland–An essence of the institutions and their activities." http://www.scribd.com/doc/51638389/Local-Self-Governance-in-Nagaland-India?olddoc accessed on 23.2.2012.

Jamir, Moanaro Imchen. "The Role of Ao Women in Church and Society." *Tribal Journal of Theology* www.biblicalstudies.org.uk/pdf/ijt/37-1_045.pdf accessed on 25.4.2013.

Jamir, Toshimenla. "Gender Dimensions of Electoral Politics in Nagaland." https://indianfolklore.org/journals/index.php/Ish/article/viewFile/522/612 accessed on 20.7.2012.

Jitendra. "Naga women approach Supreme Court for reservation of seats in local bodies." *Down To Earth*. http://www.downtoearth.org.in/content/naga-women-approach-supreme-court-reservation-seats-local-bodies accessed on 20.9.2013.

"Historic Liberation." http://www.china.org.cn/e-white/chinesewoman/11-2.htm, accessed on 26.4.2014.

Questionnaire

Please tick [√] the answer or write wherever necessary

1. Age: [ ] 15-25 [ ] 26-35
   [ ] 36-45 [ ] 46 & above

2. Sex: [ ] Male [ ] Female

3. Profession: [ ] Farmer [ ] Government Employed
   [ ] Student [ ] Pastor/Associate Pastor/Church leader [ ] Any other

4. Organisations/bodies you are involved directly in: (tick wherever appropriate)
   [ ] *Ao Senden* [ ] Village Council [ ] *Watsü Mungdang*
   [ ] ABAM [ ] Student Council

5. At present I am living in the: [ ] village
   [ ] Town
   [ ] Cities
   [ ] with any other (specify) ....

6. My Local Church: ....

7. My Area/range: ....

8. Do you think 'Voice' is important for speaking, sharing and responding to each other?
   [ ] Yes [ ] No [ ] Do not know

9. What if one's 'Voice' is debarred from speaking?
   [ ] She/he is dead [ ] She/he is not a complete being [ ] No problem

10. Do you think the traditional structures that do not allow women to participate in the decision making bodies are still relevant today?
    [ ] Yes [ ] No [ ] Can't say

11. What are the reasons behind denying women participation in decision making bodies in Ao Naga tribal community?

    [ ] Traditional socio-cultural practices must not be changed

    [ ] This must be done only by men

    [ ] Due to other responsibilities taken by her, such as child rearing, caring etc.

    Any other reason: ....

12. Are you aware of the denial of rights to half of the population, i. e., women, in the decision making bodies in our community?

    [ ] Yes [ ] No [ ] Not aware

13. Would you be willing to change the traditional system of decision making in the village council, *yimten, senso* etc., and allow women to participate?

    [ ] Yes [ ] No [ ] Do not know

    Any other reasons please explain: ....

    ....

14. Do women resist and challenge the traditional functioning of decision making body which does not give voice to women?

    [ ] Yes [ ] No [ ] Do not know (Can't say)

15. Do you think both women and men sharing and exchanging ideas in the decision making bodies would be better?

    [ ] Yes [ ] No [ ] Do not know

16. Would you still willingly participate in the decision making bodies if you have an option to do otherwise? (*for men only*)

    [ ] Yes [ ] No [ ] Do not know

    Would you willingly participate in the decision making bodies if you have an option to do so? (*for women only*)

    [ ] Yes [ ] No [ ] Do not know

17. Do you have the awareness that denial of a person's voice amounts to a negation of the basic principles of Christian communication, i.e., the right to participation and right to information?

    [ ] Yes [ ] No [ ] Do not know

18. Are you aware that democracy and the democratic process should include everyone?

    [ ] Yes [ ] No [ ] Do not know

19. Do you believe that, because men in general are stronger than women, women cannot and should not join in any of the socio-cultural, religious and political affairs?

    [ ] Yes [ ] No [ ] Do not know

20. Do you still hold on to the traditional belief that a child born out of wedlock is impure and hence, does not have any share (to hold office) in the village council?

    [ ] Yes [ ] No [ ] Do not know

21. Do you find the achievements brought by Ao women's Association (Watsü Mungdang) for the community praiseworthy?

    [ ] Yes [ ] No [ ] cannot say

22. Do you value women's (your wife, mother, sister, and daughter) voice when she gives you advice or suggest some innovative ideas at home?

    [ ] Yes [ ] No [ ] Do not know

23. Do you value your age-group (*zünga*) women voice whenever she advices or suggests some innovative ideas in the social gatherings?

    [ ] Yes [ ] No [ ] Do not know

24. Do you agree with the statement "Church and state cannot be separated from one another but must complement each other"?

    [ ] Yes [ ] No [ ] Do not know

25. Do your local church provide platform for both women and men in the decision making bodies?

    [ ] Yes [ ] No [ ] Do not know

26. Do you think that we need women deacons/elders in the church today?

    [ ] Yes [ ] No [ ] Do not know

    a. If yes, why do we need women deacons/elders in the church? (Tick more answers).

    [ ] women and men together will achieve more.

    [ ] women's contribution will make a difference.

    [ ] God created both female and male in God's likeness.

    b. If no, why do we not need women deacons/elders in the church?

    [ ] the Bible does not permit.

    [ ] she is not willing to take up the post.

    [ ] our church has not tried implementing this before.

27. Are you aware that the Village Councils in Ao villages do not allow participation of women in decision making?

[ ] Yes [ ] No [ ] Do not know

28. Are you aware that the 25% of the Management Committee of the Village Development Board (VDBs) should be composed of women?

[ ] Yes [ ] No [ ] Do not know

29. How would you rate the level of cooperation between these two bodies, the Village Council and the Village Development Board (VDB), in your village?

[ ] Very good [ ] Good [ ] Acceptable [ ] Not good at all

30. Do you like to make any suggestion towards decision making bodies in Ao Naga tribal community?

....

....

31. Any comment regarding the above questionnaire?

....

....